Twenty-Third Edition 2013

The State
of
Church Giving
through 2011

A Report by empty tomb, inc.:
A Comparison of the Growth in Church Contributions with United States Per Capita Income (1988)

Previous Editions in *The State of Church Giving* Series:

The State of Church Giving, through 1989 (1991)
   "Observations and Reflections"

The State of Church Giving through 1990 (Second Edition, 1992)
   "Church Member Giving in Recession Years: 1970, 1974, 1980, 1982 and 1990"

The State of Church Giving through 1991 (Third Edition, 1993)
   "Denominational Giving Data and Other Sources of Religious Giving Information"
   "Church Member Giving Trends Based on 1968–1991 Data"

The State of Church Giving through 1992 (Fourth Edition, 1994)
   "Church Giving in Perspective: Can Church Members Afford to Give More?"

The State of Church Giving through 1993 (Fifth Edition, 1995)
   "Exploration of Roman Catholic Giving Patterns"
   "A Unified Theory of Church Giving and Membership"

The State of Church Giving through 1994 (Sixth Edition, 1996)
   "Retrospective of *The State of Church Giving* Series"

The State of Church Giving through 1995 (Seventh Edition, 1997)
   "The Theological Implications of Church Member Giving Patterns"

The State of Church Giving through 1996 (Eighth Edition, 1998)
   "Church Member Giving in Perspective: Can Religion Influence the Middle Class"

The State of Church Giving through 1997 (Ninth Edition, 1999)
   "Future of Congregational Giving: The Need for Creative Church Policy"

The State of Church Giving through 1998 (Tenth Edition, 2000)
   "Systems and Subsystems Analysis: A Case Study"

The State of Church Giving through 1999 (Eleventh Edition, 2001)
   "National Church Leaders Response Form"

The State of Church Giving through 2000 (Twelfth Edition, 2002)
   "Two Solutions for the Vacuum of Leadership in the Church in the U.S."

The State of Church Giving through 2001 (Thirteenth Edition, 2003)
   "Reversing the Decline in Benevolences Giving: A Country-by-Country Needs Analysis"

The State of Church Giving through 2002 (Fourteenth Edition, 2004)
   "Helping Church Members to Care Effectively: Yoking Map Twenty-Year Update"

The State of Church Giving through 2003 (Fifteenth Edition, 2005)
   "Giving Trends and the Church's Priorities"

The State of Church Giving through 2004: Will We Will? (Sixteenth Edition, 2006)

The State of Church Giving through 2005: Abolition of the Institutional Enslavement of Overseas Missions (Seventeenth Edition, 2007)

The State of Church Giving through 2006: Global Triage, MDG4, and Unreached People Groups (Eighteenth Edition, 2008)

The State of Church Giving through 2007: What Are Our Christian Billionaires Thinking—Or Are They? (Nineteenth Edition, 2009)

The State of Church Giving through 2008: Kudos to Wycliffe Bible Translators and World Vision for Global At-Scale Goals, But Will Denominations Resist Jesus Christ And Not Spend $1 to $26 Per Member to Reach The Unreached When Jesus Says, "You Feed Them"? (Twentieth Edition, 2010)

The State of Church Giving through 2009: Jesus Christ, the Church in the U.S., & the 16 No-Progress-in-Child Deaths Nations, 10 Being 84% Christian (Twenty-First Edition, 2011)

The State of Church Giving through 2010: Who's in Charge Here? A Case for a Positive Agenda for Affluence (Twenty-Second Edition, 2012)

Note: Special focus chapters, indicated by quote marks above, were not listed as subtitles until the sixteenth edition.

Twenty-Third Edition 2013

The State
of
Church Giving
through 2011

The Kingdom of God,
Church Leaders & Institutions,
Global Triage Needs, and the
Promises of Jesus

John L. Ronsvalle

Sylvia Ronsvalle

empty tomb, inc.
Champaign, Illinois

The State of Church Giving through 2011:
The Kingdom of God,
Church Leaders and Institutions
Global Triage Needs, and the
Promises of Jesus
by John and Sylvia Ronsvalle
Published by empty tomb, inc.
First printing, September 2013

empty tomb, inc.
301 N. Fourth Street
P.O. Box 2404
Champaign, IL 61825-2404
Phone: (217) 356-9519
Fax: (217) 356-2344
www.emptytomb.org
See www.emptytomb.org/pubs.html for updates and corrigenda.

ISBN 978-0-9843665-3-8
ISSN 1097-3192

The Library of Congress has catalogued this publication
as follows:
The state of church giving through ... — 19uu- Champaign, Ill. :
Empty Tomb, Inc.,
v. : ill. ; 28 cm. Annual.
1. Christian giving Periodicals.
2. Christian giving Statistics Periodicals.
3. Church finance—United States Periodicals.
4. Church finance—United States Statistics Periodicals.
    BV772 .S32 98-640917

CONTENTS

TABLES, FIGURES AND ABBREVIATIONS ———————————

List of Tables:

List of Figures:

List of Abbreviations:

BEA .... U.S. Bureau of Economic Analysis
BLS .... U.S. Government Dept. of Labor Bureau of Labor Statistics
CE .... Consumer Expenditure Survey
CPI .... Consumer Price Index
CU .... Consumer Unit
DPI .... Disposable Personal Income
GDP .... Gross Domestic Product
IMB .... International Mission Board (of the SBC)
KJV .... King James Version of the Holy Bible
MDG .... Millennium Development Goal
NAB .... New American Bible
NAE .... National Association of Evangelicals
NCC .... National Council of the Churches of Christ in the U.S.A.
NIV .... New International Version of the Holy Bible (1984)
NRSV .... New Revised Standard Version of the Holy Bible
OCD .... *The Official Catholic Directory*
SBC .... Southern Baptist Convention
SCG .... *State of Church Giving*
UMC .... United Methodist Church
UNICEF .... United Nations Children's Fund
YACC .... *Yearbook of American and Canadian Churches*

PREFACE

"… we administer in order to honor the Lord himself" (2 Cor. 8:19b, NIV).

The church in the United States is indeed fortunate that faithful men and women use their gifts of administration to serve through the various communions to provide the numbers analyzed in this volume. Allowing God to use their talents to collect, aggregate, and publish these numbers, that reflect a vast array of congregations throughout the country, provides a vital historical data stream that helps to describe the story of the church in the U.S. We thank God for each one.

The *Yearbook of American and Canadian Churches* series, publishing the data from many denominations, made it available for researchers, scholars, church professionals, and the general public. Eileen W. Lindner, Ph.D., editor of this important effort for the last 15 published *YACC* editions, 1998 through 2012, continued the data collection that extends back to the first publication in the series, *Federal Council Year Book* (1916). For the most recent numbers, Eileen Lindner and her assistant, Cecilia Rosas, worked in a manner that can only be described as heroic, carrying on the correspondence to request the 2011 data from the denominations.

The staff, volunteers, and donors of empty tomb, inc., deserve a great deal of credit for encouraging and supporting this national research effort, in the midst of the other ongoing works of the organization. These coworkers, coordinated by Shannon Cook, contribute in important ways to the realization of this series.

The assistance of Joy Bonczek in moving the publication from spreadsheets and drafts to the finished pages that follow has been absolutely essential. We are grateful for her bravery in learning software, as well as her willingness to use her talents in the developing the presentation of this volume. We are also grateful for the efforts of what might be termed a merry band of volunteer proofers, who each took on the task with energy. This group includes David Anderson, Linda Garrett, Susan Gundy, Janet Marquissee, Fred Neumann, Lorraine Pryor, Carol Schuster, and Carol Thomas.

The analyses that follow, both numerical and conceptual, are offered in hope and the belief that the church is given works to do for the glory of God. Our prayer each year is that the research and information will inspire and challenge Christians, particularly in the U.S., to embrace God's agenda for loving a hurting world in Jesus' name. We trust God to do more than we can ask or imagine (Ephesians 3:20-21).

John L. Ronsvalle, Ph.D.
Sylvia Ronsvalle

Champaign, Illinois
August 2013

SUMMARY _____

The State of Church Giving through 2011 is the most recent report in an annual series that began with *The State of Church Giving through 1989*. These analyses consider denominational giving data for a set of denominations first analyzed in a study published in 1988. The present report reviews data for a composite set of denominations from 1968 through 2011 that includes 26.7 million full or confirmed members, and just over 100,000 of the estimated 350,000 religious congregations in the U.S.

The findings of the present church member giving analysis include the following.

- In chapter 1, per member giving for the composite set of denominations was analyzed for 1968 through 2011. As a portion of income, and in inflation-adjusted dollars, per member giving to Total Contributions, Congregational Finances, and Benevolences decreased from 2010 to 2011. In current dollars, per member giving to Total Contributions declined in 2008, 2009, and 2011, after not declining from one year to the next in current dollars from 1969 through 2007.

- In chapter 2, data for an additional 15 denominations was available for 2010-2011, allowing an expanded analysis for two years of 38 Protestant communions, with 36 million members. The 2010-2011 pattern in the expanded set was similar to that found in the composite set.

- In chapter 3, an analysis of data for a subset of mainline Protestant denominations and a subset of evangelical Protestant denominations found giving higher, but a steeper decline in giving as a portion of income, in the evangelical Protestant denominations over the 1968-2011 period.

- In chapter 4, a review of giving and membership patterns in 11 Protestant denominations from 1921 to 2011 found that per member giving in inflation-adjusted dollars declined in 2008, 2009, 2010, and 2011. This four-year decline was the longest since the seven years of 1928 through 1934, six of those years occurring in the Great Depression.

- In chapter 5, data was analyzed using both linear and exponential regression. Both giving and membership data were reviewed for how past patterns may influence the future for various sets of denominational groups. Expenditures on new religious construction in the U.S. were compared for the period 1964 through 2011.

- In chapter 6, a survey of denominations' overseas missions income in 2003 through 2011 found that, for the group as a whole, denominations' overseas ministries income was 2¢ for every dollar donated to congregations in 2011. The cost per church member for addressing global needs, such as world evangelization and helping to stop, in Jesus' name, global child deaths, was calculated for various church populations. If church members were to reach a congregation-wide average of 10% giving, a low estimate suggests that an additional $172 billion would be available to assist both local and global neighbors in need. If native-born church members in the U.S. were to support international ministry at the level that foreign-born residents of the U.S. send remittances to their home countries, there would have been an additional $385 billion available for international ministry through churches in 2011.

- In chapter 7, charitable giving data for the U.S. Bureau of Labor Statistics, Consumer Expenditure Survey, 2011, was analyzed by age, income level, and region of residence. Donors in every age group, in 11 of 12 income groups, and in three of four regions of the country identified gifts to "church, religious organizations" as the primary focus of their charitable activity. Giving to that category represented 69% of total contributions in 2011. Three estimates for Total Giving by Living Individuals in 2009 were compared, the latest year for which the three sources had available data. The data in the analysis was obtained from the U.S. Bureau of Labor Statistics Consumer Expenditure Survey, the Internal Revenue Service Form 990 series, and the *Giving USA* publication, based in part on IRS charitable deduction information for itemizers. The numbers differed. For example, the 2009 *Giving USA* estimate for total charitable giving exceeded the Consumer Expenditure Survey figure by 31 percent.

- Chapter 8 explores the interrelationship of the kingdom of God, church leaders and institutions, global triage needs, and the promises of Jesus, in light of the data presented in the first seven chapters of this edition.

INTRODUCTION _____

A historical series of financial and membership data in the United States extends back to 1916. Church statesmen took a broad overview of organized religion as a major social institution. They collected and preserved the data through publications and archives.

This information tradition continues through the present. Individual congregations initially provide the data to the regional or national denominational office with which the congregation is affiliated. The denominational offices then compile the data. The *Yearbook of American and Canadian Churches* (*YACC*), of the National Council of the Churches of Christ in the U.S.A., requests the data from the national denominational offices, publishing it in annual *YACC* editions.

The data published by the *YACC*, in some cases combined with data obtained directly from a denominational source during the preparation of this volume (as noted in the series of tables in Appendix B), serves as the basis for the present report. The numbers on the following pages are not survey reports. Rather, they represent the actual dollar records included in reports submitted by pastors and lay congregational leaders to their own denominational offices.

By following the same data set of denominations over a period of years, trends can be seen among a broad group of church members. In addition, since the data set includes communions from across the theological spectrum, subsets of denominations within the larger grouping provide a basis for comparing patterns between communions with different perspectives.

In an ongoing fashion, efforts are made to use the latest information available. As a result, *The State of Church Giving through 2011* provides information available to date.

Definition of Terms. The analyses in this report use certain terms that are defined as follows.

Full or Confirmed Members are used in the present analysis because it is a relatively consistent category among the reporting denominations. Certain denominations also report a larger figure for Inclusive Membership, which may include, for example, children who have been baptized but are not yet eligible for confirmation in that denomination. In this report, when the term "per member" is used, it refers to Full or Confirmed Members, unless otherwise noted.

The terms "denomination" and "communion" are used interchangeably. Both refer to a group of church people who share a common identity defined by traditions and stated beliefs.

The phrase "historically Christian church" refers to that combination of believers with a historically acknowledged confession of the faith. The broad spectrum of communions represented in the National Church Leaders Response Form list indicates the breadth of this definition.[1]

Total Contributions Per Member refers to the average contribution in either dollars or as a percent of income which is donated to the denominations' affiliated congregations by Full or Confirmed Members in a given year.

Total Contributions combines the two subcategories of Congregational Finances and Benevolences. The definitions used in this report for these two subcategories are consistent with the standardized *YACC* data request questionnaire.

The first subcategory of Congregational Finances includes contributions directed to the internal operations of the individual congregation, including such items as the utility bills and salaries for the pastor and office staff, as well as Sunday school materials and capital programs.

The second subcategory is Benevolences. This category includes contributions for the congregation's external expenditures, beyond its own operations, for what might be termed the larger mission of the church. Benevolences includes international missions as well as national and local charities, through denominational channels as well as programs of nondenominational organizations to which the congregation contributes directly. Benevolences also includes support of denominational administration at all levels, as well as donations to denominational seminaries and schools.

As those familiar with congregational dynamics know, an individual generally donates an amount to the congregation that underwrites both Congregational Finances and Benevolences. During the budget preparation process, congregational leadership considers allocations to these categories. The budget may or may not be reviewed by all the congregation's members, depending on the communion's polity. However, the sum of the congregation's activities serves as a basis for members' decisions about whether to increase or decrease giving from one year to the next. Also, many congregations provide opportunities to designate directly to either Congregational Finances or Benevolences, through fundraising drives, capital campaigns, and special offerings. Therefore, the allocations between Congregational Finances and Benevolences can be seen to fairly represent the priorities of church members.

When the terms "income," "per capita income," and "giving as a percent of income" are used, they refer to the U.S. Per Capita Disposable (after-tax) Personal Income series from the U.S. Department of Commerce Bureau of Economic Analysis (BEA), unless otherwise noted.

The Implicit Price Deflator for Gross National Product was used to convert current dollars to 2005 dollars, thus factoring out inflation, unless otherwise specified.

Appendix C includes both U.S. Per Capita Disposable Personal Income figures and the Implicit Price Deflator for Gross National Product figures used in this study.

Analysis Factors. *Chained Dollars.* The analyses in *The State of Church Giving through 2011* are keyed to the U.S. BEA series of "chained (2005) dollars."

Income Series. The U.S. Department of Commerce Bureau of Economic Analysis has published the 13th comprehensive ('benchmark") revision of the national income and product accounts, with the reference year being 2005. The U.S. Per Capita Disposable Personal Income series used in the present *The State of Church Giving through 2011* is drawn from this national accounts data.

Rate of Change Calculations, 1985–2011. The following methodology is used to calculate the rate of change between 1985 and the most recent calendar year for which data is available, in the present case, 2011.

The rate of change between 1968 and 1985 was calculated by subtracting the 1968 giving as a percent of income figure from the 1985 figure and then dividing the result by the 1968 figure.

The rate of change between 1985 and 2011 was calculated as follows. The 1968 giving as a percent of income figure was subtracted from the 2011 figure and divided by the 1968 figure, producing a 1968–2011 rate of change. Then, the 1968–1985 rate of change was subtracted from the 1968–2011 figure. The result is the 1985–2011 rate of change, which may then be compared to the 1968–1985 figure.

Rounding Calculations. In most cases, Total Contributions, Total Congregational Finances, and Total Benevolences for the denominations being considered were divided by Full or Confirmed Membership in order to obtain per capita, or per member, data for that set of denominations. This procedure occasionally led to a small rounding discrepancy in one of the three related figures. That is, by a small margin, rounded per capita Total Contributions did not equal per capita Congregational Finances plus per capita Benevolences. Similarly, rounding data to the nearest dollar for use in tables and graphics led on occasion to a small rounding error in the data presented in tabular or graphic form.

Giving as a Percent of Income. The most useful way to look at church member giving is in terms of giving as a percent of income. Rather than indicating how much money the congregation has to spend, as when one considers dollars donated, giving as a percent of income indicates how the congregation, shown through giving, rates in light of church members' total available incomes. Has the church sustained the same level of support from its members in comparison to previous years, as measured by what portion of income is being donated by members from the changing total resources available to them?

Percent of income is a valuable measure because incomes change. Just as inflation changes the value of the dollar so $5 in 1968 is not the same as $5 in 2011, incomes, influenced by inflation and real growth, also change. For example, per capita income in 1968 was $3,112 in current dollars; if a church member gave $311 that year, that member would have been tithing, or giving the standard of ten percent. In contrast, 2011 per capita income had increased to $37,013 in current dollars; and if that church member had still given $311, the member would have been giving less than 1% of income. The church would have commanded a smaller portion of the member's overall resources.

Thus, while dollars donated provide a limited picture of how much the church has to spend, giving as a percent of income provides both a measure of the church member's level of commitment to the church in comparison to other spending priorities, as well as a measure of whether the church's income is keeping up with inflation and growth in the economy. One might say that giving as a percent of income is an indication of the church's "market share" of church members' lives.

In most cases, to obtain giving as a percent of income, total income to a set of denominations was divided by the number of Full or Confirmed Members in the set. This yielded the per member giving amount in dollars. This per member giving amount was divided by per capita Disposable Personal Income.

Giving in Dollars. Per member giving to churches can be measured in dollars. The dollar measure indicates, among other information, how much money religious institutions have to spend.

Current dollars indicate the value of the dollar in the year it was donated. However, since inflation changes the amount of goods or services that can be purchased with that dollar, data provided in current dollars has limited information value over a time span. If someone donated $5 in 1968 and $5 in 2011, on one level that person is donating the same amount of money. On another level, however, the buying power of that $5 has changed a great deal. Since less can be bought with the $5 donated in 2011 because of inflation in the economy, on a practical level the value of the donation has shrunk.

To account for the changes caused by inflation in the value of the dollar, a deflator can be applied. The result is inflation-adjusted 2005 dollars. Dollars adjusted to their chain-type, annual-weighted measure through the use of a deflator can be compared in terms of real growth over a time span since inflation has been factored out.

The deflator most commonly applied in this analysis designated the base period as 2005, with levels in 2005 set equal to 100. Thus, when adjusted by the deflator, the 1968 gift of $5 was worth $22.71 in inflation-adjusted 2005 dollars, and the 2011 gift of $5 was worth $4.41 in inflation-adjusted 2005 dollars.

Data Appendix and Revisions. Appendix B includes the aggregate denominational data used in the analyses in this study. In general, the data for the denominations included in these analyses appears as it was reported in editions of the *YACC*. In some cases, data for one or more years for a specific denomination was obtained directly from the denominational office. Also, the denominational giving data set has been refined and revised as additional information has become available. Where relevant, this information is noted in the appendix.

---

[1]   John Ronsvalle and Sylvia Ronsvalle; "National Church Leaders Response Form"; *The State of Church Giving through 1998* (2000 edition); <http://www.emptytomb.org/survey1.html>.

chapter 1

Church Member Giving,
1968–2011

"Why be like the pagans who are so deeply concerned about these things? Your heavenly Father already knows all your needs, and he will give you all you need from day to day if you live for him and make the Kingdom of God your primary concern."
　　　　　　　—Jesus Christ quoted in Matthew 6:32-33 (New Living Translation)

"For whoever wishes to save his life will lose it, but whoever loses his life for my sake will find it."
　　　　　　　—Jesus Christ quoted in Matthew 16:25 (New American Bible)

"I tell you the truth, anyone who has faith in me will do what I have been doing. He will do even greater things than these, because I am going to the Father."　　　　　　—Jesus Christ quoted in John 14:12 (New International Version)

The Importance of Church Giving Numbers

To measure church member giving is to develop a sense of the priority that members place on their church involvement.

To measure church member giving is also to observe how effectively church leaders are guiding members in the formation of those priorities. Chapter 8 considers how church leaders and church institutions intersect with the kingdom of God, and the promises of Jesus Christ.

It is in the first seven chapters of this volume that the foundation is laid for that discussion. A review of present giving and membership patterns, as well as a consideration of potential giving, lays the groundwork of facts that may help move the conversation from well-meaning wishful thinking to well-founded mobilization.

The working assumption is that church member giving numbers provide an objective measurement of the value church members place on their faith activities compared to other spending options available to them. The chapters that follow build on this working assumption.

In a related fashion, one may also consider church leader and church institutional priorities, revealed through spending patterns, by comparing the percent of expenses focused on the internal services to current members, and the percent focused on external activities that reflect broader issues highlighted by Jesus, what might be termed kingdom of God priorities found in global triagic needs.

Voluntary Transparency. The church member giving analyses are possible because of a long history of voluntary transparency within the church in the U.S.[1]

The *1916 Federal Council Year Book* began a series of surveys of Christian denominations regarding their "foreign missions" activity. In the *1919 Yearbook of the Churches*, general giving information was added to the foreign missions statistics.[2] The *Yearbook of American and Canadian Churches (YACC)* has continued to publish general church member giving numbers voluntarily provided by denominations. For example, information for a set of denominations that include over 100,000 (based on *YACC 2012*) of the estimated 350,000 religious congregations in the U.S. is available for the 1968–2011 period, largely through data published in the *YACC* series, although supplemented in some cases through direct contact with the denominations. This consistent set of data is useful for identifying, and to some degree understanding, trends in church member giving patterns during this more than four-decade period. Other data for a smaller group of denominations extends back as far as 1921 (see chapter 4). The publication by the *YACC* of voluntarily provided denominational data serves as an invaluable historical data stream, captured faithfully on an annual basis by generations of servant editors and denominational officials concerned about the general good of the church and the larger society in which it exists.

Two Troubling Trends. However, more recently, two troubling developments have surfaced in the voluntary transparency of church communions in the U.S. These trends have occurred at a time when the nature of being a nonprofit is under close review in the U.S.

As observed in a May 2011 *Chronicle of Philanthropy* column: "Charities are under a magnifying glass like never before. Advances in technology have created an era of transparency. No longer can charities rely on just the good will of their name and historical record. Now they must continually justify their relevance and nurture and protect their credibility. Public trust is of paramount importance, and to lose it may mean losing everything."[3]

Five Denominations No Longer Voluntarily Report. A first concern is that five denominations no longer voluntarily report their church member giving numbers on a regular basis.

The *State of Church Giving (SCG)* series analysis is largely based on a composite set of denominations that published data in 1968 and 1985. By 2011, five of these original 31 communions were no longer making their church member giving numbers public.

The historical data stream is a fragile resource. If the data is not collected on a contemporary basis, it is difficult if not impossible to recover the information in subsequent years. It is therefore a regrettable development that these threads in the giving data tapestry of the church in the U.S. are no longer visible.

1. The Friends United Meeting stopped reporting giving data in 1991.

2. The Church of God (Anderson, IN) stopped reporting giving data in 1998.

3. The Mennonite Church USA reported general giving data only in 1999, the year it resulted from the merger of the Mennonite Church and the Mennonite Church, General Conference; these two individual antecedent denominations had provided church member giving data back to at least 1968.

4. The North American Baptist Conference stopped providing membership and giving data in 2005.

5. The Evangelical Covenant Church did not report membership or giving data for 2008 through 2011.

In each case, the historical data series extends back to at least 1968, in some cases even further.

Some of these denominations have explained that the central office in that communion has had to cut back on budgets, and therefore does not have the staff to obtain the numbers from the congregations and aggregate them. This trend is a logical consequence of the long-term decline in spending on Benevolences, including denominational support, by congregations (see the discussion on Table 1). Other denominations suggest that the relationship between the national denominational office and the related congregations has weakened to the degree that congregations no longer feel accountable to the national office regarding the reporting of numbers.

In addition, for the 2011 data, two other communions were not able to provide data. In one case, the Fellowship of Evangelical Bible Churches, data was not available for the specific year of 2011, although denominational staff said that collection of data for 2012 was underway. In the other case, the Brethren in Christ Church, the national staff was not able to provide the 2011 data in time for the current edition's deadline, indicating that the data would be available later.

Further, in this edition, an adjustment has been made to the data series because the California Baptist Convention has not collected information about Total Contributions from its constituent congregations since 2005. This choice by the California Baptist Convention interrupts a 160-year voluntary financial data stream of the Southern Baptist Convention that extends back at least 125 years, to 1885–1890, with uninterrupted data from 1896.[4]

This trend toward a lack of public accountability by denominations, or regions within denominations, evident in a lack of voluntary aggregate reporting to the society in general, is occurring at the same time that the second troubling trend is emerging.

Proposed Government Intervention. The second troubling development is a possible move toward increased regulation of denominations and congregations by external entities.

The second troubling development is a possible move toward increased regulation of denominations and congregations by external entities.

Traditionally, the church has enjoyed exemptions from governmental control. The church has been regarded as representing many of the higher ideals that have influenced the general social fabric of the nation. The church as a safeguard of these higher ideals, "providing beneficial services for society"[5] related to those ideals—both to members and to the public—has earned various privileges in society, including exemption from taxes and other real-world privileges.

The church has returned this trust from society through voluntary transparency. Reporting of numbers demonstrates trustworthiness on the part of church institutions. Voluntary reporting also has served to call the society in general to values beyond one's individual needs, values that emphasize the common, or greater, good. Altruistic spending patterns model a set of values that demonstrate and embody higher ideals, emphasizing "the least" in the U.S. and the global community. The church as an institution can serve as a tether to the perspectives that keep the society in general focused on values insuring a broader social context, including the needs of everyone, especially those with no other voice than the voluntary concern of those of good will.

The voluntary reporting has also served to call the society in general to values beyond one's individual needs, values that emphasize the common, or greater, good.

Therefore, those who care about the church in the U.S. should regard with concern a move away from voluntary transparency on the part of Christian traditions within the U.S. An unwillingness to be accountable to a society from which the church, as an institution, expects special privileges, could lead to the withdrawal of those privileges. Such a change would weaken not only the church, but also the society, which the church is supposed to be influencing.

Yet, there appears to be a trend taking shape that regards the church not as a special entity but as another nonprofit institution that requires regulation. Consider the following developments.

Tax-exemption privileges for churches and nonprofits. Some of the developments could affect the tax-exempt nature of the church, as well as nonprofits in general.

1. In a move affecting all nonprofits, including churches, the December 2010 report of the deficit commission advising President Barak Obama proposed the end of the charitable tax deduction available to itemizers, substituting a "12% non-refundable tax credit available to all taxpayers; available above 2% of Adjusted Gross Income (AGI) floor."[6] In July 2011, a proposal to "curb" charitable deductions was made by a bipartisan group of U.S. senators, seeking to address the national deficit and the U.S. debt ceiling.[7]

2. Looking for additional revenue, the City of Boston previously asked large nonprofits to make "payments in lieu of taxes (PILOTs)" for a portion of what would otherwise be property taxes. In 2011, the city began exploring the arrangement for all tax-exempt organizations. The news report about this development did not mention whether or not churches would be excluded from that expansion.[8]

3. Municipalities are levying "fees" on churches, as opposed to taxes. The fee in Mission, Kansas, specifically is based on a multiplier that combines an estimated average number of round trips to a church and "each seat in a sanctuary."[9]

General operations such as pensions under review. Some denominations have pension funds that are "sufficiently funded to meet future obligations ... [and] rank among the nation's largest …" One report indicated that The Episcopal Church, the Presbyterian Church (USA), and The United Methodist Church are in this category. A spokesman for Guidestone Financial Services of the Southern Baptist Convention was also quoted as affirming that organization's stability. However, other denominations report underfunding of their commitments. One mainline Protestant denomination's defined benefit program "has been closed to new participants since January 1, 2010." Denominations have been exempt from enrolling in the Pension Benefit Guaranty Corporation for federal insurance, and therefore have been exempt from the related regulations. Some observers, such as the director of the Pension Rights center, "a Washington-based watchdog group," have suggested recently that participants in "so-called church plans are far more at risk."[10]

Reporting requirements. The Evangelical Council for Financial Accountability (ECFA) was asked for assistance by Senator Charles Grassley, then ranking member of the Senate Finance Committee that has "tax-exempt oversight responsibilities." ECFA formed the Commission on Accountability and Policy for Religious Organizations. The commission was "tasked with gathering input from the sector and providing feedback to the senator's office, with the goal of improving accountability and policy in the religious sector." Issues within the commission's purview included whether churches should file the detailed Form 990 or a similar form, whether the clergy housing allowance exclusion should be continued, and whether "legislation is needed to clarify 'love offerings' to ministers."[11]

The Commission's Report was issued in December 2012. While the Report recommended against churches having to file Form 990, the report stated, "Churches and their leaders should not engage in abusive financial activities, nor should they improperly exploit the exemption from filing Form 990, because doing so undermines the credibility of their organizations and the religious community as a whole."[12]

The Report observed that the Internal Revenue Service already has the right to "initiate a church inquiry or examination so long as certain criteria are met" as a result of the Church Audit Procedures Act, Section 7611 of the Internal Revenue Code, although implementation of this act is currently under review.[13]

The Report discussed various strategies for churches to pursue in order to maintain financial integrity, including: "Robust and meaningful financial oversight by a denominational organization is another method for churches that are part of hierarchical structure" (although it may be noted that the strength or looseness of denominational hierarchy structures varies widely based on church polity). The Commission Report further asserted, "As mentioned in our recommendations, churches should verifiably demonstrate their commitment to proper oversight and accountability."[14]

One assessment of the church's commitment to such voluntary accountability was voiced by *The NonProfit Times* when it named ECFA president Dan Busby one of it's "2013 Power & Influence Top 50":

> There might be a day in the not-too-distant future when tax law mandates financial transparency for religious organizations. Busby's members will be ready. He has put his neck out to make financial accountability a near creed within a membership often not happy about drawing the curtains back and letting the light shine in.[15]

The Commission Report further asserted, "As mentioned in our recommendations, churches should verifiably demonstrate their commitment to proper oversight and accountability."

Voluntary transparency by congregations through their denominations may be a vital line of defense against a change in the larger culture's attitude about the value of the church receiving certain exemptions due to its unique status in society.

Areas for Further Research. There are at least two areas of further research that may prove helpful to those concerned with church giving data. One could explore what proportion of the congregations affiliated with a broad representation of denominations continue to report financial and membership data to those denominations. How much variation is there by year? Has the number changed over the decades, and what trends are suggested by the numbers?

Second, when congregations disaffiliate with a denomination, does that same denomination experience other congregations affiliating with that same denomination? To what extent is the total number of congregations affected? To what extent is the total number of membership affected?

Many Denominations Continue Voluntary Reporting of Church Giving Data. The trends considered above could have serious implications for the status of the church in U.S. society, and the church's ability to pursue its own agenda. Fortunately, a large number of denominations continue the rich tradition of making voluntarily reported data available for review by scholars, academics, and members of the general public who recognize the importance of the role of the church in U.S. society. The willingness of these denominational officials to share this information serves as a counterweight to any who would reduce the church to the status of just another institution to be regulated. The faithfulness of these denominational officials distinguishes the church through their voluntary transparency and modeling of self-disclosure, underscoring the basis for recognizing the church as an acknowledged practitioner of core values, and as embodying many of the higher ideals, of society. The information these denominational officials have shared extends the historical data stream through 2011.

> The willingness of these denominational officials to share this information serves as a counterweight to any who would reduce the church to the status of just another institution to be regulated.

Overview of Church Member Giving, 1968 through 2011

Giving Categories. When a dollar is given to the church, it is allocated into one of two major subcategories, as defined by the annual reporting form of the *Yearbook of American and Canadian Churches (YACC)*.

The first subcategory is Congregational Finances. This subcategory refers to those expenditures that support the operations of the local congregation, such as building and utilities, pastor and staff salaries, insurance, music, and Sunday school materials.

The second is Benevolences, which generally refers to expenditures for what might be termed the broader mission of the church, beyond the local congregation. Benevolences includes everything from support of regional and national denominational offices to the local soup kitchen, from seminaries to international ministries.

Total Contributions is the sum of Congregational Finances and Benevolences.

Giving as a Percent of Income, 1968–2011. The format of the measurement tool of church member giving can be the number of dollars given, or the portion of income given. To understand how much church members have available to address, in Jesus' name, the needs in front of them, the percent of income given provides a better overview.

Even factoring out inflation, few people had the same amount of income in 2011 as in 1968. This real growth in income is taken into account in giving as a percent of income, since the number of dollars given is placed in the context of the total amount of resources available to the donor. If income goes up faster than the amount of dollars given, in a very real sense giving has decreased in the donor's priorities, because the dollars given represent a smaller percent of the donor's total spending.

If the rate of increase in income slows, and yet church giving remains steady or even increases, then the percent of income given will increase, thus suggesting a sustained level of commitment to the church even in difficult economic times.

Considering giving as a percent of income provides insight not only into the amount given by church members, but also into the priority that the members are placing on those donations, compared to other categories that attract the church members' spending.

Figure 1 presents per member giving as a portion of income to the church among the members of the basic set of denominations in this analysis, referred to as the composite data set. As can be observed from this chart, giving as a portion of income declined in all three categories of Total Contributions, Congregational Finances, and Benevolences between 1968 and 2011, each reaching in 2011 their lowest level in the 1968–2011 period. The overall decline in giving as a portion of income from 1968 to 2011 suggests that the church is commanding less of church members' attention compared to other spending priorities.

Figure 1: Per Member Giving to Total Contributions, Congregational Finances, and Benevolences, Percent of Income, 1968–2011

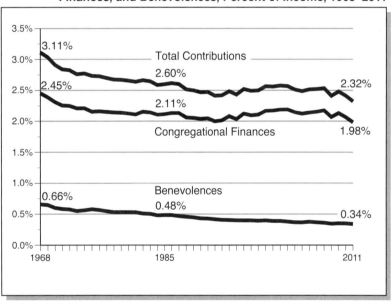

Source: empty tomb analysis; *YACC* adjusted series; U.S. BEA   empty tomb, inc. 2013

The portion of income contributed to the church, as represented in Total Contributions, decreased from 3.11% in 1968 to 2.32% in 2011, a decline of 25% from the 1968 base.

Overall, giving to Congregational Finances as a percent of income decreased from 2.45% in 1968 of income to 1.98%, a decline of 19%. In 1993, giving to Congregational Finances began an intermittent recovery from the previous low point in 1992. However, since 2003, declines outnumbered increases from year to year.

The portion of income directed to Benevolences demonstrated a fairly steady decline throughout the period. Beginning in 1968, the portion of income directed to

13

Benevolences was 0.66%. By 2011, the level had declined to 0.34%, in unrounded numbers lower than the 2008 figure. This 1968–2011 change represented a decrease of 48% in the portion of income directed to the category of Benevolences.

Implications of Giving in 2010 Compared to 2011. Sometimes the change in the portion of income given can be very small from one year to the next. Yet, because there are so many members involved, even small changes are magnified. To explore the implications of these changes, consider the impact of the difference in the portion of income given to Benevolences between 2010 and 2011. For this analysis, information for the 23 denominations that reported data for both 2010 and 2011 is compared.

In 2010, per member giving to Benevolences as a portion of income measured 0.35%. In 2011, the amount again measured 0.34%.

The implications of this change can be understood when translated to dollars. The unrounded difference between 2010 and 2011 Benevolences as a portion of income was -0.008823% of per capita income. When multiplied by the 2011 current dollar U.S. per capita income figure of $37,013, that change translated into a decrease in 2011 of $3.27 given by each of the 26,700,466 members in these denominations. The combination of these individual dollar decreases meant that the composite communions had $87,196,174 less to spend in 2011 on the larger mission of the church, compared to the 2010 level.

Potential Giving. Another approach is to consider what would have been the situation in 2011 if giving had at least maintained the 1968 percentages of income donated.

The implications of the difference become clearer when aggregate totals are calculated. The levels of giving as a percent of income in 1968 were multiplied by 2011 income. The resulting per member dollar figure was then multiplied by the number of members reported by these denominations in 2011. If the same portion of income had been donated in 2011 as in 1968, aggregate Total Contributions would have been $30.3 billion rather than the actual amount given of $22.9 billion, a difference of $7.4 billion, or an increase of 32%.

Aggregate Congregational Finances would have been $24.0 billion rather than $19.6 billion, a difference of $4.4 billion, or an increase of 22%.

There would have been a 90% increase in the total amount received for Benevolences. Instead of receiving $3.4 billion in 2011, as these church structures did, they would have received $6.4 billion, a difference of $3.0 billion available for the larger mission of the church. The additional $3.0 billion for Benevolences would have resulted, not from an increase in the portion of income given, but if giving as a percent of income had not declined between 1968 and 2011. The additional $3.0 billion could have provided the millions of dollars that some denominations lament are not available for global evangelization. The balance could have had a significant impact on the number of child deaths prevented.

It may be tempting for denominational officials to reflect on how the $3.0 billion could have benefited their organizational structures, as many denominations cut back on operations. However, a word of caution may be in order on that point. Church

If the same portion of income had been donated in 2011 as in 1968 ... There would have been a 90% increase in the total amount received for Benevolences.

members were offered the opportunity to maintain those structures between 1968 and 2011 and chose not to do so, as evidenced by the actual giving patterns.

Another question could impact how denominations relate to congregations from this point forward. That is, would church members have maintained the 1968 level of giving as a portion of income if they had the option to apply the entire amount of those funds through the denomination to the global triage tasks of expanding global evangelization and/or the prevention of child deaths? Since no denomination offered members the option of favoring the task of evangelization or preventing child deaths over structure maintenance, the possibilities remain in the realm of conjecture.

In any case, the difference between the 1968 and 2011 portions of income given impacts the ministry of the church in very real ways.

Chapters 6 and 8 of this volume consider some of the implications and consequences of the difference between actual and potential giving levels among church members.

Giving in Dollars, 1968 through 2011. Per member giving measured in current dollars (the value the dollar had in the year it was given) increased overall from 1968 through 2011.[16] This increase was evident in giving to Total Contributions, and to the two subcategories of Congregational Finances and Benevolences, as presented in Figure 2.

Of course, dollars did not have the same purchasing power in both 1968 and 2011. To be able to compare dollars across different years, a deflator is used to factor out the effects of inflation. When inflation is factored out, the value that the dollars had in the same year the dollars were given ("current" dollar value) is converted to the value those adjusted dollars would have in a standard year ("inflation-adjusted" dollar value). The year 2005 serves as the standard year for the deflator series used in these analyses. Applying this deflator series, a gift of $5.00 in 1968 had the value, or purchasing power, of $22.71 in the year 2005, and a gift of $5.00 in the year 2011 had the value of $4.41 in the year 2005. By factoring out inflation, gifts in dollars can be compared across years in a more meaningful way.

Figure 2 presents the changes in inflation-adjusted dollar contributions to Total Contributions, and the two subcategories of Congregational Finances and Benevolences. As can be observed in Figure 2, giving to each of the categories of Total Contributions, Congregational Finances, and Benevolences declined in some years.

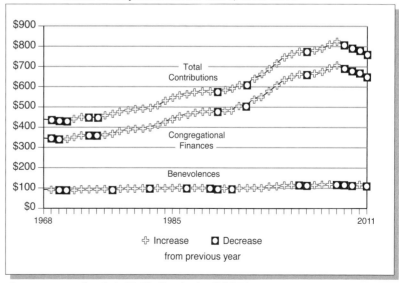

Figure 2: Changes in Per Member Giving to Total Contributions, Congregational Finances, and Benevolences, Inflation-Adjusted 2005 Dollars, 1968–2011

Source: empty tomb analysis; *YACC* adjusted series; U.S. BEA   empty tomb, inc. 2013

15

Of the total inflation-adjusted dollar increase between 1968 and 2011, 94% was directed to Congregational Finances. Stated another way, of each additional inflation-adjusted dollar donated in 2011 compared to 1968, 94¢ was directed to Congregational Finances. This emphasis on the internal operations of the congregation helps explain the finding that Benevolences represented 21% of all church activity in 1968, and 15% in 2011.

Figure 3: Per Member Giving to Congregational Finances and Benevolences, and U.S. Per Capita Disposable Personal Income, Inflation-Adjusted 2005 Dollars, 1968–2011

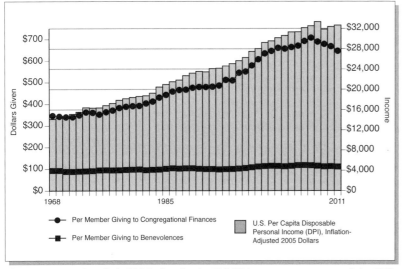

Source: empty tomb analysis; *YACC* adjusted series; U.S. BEA   empty tomb, inc. 2013

From 1968 to 2011, per member giving to Total Contributions increased 72% in inflation-adjusted dollars. However, during this same period, U.S. Per Capita Disposable (after-tax) Personal Income increased 131%. The fact that incomes increased faster than giving explains why per member giving increased overall from 1968 through 2011 in dollars, but shrank as a portion of income.

Figure 3 provides a comparison of per member giving to the categories of Congregational Finances and Benevolences with changes in U.S. per capita DPI, both in inflation-adjusted 2005 dollars.

Details of Church Member Giving, 1968 through 2011

The Composite Denominations. The first study that provided a basis for the present series was published in 1988. The *Yearbook of American and Canadian Churches* (*YACC*) series publishes church member giving data. Data for the years 1968 and 1985 could be confirmed for 31 denominations.[17] The data year 1968 was selected because, beginning that year, a consistent distinction was made between Full or Confirmed Membership and Inclusive Membership in the *YACC* series. The denominations that published data for both 1968 and 1985 included 29,476,782 Full or Confirmed Members in 1985. The current composite denomination set comprises approximately 100,000 of the estimated 350,000 religious congregations in the U.S.

The present church member giving report series extended the analysis for the original set of denominations beyond 1985. The current report analyzes the data set through 2011, the most recent year for which data was available at the time the report was written.[18] Also, data for the intervening years of 1969 through 1984, and 1986 through 2010, was included in the composite data set, as available.[19]

Financial Categories. Calculating contributions on a per member basis accounts for any changes in membership, either through growth or decline, which might have taken place during the period under review. The dollars given can be considered from two points of view. The *number of dollars given* by members indicates how much money the church has to spend. On the other hand, *giving as a percent of income* places donations in the larger context of the income available to church members, and demonstrates how the church fared compared to other church member spending priorities.

The key general category is giving as a percent of income. This category considers not only the dollars given, but also what portion those dollars represent of the resources available to the church member who gave them. One might say that considering giving as a percent of income reflects how the donation rated in the donor church member's overall lifestyle choices, a sort of thermometer to gauge the warmth of the member's commitment. Therefore, since the point of interest is in the level of priority members place on their church giving, the more useful category is giving as a percent of income.

Giving as a percent of income is, of course, based on the dollars given, set in the context of dollars available as income. Within the category of dollars given, there are two approaches: (1) current dollars; and (2) inflation-adjusted dollars.

Current dollars refers to the value that the dollar had in the year it was donated. However, inflation affects the value of dollars. A dollar in 2011 bought fewer goods or services than it did in 1968. In order to account for this factor, a deflator is applied to the current dollar values, to translate the dollars into the value they would have in a standard year, thereby neutralizing the economic impact of inflation.

Giving as a Percent of Income, 1968–2011.

The first approach to considering giving is giving as a percent of income, presented in Table 1. Unlike dollars, there is no distinction between current or inflation-adjusted when one is considering giving as a percent of income. So long as one compares current dollar giving to current dollar income when calculating the percent of income—or inflation-adjusted giving to inflation-adjusted income—the percent will be the same.

Table 1: Per Member Giving as a Percent of Income, 1968–2011

| Year | Per Full or Confirmed Member Giving as a Percent of Income | | | | | |
	Total Contrib.	↑↓	Cong. Finances	↑↓	Benevol.	↑↓
1968	3.11%	—	2.45%	—	0.66%	—
1969	3.03%	↓	2.39%	↓	0.65%	↓
1970	2.91%	↓	2.31%	↓	0.60%	↓
1971	2.84%	↓	2.26%	↓	0.58%	↓
1972	2.83%	↓	2.25%	↓	0.58%	↓
1973	2.76%	↓	2.21%	↓	0.55%	↓
1974	2.77%	↑	2.21%	↑	0.56%	↑
1975	2.73%	↓	2.15%	↓	0.58%	↑
1976	2.73%	↓	2.16%	↑	0.56%	↓
1977	2.70%	↓	2.15%	↓	0.55%	↓
1978	2.67%	↓	2.14%	↓	0.53%	↓
1979	2.67%	↓	2.14%	↓	0.53%	↑
1980	2.66%	↓	2.13%	↓	0.53%	↓
1981	2.64%	↓	2.11%	↓	0.53%	↓
1982	2.66%	↑	2.16%	↑	0.51%	↓
1983	2.65%	↓	2.14%	↓	0.50%	↓
1984	2.59%	↓	2.11%	↓	0.48%	↓
1985	2.60%	↑	2.11%	↑	0.48%	↑
1986	2.62%	↑	2.13%	↑	0.48%	↓
1987	2.60%	↓	2.13%	↑	0.47%	↓
1988	2.52%	↓	2.06%	↓	0.46%	↓
1989	2.50%	↓	2.05%	↓	0.45%	↓
1990	2.47%	↓	2.04%	↓	0.43%	↓
1991	2.47%	↑	2.05%	↑	0.43%	↓
1992	2.41%	↓	2.00%	↓	0.42%	↓
1993	2.42%	↑	2.01%	↑	0.41%	↓
1994	2.48%	↑	2.08%	↑	0.40%	↓
1995	2.43%	↓	2.03%	↓	0.40%	↓
1996	2.52%	↑	2.12%	↑	0.40%	↓
1997	2.49%	↓	2.09%	↓	0.40%	↓
1998	2.50%	↑	2.11%	↑	0.39%	↓
1999	2.57%	↑	2.17%	↑	0.40%	↑
2000	2.56%	↓	2.17%	↑	0.39%	↓
2001	2.58%	↑	2.19%	↑	0.39%	↑
2002	2.57%	↓	2.19%	↑	0.38%	↓
2003	2.51%	↓	2.15%	↓	0.37%	↓
2004	2.49%	↓	2.12%	↓	0.37%	↓
2005	2.52%	↑	2.14%	↑	0.38%	↑
2006	2.52%	↑	2.15%	↑	0.37%	↓
2007	2.53%	↑	2.17%	↑	0.36%	↓
2008	2.41%	↓	2.07%	↓	0.34%	↓
2009	2.48%	↑	2.13%	↑	0.35%	↑
2010	2.41%	↓	2.06%	↓	0.35%	↓
2011	2.32%	↓	1.98%	↓	0.34%	↓

Details in table may not compute to numbers shown due to rounding.
Source: empty tomb analysis; *YACC* adjusted series; U.S. BEA
empty tomb, inc. 2013

In Table 1, giving as a percent of income is presented for per member Total Contributions, and the two subcategories of Congregational Finances and Benevolences. The arrows indicate whether the percent of income in that category increased or decreased from the previous year. Inasmuch as the percent figures are rounded to the second decimal place, the arrows indicate the direction of even a slight increase or decrease for those years in which the percent provided appears to be the same numerical figure as the previous year.

A review of Table 1 yields the following information.

Overall, per member giving to Total Contributions as a percent of income decreased from 3.11% in 1968 to 2.32% in 2011, a decline of 25% in the portion of income donated to the church. Giving to Total Contributions as a percent of income decreased 28 of a possible 43 years, or 65% of the time, between 1968 and 2011.

Unlike measuring only the dollars given, considering giving as a percent of income takes into account changes in the resources available to the donor as well. U.S. per capita Disposable (after-tax) Personal Income (DPI) serves as an average income figure for the broad spectrum of church members included in the composite denominations data set.

U.S. per capita DPI was $3,112 in current dollars in 1968. When that figure was calculated in inflation-adjusted 2005 dollars, U.S. per capita DPI in 1968 was $14,136.

The current-dollar DPI figure for 2011 was $37,013. When inflation was factored out using inflation-adjusted 2005 dollars, 2011 U.S. per capita DPI was $32,653.

Thus, after-tax per capita income in inflation-adjusted dollars increased by $18,517, an increase of 131% from 1968 to 2011. During the same period, per member Total Contributions increased 72% in inflation-adjusted dollars. This difference explains how church member contributions could be increasing in inflation-adjusted dollars in most of the years from 1968 to 2011, and yet decreasing as a percent of income in most of the years from 1968 to 2011.

As a percent of income, giving to Congregational Finances, the amount spent to maintain the operations of the local congregation, decreased from one year to the next 56% of the time in the 1968–2011 period. Congregational Finances declined from 2.45% in 1968 to 1.98% in 2011, a percent decrease of 19% from the 1968 base in giving as a percent of income. Giving to Congregational Finances as a percent of income declined in more years than it increased between 1968 and 1993. In 1993, an intermittent increase in this category began, with giving to Congregational Finances as a percent of income increasing in more years than it declined through 2002. In 2003 through 2011, Congregational Finances as a portion of income decreased five times and increased four times. The 2011 figure was the lowest in the 1968–2011 period and for the first time fell below 2%.

As a percent of income, giving to Benevolences, church members' investment in the larger mission of the church, declined from 0.66% of income in 1968 to 0.34% in 2011, a decline of 48% as a portion of income. In the 1968–2011 period, the portion of income that went to Benevolences declined 81% of the time, from one year to the next. The decline in giving to Benevolences as a percent of income was fairly steady in the 1968 to 2011 period, never increasing more than two years in

Between 1968 and 2011, as a portion of income, church member giving to Total Contributions declined 25%, Congregational Finances 19%, and Benevolences 48%.

a row (see 1974 and 1975). The level of giving to Benevolences as a percent of income in 2008 and 2011 both measured 0.34%. In unrounded numbers, the 2011 figure was smaller than the 2008 figure.

An increase in giving to Benevolences as a percent of income in 2005 is evident. This increase appears to have been a function of the disaster response opportunities that year. The year 2005 included the Indian Ocean earthquake and related tsunami that occurred the day after Christmas in 2004, Hurricanes Katrina, Rita and Wilma, and the Pakistani earthquake. All presented opportunities for compassionate response in churches. The declines in this category that occurred in 2006–2008 and in 2010–2011 suggest that the 2005 giving was crisis-oriented, and did not represent a change in the pattern of long-term decline.

Giving in Current Dollars, 1968–2011.
Table 2 presents per member contributions in current dollars for the composite denominations data set. Per member giving is presented as Total Contributions, and the two subcategories of Congregational Finances and Benevolences. U.S. per capita DPI is also included. The last column includes the Benevolences dollar figures divided by the DPI, yielding Benevolences as a percent of income, which is also presented in Table 1.

As can be seen in Table 2, the per member amount given to Total Contributions, Congregational Finances, and Benevolences increased in current dollars between 1968 and 2011.

Overall, from 1968 to 2011, Total Contributions to the church in current dollars increased $762.35 on a per member basis. That amounted to an increase of 788% from the 1968 base.

Of this increase, $656.83 was allocated to Congregational Finances, for the benefit of members within the congregation, an increase of 860% for this category from its 1968 base.

Benevolences, or outreach activities of the congregation, increased by $105.52, an increase of 516% over the 1968 base level for the category. Meanwhile, U.S. per capita DPI increased from

Table 2: Per Member Giving to Total Contributions, Congregational Finances, and Benevolences, U.S. Per Capita Disposable Personal Income, Current Dollars, and Per Member Giving to Benevolences as a Percent of Income, 1968–2011

Year	Current Dollars			U.S. Per Capita Disposable Personal Income	Per Member Giving to Benevolences as % of Income
	Per Full or Confirmed Member Giving				
	Total Contrib.	Cong. Finances	Benevol.		
1968	$96.79	$76.35	$20.44	$3,112	0.66%
1969	$100.82	$79.34	$21.47	$3,324	0.65%
1970	$104.36	$82.87	$21.49	$3,586	0.60%
1971	$109.55	$87.08	$22.48	$3,859	0.58%
1972	$116.97	$93.16	$23.81	$4,140	0.58%
1973	$127.37	$102.01	$25.36	$4,615	0.55%
1974	$138.87	$110.79	$28.08	$5,010	0.56%
1975	$150.19	$118.45	$31.73	$5,497	0.58%
1976	$162.87	$129.15	$33.72	$5,972	0.56%
1977	$175.82	$140.23	$35.60	$6,514	0.55%
1978	$193.05	$154.74	$38.31	$7,220	0.53%
1979	$212.42	$170.17	$42.25	$7,956	0.53%
1980	$233.57	$186.90	$46.67	$8,794	0.53%
1981	$256.59	$205.15	$51.44	$9,726	0.53%
1982	$276.72	$223.93	$52.79	$10,390	0.51%
1983	$293.52	$237.68	$55.83	$11,095	0.50%
1984	$316.25	$257.63	$58.62	$12,232	0.48%
1985	$335.43	$272.95	$62.48	$12,911	0.48%
1986	$354.20	$288.73	$65.47	$13,540	0.48%
1987	$367.87	$301.73	$66.14	$14,146	0.47%
1988	$382.54	$313.15	$69.40	$15,206	0.46%
1989	$403.23	$331.06	$72.16	$16,134	0.45%
1990	$419.65	$346.48	$73.17	$17,004	0.43%
1991	$433.57	$358.67	$74.90	$17,532	0.43%
1992	$445.00	$368.28	$76.72	$18,436	0.42%
1993	$457.47	$380.54	$76.94	$18,909	0.41%
1994	$488.83	$409.35	$79.48	$19,678	0.40%
1995	$497.71	$416.00	$81.71	$20,470	0.40%
1996	$538.39	$453.34	$85.05	$21,355	0.40%
1997	$554.59	$466.07	$88.52	$22,255	0.40%
1998	$587.90	$495.56	$92.34	$23,534	0.39%
1999	$624.81	$527.99	$96.82	$24,356	0.40%
2000	$664.25	$563.52	$100.72	$25,946	0.39%
2001	$690.79	$586.58	$104.22	$26,816	0.39%
2002	$714.30	$609.09	$105.21	$27,816	0.38%
2003	$724.23	$618.47	$105.76	$28,827	0.37%
2004	$753.65	$642.79	$110.86	$30,312	0.37%
2005	$788.34	$670.67	$117.67	$31,343	0.38%
2006	$836.38	$714.60	$121.78	$33,183	0.37%
2007	$875.71	$751.41	$124.29	$34,550	0.36%
2008	$873.13	$748.34	$124.79	$36,200	0.34%
2009	$865.70	$743.23	$122.47	$34,899	0.35%
2010	$866.57	$741.16	$125.41	$35,920	0.35%
2011	$859.14	$733.18	$125.96	$37,013	0.34%

Details in table may not compute to numbers shown due to rounding.
Source: empty tomb analysis; *YACC* adjusted series; U.S. BEA
empty tomb, inc. 2013

$3,112 in 1968, to $37,013 in 2011, an increase of 1089% from the 1968 base. Therefore, Benevolences shrank 48% as a portion of income between 1968 and 2011.

In 2008, per member giving to Total Contributions decreased in current dollars for the first time in the 1968–2011 period. Declines were also observed in 2009 and 2011. Although per member giving to Total Contributions increased in 2010, it did not recover to the 2007 level.

Per member contributions to Congregational Finances in current dollars declined in each of the years 2008, 2009, 2010, and 2011. This period of decline is in contrast to the 1969–2007 pattern of consistent increases. In 2009, even though the current dollar amount declined that year, giving as a portion of income increased to this category.

In light of the consistent decline in giving as a percent of income to Benevolences in the 1968–2011 period, it is of interest to observe that, during the 2008–2011 period, per member giving to Benevolences in current dollars declined only in 2009, in contrast to the changes in Total Contributions and Congregational Finances.

In 2008, per member giving to Total Contributions decreased in current dollars for the first time in the 1968–2011 period.

As noted earlier, considering changes in giving in current dollars provides a limited evaluation tool. For example, while a congregation or denomination might accurately state that members in general gave more current dollars from one year to the next, the reality of inflation's impact should be taken into account, to understand how the buying power of those dollars given might be affected.

Giving in Inflation-Adjusted Dollars, 1968–2011. The U.S. Bureau of Economic Analysis (BEA) publishes the deflator series that is used to factor out inflation. This deflator series allows dollar figures to be compared more precisely across years. The current year of base comparison in the U.S. BEA series is 2005. By applying the Implicit Price Deflator for Gross National Product to the current-dollar church member giving data, the data can be reviewed across years with the effects of inflation thus factored out.

Table 3 presents per member giving in inflation-adjusted dollars, as well as U.S. per capita DPI, also in inflation-adjusted dollars. The arrows next to the three inflation-adjusted giving category columns are included to provide a quick reference as to whether giving increased or decreased from one year to the next.

When the effects of inflation were removed, one may note that per member giving decreased in a number of years. Per member giving to Total Contributions did increase overall from 1968 to 2011. However, when inflation was factored out, the percent increase was smaller than in current dollars. Per member giving to Total Contributions in inflation-adjusted dollars increased from $439.65 in 1968 to $757.93 in 2011, an increase of 72% from the 1968 base.

Congregational Finances also increased in inflation-adjusted 2005 dollars from 1968 to 2011. Overall, per member giving to Congregational Finances increased from $346.82 in inflation-adjusted dollars to $646.81 in 2011, an increase of $299.99, or 86%.

Benevolences also increased from 1968 to 2011 when adjusted for inflation, although proportionately less than Congregational Finances. From 1968 to 2011, per member giving to Benevolences in inflation-adjusted dollars increased $18.29, an increase of 20% from the 1968 base.

U.S. per capita DPI, considered in inflation-adjusted dollars, increased from $14,136 in 1968, to $32,653 in 2011, an increase of 131%.

Per member giving to Benevolences as a percent of income is again included in Table 3. The figures for this category are the same in both Tables 2 and 3. Because the same deflator is applied to both the giving dollars and the income dollars, per member giving to Benevolences as a percent of income is proportionally the same, whether the information is considered as current or inflation-adjusted dollars. As long as current dollar giving is compared to current dollar income, or inflation-adjusted giving is compared to inflation-adjusted income, giving as a percent of income will be the same for both series.

One may observe the consequences of the fact that U.S. per capita DPI increased 131% in inflation-adjusted dollars from 1968 to 2011, while per member giving to Benevolences increased 20%. The result was the overall decline of 48% to Benevolences in the portion of income given, from the 1968 base.

In the 2008–2011 period, per member giving to Benevolences decreased only once in current dollars. However, in inflation-adjusted dollars, the subcategory declined three times in the four years during that period. Per member giving in inflation-adjusted dollars to Total Contributions and Congregational Finances declined in each of the four years of 2008 through 2011.

Giving in Inflation-Adjusted Dollars, 1968 and 2011. The first report, which served as the basis for the present series on church member giving, considered data for the denominations in the composite

Table 3: Per Member Giving to Total Contributions, Congregational Finances, and Benevolences, U.S. Per Capita Disposable Personal Income, Inflation-Adjusted 2005 Dollars, and Per Member Giving to Benevolences as a Percent of Income, 1968–2011

	Inflation-Adjusted 2005 Dollars						U.S. Per Capita Disposable Personal Income	Per Member Giving to Benevolences as % of Income
	Per Full or Confirmed Member Giving							
Year	Total Contrib.	↑↓	Cong. Finances	↑↓	Benevol.	↑↓		
1968	$439.65	—	$346.82	—	$92.83	—	$14,136	0.66%
1969	$436.41	↓	$343.46	↓	$92.95	↑	$14,389	0.65%
1970	$429.13	↓	$340.76	↓	$88.37	↓	$14,745	0.60%
1971	$429.00	↓	$340.98	↑	$88.02	↓	$15,111	0.58%
1972	$439.10	↑	$349.73	↑	$89.38	↑	$15,541	0.58%
1973	$452.92	↑	$362.74	↑	$90.18	↑	$16,411	0.55%
1974	$452.79	↓	$361.24	↓	$91.55	↑	$16,336	0.56%
1975	$447.38	↓	$352.85	↓	$94.53	↑	$16,375	0.58%
1976	$458.76	↑	$363.77	↑	$94.99	↑	$16,822	0.56%
1977	$465.55	↑	$371.29	↑	$94.26	↓	$17,248	0.55%
1978	$477.62	↑	$382.85	↑	$94.77	↑	$17,863	0.53%
1979	$485.17	↑	$388.67	↑	$96.50	↑	$18,172	0.53%
1980	$488.96	↑	$391.27	↑	$97.69	↑	$18,409	0.53%
1981	$491.08	↑	$392.63	↑	$98.45	↑	$18,614	0.53%
1982	$499.15	↑	$403.93	↑	$95.21	↓	$18,742	0.51%
1983	$509.27	↑	$412.39	↑	$96.87	↑	$19,250	0.50%
1984	$528.84	↑	$430.81	↑	$98.03	↑	$20,455	0.48%
1985	$544.41	↑	$443.00	↑	$101.41	↑	$20,955	0.48%
1986	$562.46	↑	$458.50	↑	$103.96	↑	$21,501	0.48%
1987	$567.66	↑	$465.61	↑	$102.06	↓	$21,829	0.47%
1988	$570.69	↑	$467.17	↑	$103.53	↑	$22,685	0.46%
1989	$579.60	↑	$475.87	↑	$103.72	↑	$23,191	0.45%
1990	$580.75	↑	$479.49	↑	$101.26	↓	$23,532	0.43%
1991	$579.50	↓	$479.38	↓	$100.11	↓	$23,433	0.43%
1992	$581.05	↑	$480.87	↑	$100.18	↑	$24,072	0.42%
1993	$584.32	↑	$486.05	↑	$98.27	↓	$24,152	0.41%
1994	$611.48	↑	$512.06	↑	$99.42	↑	$24,615	0.40%
1995	$609.85	↓	$509.73	↓	$100.12	↑	$25,082	0.40%
1996	$647.37	↑	$545.10	↑	$102.27	↑	$25,678	0.40%
1997	$655.32	↑	$550.72	↑	$104.60	↑	$26,297	0.40%
1998	$686.95	↑	$579.05	↑	$107.90	↑	$27,499	0.39%
1999	$719.49	↑	$608.00	↑	$111.49	↑	$28,047	0.40%
2000	$748.70	↑	$635.17	↑	$113.53	↑	$29,245	0.39%
2001	$761.42	↑	$646.54	↑	$114.87	↑	$29,557	0.39%
2002	$774.80	↑	$660.68	↑	$114.12	↓	$30,172	0.38%
2003	$769.39	↓	$657.03	↓	$112.35	↓	$30,624	0.37%
2004	$778.71	↑	$664.16	↑	$114.55	↑	$31,320	0.37%
2005	$788.34	↑	$670.67	↑	$117.67	↑	$31,343	0.38%
2006	$810.18	↑	$692.22	↑	$117.96	↑	$32,143	0.37%
2007	$824.35	↑	$707.35	↑	$117.00	↓	$32,524	0.36%
2008	$804.07	↓	$689.15	↓	$114.92	↓	$33,337	0.34%
2009	$790.39	↓	$678.57	↓	$111.82	↓	$31,863	0.35%
2010	$780.85	↓	$667.85	↓	$113.00	↑	$32,367	0.35%
2011	$757.93	↓	$646.81	↓	$111.12	↓	$32,653	0.34%

Details in table may not compute to numbers shown due to rounding.
Source: empty tomb analysis; *YACC* adjusted series; U.S. BEA
empty tomb, inc. 2013

data set for the years 1968 and 1985. With data now available through 2011, a broader trend can be reviewed for the period under discussion, the 44-year range of 1968 through 2011.

The per member amount donated to Total Contributions in inflation-adjusted 2005 dollars was $318.28 greater in 2011 than it was in 1968 for the denominations in the composite data set. This amount represented an average increase of $7.40 a year in per member contributions over this 43-year interval.

Gifts to Congregational Finances also increased between 1968 and 2011. Per member contributions to Congregational Finances were $346.82 in 1968, in inflation-adjusted 2005 dollars, and increased to $646.81 in 2011, a total increase of $299.99, with an average annual rate of change of $6.98.

In inflation-adjusted 2005 dollars, gifts to Benevolences were $92.83 in 1968 and grew to $111.12 in 2011, an increase of $18.29, with an annual average rate of change of $0.43.

Table 4 presents per member gifts to Total Contributions, Congregational Finances, and Benevolences in inflation-adjusted 2005 dollars for the years 1968 and 2011.

Table 4: Per Member Giving to Total Contributions, Congregational Finances, and Benevolences, Inflation-Adjusted 2005 Dollars, 1968 and 2011

	Per Member Giving in Inflation-Adjusted 2005 Dollars								
	Total Contributions			Congregational Finances			Benevolences		
Year	Per Member Giving	Difference from 1968 Base	Average Annual Diff. in $ Given	Per Member Giving	Difference from 1968 Base	Average Annual Diff. in $ Given	Per Member Giving	Difference from 1968 Base	Average Annual Diff. in $ Given
1968	$439.65			$346.82			$92.83		
2011	$757.93	$318.28	$7.40	$646.81	$299.99	$6.98	$111.12	$18.29	$0.43

Details in table may not compute to numbers shown due to rounding. empty tomb, inc. 2013
Source: empty tomb analysis; *YACC* adjusted series; U.S. BEA

Giving as a Percent of Income, 1968 and 2011. Between 1968 and 2011, Total Contributions declined from 3.11% to 2.32% as a portion of income, an absolute decline of 0.79%, a decrease of more than three-quarters of a percent of income donated to the church. The percent change in the portion of income donated to the church in the 44-year period was -25%.

Per member gifts to Congregational Finances measured 2.45% of income in 1968, and 1.98% in 2011. The absolute change in giving as a percent of income was -0.47%. The percent change in the portion of income to Congregational Finances, from the 1968 base, was a decline of 19%.

From 1968 to 2011, the portion of member income directed to Benevolences decreased from 0.66% to 0.34%, an absolute difference of -0.32%, about two-thirds of the decline in Congregational Finances, even though Benevolences began from a smaller base. The decline in the portion of income given to Benevolences translated to a percent change in giving as a percent of income of -48% from the 1968 base.

Table 5 presents per member giving to Total Contributions, Congregational Finances, and Benevolences as a percent of income in 1968 and 2011.

Table 5: Per Member Giving to Total Contributions, Congregational Finances, and Benevolences, Percent of Income, 1968 and 2011

Year	Per Member Giving as a Percent of Income		
	Total Contributions	Congregational Finances	Benevolences
1968	3.11%	2.45%	0.66%
2011	2.32%	1.98%	0.34%
Absolute Difference in Per Member Giving as a Percent of Income from 1968 Base	-0.79%	-0.47%	-0.32%
Percent Change in Giving as a Percent of Income, Calculated from 1968 Base	-25%	-19%	-48%

Details in table may not compute to numbers shown due to rounding.
Source: empty tomb analysis; *YACC* adjusted series; U.S. BEA   empty tomb, inc. 2013

Notes for Chapter 1

[1]   In addition to the rich vein of voluntarily reported denominational data, there is also a set of Census Bureau data for 1850, 1860, 1870, and 1890, that provides "limited information on religious bodies (number of congregations and buildings, and value of edifices)." A Census of Religious Bodies was also carried out in 1906, 1916, 1926, and 1936. See: U.S. Bureau of the Census, *Historical Statistics of the United States, Colonial Times to 1970, Bicentennial Edition, Part 1* (Washington, DC, 1975), pp. 389-390. For further discussion about the Census of Religious Bodies data, see also: Benson Y. Landis, "The 1936 Census of Religious Bodies," in Landis, ed., *Yearbook of American Churches (Fifteenth Issue) (Biennial)*, 1941 Edition (Jackson Heights, NY: Yearbook of American Churches Press, 1941), particularly pp. 138-141.

[2]   For a discussion of the historical data categories available in the *Yearbook of American and Canadian Churches* series, see John Ronsvalle and Sylvia Ronsvalle, "Giving Trends and the Church's Priorities," *The State of Church Giving through 2003* (Champaign, Ill., empty tomb, inc., 2005), pp. 107-111, including Table 27, p. 111. This chapter is also available at: <http://www.emptytomb.org/SCG03Priorities.pdf>.

[3]   Emily Chan and Gene Takagi, "Charities Should Drink Deeply of the 'Three Cups of Tea' Scandal's Lessons," *The Chronicle of Philanthropy*, May 5, 2011, p. 31.

[4]   Wm. Robert Johnston; "SBC Giving, Financial Data"; 11/3/2008; <http://www.johnstonsarchive.net/Baptist; sbcdata2.html>; p. 1 of 7/24/2012 printout.

[5]   Adelle M. Banks, RNS; "Cash-Strapped Cities Look to Tax Churches for Road Use"; *The Christian Century*; 1/21/2011; <http://www.christiancentury.org/article/2011-01/cash-strapped-cities-look-tax-churches-road-use>; p. 1 of 7/17/2011 11:48 AM printout.

[6]   The National Commission on Fiscal Responsibility and Reform; "The Moment of Truth"; The White House; December 1, 2010; <http://www.fiscalcommission.gov/sites/fiscalcommission.gov/files/documents/TheMomentof Truth12_1_2010.pdf>; p. 31 of 7/22/2011 download.

[7]   John D. McKinnon; "Tax Plan Cuts Both Ways"; online.wsj.com; 7/21/2011; <http://online.wsj.com/article/SB10 0014240531119042334045764583620245521 34.html?mod=googlenews_wsj>; p. 2 of 7/22/2011 3:14 PM printout.

[8]   The NonProfit Times Weekly Newsletter; "Cash-Strapped Boston Going After Nonprofits"; 12/27/2010; <http://www. thenonprofittimes.com/newsletters/weekly/nptimesweeklydec372010.html#sub1>; pp. 1-2 of 7/17/2011 11:25 AM printout.

[9]   Banks, pp. 1-2.

[10]   G. Jeffrey MacDonald, RNS, appearing as "Shaky Economy Imperils Church Pensions," *The Christian Century*, January 11, 2011, pp. 14-15. Also: G. Jeffrey MacDonald, RNS, with contributions by Dianna L. Cagle, Biblical Recorder assistant managing editor; appearing as, "Market Bumps Raise Church Pension Concerns"; *Biblical*

Recorder; 1/4/2011; <http://www.biblicalrecorder.org/post/2011/01/04/Market-bumps-raise-church-pension-concerns.aspx>; p. 1 of 1/10/2011 7:01 PM printout.

[11] Mark Hrywna, "Evangelical Groups Avoid Legislation, For Now," *The NonProfit Times*, February 1, 2011, pp. 1, 8.

[12] Commission on Accountability and Policy for Religious Organizations; "Enhancing Accountability For The Religious And Broader Nonprofit Sector"; December 2012; Commission-Report-December-2010.pdf accessed through <http://religiouspolicycommission.org/CommissionReport.aspx>; p. 30 of 8/13/2013 6:27 PM printout.

[13] Commission on Accountability and Policy for Religious Organizations Report, pp. 34-35.

[14] Commission on Accountability and Policy for Religious Organizations Report, p. 36.

[15] *The NonProfit Times*, "2013 Power & Influence Top 50," August 1, 2013, p. 11.

[16] No adjustment was made in the composite data for missing denominational data in the 1968–2011 analysis. The 2011 composite data set membership represented 98.4% of the benchmark 1985 membership of the composite data set.

[17] John Ronsvalle and Sylvia Ronsvalle, *A Comparison of the Growth in Church Contributions with United States Per Capita Income* (Champaign, IL: empty tomb, inc., 1988).

[18] Two of the original 31 denominations merged in 1987, bringing the total number of denominations in the original data set to 30. As of 1991, one denomination reported that it no longer had the staff to collect national financial data, resulting in a maximum of 29 denominations from the original set, which could provide data for 1991 through 2011. Of these 29 denominations, one reported data for 1968 through 1997, but did not have financial data for 1998 through 2011. A second denomination merged with another communion not included in the original composite set but has since been added; having merged, this new denomination has not collected financial data for 2001–2011 from its congregations, although it did do a survey of congregations for one year. A third denomination indicated that the national office would no longer provide data after 2006 in order to focus on other priorities. Another denomination did not provide for 2008 through 2011 data. Two additional denominations indicated that they could not provide 2011, but hoped to do so in the future. Therefore, the composite data for 2011 includes information from 23 communions in the data set. Throughout this report, what was an original set of 31 denominations in 1985 will be referred to as the composite denominations. Data for 31 denominations will be included for 1968 and 1985, as well as for intervening years, as available.

[19] For 1986 through 2011, annual denominational data has been obtained which represented for any given year at least 98.4% (the 2011 percent) of the 1985 Full or Confirmed Membership of the denominations included in the 1968–1985 study. For 1986 through 2011, the number of denominations for which data was available varied from a low of 23 denominations of a possible 30 in 2011 to a high of 29 in 1987 through 1997. For the years 1969 through 1984, the number of denominations varied from a low of 28 denominations of a possible 31 in 1971–1972 and 1974–1975 to 31 in 1983, representing at least 99.59% of the membership in the data set. No computation was made to adjust the series for missing data in this chapter. The denominational giving data considered in this analysis was obtained either from the *Yearbook of American and Canadian Churches* series, or directly in correspondence with a denominational office. For a full listing of the data used in this analysis, including the sources, see Appendix B-1.

chapter 2

Church Member Giving for 38 Denominations, 2010 to 2011

Overview of Giving for 38 Denominations, 2010–2011

The composite denominations data set considered in chapter 1 was expanded to include 15 additional denominations for which 2010 and 2011 data was also available.

The composite set and the expanded set of 38 denominations demonstrated similar patterns of change from 2010 to 2011 when per member giving was considered in current and inflation-adjusted dollars, as well as a percent of income.

Details of Giving for 38 Denominations, 2010–2011

The 1968–2011 analysis in chapter 1 considers data for a group of denominations that published their membership and financial information for 1968 and 1985 in the *Yearbook of American and Canadian Churches (YACC)* series. That initial set of communions, considered in the first report on which the present series on church giving is based, has served as a denominational composite set analyzed for subsequent data years.

For the two most recent years, a subset of 23 denominations in the composite set reported data for both 2010 and 2011.

Data for both 2010 and 2011 for an additional 15 denominations was either published in the relevant editions of the *YACC* series, or obtained directly from denominational offices. By adding the data for these 15 denominations to that of the composite group for these two years, giving patterns in an expanded set of 38 communions can be considered.

In this enlarged comparison, the number of 2011 Full or Confirmed Members increased from 26.7 million in the composite set to 36,590,981 in the expanded set, a 37% increase in the number of members considered. The number of denominations increased from 23 to 38. The larger group of denominations included both The United Methodist Church and The Episcopal Church, which were not included in the original 1968–1985 analysis because of the unavailability of confirmed 1968 data at the time of that study. A list of the denominations included in the present analysis is contained in Appendix A.

Table 6 presents the data for the 38 denominations in tabular form, including per member giving in current and inflation-adjusted 2005 dollars, and giving as a percent of income.

Table 6: Per Member Giving in 38 Denominations, Current Dollars, Inflation-Adjusted 2005 Dollars, and as a Percent of Income, 2010 and 2011

Year	Total Contributions			Congregational Finances			Benevolences		
	$ Given in Current $	$ Given in Inflation-Adj. '05 $	Giving as % of Income	$ Given in Current $	$ Given in Inflation-Adj. '05 $	Giving as % of Income	$ Given in Current $	$ Given in Inflation-Adj. '05 $	Giving as % of Income
2010	$902.08	$812.85	2.51%	$761.25	$685.95	2.12%	$140.83	$126.90	0.39%
2011	$901.12	$794.97	2.43%	$759.07	$669.65	2.05%	$142.06	$125.32	0.38%
Difference from the 2010 Base	-$0.96	-$17.88	-0.08%	-$2.18	-$16.30	-0.07%	$1.22	-$1.58	-0.01%
% Change in Giving as % of Income from the 2010 Base			-3.1%			-3.2%			-2.1%

Details in table may not compute to numbers shown due to rounding.　　　　　empty tomb, inc. 2013
Source: empty tomb analysis; *YACC* adjusted series; U.S. BEA

Per Member Giving as a Percent of Income. For the 23 denominations in the composite subset that had data for from 2010 to 2011, giving as a percent of income decreased to Total Contributions, and to the subcategories of Congregational Finances and Benevolences, as follows:

- Total Contributions: 2.41% in 2010 to 2.32% in 2011, a percent change of -3.8% from the 2010 base.

- Congregational Finances: 2.06% in 2010 to 1.98% in 2011, a percent change of -4.0% from the 2010 base.

- Benevolences: 0.35% in 2010 and 0.34% in 2011, a percent change of -2.5% from the 2010 base.

In the expanded group of 38 denominations, a decline in giving as a percent of income to Total Contributions and to the subcategories of Congregational Finances and Benevolences was also observed. It may be noted that the percent of income given in the expanded set was higher than the composite set.

In the expanded set, the percent of income given on a per member basis to Total Contributions measured 2.51% in 2010 and 2.43% in 2011, a percent change of -3.1% in giving as a percent of income from the 2010 base.

Congregational Finances was 2.12% in 2010 and decreased to 2.05% in 2011, a change of -3.2% from the 2010 base.

Benevolences measured 0.39% in 2010 and 0.38% in 2011, a percent change of -2.1% from the 2010 base.

Giving in Dollars. Per member giving in current dollars for the 23 denominations in the composite subset was as follows:

- Total Contributions: from $866.57 in 2010 to $859.14 in 2011, a decrease of $7.43.

- Congregational Finances: from $741.16 in 2010 to $733.18 in 2011, a decline of $7.98.

- Benevolences: from $125.41 in 2010 to $125.96 in 2011, an increase of $0.55.

When the 2010 and 2011 data was adjusted for inflation, per member giving in the composite subset was as follows:

- Total Contributions: from $780.85 in 2010 to $757.93 in 2011, a decline of $22.92.

- Congregational Finances: from $667.85 in 2010 to $646.81 in 2011, a decline of $21.04.

- Benevolences: from $113.00 in 2010 to $111.12 in 2011, a decrease of $1.88

As can be seen in Table 6, in the expanded set, per member giving to Total Contributions in current dollars demonstrated the same pattern as the composite set, decreasing to Total Contributions and the subcategory of Congregational Finances, while increasing to Benevolences.

When the 2010 and 2011 data was adjusted for inflation, again, the expanded set of denominations demonstrated the same pattern as the composite set. Per member giving to Total Contributions and the subcategories of Congregational Finances and Benevolences decreased.

Summary. When the 23 denominations in the composite set that reported data for 2010 and 2011, considered in chapter 1 of this volume, was expanded to include 15 additional denominations, the number of church members in the giving analysis increased by 37%. The pattern of change from 2010 to 2011 was the same in both the composite subset and the expanded set of denominations, whether per member giving to the three categories was considered in current dollars, inflation-adjusted dollars, or giving as a percent of income.

chapter 3

Church Member Giving in Denominations Defined by Organizational Affiliation, 1968, 1985, and 2011

Overview of Giving by Organizational Affiliation, 1968, 1985, and 2011

The communions included in the composite denominations data set considered in chapter 1 of this volume span the theological spectrum. Reviewing data for defined subsets within the composite group allows for additional analysis.

For example, the theory that evangelical Protestants donate more money to their churches than do members of mainline Protestant denominations can be tested by comparing giving patterns in two subgroups of communions within the composite denominations data set.

Of course, there is diversity of opinion within any denomination, as well as in multi-communion groupings. For purposes of the present analysis, however, two groups may serve as general standards for comparison, since they have been characterized as representing certain types of denominations. Specifically, the National Association of Evangelicals (NAE) has, by choice of its title, defined its denominational constituency. And traditionally, the National Council of the Churches of Christ in the U.S.A. (NCC) has counted mainline denominations among its members.

Recognizing that there are limitations in defining a denomination's theological perspectives merely by membership in one of these two organizations, a review of giving patterns of the two subsets of denominations may nevertheless provide some insight into how widely spread current giving patterns may be. Therefore, an analysis of 1968, 1985, and 2011 giving patterns was completed for the two subsets of those denominations that were affiliated with one of these two interdenominational organizations.

During the 1968–2011 period, members of evangelical Protestant denominations gave larger portions of income to their churches than did members of mainline Protestant denominations.

Also of note, the 1968–2011 decline in giving as a portion of income to Total Contributions was greater among the members of the evangelical denominations than it was among the members of the mainline denominations.

Figure 4: Per Member Giving to Total Contributions, Congregational Finances, and Benevolences as a Percent of Income, Six NAE and Eight NCC Denominations, 1968, 1985, and 2011

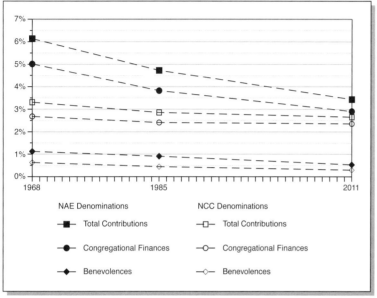

Source: empty tomb analysis; *YACC* adjusted series; U.S. BEA   empty tomb, inc. 2013

Figure 5: Per Member Giving to Total Contributions, Congregational Finances, and Benevolences, Six NAE and Eight NCC Denominations, Inflation-Adjusted 2005 Dollars, 1968, 1985, and 2011

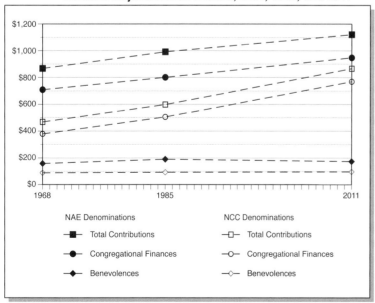

Source: empty tomb analysis; *YACC* adjusted series; U.S. BEA   empty tomb, inc. 2013

Giving as a portion of income to Congregational Finances declined among the NAE-affiliated denominations from 1968 to 1985, and again to 2011. The level of giving to Congregational Finances in the NCC-affiliated denominations also declined during the 1968 to 1985, and 1985 to 2011 period, although to a lesser degree than among the NAE-affiliated denominations.

Per member giving as a portion of income to Benevolences declined in both the evangelical and the mainline communions from 1968 to 1985, and again in 2011.

Figure 4 presents data for giving as a percent of income to Total Contributions, Congregational Finances, and Benevolences for both the NAE- and NCC-affiliated denominations in graphic form for the years 1968, 1985 and 2011.

In the NAE-affiliated denominations, per member giving in inflation-adjusted dollars increased to all three categories in 1985. In 2011, per member giving in these communions increased to Total Contributions and Congregational Finances, but declined to Benevolences. In the NCC-affiliated denominations, per member giving in inflation-adjusted dollars increased to all three categories in 1985 and again in 2011. Figure 5 presents the data for per member contributions in inflation-adjusted 2005 dollars in graphic form for the years 1968, 1985, and 2011 for both the NAE-affiliated and NCC-affiliated denominations.

Changes in membership were considered in combination with the giving patterns.

Membership in the evangelical denominations grew between 1968 and 2011, in contrast to the mainline denominations, which decreased in membership. Therefore, although evangelicals were receiving a smaller portion of income per member in 2011 than was donated in 1968, aggregate donations in inflation-adjusted dollars were higher in 2011 than in 1968 for this group.

Among the mainline denominations, membership decreased from 1968 to 2011. This fact, in combination with the increase in inflation-adjusted dollars being directed to Congregational Finances, may account in part for the finding that aggregate Benevolences donations in inflation-adjusted dollars were 40 percent smaller in 2011 than in 1968 for these communions.

Details of Giving by Organizational Affiliation, 1968–2011

In the composite group, membership and financial data is available for 1968, 1985 and 2011 for six communions affiliated with the National Association of Evangelicals (NAE). This analysis is impacted by the trend in the number of denominations reporting data, as discussed in chapter 1. Two of the composite communions that were not able to provide 2011 data were NAE-affiliated denominations.

Eight communions affiliated with the National Council of the Churches of Christ in the U.S.A. (NCC) in the composite set had membership and financial data available for 1968, 1985 and 2011.

Using 1985 data as the reference point, the six denominations affiliated with the NAE in the present analysis represented 13% of the total number of NAE-member denominations listed in the *Yearbook of American and Canadian Churches* (*YACC*) series. These six denominations represented 21% of the total number of NAE-member denominations with membership and financial data listed in the *YACC*, and approximately 15% of the total membership of those NAE-member denominations that provided membership data in the *YACC*.[1]

Data for 2011 was also available for eight NCC-member denominations. In 1985, these eight denominations represented 24% of the total number of NCC constituent bodies listed in the *YACC*; 29% of the NCC constituent bodies with membership and financial data listed in the *YACC*; and approximately 27% of the total membership of those NCC constituent bodies with membership data listed in the *YACC*.[2]

Per Member Giving to Total Contributions, 1968, 1985 and 2011.
Per member giving as a percent of income to Total Contributions for a composite of the six NAE-member denominations was 6.14% in 1968. That year, per member giving as a percent of income to Total Contributions was 3.31% for a composite of the eight NCC-member denominations.

In 1985, the NAE denominations' per member giving as a percent of income level was 4.73%, while the NCC level was 2.85%.

Per member giving as a portion of income to Benevolences declined in both the evangelical and the mainline communions from 1968 to 1985, and again in 2011.

Table 7: **Per Member Giving to Total Contributions as a Percent of Income, Six NAE and Eight NCC Denominations, 1968, 1985, and 2011**

	Total Contributions										
	NAE Denominations					NCC Denominations					
Year	Number of Denom. Analyzed	Total Contrib. Per Member as % of Income	Diff. in Total Contrib. as % of Income from Previous Base	Percent Change in Total Contrib. as % of Income Figured from Previous Base	Avg. Annual Percent Change in Total Contrib. as % of Income	Number of Denom. Analyzed	Total Contrib. Per Member as % of Income	Diff. in Total Contrib. as % of Income from Previous Base	Percent Change in Total Contrib. as % of Income Figured from Previous Base	Avg. Annual Percent Change in Total Contrib. as % of Income
1968	6	6.14%				8	3.31%			
1985	6	4.73%	-1.41%	-22.91% from '68	-1.35%	8	2.85%	-0.45%	-13.73% from '68	-0.81%
2011	6	3.43%	-1.30%	-21.13% from '85	-0.81%	8	2.65%	-0.20%	-6.09% from '85	-0.23%

Details in the above table may not compute to the numbers shown due to rounding.   empty tomb, inc. 2013
Source: empty tomb analysis; *YACC* adjusted series; U.S. BEA

As noted in Table 7, the data shows the NAE-member denominations received a larger portion of their members' incomes than did NCC-affiliated denominations in both 1968 and 1985. This information supports the assumption that denominations identifying with an evangelical perspective received a higher level of support than denominations that may be termed mainline.

The analysis also indicates that the decline in levels of giving observed in the larger composite denominations set was evident among both the NAE-member denominations and the NCC-member denominations. While giving levels decreased for both sets of denominations between 1968 and 1985, the decrease in Total Contributions was more pronounced in the NAE-affiliated communions. The percent change in the percent of income donated in the NAE-member denominations, in comparison to the 1968 base, was -23% between 1968 and 1985, while the percent change in percent of income given to the NCC-member denominations was -14%.

A decline in giving as a percent of income continued among the six NAE-member denominations during the 1985–2011 period. By 2011, per member giving as a percent of income to Total Contributions had declined from the 1985 level of 4.73% to 3.43%, a percentage change of -21% in the portion of members' incomes donated over that 27-year period.

The eight NCC-affiliated denominations also declined in giving as a percent of income to Total Contributions during 1985–2011, from the 1985 level of 2.85% to 2.65% in 2011. The percent decrease from the 1985 base was 6%.

In 2011 the difference in per member giving as a percent of income between the NAE-affiliated denominations and the NCC-affiliated denominations was not as large as it had been in 1968. Comparing the two rates in giving as a percent of income to Total Contributions between the NAE-member denominations and the NCC-member denominations in this analysis, the NCC-affiliated denominations received 54% as much of per capita income as the NAE-member denominations did in 1968, 60% as much in 1985, and 77% in 2011.

For the NAE-affiliated denominations, during the 1985 to 2011 period, the rate of decrease in the average annual percent change in per member giving as a percent of income to Total Contributions slowed in comparison to the 1968–1985 annual percent change from the 1968 base. The 1968–1985 average annual percent change was -1.35%. The annual rate of change for 1985–2011 was -0.81%.

In the NCC-member denominations, during the 1968–1985 period, the average annual percent change from the 1968 base in giving as a percent of income was -0.81%. Between 1985 and 2011, the average annual change from 1985 was -0.23%.

Per Member Giving to Congregational Finances and Benevolences, 1968, 1985 and 2011. Were there any markedly different patterns between the two subsets of denominations defined by affiliation with the NAE and the NCC in regards to the distribution of Total Contributions between the subcategories of Congregational Finances and Benevolences?

In the subcategory of Congregational Finances, both the NAE-affiliated and the NCC-affiliated denominations declined in giving as a portion of income between 1968 and 2011. However, the decline was more pronounced among the NAE-affiliated denominations. Therefore, the percent of per capita income that the NCC-affiliated denominations received in 1968 was 53% of the percent received by the NAE-affiliated denominations, 63% in 1985, and 81% in 2011. Table 8 presents the Congregational Finances giving data for the NAE and NCC denominations in 1968, 1985 and 2011.

Table 8: Per Member Giving to Congregational Finances as a Percent of Income, Six NAE and Eight NCC Denominations, 1968, 1985, and 2011

		Congregational Finances								
		NAE Denominations					NCC Denominations			
Year	Number of Denom. Analyzed	Cong. Finances Per Member as % of Income	Diff. in Cong. Finances as % of Income from Previous Base	Percent Change in Cong. Finances as % of Income Figured from Previous Base	Avg. Annual Percent Change in Cong. Finances as % of Income	Number of Denom. Analyzed	Cong. Finances Per Member as % of Income	Diff. in Cong. Finances as % of Income from Previous Base	Percent Change in Cong. Finances as % of Income Figured from Previous Base	Avg. Annual Percent Change in Cong. Finances as % of Income
1968	6	5.01%				8	2.68%			
1985	6	3.82%	-1.19%	-23.77% from '68	-1.40%	8	2.41%	-0.27%	-10.05% from '68	-0.59%
2011	6	2.90%	-0.92%	-18.37% from '85	-0.71%	8	2.36%	-0.05%	-1.99% from '85	-0.08%

Details in the above table may not compute to the numbers shown due to rounding.
Source: empty tomb analysis; *YACC* adjusted series; U.S. BEA

empty tomb, inc. 2013

In the subcategory of Benevolences, both groups posted declines in the portion of income directed to that category between 1968 and 2011. The NCC-affiliated denominations received 56% as much of per capita income for Benevolences in 1968

Table 9: **Per Member Giving to Benevolences as a Percent of Income,
Six NAE and Eight NCC Denominations, 1968, 1985, and 2011**

	Benevolences									
	NAE Denominations					NCC Denominations				
Year	Number of Denom. Analyzed	Benevol. Per Member as % of Income	Diff. in Benevol. as % of Income from Previous Base	Percent Change in Benevol. as % of Income Figured from Previous Base	Avg. Annual Percent Change in Benevol. as % of Income	Number of Denom. Analyzed	Benevol. Per Member as % of Income	Diff. in Benevol. as % of Income from Previous Base	Percent Change in Benevol. as % of Income Figured from Previous Base	Avg. Annual Percent Change in Benevol. as % of Income
1968	6	1.12%				8	0.63%			
1985	6	0.91%	-0.21%	-19.08% from '68	-1.12%	8	0.44%	-0.18%	-29.36% from '68	-1.73%
2011	6	0.53%	-0.38%	-33.51% from '85	-1.29%	8	0.30%	-0.15%	-23.55% from '85	-0.91%

Details in the above table may not compute to the numbers shown due to rounding.   empty tomb, inc. 2013
Source: empty tomb analysis; *YACC* adjusted series; U.S. BEA

as did the NAE-affiliated denominations, 49% in 1985, and 56% in 2011. Table 9 presents the Benevolences giving data for the NAE and NCC denominations in 1968, 1985 and 2011.

In 1968, the NAE-affiliated members were giving 6.14% of per capita income to their churches. Of that, 5.01% went to Congregational Finances, while 1.12% went to Benevolences. In 1985, of the 4.73% of income donated to Total Contributions, 3.82% was directed to Congregational Finances. This represented a percent change in the portion of income going to Congregational Finances of -24% from the 1968 base. Per member contributions to Benevolences among these NAE-member denominations declined from 1.12% in 1968 to 0.91% in 1985, representing a percent change of -19% from the 1968 base in the portion of income donated to Benevolences.

In 2011, the 3.43% of income donated by the NAE-member denominations to their churches was divided between Congregational Finances and Benevolences at the 2.90% and 0.53% levels, respectively. The percent change between 1985 and 2011 in contributions to Congregational Finances as a percent of income was a decline of 18%. In contrast, the percent change in contributions to Benevolences as a percent of income was a decline of 34% over the same 27-year period. The annual rate in the percent change in giving as a percent of income to Benevolences increased, from -1.12% from 1968 to 1985 to -1.29% from 1985 to 2011.

In 1968, the NCC-member denominations were giving 3.31% of per capita incomes to their churches. Of that, 2.68% went to Congregational Finances. In 1985, of the 2.85% of income donated to these communions, 2.41% went to Congregational Finances. This represented a percent change from the 1968 base in the portion of income going to Congregational Finances of -10%. In contrast, per member contributions as a percent of income to Benevolences among these same NCC-affiliated denominations had declined from 0.63% in 1968 to 0.44% in 1985, representing a percent change of -29% from the 1968 base in the portion of income donated to Benevolences.

In 2011, the 2.65% of income donated by the NCC-affiliated members to their churches was divided between Congregational Finances and Benevolences at the 2.36% and 0.30% levels, respectively. Congregational Finances decreased from 2.41% in 1985 to 2.36% in 2011. The 2011 percent change in contributions to Congregational Finances as a percent of income from 1985 was a decrease of 2%.

The portion of income directed to Benevolences by these NCC-member denominations declined from 1968 to 1985, and continued to decline from 1985 to 2011. The percent change in contributions to Benevolences as a percent of income declined from 0.44% in 1985 to the 2011 level of 0.30%, a decline of 24% over this 27-year period. The annual percent change from the 1985 base in giving as a percent of income to Benevolences indicated a lower rate of decline at -0.91% between 1985 and 2011, compared to the 1968–1985 annual rate of -1.73%.

Changes in Per Member Giving, 1968 to 2011.

For the NAE-affiliated denominations, per member giving as a percent of income to Congregational Finances declined from 5.01% in 1968 to 2.90% in 2011, a change of -42% from the 1968 base. In Benevolences, the -53% change reflected a decline from 1.12% in 1968 to 0.53% in 2011.

For the NCC-affiliated denominations, in the subcategory of Congregational Finances, per member giving as a percent of income was 2.68% in 1968, and 2.36% in 2011, a decline of 12%. In the subcategory of Benevolences, the level of giving decreased from 0.63% in 1968 to 0.30% in 2011, which produced a decline similar to that of the NAE-affiliated denominations, that is, a 53% decline in the portion of income donated to this subcategory.

Table 10 presents the 1968–2011 percent change in per member giving as a percent of income to Total Contributions, Congregational Finances, and Benevolences in both the NAE- and NCC-affiliated communions.

Table 10: Percent Change in Per Member Giving as a Percent of income, Six NAE and Eight NCC Denominations, 1968 to 2011

Year	NAE Denominations				NCC Denominations			
	Number of Denom. Analyzed	Total Contrib.	Cong. Finances	Benevol.	Number of Denom. Analyzed	Total Contrib.	Cong. Finances	Benevol.
1968	6	6.14%	5.01%	1.12%	8	3.31%	2.68%	0.63%
2011	6	3.43%	2.90%	0.53%	8	2.65%	2.36%	0.30%
% Chg. 1968-'11	6	-44%	-42%	-53%	8	-20%	-12%	-53%

Details in the above table may not compute to the numbers shown due to rounding.
Source: empty tomb analysis; *YACC* adjusted series; U.S. BEA   empty tomb, inc. 2013

Per Member Giving in Inflation-Adjusted 2005 Dollars.

The NAE-affiliated group's level of per member support to Total Contributions in inflation-adjusted 2005 dollars was $867.31 in 1968. This increased to $991.12 in 1985, and by 2011 increased to $1,121.06.

For the NAE-affiliated denominations, per member contributions in inflation-adjusted 2005 dollars to the subcategory of Congregational Finances increased from 1968 to 1985, and again from 1985 to 2011. Per member contributions in inflation-adjusted 2005 dollars to Benevolences increased between 1968 and 1985, and, decreased between 1985 and 2011. Of the increased per member giving in inflation-adjusted dollars between 1968 and 2011, 94% went to Congregational Finances.

Table 11: Per Member Giving in Six NAE and Eight NCC Denominations, Inflation-Adjusted 2005 Dollars, 1968, 1985, and 2011

	NAE Denominations					NCC Denominations				
Year	Number of Denom. Analyzed	Total Contrib.	Cong. Finances	Benevol.	Benevol. as % of Total Contrib.	Number of Denom. Analyzed	Total Contrib.	Cong. Finances	Benevol.	Benevol. as % of Total Contrib.
1968	6	$867.31	$708.89	$158.42	18%	8	$467.77	$378.79	$88.98	19%
1985	6	$991.12	$801.08	$190.04	19%	8	$598.23	$505.05	$93.18	16%
2011	6	$1,121.06	$947.57	$173.49	15%	8	$866.35	$769.56	$96.80	11%
$ Diff. '68-'11		$253.75	$238.68	$15.07			$398.59	$390.77	$7.81	
% Chg. '68-'11		29%	34%	10%			85%	103%	9%	

Details in the above table may not compute to the numbers shown due to rounding.

Source: empty tomb analysis; *YACC* adjusted series; U.S. BEA

empty tomb, inc. 2013

The NCC-affiliated group also experienced an increase in inflation-adjusted per member Total Contributions between 1968 and 2011. The 1968 NCC level of per member support in inflation-adjusted 2005 dollars was $467.77. In 1985, this had increased to $598.23, and in 2011 the figure was $866.35.

The NCC-member denominations experienced an increase in inflation-adjusted per member donations to Congregational Finances in both 1985 and 2011 as well. Although 98% of the increase between 1968 and 2011 was directed to Congregational Finances, gifts to Benevolences also increased in inflation-adjusted 2005 dollars between 1968 and 1985, and again between 1985 and 2011.

As a portion of Total Contributions, the NAE-member denominations directed 18% of their per member gifts to Benevolences in 1968, 19% in 1985, and 15% in 2011. The NCC-member denominations directed 19% of their per member gifts to Benevolences in 1968, 16% in 1985, and 11% in 2011.

Table 11 presents the levels of per member giving to Total Contributions, Congregational Finances, and Benevolences, in inflation-adjusted 2005 dollars, and the percentage of Total Contributions that went to Benevolences in 1968, 1985 and 2011, for both sets of denominations. In addition, the percent change from 1968 to 2011 contributions, from the 1968 base, in per member inflation-adjusted 2005 dollars is noted.

Aggregate Dollar Donations, 1968 and 2011. The NCC-member denominations and the NAE-member denominations differed in terms of changes in membership. The impact of this difference was evident at the aggregate dollar level.

Table 12 considers aggregate giving data for the six NAE-member denominations included in this analysis. Membership in these six NAE-member denominations increased 55% from 1968–2011.

As measured in current aggregate dollars, giving in each of the three categories of Total Contributions, Congregational Finances, and Benevolences was greater in

**Table 12: Aggregate Giving, Six NAE Denominations,
Current and Inflation-Adjusted 2005 Dollars, 1968 and 2011**

Year	Number of Denom. Analyzed	Membership	Current Dollars			Inflation-Adjusted 2005 Dollars		
			Total Contributions	Congregational Finances	Benevolences	Total Contributions	Congregational Finances	Benevolences
1968	6	525,199	$100,280,739	$81,963,632	$18,317,107	$455,510,965	$372,308,117	$83,202,848
2011	6	814,762	$1,035,367,031	$875,135,961	$160,231,070	$913,400,643	$772,044,817	$141,355,826
% Chg.		55%	932%	968%	775%	101%	107%	70%

Details in the above table may not compute to the numbers shown due to rounding.   empty tomb, inc. 2013
Source: empty tomb analysis; *YACC* adjusted series; U.S. BEA

2011 than in 1968 for the NAE-member denominations. This was true even though per member giving as a portion of income declined to all three categories during this period.

The same can be said for the three aggregate categories when inflation was factored out by converting the current dollars to inflation-adjusted 2005 dollars. These denominations have been compensated for a decline in giving as a percent of income to all three categories by the increase in total membership. As long as these denominations continue to grow in membership, their national and regional programs may not be affected in the immediate future by the decline in the portion of income donated.

Table 13 below considers aggregate data for the eight NCC-member denominations. The NCC-related denominations experienced a membership decline of 45% between 1968 and 2011. The increase in current dollar donations was sufficient to result in an increase in aggregate current dollars in each of the three categories of Total Contributions, Congregational Finances, and Benevolences.

However, the figures in the inflation-adjusted 2005 dollars account for the acknowledged financial difficulties in many of these communions, particularly in the category of Benevolences. The impact of the decline in membership was evident at the aggregate dollar level. The increase in giving to Congregational Finances as a portion of income noted above was tempered by a loss of members. Between 1968

**Table 13: Aggregate Giving, Eight NCC Denominations,
Current and Inflation-Adjusted 2005 Dollars, 1968 and 2011**

Year	Number of Denom. Analyzed	Membership	Current Dollars			Inflation-Adjusted 2005 Dollars		
			Total Contributions	Congregational Finances	Benevolences	Total Contributions	Congregational Finances	Benevolences
1968	8	12,876,821	$1,326,045,714	$1,073,798,710	$252,247,004	$6,023,373,672	$4,877,577,606	$1,145,796,066
2011	8	7,056,605	$6,929,859,472	$6,155,603,744	$774,255,728	$6,113,521,011	$5,430,472,721	$683,048,290
% Chg.		-45%	423%	473%	207%	1%	11%	-40%

Details in the above table may not compute to the numbers shown due to rounding.   empty tomb, inc. 2013
Source: empty tomb analysis; *YACC* adjusted series; U.S. BEA

and 2011, while the NCC-related communions experienced an increase of 85% in per member giving to Total Contributions in inflation-adjusted 2005 dollars—from $467.77 in 1968 to $866.35 in 2011—aggregate Total Contributions in 2011 to these eight denominations measured 1% larger in inflation-adjusted 2005 dollars in 2011 than in 1968.

Further, Congregational Finances absorbed all of the increased giving at the aggregate level, with aggregate dollars to Congregational Finances increasing 11%. The resulting 40% decline in aggregate Benevolences receipts in inflation-adjusted 2005 dollars between 1968 and 2011 provides insight into the basis for any cutbacks at the denominational level.

Notes for Chapter 3

[1] The 1985 total church membership estimate of 3,388,414 represented by NAE denominations includes *YACC* 1985 membership data for each denomination where available or, if 1985 membership data was not available, membership data for the most recent year prior to 1985. Full or Confirmed membership data was used except in those instances where this figure was not available, in which case Inclusive Membership was used.

[2] The 1985 total church membership estimate of 39,621,950 represented by NCC denominations includes *YACC* 1985 membership data for each denomination where available or, if 1985 membership data was not available, membership data for the most recent year prior to 1985. Full or Confirmed membership data was used except in those instances where this figure was not available, in which case Inclusive Membership was used.

chapter 4

Church Member Giving and Membership in 11 Denominations, 1921–2011

Overview of Giving and Membership, 1921–2011

A continuing feature in this ongoing series on church member giving is an analysis of available giving data throughout this century. Because of the fixed nature of the data source, the analysis remains fairly static. However, the data can now be updated to include information through 2011. This data makes use of the U.S. Bureau of Economic Analysis (BEA) per capita Disposable (after-tax) Personal Income (DPI) series, with the benchmark year being 2005 to adjust current dollars for inflation.

For the period 1921 through 2011, the preferable approach would be to analyze the entire composite denominations data set considered in chapter 1 of this volume. Unfortunately, comparable data since 1921 is not readily available for these communions. However, data over an extended period of time is available in the *Yearbook of American and Canadian Churches* (*YACC*) series for a group of 11 Protestant communions, or their historical antecedents. This set includes 10 mainline Protestant communions and the Southern Baptist Convention.

The available data has been reported fairly consistently over the time span of 1921 to 2011.[1] The value of the multiyear comparison is that it provides a historical time line over which to observe giving patterns.

A review of per member giving as a portion of income during the 1921 through 2011 period found that the portion of income given was above three percent during two multiyear periods. From 1922 through 1933 and then again from 1958 through 1962, per member giving as a percent of income was at or above 3%. This relatively high level of giving is particularly interesting because per capita DPI was also increasing from 1922–1927 (with the exception of 1925), and from 1959 through 1962. However, unlike after 1933, when the country was experiencing the Great

Figure 6: Per Member Giving in 11 Denominations as a Percent of Income, and U.S. Per Capita Disposable Personal Income, Inflation-Adjusted 2005 Dollars, 1921–2011

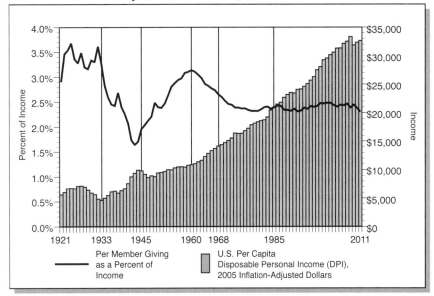

Source: empty tomb analysis; *YACC* adjusted series; U.S. BEA   empty tomb, inc. 2013

Depression followed by World War II, no major national catastrophes explain the drop below 3% after 1962.

Per member giving as a percent of income was at a low point during World War II, recovered during the 1950s, and then declined fairly steadily during the 1960s. The decline in giving as a percent of income that began after the peak in 1960 continued with little interruption until 1980, when giving began to alternate increases with decreases. Giving as a portion of income was 2.31% in 1992, the lowest level since 1948. An intermittent upward trend in giving was again visible beginning in 1993 until 2002, when an intermittent overall downward trend began. By 2011, the level of giving as a percent of income was at 2.30%, the lowest percentage since 1948.

Figure 6 contrasts per member giving as a percent of income for a group of 11 Protestant denominations, with U.S. per capita DPI in inflation-adjusted 2005 dollars, for the period 1921 through 2011.

By 2011, U.S. per capita DPI had increased 481% since 1921 in inflation-adjusted 2005 dollars, and 602% since 1933—the depth of the Great Depression.

Meanwhile, by 2011, per member giving in inflation-adjusted 2005 dollars had increased 361% since 1921, and 395% since the depth of the Great Depression.

Consequently, per member giving as a percent of income was lower in 2011 than in either 1921 or 1933. In 1921, per member giving as a percent of income was 2.9%. In 1933, it was 3.3%. In 2011, per member giving as a percent of income was 2.3% for the group of the 11 denominations considered in this section. By 2011, the percent change in the per member portion of income donated to the church had declined by 21% from the 1921 base, and by 30% from the 1933 base.

Membership in absolute numbers increased for the group of 11 denominations on a fairly regular basis from 1921 until 1968, when it peaked. However, as a portion of U.S. population, the group's peak was earlier, in 1961, when membership in the 11 denominations represented 20% of the U.S. population. The decline in membership as a percent of U.S. population that began in 1962 continued through 2011.

It is of some interest to note that the ongoing decline in membership as a percent of U.S. population in the set of 11 denominations began in 1962, one year after the decline in giving as a percent of income that occurred in 1961, the first such decline since 1951. While giving as a portion of income displayed a pattern of increase in some years and decline in others after 1961, the decline in membership as a percent of U.S. population that began in 1962 continued uninterrupted through the year 2011.

Figure 7 presents both per member giving as a percent of income and membership as a percent of U.S. population, for the group of 11 Protestant denominations, from 1921 through 2011.

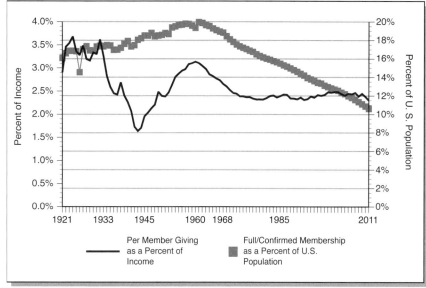

Figure 7: Per Member Giving as a Percent of Income, and Membership as a Percent of U.S. Population, 11 Denominations, 1921–2011

Source: empty tomb analysis; *YACC* adjusted series; U.S. BEA

empty tomb, inc. 2013

Details of Giving and Membership, 1921–2011

Giving as a Percent of Income. The period under consideration in this section of the report began in 1921. At that point, per member giving as a percent of income was 2.9%. In current dollars, U.S. per capita DPI was $555, and per member giving was $16.10. When inflation was factored out by converting both income and giving to 2005 dollars, per capita income in 1921 measured $5,617 and per member giving was $163.05.

From 1922 through 1933, giving as a percent of income stayed above the 3% level. The high was 3.7% in 1924, followed closely by the amount in 1932, when per member giving measured 3.6% of per capita income. This trend is of particular interest inasmuch as per capita income was generally increasing in inflation-adjusted dollars between 1921 and 1927, with the exception of 1925. Even as people were increasing in personal affluence, they also continued to maintain a giving level of more than 3% to their churches. Even after income began to decline, including the economic reverses in the early years of the Great Depression, giving measured above 3% from 1929 through 1933.

The year 1933 was the depth of the Great Depression. Per capita income was at the lowest point it would reach between 1921 and 2011, whether measured in current or inflation-adjusted dollars. Yet per member giving as a percent of income was 3.3%. Income had decreased by 17% between 1921 and 1933 in inflation-adjusted 2005 dollars, from $5,617 to $4,649. Meanwhile, per member giving had decreased 7%, from $163.05 in 1921 to $151.80 in 1933, in inflation-adjusted dollars. Therefore, giving as a percent of income actually increased from 2.9% in 1921 to 3.3% in 1933, an increase of 12% in the portion of income contributed to the church.

Giving in inflation-adjusted 2005 dollars declined from 1933 to 1934, although income began to recover in 1934. Giving then began to increase again in 1935.

In inflation-adjusted dollars, giving did not surpass the 1927 level of $250.25 until 1953, when giving grew from $239.85 in 1952 to $264.04 in 1953.

During World War II, incomes improved rapidly. Meanwhile, church member giving increased only modestly in current dollars. When inflation was factored out, per member giving was at $157.05 in 1941, the year the United States entered the war. It declined to $152.23 in 1942, increased in 1943 to $154.12, and then to $169.65 in 1944. However, income in inflation-adjusted dollars grew from $7,583 in 1941 to $8,792 in 1942, $9,395 in 1943, and reached a high for this period of $9,938 in 1944, an income level that would not be surpassed again until 1953. Thus, giving as a percent of income reached a low point during the three full calendar years of formal U.S. involvement in World War II, at levels of 1.73% in 1942, 1.64% in 1943, and 1.71% in 1944.

In 1945, the last year of the war, U.S. per capita income was $9,825 in inflation-adjusted dollars. Giving in inflation-adjusted dollars increased from $169.65 in 1944, to $192.25 in 1945, the highest inflation-adjusted dollar amount it had been since 1930. Although per member giving increased 27% between 1933 and 1945, per capita income increased 111%. Giving as a percent of income therefore declined from the 3.3% level in 1933, to 2.0% in 1945.

The unusually high level of per capita income slumped after the war but had recovered to war levels by the early 1950s. By 1960, U.S. per capita income was 11% higher in inflation-adjusted 2005 dollars than it had been in 1945, increasing from $9,825 in 1945 to $10,865 in 1960. Meanwhile, per member giving in inflation-adjusted dollars increased 77%, from $192.25 in 1945 to $340.76 in 1960. Giving as a portion of income recovered to the level it had been from 1922 through 1933, and stayed above 3% from 1958 through 1962. Giving as a percent of income reached a postwar high of 3.14% in 1960, and then began to decline.

For the second time in the century, giving levels were growing to, or maintaining a level above, three percent of income even while incomes were also expanding. From 1921–1928, incomes expanded 24%. During this time giving grew to above 3% and stayed there. From 1950–1962, incomes grew 20%. Again, giving grew to above 3% in 1958 and stayed there through 1962. In both cases, church members increased or maintained their giving levels, even as their incomes increased.

In the 1920s, the economic expansion was interrupted by the Great Depression, followed by World War II.

In contrast to the economic upheaval earlier in the century, however, the economy continued to expand through the 1960s. Yet the portion of income given was not sustained above 3%. By 1968, giving as a percent of income declined to 2.7% for this group of 11 communions. U.S. per capita income increased 30% in inflation-adjusted 2005 dollars between 1960 and 1968, from $10,865 in 1960 to $14,136 in 1968. In comparison, per member giving increased 10% in inflation-adjusted dollars, from the 1960 level of $340.76 to the 1968 level of $375.07.

By 1985, per member giving increased 34% in inflation-adjusted 2005 dollars, from $375.07 in 1968 to $501.54 in 1985. U.S. per capita income measured $20,955 in 1985, an increase of 48% over the 1968 level of $14,136. Giving as a percent of income, therefore, measured 2.4% in 1985, representing a 10% decline from the 1968 level of 2.7%.

The year 2011 was the latest year for which data was available for the 11 denominations considered in this section. In that year, per member giving as a percent of income rounded to 2.3%, a 4% decrease from the 1985 level. Per member giving increased 50% in inflation-adjusted 2005 dollars, from $501.54 in 1985 to $751.46 in 2011. U.S. per capita income increased 56% during this period, from the 1985 level of $20,955 to the 2011 level of $32,653.

Membership and Giving, 1921–2011. Membership was changing for this group of 11 denominations during the 1921–2011 period as well.

Between 1921 and 1961, the portion of U.S. population that this group of 11 denominations represented grew from 16.1% of the U.S. population to 20%, or one-fifth of the United States.

In that same year of 1961, the first decline in giving as a percent of income occurred since 1951.

The next year, in 1962, a decline in membership as a percent of U.S. population began for this group that would continue through the year 2011. Membership growth slowed and then the number of members declined between 1968 and 1969, from 37,785,048 to 37,382,659. Meanwhile, U.S. population continued to expand. Therefore, while this group represented 20% of U.S. population in 1961, by the year 2011, this group represented 10.6% of U.S. population.

During the 1961–2011 period, the Southern Baptist Convention (SBC) grew from 9,978,139 to 15,978,112. Meanwhile, the other 10 denominations, all of which might be termed mainline Protestant, declined in membership as a group, from 26,683,648[2] in 1961 to 17,134,555 in 2011.

The growth in the number of members in the SBC offset the mainline Protestant membership loss to some degree. Nevertheless, the group's membership of the combined group of 11 denominations declined, measuring 36,661,788 in 1961 and 33,112,667 in 2011. U.S. population increased from 183,742,000 in 1961, when the group of 11 denominations represented 20% of the U.S. population, to 312,036,000 in 2011, when the 11 denominations represented 10.6% of the U.S. population.

Although the decrease in giving as a percent of income that began in 1961 resulted in giving levels varying between 2.34% and 2.32% during 1977 through 1980, the level of giving as a portion of income recovered to 2.41% by 1983 and was at 2.43% in 1986, and 2.42% in 1987. The level of giving as a percent of income went up and down until it reached a low of 2.31% in 1992. An intermittent increase occurred through 2001 and 2002, when the percent given was 2.48%. An intermittent decline began in 2002 until the level of giving as a percent of income was 2.30% in 2011.

In contrast, membership as a percent of population for the 11 denominations as a group began a decline in 1962 that continued uninterrupted through the year 2011.

The next year, in 1962, a decline in membership as a percent of U.S. population began for this group that would continue through the year 2011.

Change in Per Member Giving and Total Membership. In Table 14, giving as a percent of U.S. per capita DPI is presented for the first and last year in the period noted. The difference between giving in these two years was calculated and then divided by the number of annual intervals in the period to produce the Average Annual Change.

When considered as a portion of income, the period of 1950–1955 posted the highest Average Annual Change in giving as a percent of income, followed by the 1955–1960 period. Giving grew to 3.1% in 1958, and a level above 3% was maintained through 1962. However, the 1960–1964 period also was the period within which giving as a portion of income began to decline. It is clear from the Average Annual Change column that giving as a portion of income began a downward trend in the 1960–1964 period that continued through the 1975–1980 period. Reversing in the 1980–1985 period, the average annual change was again negative in the 1985–1990 period. During the 1990–1995 and 1995–2000 periods, positive change was measured, but the increases did not recover to the 1950–1960 Average Annual Change levels. The Average Annual Change for the 2000–2005, the 2005–2010, and the 2010–2011 periods were again negative. The single-year change from 2010 to 2011 was the largest since the 2007–2008 change.

Meanwhile, during the 1950–2011 period, the group of 11 denominations shrank as a portion of U.S. population. The 1950–1955 period posted an average annual increase of 0.21% in the portion of U.S. population that these denominations represented. The 1955–1960 period posted a decline. The group of 11 denominations nevertheless peaked in 1961 at 20% of U.S. population. In 1964–1970, a period of decline began that continued through 2011.

Table 14: Average Annual Change in Per Member Giving as a Percent of U.S. Disposable Personal Income and in Membership as a Percent of U.S. Population, 11 Denominations, 1950–2011

Time Period	Per Member Giving as % of Income			Membership as % of U.S. Population		
	First Year in Period	Last Year in Period	Average Annual Change	First Year in Period	Last Year in Period	Average Annual Change
1950–1955	2.40%	2.88%	0.10%	18.58%	19.64%	0.21%
1955–1960	2.88%	3.14%	0.05%	19.64%	19.34%	-0.06%
1960–1964 [3]	3.14%	2.86%	-0.07%	19.34%	19.53%	0.05%
1964–1970 [3]	2.86%	2.52%	-0.06%	19.53%	18.10%	-0.24%
1970–1975	2.52%	2.37%	-0.03%	18.10%	17.05%	-0.21%
1975–1980	2.37%	2.32%	-0.01%	17.05%	16.16%	-0.18%
1980–1985	2.32%	2.39%	0.01%	16.16%	15.48%	-0.14%
1985–1990	2.39%	2.32%	-0.01%	15.48%	14.59%	-0.18%
1990–1995	2.32%	2.36%	0.01%	14.59%	13.59%	-0.20%
1995–2000	2.36%	2.47%	0.02%	13.59%	12.82%	-0.16%
2000–2005	2.47%	2.44%	-0.01%	12.82%	11.97%	-0.14%
2005–2010	2.44%	2.38%	-0.01%	11.97%	10.87%	-0.22%
2010–2011	2.38%	2.30%	-0.08%	10.87%	10.61%	-0.26%

Details in the above table may not compute to the numbers shown due to rounding.   empty tomb, inc. 2013
Source: empty tomb analysis; *YACC* adjusted series; U.S. BEA

Change in Per Member Giving and U.S. Per Capita Disposable Personal Income, in Inflation-Adjusted 2005 Dollars. For this group of 11 communions, per member giving in inflation-adjusted 2005 dollars increased half the time during the 1921–1947 period. Per member giving in inflation-adjusted dollars decreased from 1924 to 1925. While it increased from 1925 to 1926 and again in 1927, giving began a seven-year decline in 1928. This seven-year period, from 1928 to 1934, included some of the worst years of the Great Depression. Giving increased again in 1935. Declines in 1939, 1940, 1942, 1946 and 1947 alternated with increases in the other years.

Then, from 1948 through 1968,[4] the members in these 11 communions increased per member giving in inflation-adjusted 2005 dollars each year. During the first 12 years of this period, 1948–1960, per member giving averaged an increase of $11.93 a year. Although giving continued to increase for the next few years, it was at the slower rate of $4.29 per year. Overall, in inflation-adjusted 2005 dollars, income grew 58% from 1948 to 1968, while per member giving increased 90%, resulting in the recovery of giving levels to 3% or more in the late 1950s and early 1960s.

Per member giving in inflation-adjusted dollars declined in 1969, 1970 and 1971, followed by two years of increase and two years of decline.

The longest sustained period of average annual increases in per member giving in inflation-adjusted dollars during the 91-year period occurred during the 27 years that include 1976 through 2002. During this time, income increased an average of $513.48 annually in inflation-adjusted 2005 dollars. Meanwhile, per member giving increased $13.46 on average each year, a higher overall rate than during the 21 years including 1948 through 1968, when the annual increase was $8.87. However, while giving increased 88% from 1976 to 2002, it increased 90% from 1948–1968. U.S. per capita income increased 79% from 1976 to 2002. Because giving increased at a faster rate than income during the 1976 to 2002 period, giving as a percent of income was 2.37% in 1976 and 2.48% in 2002.

By reviewing this data in smaller increments of years from 1950 to 2011, the time period in which giving began to decline markedly can be identified. Data for the first and last year in each period is presented. The difference between these two years was calculated and then divided by the number of annual intervals in the period. The Average Annual Change in Giving as a Percent of the Average Annual Change in Income column presents the Per Member Giving Average Annual Change divided by the U.S. Per Capita Income Average Annual Change.

As indicated in Table 15 on the following page, during the 1950 to 2011 period, the highest increase in the average annual change in per member giving measured in inflation-adjusted 2005 dollars occurred from 1995–2000. However, when the average annual change in per member giving was considered as a portion of the average annual change in per capita income, the largest increase occurred in the 1955–1960 period, followed by the 1950–1955 period. In 1995–2000, the annual dollar increase in giving of $25.97 represented 3% of the average annual increase in U.S. per capita income, compared to the 8% represented by the increased dollars given during 1950–1955 and 1955–1960.

The longest sustained period of average annual increases in per member giving in inflation-adjusted dollars during the 91-year period occurred during the 27 years that include 1976 through 2002.

Between 1960 and 1964 in these communions, the average annual change in per member giving declined markedly from the previous five years. While income was increasing at an annual rate of $361.02 in this four-year period, the average annual increase in per member contributions in inflation-adjusted 2005 dollars was $2.85 in 1960–1964, only a third of the $8.68 annual rate of increase in the 1955–1960 period.

The 1960–1964 period predates many of the controversial issues often cited as reasons for declining giving as a percent of income. Also, it was in the 1960–1964 period when membership as a percent of population began to decrease in mainline denominations, 10 of which are included in this group. Therefore, additional exploration of that period of time might be merited.

Increases in per member giving were consistently low from 1960–1975, compared to all but the two most recent segments in the 1950–2011 period, as indicated in Table 15. The annual rates of increase of $2.85 per year from 1960 to 1964, $3.31 from 1964 to 1970, and $3.21 from 1970 to 1975, were the lowest in the 1950 to 2005 period. From 1960 to 1975, the increase in dollars given represented less than one percent of the average annual increase in per capita income.

Table 15: Average Annual Change in U.S. Per Capita Disposable Personal Income and Per Member Giving, 11 Denominations, Inflation-Adjusted 2005 Dollars, 1950–2011

Time Period	U.S. Per Capita Income			Per Member Giving			Avg. Ann. Chg. Giv. as % Avg. Annual Chg. in Income
	First Year in Period	Last Year in Period	Average Annual Change	First Year in Period	Last Year in Period	Average Annual Change	
1950–1955	$9,455	$10,330	$175.13	$226.60	$297.34	$14.15	8.08%
1955–1960	$10,330	$10,865	$106.88	$297.34	$340.76	$8.68	8.13%
1960–1964 [3]	$10,865	$12,309	$361.02	$340.76	$352.14	$2.85	0.79%
1964–1970 [3]	$12,309	$14,745	$406.02	$352.14	$371.98	$3.31	0.81%
1970–1975	$14,745	$16,375	$325.93	$371.98	$388.01	$3.21	0.98%
1975–1980	$16,375	$18,409	$406.94	$388.01	$427.05	$7.81	1.92%
1980–1985	$18,409	$20,955	$509.04	$427.05	$501.54	$14.90	2.93%
1985–1990	$20,955	$23,532	$515.41	$501.54	$546.97	$9.09	1.76%
1990–1995	$23,532	$25,082	$310.14	$546.97	$592.59	$9.12	2.94%
1995–2000	$25,082	$29,245	$832.48	$592.59	$722.43	$25.97	3.12%
2000–2005	$29,245	$31,343	$419.64	$722.43	$766.21	$8.76	2.09%
2005–2010	$31,343	$32,367	$204.81	$766.21	$770.11	$0.78	0.38%
2010–2011	$32,367	$32,653	$285.80	$770.11	$751.46	($18.65)	-6.52%

Details in the above table may not compute to the numbers shown due to rounding.
Source: empty tomb analysis; *YACC* adjusted series; U.S. BEA

empty tomb, inc. 2013

In the 1975–1980 period, the average annual increase in giving grew to $7.81, representing 1.92% of the average annual increase in per capita income.

From 1980 to 1985, the average annual increase in giving of $14.90 represented 2.93% of the average annual increase in income during this period.

The annual average change in giving as a percent of the average annual income increase during 1985 to 1990 fell from the 1980 to 1985 period. The 1990–1995 Average Annual Change in Giving as a Percent of the Average Annual Change in Income increased from the 1985–1990 figure, although the Average Annual Change in

Per Member Giving was comparable in the two periods. Because of the slower growth in income during the 1990–1995 period, the increase in dollars given represented a larger portion of the increase in income.

In the 1995–2000, the average annual change in giving as a percent of the average annual change in income increased from the 1990–1995 period. The average annual change in the number of dollars given on a per member basis was more than double that of the previous period. However, during the 1995–2000 segment, income increased at the fastest rate in the 1950–2011 period, in terms of per capita inflation-adjusted dollars. Thus, the rate of growth in giving from 1995–2000 was less than half the rate during the 1950–1960 period, when considered as a portion of the income increases.

For the period 2000–2005, the average annual change in dollars given as a percent of the annual change in income was an increase of 2.09%.

Of the 13 periods under review within the years from 1950 through 2011, the 2005–2010 period posted the third lowest annual increase in U.S. per capita income in inflation-adjusted dollars. The 2005–2010 period also posted a per member giving increase of an average of 78¢ a year in inflation-adjusted dollars.

The annual per member giving change measured $16.19 from 2005 to 2006, and $19.13 from 2006 to 2007. During the economic downturn from December 2007 to mid-2009, giving decreased in both 2008 and 2009. From 2007 to 2008, per member giving in inflation-adjusted dollars declined $5.42, and from 2008 to 2009 giving again declined, this time by $17.14. From 2009 to 2010, the decline was $8.87. For the 2005–2010 period, the total overall increase measured $3.89, increasing from $766.21 in 2005 to $770.11 in 2010. As a result of the combination of increases and decreases, the annual average increase was $0.78 a year for this period, the only time the average annual increase measured less than $1.00.

The 2010–2011 posted a negative annual change of $18.65 in this abbreviated period. It may be noted that the period of 2008–2011 posted four years in a row of decline in per member giving in inflation-adjusted dollars. This four-year period was the longest series of annual decline in this category since the seven years from 1928 through 1934, that included six years of the Great Depression.

Appendix A contains a listing of the denominations contained in the 1921–2011 analysis in this chapter.

This four-year period was the longest series of annual decline in this category since the seven years from 1928 through 1934, that included six years of the Great Depression.

Notes for Chapter 4

[1] Data for the period 1965–1967 was not available in a form that could be readily analyzed for the present purposes. Therefore data for these three years was estimated by dividing the change in per member current dollar contributions from 1964 to 1968 by four, the number of years in this interval, and cumulatively adding the result to the base year of 1964 data and subsequently to the calculated data for the succeeding years of 1965 and 1966 in order to obtain estimates for the years 1965–1967.

[2] The difference is due to rounding. See Appendix B Series introduction, Appendix B-3 for a discussion of the calculation of membership for 1953 through 1964.

[3] Use of the intervals 1960–1964 and 1964–1970 allows for the use of years for which there is known data, avoiding the use of the 1965 through 1967 years for which estimated data is used in this chapter.

[4] For the years 1965 through 1967, estimated data is used. See Note 1 above.

chapter 5

Church Member Giving and Membership Trends Based on 1968–2011 Data

Overview of Church Member Giving and Membership Trends, 1968–2011

Information as a Tool. The rich historical data series in the *Yearbook of American and Canadian Churches* (*YACC*) has, in this volume, been supplemented with and revised by additional denominational data for the 1968–2011 period.

Analysis of this data has been presented in the *State of Church Giving (SCG)* series since the early 1990s. When first published, the finding that giving as a portion of income was shrinking was received with some surprise and intense interest in many quarters.

Now the series has continued for over two decades. The trends identified in earlier analyses impact current activities. Various denominations continue to face decisions about staff cuts and, in some cases, whether to decrease missionary forces. The emphasis on local internal operations indicated by the trend in giving to Congregational Finances has, in fact, resulted in changed dynamics between local congregations and national church offices. The numbers did not cause such changes to occur. The numbers only described symptoms of priorities. These priorities produced behaviors resulting in the changed relationships.

It is generally acknowledged that most individuals do not decide how much to give based on academic information such as that contained in these analyses. However, it is possible for institutional leaders at all levels of the church, local as well as national, to make use of trend information to formulate strategies in response to the findings. For example, the data indicated that giving to Congregational Finances began to increase as a portion of income in 1993, and continued a general trend in an upward direction through 2002. It is possible that local church leadership had recognized a negative general trend in giving as a percent of income observed from 1968 to 1992 in Table 1 Chapter 1, and took steps to address it. The fact that the upturn in giving that began in 1993 essentially benefited local expenses, with only a slowing of the decline to Benevolences, indicates that church leadership may yet be operating with a limited vision of whole-life stewardship. Since 2003, an overall pattern of decline in giving as a percent of income to Congregational Finances was observed. On the one hand, the decline could reflect the December 2007 to mid-2009 recession. On the other, the decline in donations for Congregational Finances that began to reoccur in 2003 may suggest support for the internal operations of the congregation will not remain robust over time if not accompanied by a broader vision reflected in support for Benevolences. In either case, the uptick from 1993 through 2002 also indicates that the direction of trends can change.

Facts and figures may be useful to those responsible for promoting the health of the church. The analyses in this chapter are presented in an effort to expand the available information base.

The Meaning of Trends.
Projections produced by statistical regression models are a tool to help leaders plan in response to reported data. Experts evaluate trends in weather to plan strategies that will safeguard agriculture. Demographers map out population change trends to help government at local, national, and international levels plan for needs in education, aging, and trade.

For example, a business-focused Web site posted an article that reviewed trends describing what to expect the world to be like in the year 2100. Topics considered included population location, the number of languages that will be spoken, the age of the population, and cultural diversity within nations.[1]

Meanwhile, an article on the University of Southampton (United Kingdom) Web site reviewed trends in sea level rise up to the year 2100 that could affect the U.S. Atlantic and Gulf Coasts. The Abstract to the article read in part, "Ignoring sea-level rise will lead to unwise decisions and increasing hazards with time."[2]

Statistical techniques can also be used to suggest both consequences and possibilities regarding church giving and membership patterns. Of course, trend data only indicates future directions. Data does not dictate what will happen. Available information, including trend analysis, can help formulate intelligent responses to identified factors. Church leaders and members can help decide, through action or inaction, what the future will look like.

Trend analysis was first included in this series partly in response to developments in national church offices. After talking with a number of denominational officials who were making painful decisions about which programs to cut, in light of decreased Benevolences dollars being received, it seemed useful to see where the present patterns of giving might lead if effective means were not found to alter present behavior. Were current patterns likely to prove a temporary setback, or did the data suggest longer-term implications?

The data for both Benevolences and Congregational Finances can be projected using linear and exponential regression analysis. Linear regression is sometimes called a "straight-line" projection. An exponential regression is also labeled a "decay" model. To determine which type of analysis more accurately describes the data in a category's giving pattern, the data for 1968–1985 was projected using both techniques. Then, the actual data for 1986 through 2011 was plotted. The more

Church leaders and members can help decide, through action or inaction, what the future will look like.

accurate projection was judged to be the procedure that produced the trend line most closely resembling the actual 1986–2011 data.

General Trends in Church Member Giving. As noted in earlier chapters, the category of Total Contributions from church members is divided into the two general categories of Congregational Finances and Benevolences. In the category of Congregational Finances, giving as a portion of income declined overall between 1968 and 2011 for the composite denominations. Yet a trend toward increase in the level of giving to this category was observed beginning in 1993. These intermittent increases from one year to the next were in contrast to the decline indicated by an exponential projection through 2011, based on 1968–1985 giving data. However, in the 2003–2011 time span, the actual data for giving as a percent of income for this category increased four times from one year to the next, and decreased five times. Although giving to this category exceeded levels suggested by either the linear or exponential trends, the recent declines suggest the data bears monitoring.

The continued decline in actual data for giving to Benevolences as a portion of income throughout the 1968–2011 period in the composite denominations initially followed the linear trend. In 1993, the rate of decline began to slow, although the level of giving remained closer to the linear trend. In 1999, the actual data moved above the exponential trend. Although Benevolences may be expected to be above either trend line, if the pattern of decline observed in the 1968–2011 period continues, Benevolences may represent a substantially reduced portion of income throughout the current century.

General Trends in Church Membership. Membership trends across the theological spectrum point to a decline when membership was considered as a percent of U.S. population.

Eleven mainline Protestant denominations represented 13.2% of the population in 1968, and 5.5% in 2011, a decline of 58% from the 1968 base.

The composite data set communions analyzed in earlier chapters of this volume measured 14% of U.S. population in 1968 and 9.1% in 2011, down 35% as a portion of U.S. population from the 1968 base.

A set of 15 evangelical denominations grew 47% in the number of members between 1968 and 2011, but posted a 5% decline as a portion of U.S. population, since U.S. population expanded at a faster rate. The growth as a percent of population for this group peaked in the mid-1980s, and then began a slow decline, reaching its lowest point of the period in 2011.

Membership in a set of 35 Protestant denominations, including some of the fastest growing denominations in the U.S., and the Roman Catholic Church represented 45% of U.S. population in 1968, and 35% in 2011, a decline of 22% from the 1968 base. An exponential trend line for this set of denominations suggests that the group will represent less than one-quarter of the U.S. population by 2100, and 15% in 2200, if current patterns continue.

New Religious Construction. When considered as a portion of income, spending on new construction of religious buildings was higher in 1965 than in 2011. Per capita spending on new religious construction in 1965 was also higher than in 2011, when considered in inflation-adjusted dollars. Again in inflation-adjusted

Membership in a set of 35 Protestant denominations, including some of the fastest growing denominations in the U.S., and the Roman Catholic Church represented 45% of U.S. population in 1968, and 35% in 2011, a decline of 22% from the 1968 base.

dollars, the aggregate billions spent in 2001 were the highest annual amount spent in the 1964–2011 period.

Details of Church Giving and Membership Trends, 1968–2011

The Current Trends in Church Giving. The first chapter in this report indicates that per member giving as a percent of income decreased between 1968 and 2011. Further, contributions to the category of Benevolences were declining proportionately faster than those to Congregational Finances between 1968 and 2011.

The data for the composite denominations analyzed for 1968 through 2011 has been projected in the *SCG* series, beginning with the edition that included 1991 data.[3] The most recent projection is based on data from 1968 through 2011.

The Trend in Congregational Finances. The 1968–2011 church giving data contained in this report indicates that giving for Congregational Finances as a percent of income declined from 2.45% in 1968, to 1.98% in 2011, a decline of 19%.

Both linear and exponential regression were used to analyze the data for giving to Congregational Finances as a percent of income for the 17-year interval of 1968 through 1985. Then the actual data for 1986 through 2011 was plotted. The actual data for 1986–1992 declined but still exceeded the exponential curve. In 1993, giving to Congregational Finances as a percent of income began to increase in some years, unlike either projection. However starting in 2003, annual declines in the giving level appeared more frequently than in the 1993–2002 period of general increase. Although the actual data remained above the projected data of the exponential curve, the decrease in 2011 meant giving as a portion of income to this category was at the lowest level in the 1968–2011 period, measuring below 2.0% for the first time. The results are shown in Figure 8.

The upturn in giving as a percent of income to Congregational Finances in 1993 through 2002 posted eight annual increases and two decreases. This pattern differed from the 1968 through 1992 period, when annual declines occurred in 76% of the annual changes. This 1993 through 2002 period of increase was followed from 2003 to 2011 by four increases and five declines in giving as a portion of income to Congregational Finances. By 2011, there was an overall decline from the 1968 base to 1.98%. The 1993–2002 decade of general increase was not robust enough to sustain a positive trend. The 2008, 2010, and 2011 decreases in giving to Congregational Finances may reflect ongoing economic challenges faced by church

Figure 8: Projected Trends for Composite Denominations, Per Member Giving to Congregational Finances as a Percent of Income, Using Linear and Exponential Regression Based on Data for 1968–1985, with Actual Data for 1986–2011

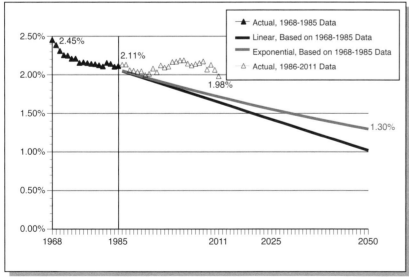

Source: empty tomb analysis, *YACC* adjusted series; U.S. BEA   empty tomb, inc., 2013

members resulting from the 2007–2009 recession. However, declines in giving as a percent of income to this category began to appear in 2003, before the recession years of 2008 to mid-2009.

There may be an interaction between giving and membership that affects the amount of giving to the category of Congregational Finances. The trends in membership are considered below. In cases where membership is declining, levels of giving to Congregational Finances may initially be maintained or even increased on a per member basis, in an effort to keep basic operations at current levels. In these instances, Benevolences may be seen as an optional expenditure and decreased as a cost-cutting strategy. However, over time, Congregational Finances may also decline, since maintenance of congregational operations may not be perceived as a strong enough reason to continue giving to the church at the same level in light of other lifestyle expenditure choices.

This hypothesis suggests that an increase in per member giving to the internal operations of the church, which may initially accompany a decline in membership, will not be maintained over time if there is not also a broader vision attracting church member support for the category of Benevolences as well.

Data for additional years could help to demonstrate whether the downturn in giving as a portion of income to Congregational Finances that began in 2003 was an interruption in the 1993–2002 pattern of increase, or if the 1993–2002 trend of increase was a temporary reversal in an overall pattern of decline in giving to this category.

The Trend in Benevolences. Per member contributions to Benevolences as a percent of income decreased from 0.66% in 1968 to 0.34% in 2011, the lowest point in the 1968–2011 period. The 2011 level of giving as a percent of income represented a decline of 48% from the 1968 base.

The data for giving to Benevolences as a percent of income for the 17-year interval of 1968 through 1985 was also projected using both linear and exponential regression. The actual data for 1986 through 2011 was then plotted. The results are shown in Figure 9.

Reported per member giving to Benevolences as a percent of income was near or below the projected value of the linear regression for 1989 through 1993. In 1994, the rate of decline slowed to the point that the actual data was above, but still closer to, the linear trend line. However, from 1999–2011, giving to Benevolences as a percent of income moved above the exponential line, suggesting

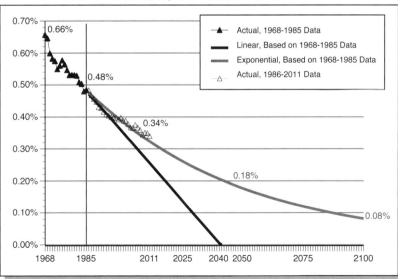

Figure 9: Projected Trends for Composite Denominations, Per Member Giving to Benevolences as a Percent of Income, Using Linear and Exponential Regression Based on Data for 1968–1985, with Actual Data for 1986–2011

Source: empty tomb analysis, *YACC* adjusted series; U.S. BEA   empty tomb, inc., 2013

53

that, although the negative trend continued, the rate of decline slowed. In 2008, per member giving as a portion of income to Benevolences measured 0.34%, and then increased to 0.35% in 2009 and 2010. In 2011, per member giving as a portion of income to Benevolences declined to 0.34%, below the 2008 figure in unrounded numbers. As discussed in chapter 1, it appears that the external factors of tsunami and hurricane relief efforts contributed to the increase observed in this category in 2005, since data for 2006, 2007, 2008, 2010, and 2011 again posted declines.

In summary, although giving to Benevolences as a portion of income between 1968 and 2011 exhibited a pattern of decline throughout, the rate slowed toward the end of that period, shown in Figure 9.

In addition to the 1968–1985 projection, a second analysis was done on the entire period from 1968–2011. A linear trend based on the entire period of 1968–2011 data indicated that per member giving as a portion of income to the category of Benevolences would reach 0.05% of income in the year A.D. 2050, based on the 1968–2011 numbers. The exponential curve based on 1968–2011 data indicated that giving in 2050 would be 0.19%, down 48% from the 0.34% level in 2011.[4] Extending the exponential trend to 2100, Benevolences would represent 0.09% of income in that year.

These trend lines may be more useful to predict the general level of giving, rather than precise numbers. However, the overall direction suggests that by 2050 the amount of income going to support Benevolences, including denominational structures, would be severely reduced, if the overall pattern of the last 44 years continues.

Trends in Church Membership as a Percent of U.S. Population, 1968–2011.[5]

Membership data for various church groupings is available for review for the years 1968 through 2011. When the reported data is considered as a percent of U.S. population, the membership data is placed in the larger context of the changing environment in which the church exists. This measurement is similar to giving as a percent of income, which reflects how much a financial donation represents of the resources available to the donor. In a similar way, measuring membership as a percent of U.S. population takes into account the fact that the potential population for church membership also changed as a result of growth in the number of people in the U.S.

The State of Church Giving through 1993 included a chapter entitled, "A Unified Theory of Giving and Membership."[6] The hypothesis explored in that discussion was that there is a relationship between a decline in church member giving and membership patterns. One proposal considered in that chapter was that a denomination that is able to involve its members in a larger vision, such as mission outreach, as evidenced in levels of giving to support that idea, will also be attracting additional members.

In the present chapter, discussion will focus on patterns and trends in membership as a percent of U.S. population.

Membership in the Composite Denominations, 1968–2011. The composite denominations, which span the theological spectrum, included 28,147,568 Full or Confirmed Members in 1968. By 2011, these communions included 28,522,245 members, an increase of 1%.[7] However, during the same 43-year interval, U.S. population increased from 200,745,000 to 312,036,000, an increase of 55%. Therefore, while this church member grouping represented 14% of the U.S. population

... measuring membership as a percent of U.S. population takes into account the fact that the potential population for church membership also changed as a result of growth in the number of people in the U.S.

in 1968, it included 9.1% in 2011, a decline of 35% from the 1968 base. Figure 10 presents membership as a percent of U.S. population, and giving as a percent of income, for the composite denominations, 1968–2011.

Membership Trends in Three Church Groups. Membership data for three subgroups within the historically Christian church in the U.S. is available. Data was analyzed for 11 Protestant mainline denominations, 15 Protestant evangelical denominations, and the Roman Catholic Church. Figure 11 presents the membership data for these groups of communions.

The declining membership trends have been noticed most markedly in the mainline Protestant communions. Full or Confirmed Membership in 11 mainline Protestant denominations affiliated with the National Council of the Churches of Christ in the U.S.A.[8] decreased as a percent of U.S. population between 1968 and 2011. In 1968, this group included 26,508,288, or 13.2% of U.S. population. In 2011, the

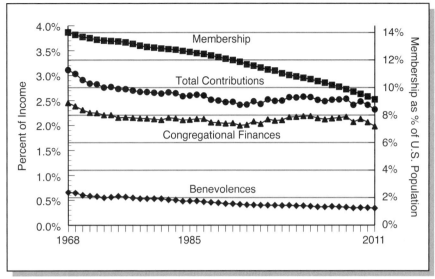

Figure 10: Membership as a Percent of U.S. Population and Giving as a Percent of U.S. Per Capita Disposable Personal Income, Composite Denominations, 1968–2011

Source: empty tomb analysis, *YACC* adjusted series; U.S. BEA   empty tomb, inc., 2013

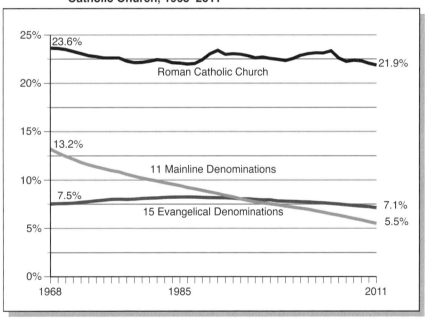

Figure 11: Membership as a Percent of U.S. Population, 15 Evangelical Denominations, 11 Mainline Denominations, and the Roman Catholic Church, 1968–2011

Source: empty tomb analysis, *YACC* adjusted series; U.S. BEA   empty tomb, inc., 2013

11 denominations included 17,170,055, or 5.5% of U.S. population, a decline of 58% from the 1968 base, as a portion of U.S. population.

Data is also available for a group of 15 denominations that might be classified on the evangelical end of the theological spectrum.[9] Although one or more of the communions in this grouping might prefer the term "conservative" to "evangelical" as a description, the latter term in its current sociological usage may be useful. These communions included some of the fastest growing denominations in the United States. This group grew 47% in membership, from 15,101,542 in 1968 to 22,229,861, in

2011, while U.S. population grew 55%. As a result, this group measured 7.52% of U.S. population in 1968, and 7.12% in 2011, a decline of 5% in the portion of the U.S. represented by these communions. In the mid-1980s, the group peaked at 8.23% as a portion of U.S. population peaked, and then declined to 7.12% by 2011, a decline of 13% as a portion of U.S. population from the 1986 peak. In 1993, these 15 evangelical communions surpassed the 11 mainline communions in the portion of U.S. population that they represented.

The Roman Catholic Church included 47,468,333 members in 1968, or 24% of U.S. population. Although the church's membership grew 44%, to 68,229,841 in 2011, it decreased to 22% as a portion of the faster-growing U.S. population, a decline of 8%.

Projected Membership Trends in 11 Mainline Denominations. As with giving to Congregational Finances and Benevolences as a percent of income, trend lines using both linear and exponential regression were developed for the 11 mainline Protestant communions discussed above, using their 1968–1985 membership data. The actual 1986 through 2011 data was also plotted. As shown in Figure 12, the actual 1986–2011 data followed closely the exponential curve for these denominations. In 2009–2011, the actual membership as a percent of U.S. population was slightly below the exponential trend figure.

An exponential curve based on the entire 1968–2011 reported data series suggested that these denominations would represent 2.8% of the U.S. population in 2050, if the present rate of decline continues.

Figure 12: Trend in Membership as a Percent of U.S. Population,
11 Mainline Protestant Denominations, Linear and Exponential
Regression Based on Data for 1968–1985,
with Actual Data 1986–2011

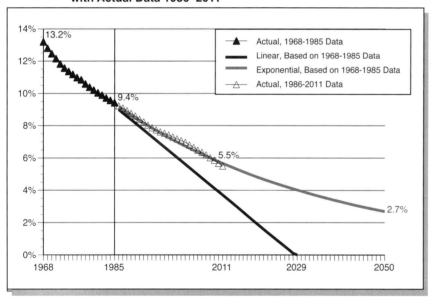

Source: empty tomb analysis, *YACC* adjusted series; U.S. BEA   empty tomb, inc., 2013

Projected Membership Trends in the Composite Denominations. Nine of the 11 mainline Protestant denominations discussed above are also included in the composite set of denominations that have been considered in earlier chapters of this report. Regression analysis was carried out on the 1968–1985 membership data for the composite denominations to determine if the trends in the larger grouping differed from the mainline denomination subset. The results were then compared to the actual 1986 through 2011 membership data for the composite data set.

The composite denominations represented 14% of the U.S. population in 1968, and 12.6% in 1985. Linear trend analysis of the 1968–1985 data suggested that this grouping would have represented 10.5% of U.S. population in 2011, while exponential regression suggested it would have included 10.8%. In fact, this composite grouping of communions represented 9.1% of the U.S. population in 2011, a smaller figure than that indicated by linear regression, suggesting the trend is closer to that predicted by linear regression than the exponential curve. By 2050, these composite denominations would represent 7.5% of the U.S. population if a linear trend remains the more accurate analysis. Figure 13 presents this information in graphic form.

Membership and Projected Membership Trends in 36 Communions. In 1968, a set of 35 Protestant denominations and the Roman Catholic Church included a total of 90,143,836 members. The Protestant churches in the dataset included a broad representation of the theological spectrum, and also included some of the fastest growing denominations in the U.S. With the U.S. population at 200,745,000, these Christians constituted 45% of the 1968 U.S. population. By 2011, the group had grown to 109,501,294 members. However, with U.S. population having grown to 312,036,000 in 2011, these Christians comprised 35% of the American population, a percent change of -22% from the 1968 base.

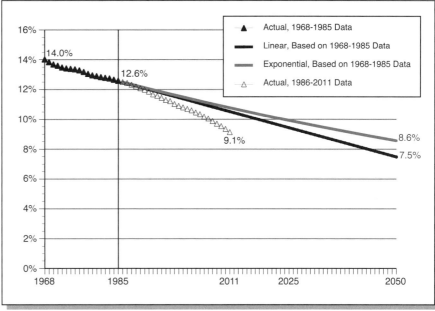

Figure 13: Trend in Membership as a Percent of U.S. Population, Composite Denominations, Linear and Exponential Regression Based on Data for 1968–1985, with Actual Data 1986–2011

Source: empty tomb analysis, *YACC* adjusted series; U.S. BEA empty tomb, inc., 2013

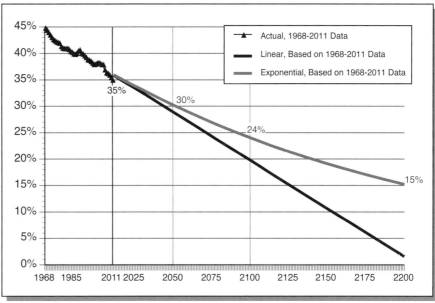

Figure 14: Trend in Membership as a Percent of U.S. Population, 36 Denominations, Linear and Exponential Regression Based on Data for 1968–2011

Source: empty tomb analysis, *YACC* adjusted series; U.S. BEA empty tomb, inc., 2013

Figure 14 presents the findings in graphic form. Because of the broad nature of the sampling of these historically Christian communions, a projection was extended to 2200, based on membership data for the entire period of 1968 through 2011. The purpose was to forecast, based on past patterns, the role this group of denominations would play at the end of the next century. The linear projection suggested the group will have declined from representing 35% of the U.S. population in 2011 to include 29% in 2050. The exponential projection forecasted 30% in 2050. By the year 2100, the linear trend projected 20% while the exponential trend projected 24% of the U.S. population will be affiliated with these 36 communions. If the trends continue long term, in 2200 this group of communions will represent 15.2% of U.S. population, according to the exponential curve, or 1.7%, if the linear trend proves more accurate.

Trends in One Denomination. The quality of trend data will be affected by the measurements taken. An example from one denomination may illustrate the point.

The United Methodist Church (UMC) resulted from the merger of The Methodist Church and The Evangelical United Brethren in 1968. In 2008, the last year with data available for the category of "Connectional Clergy Support" in the following analysis,[10] The United Methodist Church was the second largest Protestant denomination, and third largest communion overall in the U.S. While The Methodist Church reported data for 1968 in the 1970 *YACC* edition, the Evangelical United Brethren did not. Therefore, data for the UMC, including both The Methodist Church and the Evangelical United Brethren, was not available in 1968, and as a result this communion was not included in the composite denominations.

Two years after the merger, in 1971, the UMC changed its reporting methodology for its information published in the *YACC* series. Specifically, the category of Connectional Clergy Support was switched from Congregational Finances to Benevolences. UMC Connectional Clergy Support included district superintendents and Episcopal salaries, which would standardly be included in Benevolences for other communions as well. However, UMC Connectional Clergy Support also included pastor pension and benefits, including health insurance, and a category of Equitable Salary Funds, which would be included in Congregational Finances in most denominations.

UMC Connectional Clergy Support increased fairly rapidly between 1969 and 2008. When UMC Connectional Clergy Support was included in per member giving to the UMC Benevolences series as a percent of income, Benevolences increased from 0.40% in 1969 to 0.43% in 2008, a 9% increase from the 1969 base.

As of 2009, the data for Connectional Clergy Support was no longer collected, although Benevolences for those years presumably still included that category. By 2011, the increase in per member giving as a percent of income to Benevolences displayed an increase of 13% from the 1969 base.

However, when UMC Connectional Clergy Support was taken out of the UMC Benevolences series for 1971 to 2008, giving to Benevolences as a portion of income in the UMC declined from 0.40% in 1969 to 0.26% in 2008, a decrease of 34%.

Per member giving as a portion of income to the single category of UMC Connectional Clergy Support increased 35% from 1969 to 2008.

Figure 15 illustrates the two trends in Benevolences giving, based on whether the category includes Connectional Clergy Support or not.

The two different trends in UMC Benevolences illustrate the point that definitions of the categories being measured are important.

The linear projection suggested the group will have declined from representing 35% of the U.S. population in 2011 to include 29% in 2050.

If the traditional definition of Benevolences is used, which would place pastor health insurance and other benefits in Congregational Finances, then Benevolences giving in the UMC declined as a portion of income in a noticeable fashion between 1969 and 2008. If, however, a category that was initially included in Congregational Finances is transferred to Benevolences, the UMC Benevolences giving as a portion of income increased between 1969–2008.

The former definition of Benevolences, that excludes those congregationally-based expenses, provides a more specific measurement of member support for the larger mission of the church. The latter definition, which includes pastor health insurance and other benefits with broader church activities, weighted the measurement toward the funding of institutional operations.

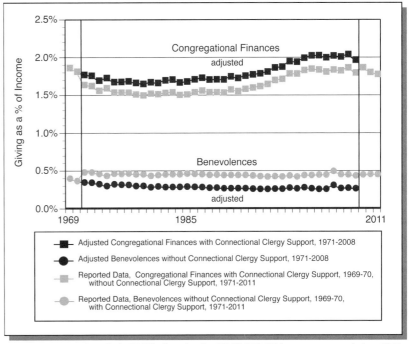

Figure 15: **The United Methodist Church, Per Member Giving to Congregational Finances and Benevolences as a Percent of Income, 1971–2011, with Connectional Clergy Support in Benevolences, and Adjusted, 1971–2008, with Connectional Clergy Support in Congregational Finances**

Source: empty tomb analysis, *YACC* adjusted series; UMC; U.S. BEA   empty tomb, inc., 2013

The denominational leadership needs to be clear about its primary goal, whether it is focused on maintaining an institution or mobilizing church members to increased mission outreach through denominational channels. When that priority has been identified, the denomination can choose the most accurate definition to measure progress toward the goal.

New Religious Construction. How does 2011 construction activity among churches in the U.S. compare to other years?

Census Bureau data provides information on the new construction of religious buildings.[11] According to the data, current dollar aggregate construction of religious buildings was $1.04 billion dollars in 1964, compared to $4.2 billion in 2011. On a current-dollar aggregate level, more building was going on in 2011 than in the mid-1960s.

However, as has been emphasized in previous chapters of this volume, aggregate numbers considered apart from inflation, or that do not take into account changes in population and income, do not give a complete picture.

When inflation was factored out, the data indicated that the aggregate sum of new religious building construction for the five-year period of 2007–2011 was $27.8 billion in inflation-adjusted 2005 dollars, which was higher than the 1964–1968 period spending of $28.0 billion. The highest single year inflation-adjusted amount in the 1964–2011 period was the 2001 level of $9.3 billion. The 1965 level of $6.3 billion had been the highest amount of aggregate, inflation-adjusted dollars spent on the construction of new religious buildings from 1964 through 1996. In 1997, aggregate inflation-adjusted spending passed the 1965 level, and religious building expenditures continued to increase through 2001. Expenditures were at or above $9 billion a year in inflation-adjusted 2005 dollars from 2000 through 2003, and decreased to $3.7 billion in 2011.

Yet, to obtain the most realistic picture about building patterns, changes in population and income also need to be factored into the evaluation. For example, taking population changes into account, in 1965 the per capita expenditure in the U.S. on religious buildings was $33 dollars per person in inflation-adjusted 2005 dollars. In 2011, it was $12 dollars.

The period 1964 through 1968 posted an average per capita expenditure on new religious buildings of $29. The period 2007–2011 was $18, suggesting that construction of new religious buildings was higher in the earlier period, when changes in population were taken into account.

Of course, a smaller portion of the entire U.S. population may have been investing in religious buildings in the late 1990s through 2011 than in the mid-1960s. To have the most meaningful comparison, changes in membership as a portion of population would have to be taken into account. Data considered above suggests that membership in historically Christian churches declined as a portion of the U.S. population between 1964 and 2011. However, other religions were added to the religious milieu of the United States during this period. The Census data includes all religious construction, not just Christian churches. So the rough estimate may be fairly useful as a first approximation.

Even comparing per capita inflation-adjusted dollars spent is of limited use because it does not account for the difference in incomes in the two periods. To review, the $33 per capita spent on religious buildings in 1965 represented a different portion of income than the $12 spent in 2011. In fact, as a portion of income, Americans spent 0.25% on the construction of new religious buildings in 1965, compared to 0.04% in 2011.

One must conclude, therefore, that the population was investing a higher portion of available resources in religious buildings in the mid-1960s than at the beginning of this century. The building activity occurring in the late 1990s through 2011

Figure 16: Construction of Religious Buildings in the U.S., Aggregate Inflation-Adjusted 2005 Dollars, Per Capita Inflation-Adjusted 2005 Dollars, and Percent of U.S. Per Capita Disposable Personal Income, 1964–2011

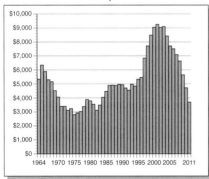
Aggregate Millions of Inflation-Adjusted Dollars

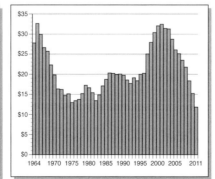
Per Capita in Inflation-Ajusted Dollars

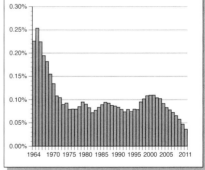
Per Capita as Percent of Income

Source: empty tomb analysis, U.S. Census Bureau; U.S. BEA   empty tomb, inc., 2013

has to be evaluated in the context of the general affluence produced by decades of economic expansion in the U.S., in order to make an intelligent evaluation of whether religious construction has in fact increased over the mid-1960s level. This fact is clear from the three charts in Figure 16. These charts contrast: (1) the annual aggregate inflation-adjusted 2005 dollar value of new religious building construction with, (2) the per capita expenditures in inflation-adjusted 2005 dollars, and (3) the per capita expenditure as a portion of U.S. per capita income, for the 1964–2011 period. One can observe that the picture is very different when the per person cost of the building is set in the context of the income available to the people paying for the building.

The Response to the Trends. As in other sectors, trend lines in church giving and membership are designed to provide an additional source of information. Planning, evaluation and creative thinking are some of the types of constructive responses that can be made in light of projections. The information on church member giving and membership trends is offered as a possible planning tool.[12] The trend lines are not considered to be dictating what must happen, but rather are seen as providing important indicators of what might happen if present conditions continue in an uninterrupted fashion. Trends in church giving and membership, if used wisely, may be of assistance in addressing conditions present in the body of Christ in the United States.

Notes for Chapter 5

[1] Eric Goldschein and Robert Johnson; "The World in 2100: Ten Billion People, No Oil and Not Enough Food"; Business Insider; 10/29/2011; <http://www.businessinsider.com/10-trends-we-can-expect-to-see-in-the-year-2100-2011-10?op=1>; pp. 1-10 of 8/9/2013 2:40 PM printout.

[2] Robert J. Nicholls and Stephen P. Leatherman; "Adapting to Sea-Level Rise: Relative Sea Level Trends to 2100 for the United States, Description/Abstract"; University of Southampton, UK; 6/18/2013; <http://eprints.soton.ac.uk/353013/>; p. 1 of 8/9/2013 2:44 PM printout.

[3] John Ronsvalle and Sylvia Ronsvalle, *The State of Church Giving through 1991* (Champaign, IL: empty tomb, inc., 1993), and subsequent editions in the series. The edition with data through 1991 provides a discussion of the choice to use giving as a percent of income as a basis for considering future giving patterns.

[4] In the linear regression for the 1968–2011 data, the value for the correlation coefficient, or r_{XY}, for the Benevolences data is -.98. The strength of the linear relationship in the present set of 1968–2011 data, that is, the proportion of variance accounted for by linear regression, is represented by the coefficient of determination, or r^2_{XY}, of .96 for Benevolences. In the exponential regression, the value for r_{XY}, for the Benevolences data is -.99, while the strength of the exponential relationship is .98. The Benevolences F-observed values of 912.51 for the linear, and 1,764.29 for the curvilinear, regression are substantially greater than the F-critical value of 7.28 for 1 and 42 degrees of freedom for a single-tailed test with an Alpha value of 0.01. Therefore, the regression equation is useful at the level suggested by the r^2_{XY} figure in predicting giving as a percent of income.

[5] The denominations analyzed in this section include the composite data set whose financial patterns were analyzed in earlier chapters. The data for the composite communions is supplemented by the data of eight denominations included in an analysis of church membership and U.S. population by Roozen and Hadaway in David A. Roozen and Kirk C. Hadaway, eds., *Church and Denominational Growth* (Nashville: Abingdon Press, 1993), 393-395.

[6] This article is available on the Internet at: <http://www.emptytomb.org/UnifiedTheory.pdf>.

[7] See Appendix B-1 for details of the composite denomination data included in these analyses. The larger Southern Baptist Convention membership figure is used in the membership analyses in this chapter. Consult Appendix B-4 for the total Full or Confirmed Membership numbers used for the American Baptist Churches in the U.S.A. The year-specific data for the North American Baptist Church and the Evangelical Covenant Church are included in the giving as a percent of income analyses, but data for these two communions is not included in the membership

as a percent of population analyses. See Appendix B-3.3 and Appendix B-4 for the membership data of the other denominations included in subsequent analyses in this chapter that are not one of the composite denominations, and that may not have provided giving as well as membership data. Missing membership data may be calculated for denominations that did not provide complete data sets for the entire period.

[8] These eleven denominations include nine of the communions in the composite set of denominations as well as The Episcopal Church and The United Methodist Church.

[9] A list of the communions in this set is presented in Appendix A.

[10] In correspondence dated March 14, 2011, a denominational representative indicated that data for the category of United Methodist Church Connectional Clergy Support was no longer collected as of 2009.

[11] For a series beginning in 1964 titled "Annual Value of Construction Put in Place," the Census Bureau defined its Religious category as follows: "*Religious* includes houses of worship and other religious buildings. Certain buildings, although owned by religious organizations, are not included in this category. These include education or charitable institutions, hospitals, and publishing houses." (U.S. Census Bureau, Current Construction Reports, C30/01-5, *Value of Construction Put in Place*: May 2001, U.S. Government Printing Office, Washington, DC 20402, Appendix A, "Definitions," p. A-2). A 2003 revision of this series presented the definitions as follows: "Religious: Certain buildings, although owned by religious organizations, are not included in this category. These include educational or charitable institutions, hospitals, and publishing houses. House of worship: Includes churches, chapels, mosques, synagogues, tabernacles, and temples. Other religious: In addition to the types of facilities listed below, it also includes sanctuaries, abbeys, convents, novitiates, rectories, monasteries, missions, seminaries, and parish houses. Auxiliary building—includes fellowship halls, life centers, camps and retreats, and Sunday schools." (U.S. Census Bureau; "Definitions of Construction"; July 30, 2003; <http://www.census.gov/const/C30/definitions. pdf>; 8/17/2003 PM printout.) Although documentation for the revised series stated that the 1993 through 2001 data was not comparable to the earlier 1964–2000 data, a comparison of the two series found that there was an average of 0.1% difference between the estimated millions of dollars spent on construction of religious buildings from 1993–2000. For the purposes of the present discussion, the difference in the two series was not deemed sufficient to impact the multi-decade review to the degree that discussion would not be useful. Table 16 shows the aggregate current dollar data.

The source for the religious construction data is:

- U.S. Census Bureau; Table 1: Annual Value of Construction Put in Place in the U.S.: [Year-Year], p. 1: Current $s & Constant (1996) $s; last revised July 1, 2002; confirmed on August 17, 2003;

  1964: 1964–1968; <http://www.census.gov/ pub/const/C30/tab168.txt>

  1965–1969: 1965–1969; <http://www. census.gov/pub/const/C30/tab169.txt>

  1970–1974: 1970–1974; <http://www. census.gov/pub/const/C30/tab174.txt>

  1975–1979: 1975–1979; <http://www. census.gov/pub/const/C30/tab179.txt>

Table 16: New Religious Construction, Aggregate Millions Current $, 1964–2011

Year	Millions of Current $	Year	Millions of Current $	Year	Millions of Current $	Year	Millions of Current $
1964	$1,044	1976	$1,040	1988	$3,271	2000	$8,030
1965	$1,263	1977	$1,144	1989	$3,449	2001	$8,393
1966	$1,205	1978	$1,367	1990	$3,566	2002	$8,335
1967	$1,118	1979	$1,701	1991	$3,521	2003	$8,559
1968	$1,135	1980	$1,811	1992	$3,485	2004	$8,153
1969	$1,044	1981	$1,853	1993	$3,894	2005	$7,715
1970	$988	1982	$1,730	1994	$3,871	2006	$7,740
1971	$867	1983	$2,009	1995	$4,348	2007	$7,522
1972	$907	1984	$2,418	1996	$4,537	2008	$7,197
1973	$877	1985	$2,751	1997	$5,782	2009	$6,177
1974	$993	1986	$3,076	1998	$6,604	2010	*$5,237*
1975	$941	1987	$3,178	1999	$7,371	2011	$4,191

1980–1984: 1980–1984; <http://www.census.gov/pub/const/C30/tab184.txt>

1985–1989: 1985–1989; <http://www.census.gov/pub/const/C30/tab189.txt>

1990: 1990; <http://www.census.gov/pub/const/C30/tab190.txt> [confirmed on August 16 & 17, 2003]

1991–1992: 1991–1995; <http://www.census.gov/pub/const/C30/tab195.txt>

- 1993–2001: U.S. Census Bureau; Annual Value of Construction Put in Place in the U.S.: 1993–2002, p. 1: Current $s & Constant (1996) $s; July 29, 2003; <http://www.census.gov/const/C30/Private.pdf>

- 2002–2012: U.S. Census Bureau; Annual: Annual Value of Construction Put in Place in the U.S.: 1993–2012, p. 1: Current $s; created: January 31, 2013 6:57:14 PM; <http://www.census.gov/construction/c30/pdf/total.pdf>

[12] For additional discussion of the implications of the trends, see Ronsvalle and Ronsvalle, *The State of Church Giving through 1991*, pp. 61-67.

Chapter 6

The Potential of the Church

The analyses in the first five chapters of this volume provide an overview of church member giving through the year 2011.

Chapter 8 will discuss how those patterns intersect with the responsibility to implement the kingdom of God, a task given to the church by King Jesus.

If Jesus expects those who regard Jesus as King to do greater things than Jesus did (i.e., John 14:12), those responsible for implementing that agenda may reasonably want to know what power, spiritual yes, but also fungible, is available to apply to the task.

While the previous chapters have generally reflected on what has happened in church giving in the past, the current chapter considers what potential resources the church has in light of those church member giving numbers, a potential that church leaders could mobilize on behalf of implementing God's agenda.

Overview of the Potential of the Church

The analyses in this chapter compare present levels of church member giving with a few standards of potential giving.

In chapter one of this volume, a brief discussion was presented of one standard of potential giving—the resources that would have been available if church members in 2011 gave the same portion of income as church members gave in 1968. If church members had given the same portion of income in 2011 as was given in 1968, an additional $3 billion would have been available for the church to spend on the larger mission of the church through Benevolences. In this case, the level of potential giving would have required church members not to increase their giving, but rather, not to let giving decline in relationship to other spending priorities.

One standard of increased giving, by which giving can be evaluated, is the classic tithe, or giving ten percent of income.[1] Calculating that difference between current giving levels and a congregationwide average of 10%, the result suggests that there would have been an additional $172 billion available for the work of the church in 2011, if historically Christian church members had given 10% of income, instead of the 2.32% that was donated. If church members had chosen to allocate 60% of this additional giving to global word and deed need, there would have been an additional $103 billion available, an amount substantially greater than estimates of the most urgent global word and deed need costs. If 20% had been directed to domestic need in the U.S., an additional $34 billion would have been available to address domestic needs including poverty, with an equal amount available for costs related to the increased international and domestic activity.

These resources are presumably provided for application to the kingdom of God priorities. As revealed through Jesus Christ, God's priorities might be summarized in the Great Commission and the Great Commandment. In the Great Commission, Jesus told his followers to go into all the world, baptizing and teaching new converts to obey the tenets of the faith (see Matthew 28:18-20 and Acts 1:8). This assignment sits in the context of the Great Commandment—to love God and therefore love the neighbor (see Mark 12:28-31). Reaching out to others, often summarized by the phrase "the church's mission," seems to be a core responsibility that Jesus passed on to those who would serve God.

One measure of the church's commitment to mission is the level of spending on international missions. In response to a survey sent out by empty tomb, inc., a set of denominations, for which 2003 through 2011 Total Contributions data was available, also provided Overseas Missions Income data for the years 2003 through 2011. The weighted average in 2011 for the group was 2.1% of Total Contributions being directed to denominational overseas ministries. Stated another way, of every dollar donated to a congregation, about two cents was spent on denominational overseas missions. In 2011, one communion within the group of 32 gave more than 10¢ of each dollar to overseas missions, while seven denominations each gave about 1¢ or less.

In general, the level of support for denominational overseas missions was lower in 2011 than in the 1920s.

Analysis resulted in an estimate that an additional $1 billion a year could have a significant impact on the goal of meeting global evangelism needs. The cost would be only cents per day for various groups of church members.

If the goal were expanded to include not only evangelization, but also the cost of helping to stop, in Jesus' name, global child deaths, providing primary education for all children around the world, and providing additional funds for addressing poverty in the U.S., then the bottom line would increase and yet still only require less than a quarter per day per every church member in the U.S. If wealthy church members donated half the costs, then the daily cost would decrease for the other church members.

As revealed through Jesus Christ, God's priorities might be summarized in the Great Commission and the Great Commandment.

A potential giving number was calculated for nine Roman Catholic archdioceses in the U.S. led by cardinals as of *The Official Catholic Directory (OCD) 2005*, or subsequently. The calculation indicated an increased level of giving among Catholics in these nine archdioceses would have resulted in a combined total of billions of additional dollars that could be applied to international needs, as well as domestically, for example, to inner-city Catholic schools.

A review of global remittances suggested that foreign-born residents of the U.S. were less than one-fourth the number of the native-born church member population in the U.S., and yet sent about seven times the amount of money internationally than did the native-born church members.

Details of the Potential of the Church

Potential Giving at 10% of Income in 2011. If members of historically Christian churches had chosen to give 10% to their congregations in 2011, rather than the 2.32% given that year, there would have been an additional $172 billion available for work through the church.[2]

Further, if those members had specified that 60% of their increased giving were to be given to international missions, there would have been an additional $103 billion available for the international work of the church. That would have left an additional $34 billion for domestic missions, including poverty conditions in the U.S., and an equal amount for costs related to the increased missions activity.[3]

Figure 17 displays the potential giving levels, and issues of global need that could be addressed by the increased giving.

This level of giving could have made a major impact on global need. One estimate is that an additional $70 to $80 billion a year could address the basic needs of the poorest people around the world.[4] Basic primary education for all children around the globe would cost $7 billion a year.[5] Of the estimated 6.9 million children under five dying around the globe

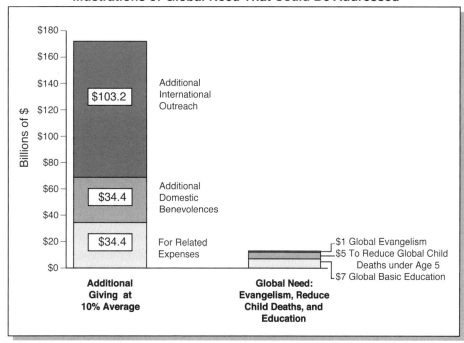

Figure 17: Potential Additional Church Giving at a 2011 Average of 10%, and Illustrations of Global Need That Could Be Addressed

Source: empty tomb analysis; UNICEF

empty tomb, inc., 2013

each year,[6] about two-thirds are dying from causes that could be addressed through lost-cost solutions, according to one international study. The report stated: "Our findings show that about two-thirds of child deaths could be prevented by interventions that are available today and are feasible for implementation in low-income countries at high levels of population coverage."[7] The cost for these interventions might be about $5 billion a year for the portion focused specifically on the children.[8] An annual estimate of $1 billion to cover the costs of global evangelization is discussed below.

Potential Giving at Previous Levels. A comparison in chapter 1 considered what would have happened if per member giving as a portion of income in 2011 had been the same as in 1968. That comparison found that Benevolences would have received an additional $3 billion in 2011. This additional giving would have resulted not from an increase in the portion of income given, but rather had there not been a decline in the portion of income given.

Another calculation suggests that giving to Benevolences could have been much larger if an earlier trend had continued. Giving as a portion of income was increasing between 1946 and 1960. If this rate of increase had been maintained, in 2011, total giving as a portion of income would have been 7.4% instead of 2.3%. If 60% of this additional $50 billion that would have been given had been directed to international missions, that allocation would have amounted to $30 billion, with another $10 billion available for domestic outreach. As noted in the discussion in chapter 1, although it may be tempting to envision how this money not given could have impacted denominational structures, it should be remembered that church members were offered the opportunity to fund those structures at this level, and chose not to do so. It cannot be known if church members would have extended the trend to increase the portion of income given if denominations had offered a challenge to engage global needs, such as evangelization or reducing child mortality, at a scale that might have solved, rather than coped with, the needs.

Per Capita Giving to International Missions. A survey of a group of Protestant denominations found that, on average, about two cents of each dollar donated to their affiliated congregations in 2011 funded international missions through the denominations.

The goal of the empty tomb, inc. research survey form was to discern how much of Overseas Missions Income came from living member giving. "Overseas Missions Income" was used in the title of the survey form, and "overseas ministries income" was used in the text of the questions on the survey form. In this volume, the two terms, "overseas missions" and "overseas ministry," are used interchangeably. The following questions were asked on the denominational Overseas Missions Income survey form for those denominations that had reported 2003, 2004, 2005, 2006, 2007, 2008, 2009, and 2010 data in previous years.

1. What was the amount of income raised in the U.S. during the calendar or fiscal year 2011 for overseas ministries?

2. How many dollars of the total amount on Line 1. came from endowment, foundation, and other investment income?

3. Of the total amount on Line 1., what is the dollar value of government grants, either in dollars or in-kind goods for distribution?

4. Balance of overseas ministries income: Line 1. minus Lines 2. and 3.

> This additional giving would have resulted not from an increase in the portion of income given, but rather had there not been a decline in the portion of income given.

Table 17: Overseas Missions Income, Excluding Any Investment or Government Income, as a Percent of Total Contributions to Congregations, 34 Denominations, 2003

Denomination	2003 Overseas Missions Income (Line 4)	2003 Total Contributions	Overseas Missions Income as % of Total Contributions	Cents of Each Dollar for Overseas Ministries
Allegheny Wesleyan Methodist Connection	$262,260	$5,216,941	5.0%	5¢
American Baptist Churches in the U.S.A.	$8,513,838	$452,422,019	1.9%	2¢
Associate Reformed Presbyterian Church (General Synod)	$3,332,992	$44,279,992	7.5%	8¢
Brethren in Christ Church	$1,606,911	$36,309,353	4.4%	4¢
Christian Church (Disciples of Christ)	$4,079,019	$501,756,492	0.8%	1¢
Christian and Missionary Alliance [10]	$43,160,960	$381,439,326	11.3%	11¢
Church of the Brethren [11]	$1,563,623	$93,876,819	1.7%	2¢
Church of God General Conference (Oregon, Ill., and Morrow, Ga.)	$67,193	$4,297,394	1.6%	2¢
Church of the Lutheran Confession	$155,156	$5,855,961	2.6%	3¢
Church of the Nazarene	$45,640,480	$728,931,987	6.3%	6¢
Churches of God General Conference [12]	$899,679	$27,444,027	3.3%	3¢
Conservative Congregational Christian Conference [13]	$147,805	$52,572,753	0.3%	0.3¢
Cumberland Presbyterian Church	$290,764	$49,168,885	0.6%	1¢
The Episcopal Church [14]	$13,193,855	$2,133,772,253	0.6%	1¢
Evangelical Congregational Church	$1,045,237	$19,628,647	5.3%	5¢
Evangelical Covenant Church	$7,913,682	$247,440,270	3.2%	3¢
Evangelical Lutheran Church in America [15]	$19,637,381	$2,517,027,671	0.8%	1¢
Evangelical Lutheran Synod	$246,587	$13,013,890	1.9%	2¢
Fellowship of Evangelical Churches	$912,689	$14,138,539	6.5%	6¢
Free Methodist Church of North America	$9,121,599	*$124,868,588*	*7.3%*	7¢
General Association of General Baptists	$1,858,866	$35,428,127	5.2%	5¢
Lutheran Church-Missouri Synod [16]	$13,079,041	$1,256,382,217	1.0%	1¢
Moravian Church in America, Northern Province [17]	$467,570	$17,864,570	2.6%	3¢
The Orthodox Presbyterian Church [18]	$1,214,449	$36,644,100	3.3%	3¢
Presbyterian Church in America	$24,070,885	$529,220,570	4.5%	5¢
Presbyterian Church (U.S.A.) [19]	$23,255,000	$2,743,637,755	0.8%	1¢
Primitive Methodist Church in the U.S.A. [20]	$536,903	$4,771,104	11.3%	11¢
Reformed Church in America	$7,852,464	$275,354,238	2.9%	3¢
Seventh-day Adventists, North Am. Div. [21]	$48,225,234	$1,088,682,947	4.4%	4¢
Southern Baptist Convention	$239,663,000	$9,648,530,640	2.5%	2¢
United Church of Christ	$8,373,084	$878,974,911	1.0%	1¢
The United Methodist Church [22]	$82,000,000	$5,376,057,236	1.5%	2¢
The Wesleyan Church	$8,507,914	$260,315,979	3.3%	3¢
Wisconsin Evangelical Lutheran Synod	$10,779,164	$278,209,035	3.9%	4¢
Total/Average for 34 Denominations	$631,675,283	*$29,883,535,236*	2.1%	2¢

Source: empty tomb analysis. See data notes at the end of the chapter. See Appendix B-5 for detail.   empty tomb, inc., 2013

Table 18: Overseas Missions Income, Excluding Any Investment or Government Income, as a Percent of Total Contributions to Congregations, 34 Denominations, 2004

Denomination	2004 Overseas Missions Income (Line 4)	2004 Total Contributions	Overseas Missions Income as % of Total Contributions	Cents of Each Dollar for Overseas Ministries
Allegheny Wesleyan Methodist Connection	$266,299	$5,638,852	4.7%	5¢
American Baptist Churches in the U.S.A.	$9,491,848	$432,734,941	2.2%	2¢
Associate Reformed Presbyterian Church (General Synod)	$3,954,575	$49,290,082	8.0%	8¢
Brethren in Christ Church	$1,800,963	$32,235,440	5.6%	6¢
Christian Church (Disciples of Christ)	$3,832,092	$493,377,355	0.8%	1¢
Christian and Missionary Alliance [10]	$43,534,066	$401,702,995	10.8%	11¢
Church of the Brethren [11]	$1,558,320	$90,440,250	1.7%	2¢
Church of God General Conference (Oregon, Ill., and Morrow, Ga.)	$113,497	$4,445,000	2.6%	3¢
Church of the Lutheran Confession	$206,896	$6,187,297	3.3%	3¢
Church of the Nazarene	$48,173,085	$743,526,726	6.5%	6¢
Churches of God General Conference [12]	$1,047,148	$28,360,228	3.7%	4¢
Conservative Congregational Christian Conference [13]	$149,299	$59,795,058	0.2%	0.2¢
Cumberland Presbyterian Church	$323,340	$49,800,171	0.6%	1¢
The Episcopal Church [14]	$14,781,000	$2,132,774,534	0.7%	1¢
Evangelical Congregational Church	$941,409	$22,831,988	4.1%	4¢
Evangelical Covenant Church	$8,591,574	$267,267,027	3.2%	3¢
Evangelical Lutheran Church in America [15]	$23,431,081	$2,568,013,806	0.9%	1¢
Evangelical Lutheran Synod	$266,241	$12,926,484	2.1%	2¢
Fellowship of Evangelical Churches	$847,526	$16,525,789	5.1%	5¢
Free Methodist Church of North America	$10,186,619	*$134,400,273*	*7.6%*	*8¢*
General Association of General Baptists	$1,768,537	$33,771,637	5.2%	5¢
Lutheran Church-Missouri Synod [16]	$13,177,379	$1,307,764,010	1.0%	1¢
Moravian Church in America, Northern Province [17]	$528,733	$18,514,925	2.9%	3¢
The Orthodox Presbyterian Church [18]	$1,374,254	$38,660,300	3.6%	4¢
Presbyterian Church in America	$24,319,185	$544,857,944	4.5%	4¢
Presbyterian Church (U.S.A.) [19]	$24,588,000	$2,774,907,848	0.9%	1¢
Primitive Methodist Church in the U.S.A. [20]	$526,640	$5,565,638	9.5%	9¢
Reformed Church in America	$7,284,560	$296,856,834	2.5%	2¢
Seventh-day Adventists, North Am. Div. [21]	$46,752,585	$1,121,549,712	4.2%	4¢
Southern Baptist Convention	$242,140,000	$10,171,197,048	2.4%	2¢
United Church of Christ	$7,935,678	$895,654,110	0.9%	1¢
The United Methodist Church [22]	$91,200,000	$5,541,540,536	1.6%	2¢
The Wesleyan Church	$8,881,386	$259,011,346	3.4%	3¢
Wisconsin Evangelical Lutheran Synod	$10,304,863	$296,791,013	3.5%	3¢
Total/Average for 34 Denominations	$654,278,678	*$30,858,917,197*	2.1%	2¢

Source: empty tomb analysis. See data notes at the end of the chapter. See Appendix B-5 for detail.   empty tomb, inc., 2013

Table 19: Overseas Missions Income, Excluding Any Investment or Government Income, as a Percent of Total Contributions to Congregations, 34 Denominations, 2005

Denomination	2005 Overseas Missions Income (Line 4)	2005 Total Contributions	Overseas Missions Income as % of Total Contributions	Cents of Each Dollar for Overseas Ministries
Allegheny Wesleyan Methodist Connection	$399,514	$5,383,333	7.4%	7¢
American Baptist Churches in the U.S.A.	$11,096,481	$336,894,843	3.3%	3¢
Associate Reformed Presbyterian Church (General Synod)	$4,516,302	$50,921,233	8.9%	9¢
Brethren in Christ Church	$1,920,000	$39,800,056	4.8%	5¢
Christian Church (Disciples of Christ)	$4,222,777	$503,045,398	0.8%	1¢
Christian and Missionary Alliance [10]	$54,267,422	$442,917,566	12.3%	12¢
Church of the Brethren [11]	$2,270,134	$97,940,974	2.3%	2¢
Church of God General Conference (Oregon, Ill., and Morrow, Ga.)	$80,000	$4,496,822	1.8%	2¢
Church of the Lutheran Confession	$309,823	$6,551,799	4.7%	5¢
Church of the Nazarene	$52,753,682	$765,434,742	6.9%	7¢
Churches of God General Conference [12]	$1,130,100	$32,249,551	3.5%	4¢
Conservative Congregational Christian Conference [13]	$166,875	$59,346,227	0.3%	0.3¢
Cumberland Presbyterian Church	$293,346	$54,148,837	0.5%	1¢
The Episcopal Church [14]	$15,371,967	$2,180,974,503	0.7%	1¢
Evangelical Congregational Church	$725,089	$21,408,687	3.4%	3¢
Evangelical Covenant Church	$9,008,719	$291,847,011	3.1%	3¢
Evangelical Lutheran Church in America [15]	$26,084,001	$2,604,798,005	1.0%	1¢
Evangelical Lutheran Synod	$222,204	$13,831,771	1.6%	2¢
Fellowship of Evangelical Churches	$785,676	$18,426,832	4.3%	4¢
Free Methodist Church of North America	$10,720,240	*$141,690,288*	*7.6%*	*8¢*
General Association of General Baptists	$1,924,508	$40,146,583	4.8%	5¢
Lutheran Church-Missouri Synod [16]	$17,175,578	$1,296,818,738	1.3%	1¢
Moravian Church in America, Northern Province [17]	$482,157	$17,835,255	2.7%	3¢
The Orthodox Presbyterian Church [18]	$1,856,529	$40,736,400	4.6%	5¢
Presbyterian Church in America	$25,890,591	$586,824,356	4.4%	4¢
Presbyterian Church (U.S.A.) [19]	$31,618,000	$2,814,271,023	1.1%	1¢
Primitive Methodist Church in the U.S.A. [20]	$497,845	$5,541,336	9.0%	9¢
Reformed Church in America	$10,727,347	$310,909,691	3.5%	3¢
Seventh-day Adventists, North Am. Div. [21]	$52,130,967	$1,273,399,341	4.1%	4¢
Southern Baptist Convention	$259,394,000	$10,721,544,568	2.4%	2¢
United Church of Christ	$7,652,371	$908,726,794	0.8%	1¢
The United Methodist Church [22]	$127,600,000	$5,861,722,397	2.2%	2¢
The Wesleyan Church	$9,769,938	$280,214,570	3.5%	3¢
Wisconsin Evangelical Lutheran Synod	$8,794,293	$299,324,485	2.9%	3¢
Total/Average for 34 Denominations	$751,858,476	*$32,130,124,015*	2.3%	2¢

Source: empty tomb analysis. See data notes at the end of the chapter. See Appendix B-5 for detail. empty tomb, inc., 2013

Table 20: Overseas Missions Income, Excluding Any Investment or Government Income, as a Percent of Total Contributions to Congregations, 34 Denominations, 2006

Denomination	2006 Overseas Missions Income (Line 4)	2006 Total Contributions	Overseas Missions Income as % of Total Contributions	Cents of Each Dollar for Overseas Ministries
Allegheny Wesleyan Methodist Connection	$286,781	$4,891,827	5.9%	6¢
American Baptist Churches in the U.S.A.	$8,779,170	$312,485,013	2.8%	3¢
Associate Reformed Presbyterian Church (General Synod)	$3,821,297	$48,592,174	7.9%	8¢
Brethren in Christ Church	$2,117,594	$42,357,718	5.0%	5¢
Christian Church (Disciples of Christ)	$4,421,669	$539,112,457	0.8%	1¢
Christian and Missionary Alliance [10]	$52,505,044	$458,063,183	11.5%	11¢
Church of the Brethren [11]	$1,887,202	$92,834,308	2.0%	2¢
Church of God General Conference (Oregon, Ill., and Morrow, Ga.)	$63,355	$4,421,793	1.4%	1¢
Church of the Lutheran Confession	$188,817	$6,965,144	2.7%	3¢
Church of the Nazarene	$50,969,965	$792,831,191	6.4%	6¢
Churches of God General Conference [12]	$1,233,843	$33,061,351	3.7%	4¢
Conservative Congregational Christian Conference [13]	$123,509	$65,417,224	0.2%	0.2¢
Cumberland Presbyterian Church	$290,307	$54,727,911	0.5%	1¢
The Episcopal Church [14]	$14,806,793	$2,187,308,798	0.7%	1¢
Evangelical Congregational Church	$1,326,393	$22,174,004	6.0%	6¢
Evangelical Covenant Church	$8,530,245	$313,771,228	2.7%	3¢
Evangelical Lutheran Church in America [15]	$21,541,809	$2,664,147,210	0.8%	1¢
Evangelical Lutheran Synod	$330,651	$16,412,280	2.0%	2¢
Fellowship of Evangelical Churches	$700,159	$19,031,219	3.7%	4¢
Free Methodist Church of North America	$11,878,875	*$146,550,263*	*8.1%*	*8¢*
General Association of General Baptists	$2,048,570	$35,905,960	5.7%	6¢
Lutheran Church-Missouri Synod [16]	$13,432,946	$1,355,458,558	1.0%	1¢
Moravian Church in America, Northern Province [17]	$512,828	$17,780,604	2.9%	3¢
The Orthodox Presbyterian Church [18]	$1,706,292	$45,883,300	3.7%	4¢
Presbyterian Church in America	$27,627,770	$650,091,428	4.2%	4¢
Presbyterian Church (U.S.A.) [19]	$20,964,000	$2,854,719,850	0.7%	1¢
Primitive Methodist Church in the U.S.A. [20]	$566,116	$5,080,485	11.1%	11¢
Reformed Church in America	$7,486,527	$328,793,517	2.3%	2¢
Seventh-day Adventists, North Am. Div. [21]	$48,905,616	$1,290,321,473	3.8%	4¢
Southern Baptist Convention	$275,747,000	$11,372,608,393	2.4%	2¢
United Church of Christ	$7,539,124	$920,094,107	0.8%	1¢
The United Methodist Church [22]	$83,100,000	$6,012,378,898	1.4%	1¢
The Wesleyan Church	$13,105,882	$292,826,250	4.5%	4¢
Wisconsin Evangelical Lutheran Synod	$10,468,560	$314,016,686	3.3%	3¢
Total/Average for 34 Denominations	$699,014,709	*$33,321,115,805*	2.1%	2¢

Source: empty tomb analysis. See data notes at the end of the chapter. See Appendix B-5 for detail.   empty tomb, inc., 2013

Table 21: Overseas Missions Income, Excluding Any Investment or Government Income, as a Percent of Total Contributions to Congregations, 34 Denominations, 2007

Denomination	2007 Overseas Missions Income (Line 4)	2007 Total Contributions	Overseas Missions Income as % of Total Contributions	Cents of Each Dollar for Overseas Ministries
Allegheny Wesleyan Methodist Connection	$332,511	$4,973,589	6.7%	7¢
American Baptist Churches in the U.S.A.	$9,866,010	$325,941,205	3.0%	3¢
Associate Reformed Presbyterian Church (General Synod)	$4,819,622	$49,424,200	9.8%	10¢
Brethren in Christ Church	$2,171,822	$43,936,567	4.9%	5¢
Christian Church (Disciples of Christ)	$4,774,004	$519,082,964	0.9%	1¢
Christian and Missionary Alliance [10]	$55,964,407	$467,812,148	12.0%	12¢
Church of the Brethren [11]	$1,736,654	$88,668,503	2.0%	2¢
Church of God General Conference (Oregon, Ill., and Morrow, Ga.)	$103,495	$4,378,745	2.4%	2¢
Church of the Lutheran Confession	$277,600	$7,207,712	3.9%	4¢
Church of the Nazarene	$50,591,155	$817,722,230	6.2%	6¢
Churches of God General Conference [12]	$1,118,921	$35,106,856	3.2%	3¢
Conservative Congregational Christian Conference [13]	$169,508	$74,467,155	0.2%	0.2¢
Cumberland Presbyterian Church	$352,644	$57,766,770	0.6%	1¢
The Episcopal Church [14]	$15,028,559	$2,221,167,438	0.7%	1¢
Evangelical Congregational Church	$1,464,523	$17,180,755	8.5%	9¢
Evangelical Covenant Church	$7,954,834	$323,916,976	2.5%	2¢
Evangelical Lutheran Church in America [15]	$21,747,378	$2,725,349,028	0.8%	1¢
Evangelical Lutheran Synod	$504,018	$16,104,636	3.1%	3¢
Fellowship of Evangelical Churches	$700,590	$19,031,219	3.7%	4¢
Free Methodist Church of North America	$12,478,468	*$149,855,328*	*8.3%*	8¢
General Association of General Baptists	$2,179,048	$31,385,133	6.9%	7¢
Lutheran Church-Missouri Synod [16]	$13,186,920	$1,399,774,702	0.9%	1¢
Moravian Church in America, Northern Province [17]	$524,149	$19,021,572	2.8%	3¢
The Orthodox Presbyterian Church [18]	$1,824,389	$45,730,400	4.0%	4¢
Presbyterian Church in America	$28,456,453	$686,331,677	4.1%	4¢
Presbyterian Church (U.S.A.) [19]	$40,366,000	$2,916,788,414	1.4%	1¢
Primitive Methodist Church in the U.S.A. [20]	$566,810	$4,632,031	12.2%	12¢
Reformed Church in America	$7,611,613	$338,446,877	2.2%	2¢
Seventh-day Adventists, North Am. Div. [21]	$52,038,112	$1,259,280,736	4.1%	4¢
Southern Baptist Convention	$278,313,000	$12,107,096,858	2.3%	2¢
United Church of Christ	$7,307,090	$936,862,062	0.8%	1¢
The United Methodist Church [22]	$79,500,000	$6,295,942,455	1.3%	1¢
The Wesleyan Church	$13,554,996	$321,461,982	4.2%	4¢
Wisconsin Evangelical Lutheran Synod	$10,672,195	$323,082,651	3.3%	3¢
Total/Average for 34 Denominations	$728,257,498	*$34,654,931,574*	2.1%	2¢

Source: empty tomb analysis. See data notes at the end of the chapter. See Appendix B-5 for detail.   empty tomb, inc., 2013

Table 22: Overseas Missions Income, Excluding Any Investment or Government Income, as a Percent of Total Contributions to Congregations, 33 Denominations, 2008

Denomination	2008 Overseas Missions Income (Line 4)	2008 Total Contributions	Overseas Missions Income as % of Total Contributions	Cents of Each Dollar for Overseas Ministries
Allegheny Wesleyan Methodist Connection	$306,946	$4,756,409	6.5%	6¢
American Baptist Churches in the U.S.A.	$9,846,000	$317,338,230	3.1%	3¢
Associate Reformed Presbyterian Church (General Synod)	$5,838,994	$46,948,089	12.4%	12¢
Brethren in Christ Church	$2,452,498	$44,671,975	5.5%	5¢
Christian Church (Disciples of Christ)	$4,527,471	$524,213,682	0.9%	1¢
Christian and Missionary Alliance [10]	$52,012,830	$466,388,400	11.2%	11¢
Church of the Brethren [11]	$1,748,520	$87,494,968	2.0%	2¢
Church of God General Conference (Oregon, Ill., and Morrow, Ga.)	$101,028	$4,056,759	2.5%	2¢
Church of the Lutheran Confession	$360,323	$7,073,530	5.1%	5¢
Church of the Nazarene	$53,761,093	$829,801,861	6.5%	6¢
Churches of God General Conference [12]	$1,187,253	$33,239,825	3.6%	4¢
Conservative Congregational Christian Conference [13]	$84,460	$72,677,645	0.1%	0.1¢
Cumberland Presbyterian Church	$301,245	$57,646,214	0.5%	1¢
The Episcopal Church [14]	$14,599,354	$2,294,941,221	0.6%	1¢
Evangelical Congregational Church	$1,583,478	$18,736,646	8.5%	8¢
Evangelical Covenant Church	NA	NA	NA	NA
Evangelical Lutheran Church in America [15]	$24,160,174	$2,764,009,721	0.9%	1¢
Evangelical Lutheran Synod	$619,754	$15,635,281	4.0%	4¢
Fellowship of Evangelical Churches	$724,626	$24,446,883	3.0%	3¢
Free Methodist Church of North America	$13,244,864	*$146,876,493*	*9.0%*	*9¢*
General Association of General Baptists	$2,105,841	$33,520,716	6.3%	6¢
Lutheran Church-Missouri Synod [16]	$14,505,811	$1,343,086,275	1.1%	1¢
Moravian Church in America, Northern Province [17]	$473,520	$18,268,105	2.6%	3¢
The Orthodox Presbyterian Church [18]	$1,800,305	$46,035,988	3.9%	4¢
Presbyterian Church in America	$29,173,722	$714,356,133	4.1%	4¢
Presbyterian Church (U.S.A.) [19]	$19,919,000	$2,921,571,493	0.7%	1¢
Primitive Methodist Church in the U.S.A. [20]	$542,438	$4,827,828	11.2%	11¢
Reformed Church in America	$7,642,569	$329,904,049	2.3%	2¢
Seventh-day Adventists, North Am. Div. [21]	$51,501,480	$1,195,419,795	4.3%	4¢
Southern Baptist Convention	$254,860,000	$12,121,220,925	2.1%	2¢
United Church of Christ	$7,244,977	$941,553,540	0.8%	1¢
The United Methodist Church [22]	$114,500,000	$6,300,722,381	1.8%	2¢
The Wesleyan Church	$13,669,461	$333,767,545	4.1%	4¢
Wisconsin Evangelical Lutheran Synod	$11,635,379	$319,988,294	3.6%	4¢
Total/Average for 33 Denominations	$717,035,415	*$34,385,196,899*	2.1%	2¢

Source: empty tomb analysis. See data notes at the end of the chapter. See Appendix B-5 for detail.   empty tomb, inc., 2013

Table 23: Overseas Missions Income, Excluding Any Investment or Government Income, as a Percent of Total Contributions to Congregations, 33 Denominations, 2009

Denomination	2009 Overseas Missions Income (Line 4)	2009 Total Contributions	Overseas Missions Income as % of Total Contributions	Cents of Each Dollar for Overseas Ministries
Allegheny Wesleyan Methodist Connection	$275,139	$5,053,282	5.4%	5¢
American Baptist Churches in the U.S.A.	$9,585,000	$288,839,340	3.3%	3¢
Associate Reformed Presbyterian Church (General Synod)	$4,234,871	$54,800,721	7.7%	8¢
Brethren in Christ Church	$2,473,594	$40,370,797	6.1%	6¢
Christian Church (Disciples of Christ)	$3,978,592	$495,988,245	0.8%	1¢
Christian and Missionary Alliance [10]	$52,888,984	$464,694,407	11.4%	11¢
Church of the Brethren [11]	$1,904,137	$89,631,907	2.1%	2¢
Church of God General Conference (Oregon, Ill., and Morrow, Ga.)	$166,433	$4,013,750	4.1%	4¢
Church of the Lutheran Confession	$402,162	$6,974,801	5.8%	6¢
Church of the Nazarene	$43,370,879	$823,915,528	5.3%	5¢
Churches of God General Conference [12]	$1,335,598	$35,331,543	3.8%	4¢
Conservative Congregational Christian Conference [13]	$18,397	$70,496,255	0.0%	0.03¢
Cumberland Presbyterian Church	$277,412	$56,383,201	0.5%	0.5¢
The Episcopal Church [14]	$15,611,043	$2,182,330,459	0.7%	1¢
Evangelical Congregational Church	$1,462,048	$19,594,243	7.5%	7¢
Evangelical Covenant Church	NA	NA	NA	NA
Evangelical Lutheran Church in America [15]	$24,665,494	$2,716,085,854	0.9%	1¢
Evangelical Lutheran Synod	$1,144,111	$15,919,860	7.2%	7¢
Fellowship of Evangelical Churches	$804,057	$24,323,500	3.3%	3¢
Free Methodist Church of North America	$11,720,519	*$150,143,041*	*7.8%*	*8¢*
General Association of General Baptists	$1,946,149	$38,261,252	5.1%	5¢
Lutheran Church-Missouri Synod [16]	*$15,491,786*	$1,361,537,807	*1.1%*	*1¢*
Moravian Church in America, Northern Province [17]	$503,817	$18,241,950	2.8%	3¢
The Orthodox Presbyterian Church [18]	$1,979,044	$46,575,856	4.2%	4¢
Presbyterian Church in America	$27,219,278	$696,680,887	3.9%	4¢
Presbyterian Church (U.S.A.) [19]	$21,986,831	$2,773,343,691	0.8%	1¢
Primitive Methodist Church in the U.S.A. [20]	$429,530	$4,664,330	9.2%	9¢
Reformed Church in America	$8,187,860	$301,838,760	2.7%	3¢
Seventh-day Adventists, North Am. Div. [21]	$49,538,644	$1,275,496,054	3.9%	4¢
Southern Baptist Convention	$255,427,000	$11,912,179,313	2.1%	2¢
United Church of Christ	$6,213,752	$928,638,925	0.7%	1¢
The United Methodist Church [22]	$96,920,000	$6,218,009,630	1.6%	2¢
The Wesleyan Church	$14,139,092	$323,061,444	4.4%	4¢
Wisconsin Evangelical Lutheran Synod	$11,030,819	$314,982,519	3.5%	4¢
Total/Average for 33 Denominations	$687,332,072	*$33,758,403,152*	2.0%	2¢

Source: empty tomb analysis. See data notes at the end of the chapter. See Appendix B-5 for detail.　　　empty tomb, inc., 2013

Table 24: Overseas Missions Income, Excluding Any Investment or Government Income, as a Percent of Total Contributions to Congregations, 32 Denominations, 2010

Denomination	2010 Overseas Missions Income (Line 4)	2010 Total Contributions	Overseas Missions Income as % of Total Contributions	Cents of Each Dollar for Overseas Ministries
Allegheny Wesleyan Methodist Connection	$313,920	$5,072,039	6.2%	6¢
American Baptist Churches in the U.S.A.	$12,121,000	$289,345,336	4.2%	4¢
Associate Reformed Presbyterian Church (General Synod)	$4,245,630	$54,229,638	7.8%	8¢
Brethren in Christ Church	See Appendix B-5	NA	NA	NA
Christian Church (Disciples of Christ)	$4,295,675	$489,365,802	0.9%	1¢
Christian and Missionary Alliance [10]	$53,693,745	$469,726,502	11.4%	11¢
Church of the Brethren [11]	$2,021,630	$92,270,210	2.2%	2¢
Church of God General Conference (McDonough, Ga.)	$106,015	$4,158,243	2.5%	3¢
Church of the Lutheran Confession	$405,811	$7,082,478	5.7%	6¢
Church of the Nazarene	$47,268,270	$774,827,069	6.1%	6¢
Churches of God General Conference [12]	$1,697,288	$36,429,878	4.7%	5¢
Conservative Congregational Christian Conference [13]	$10,124	$48,072,539	0.0%	0.02¢
Cumberland Presbyterian Church	$309,000	$52,531,185	0.6%	1¢
The Episcopal Church [14]	$20,051,263	$2,088,449,676	1.0%	1¢
Evangelical Congregational Church	$1,416,294	$20,221,005	7.0%	7¢
Evangelical Covenant Church	NA	NA	NA	NA
Evangelical Lutheran Church in America [15]	$22,908,625	$2,226,412,989	1.0%	1¢
Evangelical Lutheran Synod	$652,338	$14,960,758	4.4%	4¢
Fellowship of Evangelical Churches	$839,881	$24,607,538	3.4%	3¢
Free Methodist Church-USA	$12,226,510	*$150,770,675*	*8.1%*	*8¢*
General Association of General Baptists	$1,697,759	$35,457,524	4.8%	5¢
Lutheran Church-Missouri Synod [16]	$16,007,836	$1,375,784,215	1.2%	1¢
Moravian Church in America, Northern Province [17]	$493,168	$18,220,682	2.7%	3¢
The Orthodox Presbyterian Church [18]	$1,805,968	$48,356,529	3.7%	4¢
Presbyterian Church in America	$25,327,324	$703,852,802	3.6%	4¢
Presbyterian Church (U.S.A.) [19]	$31,462,380	$2,614,472,933	1.2%	1¢
Primitive Methodist Church in the U.S.A. [20]	$404,770	$5,006,926	8.1%	8¢
Reformed Church in America	$8,870,635	$302,162,041	2.9%	3¢
Seventh-day Adventists, North Am. Div. [21]	$50,392,451	$1,268,582,205	4.0%	4¢
Southern Baptist Convention	$264,924,000	$11,720,820,320	2.3%	2¢
United Church of Christ	$5,812,528	$938,000,522	0.6%	1¢
The United Methodist Church [22]	$135,240,000	$6,158,084,527	2.2%	2¢
The Wesleyan Church	$14,780,950	$316,205,810	4.7%	5¢
Wisconsin Evangelical Lutheran Synod	$9,267,581	$314,966,370	2.9%	3¢
Total/Average for 32 Denominations	$751,070,369	*$32,668,506,966*	2.3%	2¢

Source: empty tomb analysis. See data notes at the end of the chapter. See Appendix B-5 for detail.   empty tomb, inc., 2013

Table 25: Overseas Missions Income, Excluding Any Investment or Government Income, as a Percent of Total Contributions to Congregations, 32 Denominations, 2011

Denomination	2011 Overseas Missions Income (Line 4)	2011 Total Contributions	Overseas Missions Income as % of Total Contributions	Cents of Each Dollar for Overseas Ministries
Allegheny Wesleyan Methodist Connection	$244,376	$4,945,044	4.9%	5¢
American Baptist Churches in the U.S.A.	$10,003,000	$309,967,121	3.2%	3¢
Associate Reformed Presbyterian Church (General Synod)	$4,121,650	$66,774,089	6.2%	6¢
Brethren in Christ Church	See Appendix B-5	NA	NA	NA
Christian Church (Disciples of Christ)	$3,022,583	$483,723,029	0.6%	1¢
Christian and Missionary Alliance [10]	$51,740,315	$482,474,036	10.7%	11¢
Church of the Brethren [11]	$1,813,039	$86,361,373	2.1%	2¢
Church of God General Conference (McDonough, Ga.)	$81,281	$4,102,502	2.0%	2¢
Church of the Lutheran Confession	$389,457	$6,866,506	5.7%	6¢
Church of the Nazarene	$44,769,213	$747,925,798	6.0%	6¢
Churches of God General Conference [12]	$1,329,931	$36,994,255	3.6%	4¢
Conservative Congregational Christian Conference [13]	$21,855	$51,478,729	0.04%	0.04¢
Cumberland Presbyterian Church	$429,388	$49,236,085	0.9%	1¢
The Episcopal Church [14]	$19,369,172	$2,080,612,044	0.9%	1¢
Evangelical Congregational Church	$1,502,493	$18,062,552	8.3%	8¢
Evangelical Covenant Church	NA	NA	NA	NA
Evangelical Lutheran Church in America [15]	$24,387,446	$2,167,770,306	1.1%	1¢
Evangelical Lutheran Synod	$254,289	$15,399,301	1.7%	2¢
Fellowship of Evangelical Churches	$719,573	$23,895,325	3.0%	3¢
Free Methodist Church-USA	$13,633,423	$149,686,109	9.1%	9¢
General Association of General Baptists	$1,670,928	$44,318,518	3.8%	4¢
Lutheran Church-Missouri Synod [16]	$18,663,337	$1,376,155,314	1.4%	1¢
Moravian Church in America, Northern Province [17]	$491,164	$15,754,854	3.1%	3¢
The Orthodox Presbyterian Church [18]	$1,841,490	$49,363,564	3.7%	4¢
Presbyterian Church in America	$24,971,256	$704,611,711	3.5%	4¢
Presbyterian Church (U.S.A.) [19]	$22,952,028	$2,620,938,061	0.9%	1¢
Primitive Methodist Church in the U.S.A. [20]	$340,467	$5,244,894	6.5%	6¢
Reformed Church in America	$6,627,390	$310,520,618	2.1%	2¢
Seventh-day Adventists, North Am. Div. [21]	$55,292,154	$1,297,070,070	4.3%	4¢
Southern Baptist Convention	$256,882,000	$11,805,027,705	2.2%	2¢
United Church of Christ	$5,678,910	$934,824,110	0.6%	1¢
The United Methodist Church [22]	$102,600,000	$6,189,661,943	1.7%	2¢
The Wesleyan Church	$14,788,726	$329,711,022	4.5%	4¢
Wisconsin Evangelical Lutheran Synod	$11,601,216	$311,013,326	3.7%	4¢
Total/Average for 32 Denominations	$702,233,550	$32,780,489,914	2.1%	2¢

Source: empty tomb analysis. See data notes at the end of the chapter. See Appendix B-5 for detail.   empty tomb, inc., 2013

Table 26: Overseas Missions Income, Excluding Any Investment or Government Income, as a Percent of Total Contributions to Congregations and Membership, 32 Denominations, Ranked by Cents per Dollar, 2011

Rank	Deonomination	Cents of Each Dollar for Overseas Ministries	Number of Full/Conf Members
1	Christian and Missionary Alliance [23]	11¢	202,285
2	Free Methodist Church—USA	9¢	66,296
3	Evangelical Congregational Church	8¢	16,779
4	Primitive Methodist Church in the U.S.A. [23]	6¢	3,185
5	Associate Reformed Presbyterian Church (General Synod)	6¢	35,911
6	Church of the Nazarene	6¢	641,989
7	Church of the Lutheran Confession	6¢	5,891
8	Allegheny Wesleyan Methodist Connection	5¢	1,269
9	The Wesleyan Church	4¢	122,298
10	Seventh-day Adventists, North Am. Div. [23]	4¢	1,074,418
11	General Association of General Baptists	4¢	52,920
12	The Orthodox Presbyterian Church [23]	4¢	22,451
13	Wisconsin Evangelical Lutheran Synod	4¢	301,300
14	Churches of God General Conference [23]	4¢	32,647
15	Presbyterian Church in America	4¢	275,513
16	American Baptist Churches in the U.S.A.	3¢	1,300,744
17	Moravian Church in America, Northern Province [23]	3¢	16,180
18	Fellowship of Evangelical Churches	3¢	7,316
19	Southern Baptist Convention	2¢	15,978,112
20	Reformed Church in America	2¢	148,534
21	Church of the Brethren [23]	2¢	118,315
22	Church of God General Conference (McDonough, Ga.)	2¢	3,089
23	The United Methodist Church [23]	2¢	7,526,497
24	Evangelical Lutheran Synod	2¢	15,041
25	Lutheran Church-Missouri Synod [23]	1¢	1,731,522
26	Evangelical Lutheran Church in America [23]	1¢	3,107,925
27	The Episcopal Church [23]	1¢	1,542,072
28	Presbyterian Church (U.S.A.) [23]	1¢	1,952,287
29	Cumberland Presbyterian Church	1¢	67,076
30	Christian Church (Disciples of Christ)	1¢	393,677
31	United Church of Christ	1¢	1,028,324
32	Conservative Congregational Christian Conference [23]	0.04¢	29,462

Source: empty tomb analysis. See data notes at the end of the chapter.
See Appendix B-5 for detail.   empty tomb, inc., 2013

The form sent to denominations that had provided data in previous years included eight columns labeled "Reported 2003" through "Reported 2010." These columns presented on each line the data previously reported by that denomination. A column to the right of these eight columns was labeled "Newly Requested 2011" and included blank cells for each of the four lines.

A total of 32 denominations had complete data available for 2011.[9] The 32 denominations included a combined total of 37.8 million Full or Confirmed members, attending about 150 thousand congregations, in 2011.

Data for 34 denominations, including Overseas Missions Income and Total Contributions, is presented in Tables 17 through 25, for the years 2003, 2004, 2005, 2006, and 2007, respectively, for 33 denominations in 2008 and 2009, and for 32 denominations for 2010 and 2011.

The following observations can be drawn from Tables 17-25 data.

The overall weighted average of Overseas Missions Income as a percent of Total Contributions to the denominations in 2011 was 2.1%. That is, for each dollar of Total Contributions donated to a congregation, about 2¢ was spent on denominational overseas missions.

Information in the endnotes to Tables 17 through 25 indicates that several of the denominations noted in survey correspondence that the dollar figure for international mission activity provided was only for activities funded through the national denominational office, and did not include overseas missions funded directly by the congregations. That is, some of the national denominational offices were of the opinion that congregations may be doing international mission activity in addition to any contributions sent to their offices. In at least two instances, dialogue with the denominational offices resulted in the finding that the national office sends a congregation statistics report form to affiliated congregations, and that this report form does not ask the congregation to distinguish that portion of Benevolences that was spent for international mission activity other than through the national denominational office. One denomination indicated that the national office obtains

Figure 18: Cents Directed to Denominational Overseas Missions, Per Dollar Donated to the Congregation, 32 Denominations, 2011, 1 Denomination, 2009, and 1 Denomination, 2007

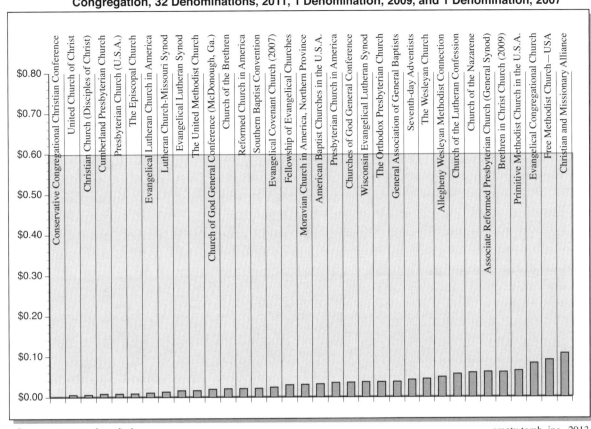

Source: empty tomb analysis

empty tomb, inc., 2013

information from the congregations about missions done both directly by the congregation, and also through the denomination.

Congregational forms, sent by denominations to their congregations to obtain annual reports, could routinely, but apparently often do not, include details of congregational global missions expenditures that are not conducted through the denomination. The denominational structures presumably monitor other congregational expenditures, such as staff compensation and payments for pastor health insurance and pension benefits, as well as the general unified budget assessments requested from the congregations.

Table 26 lists the 32 denominations with complete 2011 data in order of the level of unrounded cents per dollar donated to the congregation that was directed to denominational overseas missions. The membership for each denomination is also listed.

Figure 18 presents, in graphic form, the 2011 cents per dollar donated to the congregation that were directed to denominational overseas missions in 32 denominations in the U.S., reporting data for 2011. One additional denomination that reported data through 2007, and one that reported through 2009, are also included in the figure. The gray shading marks a potential standard of giving for overseas missions at 60¢ per dollar. As noted earlier in this chapter, this goal could be achieved if church members increased giving to a congregation-wide average of ten percent and earmarked the major portion of the increase to international missions.

Appendix B-5 lists the four lines of data for the denominations for data years 2003 through 2011.

A Comparison of Per Member Giving to Overseas Missions in Three Denominations. In the discussion immediately above, aggregate overseas missions income is set in the context of Total Contributions for each denomination.

One can also consider contributions to overseas missions income on a per member basis. A review of three denominations provided the following results.

The three denominations were selected as follows. The Church of the Nazarene, with 641,989 Full or Confirmed Members in 2011 was the largest denomination with membership in the National Association of Evangelicals that provided data. The Southern Baptist Convention, with 15,978,112 Full or Confirmed Members in 2011, was the largest Protestant denomination in the U.S. The United Methodist Church, with 7,526,497 Full or Confirmed Members in 2011, was the largest denomination with membership in the National Council of the Churches of Christ in the U.S.A. that provided data.

Dividing the amount of overseas missions income by the number of reported members resulted in a per member dollar giving level for each denomination. Since the data is for the year 2011 for all three denominations, current dollars can be effectively used in the comparison.

The dollar figure for per member giving to denominational overseas missions for the Church of the Nazarene was $70 in 2011.

The dollar figure for per member giving to denominational overseas missions for the Southern Baptist Convention was $16 in 2011.

The dollar figure for per member giving to denominational overseas missions for The United Methodist Church was $14 in 2011.

Further analysis of factors that might have contributed to the difference in the level of support for denominational overseas missions may yield insight about how denominational structures and priorities affect the level of overseas missions support.

Denominational Overseas Missions Income, 1916-1927. The *Yearbook of American and Canadian Churches* series began with the 1916 *Federal Council Year Book*. The second edition, published in 1917, and continuing through the 1927 edition, presented detailed denominational "foreign missions" information. Income as well as geographical placement and type of missionaries were presented on multi-page tables.

Changes in the level of mission support also led a group of denominations to commission a report, published in 1929, about levels of missions giving. As found in Table 27, the 1929 study provided per capita giving to Foreign Missions, Benevolences, and Total Contributions for 11 denominations.[24] With this information, it was possible to calculate per capita Foreign Missions as a percent of per capita Benevolences, and per capita Foreign Missions as a percent of per capita Total Contributions.

During the 1916-1927 period, for the group of 11 denominations, Foreign Missions Income represented about 29% of all Benevolences. The 1929 study

By 2011, some 80 years later, per capita Foreign Missions Income had decreased further, to 2.1% of Total Contributions for a set of 32 Protestant denominations.

was commissioned in response to the concern of members of the Foreign Missions Conference of North America that giving to foreign missions was declining. As seen in Table 27, per capita Foreign Missions Income had decreased to 6.54% of per capita Total Contributions in 1927.

By 2011, some 80 years later, per capita Foreign Missions Income had decreased further, to 2.1% of Total Contributions for a set of 32 Protestant denominations.

The overall average of per capita Foreign Missions Income as a percent of Total Contributions for 11 denominations for the 1916 through 1927 period was 7.9%,

Table 27: Foreign Missions, Benevolences, and Total Contributions, 11 Denominations, 1916–1927, Current Dollars

Year	Per Capita Foreign Missions Income from Living Donors	Per Capita Benevolences	Per Capita Foreign Missions as a Percent of Per Capita Benevolences (Calculated)	Per Capita Total Contributions	Per Capita Foreign Missions as a Percent of Per Capita Total Contributions (Calculated)
1916	$0.73	$2.24	32.59%	$10.11	7.22%
1917	$0.74	$2.52	29.37%	$10.75	6.88%
1918	$0.86	$2.89	29.76%	$11.44	7.52%
1919	$1.18	$3.89	30.33%	$12.90	9.15%
1920	$1.66	$5.75	28.87%	$16.45	10.09%
1921	$1.70	$5.51	30.85%	$17.20	9.88%
1922	$1.46	$5.18	28.19%	$17.19	8.49%
1923	$1.44	$5.12	28.13%	$17.69	8.14%
1924	$1.32	$4.97	26.56%	$18.44	7.16%
1925	$1.27	$4.59	27.67%	$18.74	6.78%
1926	$1.32	$4.49	29.40%	$18.94	6.97%
1927	$1.24	$4.17	29.74%	$18.95	6.54%

Source: empty tomb analysis; Charles H. Fahs, *Trends in Protestant Giving* (1929), Tables XVIII and XXIX.

compared to 2.1% for 32 denominations in 2011. The average U.S. per capita Disposable Personal Income (DPI) during the 1916–1927 period was $6,344, in inflation-adjusted 2005 dollars. That average income figure compares to the inflation-adjusted U.S. per capita DPI figure of $32,653 in 2011. Since per capita income was over five times the average in the 1916–1927 period, Americans had 415% more after-tax income in 2011 than in the earlier period. The data indicates that overseas missions support was not as high a priority in 2011 as it was in the 1920s, in spite of improved communication about global needs and a higher level of member income in 2011 compared to the 1916–1927 period.

Calculating the Cost of Missions. One area that is exclusively within the realm of the church is the cost of global evangelization. Interestingly, there have been few if any firm cost estimates for insuring that people around the globe have the opportunity to make an informed choice about responding to the Christian message. This has been true even though the accessibility to information about Christianity can be regarded as a justice issue. As a report from one international organization observed:

> There is also a tragic coincidence that most of the world's poor have not heard the Good News of the Gospel of Jesus Christ; or they could not receive it, because it was not recognized as Good News in the way in which it was brought. This is a double injustice: they are victims of oppression of an unjust economic order or an unjust political distribution of power, and at the same time they are deprived of the knowledge of God's special care for them. To announce the Good News to the poor is to begin to render the justice due to them.[25]

One term that is often used to describe the population most excluded from accessibility to the Christian message is "unreached people group" although the term "least-reached" may also be used. The Joshua Project offered a definition that reads:

A people group among which there is no indigenous community of believing Christians with adequate numbers and resources to evangelize this people group.[26]

Various factors make it complicated to define an exact number of the "unreached" people groups. In discussing these issues, the Joshua Project Web site also cites another definition:

The Lausanne 1982 people group definition says "For evangelization purposes, a people group is the largest group within which the Gospel can spread as a church planting movement without encountering barriers of understanding or acceptance."[27]

In 2013, the Joshua Project suggested there were about 7,000 such unreached people groups.[28]

In 2013, the Joshua Project suggested there were about 7,000 such unreached people groups.

One denomination that is on record as having a particular concern about unreached people groups is the Southern Baptist Convention. The Southern Baptist Convention (SBC) is the second largest communion, and the largest Protestant denomination, in the United States. As noted on the Web site of the SBC Executive Committee Director, Dr. Morris Chapman, "In 1845, a network of churches was organized into the Southern Baptist Convention for the purpose of evangelizing the world."[29] The SBC International Mission Board (IMB) is the group within the Convention that is currently charged with supervising the continuing task of global evangelization.

In 2010, the Executive Committee of the SBC asked its international mission arm, the International Mission Board (IMB), about additional needed resources to "reach all of the unreached people groups." The IMB replied that $200 million a year would field the needed additional 3,000 missionaries.[30] The figure of $200 million a year, therefore, may serve as one estimate of the additional word evangelism resources that are needed.

Another model can be developed for mission costs that could be pursued by the broad spectrum of the church.

For example, other communions are also actively pursuing the engagement of unreached people groups. Some groups opt to send cross-cultural missionaries, and others choose to work through missionaries born in the region in which the unreached people groups are located.

Two groups that build their outreach through native-born missionaries are Christian Aid Mission and Gospel for Asia.

Christian Aid Mission coordinates with native workers in various countries to "establish a witness for Christ in every unreached nation." Its Web site stated, "Approximately 100,000 of these [native missionaries] have no regular support ..." The average monthly support number cited is $50 a month.[31] At $600 a year per missionary, the cost to fund the 100,000 missionaries would be $60,000,000 a year.

Gospel for Asia also trains and coordinates a network of native missionaries through Asian countries. To reach a goal of supporting 100,000 missionaries,[32] Gospel for Asia would need to support an additional 83,500 missionaries over the current number of 16,500.[33] The costs for Gospel for Asia missionaries range from $90 to $150 a month.[34] Taking an average cost of $120 a month, the annual cost of

$1,440 was multiplied by the 83,500 figure for the number of additional missionaries needed, yielding a total need of $120,240,000 a year.

The estimate for Christian Aid Mission and Gospel for Asia additional missionaries would total $180,240,000 a year.

Other communions and para-denominational groups in the U.S. are also focused on the goal of engaging the unreached. If the cost of those efforts were on a par with the estimate for the Southern Baptist Convention, the cost would be $200,000,000.

Combining these amounts, the four sets of numbers equal $580,240,000.

If the total cost of evangelization were to be estimated, including not only expanded but also ongoing work, the increased total might not exceed $1 billion a year.[35]

Various groups could accept the challenge of funding the cost of this expanded budget for global evangelization. Table 28 indicates the daily and annual costs based on the population of each group.[36]

Table 28: Great Commandment and Great Commission Outreach Estimated Costs, Calculated Per Member for Selected Church Populations, 2011

	A. Engage Unreached People Estimate (SBC) $200,000,000	B. Combined Estimate for Global Evangelization $580,240,000	C. High Estimate for Global Evangelization $1,000,000,000	D. Stopping, in Jesus' Name Global Under-5 Child Deaths $5,000,000,000	C. + D. + Global Elementary Education + Domestic Poverty $15,000,000,000
Love Expressed in Great Commission Outreach					
Engage Unreached People Estimate (So. Baptist Conv.)	$200,000,000				
Combined Estimate for Global Evangelization		$580,240,000			
High Estimate for Global Evangelization			$1,000,000,000		$1,000,000,000
Stopping in Jesus' Name Under-Five Child Deaths				$5,000,000,000	$5,000,000,000
Global Elementary Education					$7,000,000,000
Domestic U.S. Poverty Need					$2,000,000,000
Total Per Year	$200,000,000	$580,240,000	$1,000,000,000	$5,000,000,000	$15,000,000,000
Historically Christian Church Members (59.45% US Pop. = 185,305,650)					
Annual Amount per Historically Christian Ch. Member	$1	$3	$5	$27	$81
Daily Amount per Historically Christian Church Member	Less than $0.01	$0.01	$0.01	$0.07	$0.22
Evangelical Christians (7% US Pop. = 21,819,000)					
Annual Amount per Evangelical Christian	$9	$27	$46	$229	$687
Daily Amount per Evangelical Christian	$0.03	$0.07	$0.13	$0.63	$1.88
Born Again Christians (40% US Pop. = 124,680,000)					
Annual Amount per Born Again Christian	$2	$5	$8	$40	$120
Daily Amount per Born Again Christian	Less than $0.01	$0.01	$0.02	$0.11	$0.33
National Council of the Churches of Christ in the U.S.A. (Inclusive Members = 39,664,199 [2010])					
Annual Amount per NCCC Member	$5	$15	$25	$126	$378
Daily Amount per NCCC Member	$0.01	$0.04	$0.07	$0.35	$1.04
Roman Catholic (Members = 68,229,841)					
Annual Amount per Roman Catholic Member	$3	$9	$15	$73	$220
Daily Amount per Roman Catholic Member	$0.01	$0.02	$0.04	$0.20	$0.60
Southern Baptist (Members = 15,978,112)					
Annual Amount per Southern Baptist Member	$13	$36	$63	$313	$939
Daily Amount per Southern Baptist Member	$0.03	$0.10	$0.17	$0.86	$2.57
United Methodist (Members = 7,526,497)					
Annual Amount per United Methodist Member	$27	$77	$133	$664	$1,993
Daily Amount per United Methodist Member	$0.07	$0.21	$0.36	$1.82	$5.46

Note 1: The annual and daily numbers in above table would be divided by two if wealthy Christians in that grouping provided half as matching funds.
Note 1: The NCCCUSA Calculations are based on 2010 data from the *YACC 2012*.
Source: empty tomb analysis

empty tomb, inc., 2013

Table 29: Great Commandment and Great Commission Outreach Estimated Costs, Calculated Per Household for Populations with Selected Levels of Net Worth apart from Primary Residence, 2011

	A. Engage Unreached People Estimate (SBC) $200,000,000	B. Combined Estimate for Global Evangelization $580,240,000	C. High Estimate for Global Evangelization $1,000,000,000	D. Stopping, in Jesus' Name Global Under-5 Child Deaths $5,000,000,000	C. + D. + Global Elementary Education + Domestic Poverty $15,000,000,000
Love Expressed in Great Commission Outreach					
Engage Unreached People Estimate (So. Baptist Conv.)	$200,000,000				
Combined Estimate for Global Evangelization		$580,240,000			
High Estimate for Global Evangelization			$1,000,000,000		$1,000,000,000
Stopping in Jesus' Name Under-Five Child Deaths				$5,000,000,000	$5,000,000,000
Global Elementary Education					$7,000,000,000
Domestic U.S. Poverty Need					$2,000,000,000
Total Per Year	$200,000,000	$580,240,000	$1,000,000,000	$5,000,000,000	$15,000,000,000
Historically Christian Church Households					
Greater than or Equal to $5 million (= 640,871)					
Annual Amount per Historically Christian Ch. Household	$312	$905	$1,560	$7,802	$23,406
Daily Amount per Historically Christian Church Hshld.	$0.86	$2.48	$4.28	$21.38	$64.13
Greater than or Equal to $1 million (= 5,112,700)					
Annual Amount per Historically Christian Ch. Household	$39	$113	$196	$978	$2,934
Daily Amount per Historically Christian Church Hshld.	$0.11	$0.31	$0.54	$2.68	$8.04
Greater than or Equal to $500,000 (= 8,204,100)					
Annual Amount per Historically Christian Ch. Household	$24	$71	$122	$609	$1,828
Daily Amount per Historically Christian Church Hshld.	$0.07	$0.19	$0.33	$1.67	$5.01
Evangelical Christian Households					
Greater than or Equal to $5 million (= 75,460)					
Annual Amount per Evangelical Christian Household	$2,650	$7,689	$13,252	$66,260	$198,781
Daily Amount per Evangelical Christian Household	$7.26	$21.07	$36.31	$181.53	$544.60
Greater than or Equal to $1 million (= 602,000)					
Annual Amount per Evangelical Christian Household	$332	$964	$1,661	$8,306	$24,917
Daily Amount per Evangelical Christian Household	$0.91	$2.64	$4.55	$22.76	$68.27
Greater than or Equal to $500,000 (=966,000)					
Annual Amount per Evangelical Christian Household	$207	$601	$1,035	$5,176	$15,528
Daily Amount per Evangelical Christian Household	$0.57	$1.65	$2.84	$14.18	$42.54
Born Again Christian Households					
Greater than or Equal to $5 million (= 431,200)					
Annual Amount per Born Again Christian Household	$464	$1,346	$2,319	$11,596	$34,787
Daily Amount per Born Again Christian Household	$1.27	$3.69	$6.35	$31.77	$95.31
Greater than or Equal to $1 million (= 3,440,000)					
Annual Amount per Born Again Christian Household	$58	$169	$291	$1,453	$4,360
Daily Amount per Born Again Christian Household	$0.16	$0.46	$0.80	$3.98	$11.95
Greater than or Equal to $500,000 (= 5,520,000)					
Annual Amount per Born Again Christian Household	$36	$105	$181	$906	$2,717
Daily Amount per Born Again Christian Household	$0.10	$0.29	$0.50	$2.48	$7.44
NCCCUSA Households (Note 2)					
Greater than or Equal to $5 million (= 137,177)					
Annual Amount per NCCC Household	$1,458	$4,230	$7,290	$36,449	$109,348
Daily Amount per NCCC Household	$3.99	$11.59	$19.97	$99.86	$299.58
Greater than or Equal to $1 million (= 1,094,360)					
Annual Amount per NCCC Household	$183	$530	$914	$4,569	$13,707
Daily Amount per NCCC Household	$0.50	$1.45	$2.50	$12.52	$37.55
Greater than or Equal to $500,000 (= 1,756,067)					
Annual Amount per NCCC Household	$114	$330	$569	$2,847	$8,542
Daily Amount per NCCC Household	$0.31	$0.91	$1.56	$7.80	$23.40

Note 1: The annual and daily numbers in above table would be divided by two if the general church population provided half the money in response to matching funds offered by wealthy church members.

Note 2: The NCCCUSA calculaitons are based on 2010 membership from the *YACC 2012*

Source: empty tomb analysis, empty tomb, inc., 2013

Of course, the Great Commission, in the context of the Great Commandment, would present the good news of Jesus Christ in both word and deed. Christians generally agree about God's concern for the children of the world. In 2011, about 18,942 children under the age of five died each day around the globe.[37] With about two-thirds, or 12,628, of these children dying from preventable poverty conditions for which there are low-cost immediate solutions, the church should recognize both the possibility and the responsibility inherent in this challenge. Table 28 also considers the annual and daily costs for various groups if members should choose to prevent more deaths among children under five around the globe.

However, the choice need not be between global evangelization *or* helping to stop, in Jesus' name, global child deaths, *or* primary education, *or* addressing poverty within the United States. When Jesus Christ came to announce God's love for the world in a physical body, Jesus combined the power of the spoken word with healing, feeding, clothing, and freeing those he encountered. Given the resources and the broad base of the church, the current body of Jesus Christ, Christians in the early 21st century have the power to follow Jesus' example of loving the whole person in need. The higher cost for combining evangelization, addressing global child deaths, providing primary education, and having $2 billion a year additional to address domestic poverty needs within the U.S. in Jesus' name was estimated at $15 billion a year. Table 28 also displays the annual and daily costs for various groupings of Christians to engage all of these needs simultaneously.

If creative church leadership were displayed, wealthy Christians might be found who would provide matching funds for donations from the general church population for these needs. In that case, the annual and daily costs presented in Table 28 would be divided by two.

Table 29 considers the same word and deed needs from a slightly different perspective. In this table, the size of the population with varying degrees of wealth was calculated for four sets of church groups. Annual and daily costs to meet the outlined needs are presented for households with $5 million net worth, $1 million net worth, and $500,000 net worth, apart from primary residence.[38] Again, if the general church population were to provide half the funds needed to address these needs, the numbers in the table would be divided by two.

Potential Roman Catholic Giving.

Potential Roman Catholic Giving. The Roman Catholic Church is the largest single religious body in the United States. Unfortunately, that communion has opted not to publish financial giving data on a regular basis. Therefore, any estimates of giving among this major part of the body of Christ must be only approximations. Given the size of the Catholic Church, however, such an approximation is worth exploring.

There has been some discussion in Catholic circles about the practice of the tithe in recent years.[39]

To explore that idea further, a review of potential giving levels at an average of 10% per member was conducted for nine archdioceses that were led by a cardinal as of the *OCD 2005*, or subsequently. Each archdiocese comprises certain U.S. counties. As a result, the total population[40] and the U.S. per capita DPI could be

With about two-thirds, or 12,628, of these children dying from preventable poverty conditions for which there are low-cost immediate solutions, the church should recognize both the possibility and the responsibility inherent in this challenge.

obtained for each archdiocese.[41] A general estimate of 1.2% of income was used as the current level of Catholic giving.[42]

Two observations may be made in regard to the estimate of 1.2% of per capita DPI. First, although the estimate is lower than estimates of Protestant giving, as a previous analysis in *The State of Church Giving* series demonstrated, there are certain efficiencies in the way that Catholic parishes are organized. These efficiencies allow Catholics to maintain basic operations on a par with Protestants, with a smaller per member contribution.[43]

Second, preliminary calculations based on a 2010 survey of Catholic parishes suggest that the per member contribution for "average weekly offering in U.S. parishes" was about 0.3% of income. A 1.2% estimate, for per Catholic giving as a percent of income, therefore takes into account the possibility of additional charitable contributions, including to second collections, that are three times the amount of weekly offerings.[44]

The nine archdioceses combined had a present estimated giving level of $9.9 billion dollars. If Catholics in these archdioceses increased from the current 1.2% of income given to 10% of income, the additional total would have been $72.5 billion in 2011. The increased amounts varied from $2 billion in the Archdiocese of Baltimore, to $15 billion in the Archdioceses of Los Angeles and New York.

The results of the calculations are shown in Table 30.

Table 30: Potential Additional Giving at 10% of Income, Nine Roman Catholic Archdioceses in the U.S., 2011

Area Name	Total U.S. BEA Personal Income for Counties in Archdioceses ($)	% Catholic of Total Population in Area	Calculated U.S. BEA Personal Income Available to Catholics ($)	Estimated Current Catholic Giving at 1.2% of Income ($)	Estimated Potential Additional Catholic Giving at 10% of Income ($)
Archdiocese of Baltimore	$157,258,531,000	16.2%	$25,487,879,597	$305,854,555	$2,242,933,405
Archdiocese of Boston	243,559,391,463	48.0%	116,908,523,430	1,402,902,281	10,287,950,062
Archdiocese of Chicago	284,177,657,000	39.0%	110,826,593,091	1,329,919,117	9,752,740,192
Archdiocese of Detroit	169,483,533,000	32.3%	54,768,733,446	657,224,801	4,819,648,543
Archdiocese of Galveston-Houston	288,013,030,000	19.2%	55,265,183,701	663,182,204	4,863,336,166
Archdiocese of Los Angeles	478,357,747,000	36.0%	172,208,805,193	2,066,505,662	15,154,374,857
Archdiocese of New York	394,900,891,000	45.0%	177,705,417,915	2,132,465,015	15,638,076,776
Archdiocese of Philadelphia	204,089,785,000	36.5%	74,542,671,018	894,512,052	6,559,755,050
Archdiocese of Washington	165,421,076,000	22.0%	36,392,637,911	436,711,655	3,202,552,136
Total: 9 Archdioceses with Cardinals	$2,385,261,641,463		$824,106,445,302	$9,889,277,344	$72,521,367,187

Source: empty tomb analysis. See endnotes 40-42.   empty tomb, inc., 2013

The application of this potential giving could make an impact on international need, as discussed in chapter 8. This additional giving could address domestic needs as well. For example, closings of Catholic schools have continued. A 2013 *New York Times* article on proposed closings observed, "Because finances were the most significant factor in the decisions, schools filled with children from poor and immigrant families will be hit hard."[45] Another *New York Times* article focused on the 2011 closing of Rice High School in Harlem, after the graduation of its 70th commencement class. The article noted, "With a student body that is 98 percent black or Hispanic, with 80 percent of its students requiring financial aid, virtually every graduating senior was bound for college." One observer was quoted in the article as follows:

"Given all the money that's been raised for charter schools — from the Gates Foundation, from Eli Broad, from hedge fund managers — I find it perplexing that Catholics can't raise money for their own schools that have a track record of success," Mr. Gecan said. "I don't think they've tried hard enough. They've lost focus on their core mission."[46]

A 2008 Associated Press news report on the closing of Catholic schools noted, "High school enrollment has remained roughly the same and schools are opening in suburbs, particularly in the West and Southwest. The Northeast and Midwest have been hit hardest." The same article quoted Sister Dale McDonald, the National Catholic Education Association director: "The church has always had a strong sense of mission, particularly to the poor … As it becomes more and more difficult, not only on the poor but on middle-income people, we're not really fulfilling the mission of the church to serve all if we only can afford to serve the people who can afford the big bucks."[47]

As proposed earlier in this chapter, increased giving at the ten percent level could be allocated so that 60 percent is directed to international ministries and 20 percent to domestic needs. That distribution could direct billions of additional dollars to inner-city Catholic schools in these nine archdioceses, even while providing critical resources for missions that address international need.

However, as shown earlier in Table 28, Catholics, as well as all other Christians, could make a dramatic impact on global word and deed need for much less than the cost of increasing giving to the classic tithe.

… Catholics, as well as all other Christians, could make a dramatic impact on global word and deed need for much less than the cost of increasing giving to the classic tithe.

Putting Potential into Perspective. The latest edition in a report series on global philanthropy by the Hudson Institute was *The Index of Global Philanthropy and Remittances (Index) 2012*.[48] That report included an estimate on the amount of money being sent from the United States to other countries.

The ambitious project sought to bring a broad and fresh perspective to the growing area of global philanthropy. The report was not limited to the traditional boundaries of the area, instead including, for example, "private capital flows," representing investment on market terms by for-profit businesses in developing countries, and remittances by foreign-born residents to their home countries into the mix.

The focus of the discussion in this chapter is on the potential of religious giving. The *Index 2012* is relevant to the current discussion as it included an estimate of religious giving directed to international ministries. Some preliminary calculations, based on the text descriptions in *Index 2012*, suggested that the *Index 2012*'s $7.2 billion (for 2009, the last year available in the *Index*) may be a somewhat low estimate for religious philanthropy directed to other countries. That is, in order not to double-count $6.3 billion in congregational donations to U.S.-based relief and development organizations, the *Index* included that $6.3 billion in the Private Voluntary Organization category, and subtracted that amount from its survey findings of international assistance provided by religious congregations. However, in the present discussion of religious giving to international ministry, there is no basis for excluding that $6.3 billion. When the $6.3 billion was added to the *Index*'s Religion figure of $7.2 billion, a revised 2009 total of $13.5 billion given internationally by people in the U.S. can be described as given as a function of Religion.

Two observations about the *Index*'s numbers as they were presented can be made. One observation considers the potential to stop child deaths in light of total assistance to developing countries, and the second compares religious philanthropy to remittances.

Total Assistance to Developing Countries and Child Deaths. The *Index 2012* estimated that the "Total U.S. Economic Engagement with Developing Countries, 2010" was $326.4 billion, including government and private entities, as well as remittances.[49]

As noted earlier in this chapter, a figure of $5 billion a year has been calculated as the amount needed to stop the deaths of two-thirds of the 6.9 million children under five being killed each year by preventable causes that could be addressed with available, low-cost solutions.

A comparison of the $326.4 billion economic engagement with developing countries, and the $5 billion needed to stop most of the child deaths in those countries, leads to a question of priorities. Why have the leaders responsible for the billions of dollars transmitted to developing countries not focused less than 2% of that total on the strategies available to prevent these child deaths? Or alternatively, why have the leaders not organized to increase the total slightly, with the targeted goal of applying the increase to addressing these child deaths?

The present discussion focuses on the resources available to church leaders and institutions that could be mobilized among church members to help implement God's agenda in regard to relieving global need. In that setting, how global leaders, both government and private industry, respond to global need alleviation is tangentially related to the church. However, it is church leaders who are responsible to assist church members in implementing God's agenda. What the following comparison suggests about the basis for church priorities is discussed further in chapter 8.

Church Giving to Global Need Compared to Foreign-Born Remittances. As noted above, the *Index 2012* private religious philanthropy to developing countries in 2009 was adjusted to $13.5 billion, for a maximum estimate of religious giving in the U.S. to international causes for the present analysis. When adjusted by a Gross Domestic Product factor, a 2011 estimate of $14.6 billion results. An estimate of 161,236,758 native-born members in historically Christian churches in the U.S. in 2011 was used in the comparison.[50] For purposes of the present discussion, one may attribute all of the $14.6 billion in private religious assistance to these native-born church members.

That figure of $14.6 billion from native-born church members in the U.S. can be compared to a figure of $100.17 billion figure of "U.S. Remittances" in 2011.[51] The category represents assistance "from individuals, families, and hometown associations in the United States going to developing countries" provided by "immigrants and migrant workers."[52] The aid sent home was observed to increase in 2011 from the 2010 level of $95.8. In 2010, the developing countries that received the largest amount of these remittances sent from the U.S. were Latin America and

However,
it is church
leaders who are
responsible to
assist church
members in
implementing
God's agenda.

the Caribbean, with Mexico receiving over half of that amount, as well as Asia and the Pacific, predominantly China, India, and the Philippines.[53]

A comparison of these numbers leads to questions of both potential and priorities. In 2011, there were an estimated 161,236,758 native-born church members, which was four times the 40,377,860 foreign-born people living in the U.S.[54] Yet, those foreign-born inhabitants sent seven times the amount of assistance to developing countries than did the native-born church members. Given the list of recipient countries, one might hypothesize that the foreign-born people living in the U.S. and sending remittances to developing countries are from varying economic backgrounds, and not necessarily wealthier than native-born church members. These foreign-born inhabitants have to obtain housing, food, and clothing to maintain themselves while living in the U.S., as do the native-born church members.

If the total remittances sent by foreign-born people in the United States figure is divided by the foreign-born population in the U.S., the amount is calculated to be $2,481 per capita. Following a similar procedure for the native-born church members, it is estimated that the per member contribution to international ministries in 2011 was $90. If native-born church members in the U.S. were to donate to international ministries on the same level as foreign-born people in the U.S., the additional donations would total $385 billion more.

Figure 19 presents a graphic comparison of these three figures.

The numbers in this comparison are another demonstration of the potential of church members in the U.S. to increase contributions, in this instance to approach the level of foreign-born people's remittances, in order to impact global needs. The numbers also point out the disparity of priorities between the foreign-born inhabitants and the church members. The first is presumably sending assistance to family and hometowns. The second has been given the opportunity and responsibility to further God's agenda in the world as ambassadors of King

Figure 19: Religious Giving in the U.S. for International Ministries, 2011, Level of Remittances by Foreign-Born Individuals Living in the U.S. to Other Countries, 2011, and Additional Support for International Ministries if Giving by Native-Born Church Members in the U.S. Had Been at the Level of Foreign-Born Remittances, 2011

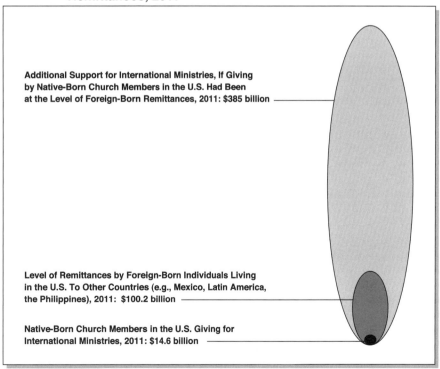

Additional Support for International Ministries, If Giving by Native-Born Church Members in the U.S. Had Been at the Level of Foreign-Born Remittances, 2011: $385 billion

Level of Remittances by Foreign-Born Individuals Living in the U.S. To Other Countries (e.g., Mexico, Latin America, the Philippines), 2011: $100.2 billion

Native-Born Church Members in the U.S. Giving for International Ministries, 2011: $14.6 billion

Source: empty tomb analysis; *The Index of Global Philanthropy and Remitttances*   empty tomb, inc., 2013

Jesus. The question may be posed, in light of the available resources, if native-born church members will honor Jesus' priorities to the same degree that foreign-born people living in the U.S. honor their families still living in their home countries.

Making Missions Giving a Priority in order to Act on the Potential.
The numbers in this chapter document the potential for church members in the U.S. to increase giving, and outline some of the impact on global word and deed need, as well as domestic need, that could be made as a result.

Various comparisons in this chapter demonstrate that the issue of meeting global and domestic need is not one of resources, but of priorities and intentions. The Biblical mandate, as well as various methodologies, are in place to lay the groundwork for impacting global word and deed need in Jesus' name.

Notes for Chapter 6

[1] See Jesus' statement in Matthew 23:23. For a discussion of various views of the tithe, see John and Sylvia Ronsvalle, *Behind the Stained Glass Windows: Money Dynamics in the Church* (Grand Rapids, MI: Baker Book House, 1996), pp. 187-193.

[2] The basis for the calculations of potential giving by historically Christian churches in the U.S. in 2011 is as follows. In chapter seven of this volume titled "Why and How Much Do Americans Give?" a 2011 figure of total giving to religion was presented in the "Denomination-Based series Keyed to 1974 Filer Estimate." That figure was $70.4 billion. A figure of 73.8% was multiplied by the 2011 figure for giving to religion of $70.4 billion to determine what amount was given by those who identify with the historically Christian church. The result was $52.0 billion. In 2011, if giving had increased to an average of 10% from the actual level of 2.32% given, instead of $52 billion, an amount of $224 billion would have been donated to historically Christian churches in the U.S. The difference between the $52 billion given and the potential of $224 billion is $172 billion, the additional money that would have been available at an average of 10% giving. The above figure of 73.8% was based on an empty tomb, inc. analysis of data published in Barry A. Kosmin and Ariela Keysar; American Religious Identification Survey [ARIS 2008] Summary Report; Hartford, Conn.: Trinity College, March 2009; p. 5 of 7/4/2009 printout, and referred to that portion of the U.S. population that identifies with the historically Christian church—those communions and traditions, such as Roman Catholic, Orthodox, evangelical and mainline Protestant, Pentecostal, and Anabaptist, that profess a commitment to the historic tenets of the faith.

[3] It may be noted that the estimate of an additional $172 billion that would be available if average giving were at 10% is at the lower end. Rather than using the calculation detailed in the previous endnote, two other estimates of $635 billion and $800 billion for 2011 were obtained based on alternate assumptions.

An alternative estimate of $635 billion was derived based on the assumption that: (1) 59.45% of Americans are members of historically Christian churches, with aggregate after-tax income of $6.9 trillion; (2) religious giving was $70.4 billion in 2011; and (3) 73.8% of religious giving was from self-identifying Christians (estimate based on Kosmin and Keysar, ARIS 2008 [March 2009]). The results indicated that the giving level was 0.76% of historically Christian church member after-tax income in 2011, rather than the 2.32% noted in the previous endnote. In that case, the difference between 2011 giving at 0.76% and 10% would have been $635 billion.

Alternatively, one could base the potential giving level calculation on the assumptions that: (1) 73.8% of Americans identify with the historically Christian church, whether or not they are members (estimate based on Kosmin and Keysar, ARIS 2008 [March 2009]); (2) this portion of Americans had an aggregate after-tax income of $8.5 trillion; and (3) the calculation considered contributions as possibly available from this 73.8% of U.S. population. Giving levels would then have been at the 0.61% of income level. In that case, the difference between self-identified

Christian giving in 2011 at the 0.61% level and a potential 10% level would have yielded an additional $800 billion in 2011. The estimate of 59.45% church member figure was an empty tomb, inc. calculation based on George H. Gallup, Jr., *Religion in America 2002* (Princeton, NJ: Princeton Religion Research Center [2002?]), pp. 28, 40. The 2011 aggregate Disposable Personal Income figure of $11.5493 trillion that was multiplied by the church member population figures in the two alternative calculations contained in this endnote above was obtained from U.S. Bureau of Economic Analysis; "Table 2.1. Personal Income and Its Disposition"; Line 27: "Disposable personal income"; National Income and Product Accounts Tables; 1969-2012: <http://www.bea.gov//national/nipaweb/SS_Data/Section2All_xls.xls>; 1969-2012 data published on March 28, 2013.

[4] Carol Bellamy, *The State of the World's Children 2000* (New York: UNICEF, 2000), p. 37.

[5] Carol Bellamy, *The State of the World's Children 1999* (New York: UNICEF, 1999), p. 85.

[6] Abid Aslam, editor, *The State of the World's Children 2013* (New York: UNICEF, 2013), p. 103.

[7] Gareth Jones, et al.; "How Many Child Deaths Can We Prevent This Year?"; *The Lancet*, vol. 362; 7/5/2003; <http://www.thelancet.com/journal/vol1362/iss9377/full/llan.362.9377.child_survival.26292.1>; p. 6 of 7/7/03 2:06 PM printout.

[8] James Grant, *The State of the World's Children 1990* (New York: Oxford University Press, 1990), p. 16, estimated that $2.5 billion a year would be needed by the late 1990s to stop preventable child deaths. An updated figure of $5.1 billion was cited in Jennifer Bryce, et al.; "Can the World Afford to Save the Lives of 6 Million Children Each Year?"; *The Lancet*, vol. 365; 6/25/2005; p. 2193; <http://www.thelancet.com/journals/lancet/article/PIIS014065667773/fulltext>; p. 1 of 1/11/2006 printout.

[9] Two additional denominations provided Overseas Missions Income for 2003 through 2011, but indicated that they were not able to provide Total Contributions for 2003 through 2011. Those denominations and their data are listed in a table in Appendix B-5. It should be noted that in 2004, Friends United Meeting changed fiscal years to end June 30, 2004, and so only six months of data was available for 2004. A third denomination provided missions data for 2011 but was not able to provide Total Contributions. Data for Tables 17-25, and the three denominations, is presented in Appendix B-5.

[10] Christian and Missionary Alliance: "Since both domestic and overseas works are budgeted through the same source (our 'Great Commission Fund'), the amount on lines 1 and 4 are actual amounts spent on overseas missions."

[11] Church of the Brethren "This amount is national denominational mission and service, i.e., direct staffing and mission support, and does not include other projects funded directly by congregations or districts, or independent missionaries sponsored by congregations and individuals that would not be part of the denominational effort."

[12] Churches of God General Conference: "[Data Year] 2008 line 2 represents a net loss in investment income included in line 1. By adding this net loss amount back, line 4 represents the amount received in contributions from donors."

[13] Conservative Congregational Christian Conference: "The structure of this communion limits the national office coordination of overseas ministries activity. By design, congregations are to conduct missions directly, through agencies of their choice. The national office does not survey congregations about these activities. The one common emphasis of affiliated congregations is a focus on Micronesia, represented by the reported numbers." Data Year 2010: "The amount raised is down because we didn't have any missionary that we sent overseas."

[14] The Episcopal Church: "The Episcopal Church (aka, The Domestic and Foreign Missionary Society) does not specifically raise money to support our non-domestic ministries. Many of the activities included in our budget are, however, involved, directly or indirectly with providing worldwide mission ... Many other expenditures (e.g., for ecumenical and interfaith relations; for federal chaplaincies; for management's participation in activities of the worldwide Anglican Communion) contain an overseas component; but we do not separately track or report domestic vs. overseas expenses in those categories."

[15] Evangelical Lutheran Church in America: "Some assumptions were made in arriving with the total income, and those remain consistent from year to year."

[16] Lutheran Church-Missouri Synod: "The Lutheran Church-Missouri Synod (LCMS) is a confessing, orthodox Lutheran church comprising 6,000 congregations and approximately 600,000 households (2.27 million baptized individuals) across North America. LCMS witness and mercy work is carried out by two distinct offices: The Office of International Mission and the Office of National Mission. These offices encompass the work of two legacy entities: LCMS World Mission and LCMS World Relief and Human Care. The information

provided in this report reflects the work of LCMS World Mission*. Annual budget income; above budget income; administrative incomes; and the special, multi-year, mission funding campaign, called *Fan into Flame*, income is included in the overseas income data. The majority of LCMS World Mission funding was supplied through direct gifts from individuals, congregations, and organizations connected to the Synod.

"(*) Note: information for LCMS World Relief and Human Care, another official LCMS entity involved in international and national ministry, is not included in the statistics provided here.

"In more recent years, the 35 districts (regional jurisdictions) of the LCMS, along with a growing number of congregations and Lutheran mission societies, began sponsoring various mission fields and projects directly. That support did not flow through LCMS World Missions. More information regarding the international work of the 35 LCMS districts can be found at www.lcmsdistricts.org and the 75-plus members of Association of Lutheran Mission Agencies at www.alma-online.org. Therefore, millions of dollars of additional support from LCMS members is raised and spent for international ministry each year which are not part of this report. Since these funds are not sent through the LCMS national office—and thus are not part of Synod's annual auditing process—the total amount cannot be verified and incorporated into this report."

[17] Moravian Church in America, Northern Province: "Data provided by the Board of World Mission, an interprovincial agency of the North American Moravian Church. The Overseas Missions Income figure was estimated for the Northern Province by the Board of World Mission of the Moravian Church. The Northern Province is the only one of the three Moravian Provinces that reports Total Contributions to the *Yearbook of American and Canadian Churches* series."

[18] Orthodox Presbyterian Church: "These figures, as in past years, reflect only what was given through our denominational committee on Foreign Missions. In addition, $122,166 was given through our Committee on Diaconal Ministries for diaconal and disaster relief ministries administered by our missionaries on various overseas fields. Local churches and individuals also give directly to a variety of overseas missions causes."

[19] Presbyterian Church (U.S.A.): "Nos. 1 & 4 Year 2005: Higher for Asian Tsunami Relief."

[20] Primitive Methodist Church in the U.S.A.: "This only includes monies passing through our Denominational Mission Board (International). Many churches send money directly to a mission field."

[21] Seventh-day Adventist, North American Division: "This estimate, prepared by the General Conference Treasury Department, is for the U.S. portion of the total donated by congregations in both Canada and the U.S."

[22] The United Methodist Church: "The above represents total income received by the General Board of Global Ministries, The United Methodist Church."

[23] See notes for Tables #6B through #6J.

[24] Charles H. Fahs, *Trends in Protestant Giving* (New York: Institute of Social and Religious Research, 1929), pp. 26, 29, 53. The eleven denominations included in the 1916-1927 figures are: Congregational; Methodist Episcopal; Methodist Episcopal, South; Northern Baptist Convention; Presbyterian Church in the U.S.; Presbyterian Church in the U.S.A.; Reformed Church in the United States; Reformed Church in America; Southern Baptist Convention; United Brethren; and United Presbyterian. For a more detailed discussion of the Fahs study, and a comparison of church member giving in the 1920s and 2003, see John and Sylvia Ronsvalle, *The State of Church Giving through 2003* (Champaign, IL: empty tomb, inc., 2005), pp. 55-60. The chapter is also available at <http://www.emptytomb.org/scg03missions.pdf>.

[25] Commission on World Mission and Evangelism of the World Council of Churches, "Mission and Evangelism—An Ecumenical Affirmation," *International Review of Mission*, vol. LXXI, no. 284 (October, 1982), p. 440.

[26] "Definitions and Terms Related to the Great Commission"; Joshua Project; n.d.; <http://www.joshuaproject.net/definitions.php?term=24>; p. 1 of 7/25/2011 4:28 PM printout.

[27] "How Many People Groups Are There?"; The Joshua Project; n.d.; <http://www.joshuaproject.net/how-many-people-groups.php>; p. 1 of 8/10/2013 5:49 PM printout.

[28] In August 2013, the Joshua Project posted a number 7,266 ("Unreached People Groups"; <http://www.joshuaproject.net>; p. 1 of 8/10/2013 5:55 PM printout).

[29] Morris Chapman; "The Conversation is Changing"; published July 1, 2006; <http://www.morrischapman.com/article.asp?is=57>; p. 1 of 8/6/06 4:48 PM printout.

[30] Bob Rodgers, Southern Baptist Convention Executive Committee vice president for Cooperative Program & stewardship; "Analysis: Are We Serious About Penetrating Lostness?"; Baptist Press; 5/28/2010; <http://www.bpnews.net/printerfriendly.asp?ID=33027>; p. 1 of 5/29/2010 10:54 AM printout.

[31] "Frequently Asked Questions"; Christian Aid Mission; n.d.; <http://www.christianaid.org/About/FAQ.aspx>; pp. 1-2 of 6/10/2008 1:58 PM printout.

[32] "F.A.Q.'s"; Gospel for Asia; <http://www.gfa.org/gfa/faqs>; p. 2 of 8/23/2005 8:48 AM printout.

[33] "Frequently Asked Questions"; Gospel for Asia; 2008; <http://www.gfa.org/faqs#q13>; p. 1 of 6/10/2008 2:42 PM printout.

[34] "Sponsorship FAQ's"; Gospel for Asia; 2008; <http://www.gfa.org/sponsore-faqs>; p. 1 of 6/10/2008 3:36 PM printout.

[35] John Ronsvalle and Sylvia Ronsvalle, *The State of Church Giving through 2005: Abolition of the Institutional Enslavement of Overseas Missions* (Champaign, IL: empty tomb, inc., 2008), pp. 66-67.

[36] Membership data for specific denominations is provided in Appendix B. The Evangelical and Born Again population percents are taken from "The Barna Update: Barna Survey Reveals Significant growth in Born Again Population"; The Barna Group; <http://www.barna.org/FlexPage.aspx?Page=BarnaUpdate&BarnaUpdateID=271>; p. 2 of 7/9/2007 9:22 AM printout. The National Council of the Churches of Christ in the U.S.A. inclusive membership figure was obtained from Eileen W. Lindner, ed., *Yearbook of American and Canadian Churches 2012* (Nashville: Abingdon, 2012); pp. 378-79.

[37] UNICEF estimated there were 6,914,000 under-five child deaths in 2011: "Statistical Tables: Table 1," *The State of the World's Children 2013*, p. 103. Dividing that number by 365 days in 2011 yields the estimate of 18,942 children a day.

[38] "Affluent Market Insights 2012"; Spectrem Group Release 3-21-12; Voice of the Investor; SpectremGroup; March 21, 2012; <http:www.spectremgroup.com/content/spectrem-group-release-3-21-12>; p. 1 of 6/11/2012 9:05 AM printout.

[39] For a brief review of this topic, see John Ronsvalle and Sylvia Ronsvalle, *The State of Church Giving through 2002* (Champaign, IL: empty tomb, inc., 2004), pp. 65-66. Also available at <http://www.emptytomb.org/scg036Potential.php>.

[40] The percent Catholic for each diocese was derived by dividing "Total Catholic Population" by "Total Population" as found in *The Official Catholic Directory (OCD)*, P.J. Kenedy & Sons, New Providence, NJ, 2012, subtitled, "Giving Status of the Catholic Church as of January 1, 2012." The population data for the Archdioceses under consideration was found in the *OCD* as follows: Baltimore (p. 73), Boston (p. 131), Chicago (p. 250), Detroit (p. 383), Galveston-Houston (p. 487), Los Angeles (p. 708-09), New York (pp. 884), Philadelphia (p. 1019-20), and Washington (p. 1468).

The percent Catholic calculated for each diocese was used to obtain an estimate of U.S. BEA Personal Income for Catholics in each Archdiocesan county. An alternative approach would have been to employ data from Dale E. Jones et al., *Religious Congregations & Membership in the United States (RCMUS), 2000* (Nashville: Glenmary Research Center, 2002). The *RCMUS* provided "Total Adherents" as a "% of Total Pop." data for Catholics as well as other denominations and religions for each county. A cursory review in 2005 of this data for selected counties suggested that this latter approach using somewhat older data would have resulted in marginal differences. The *RCMUS* is part of a series that has been published decennially.

[41] Total 2011 U.S. BEA Personal Income for Counties in Archdioceses ($s) County level U.S. BEA Personal Income data for 2011, the latest year listed, was accessed on 4/1/2013 via <http://www.bea.gov/iTable/iTable.cfm?reqid=70&step=1&isuri=1&acrdn=5 - reqid=70&step=1&isuri=1>. The Archdiocese of Boston was adjusted for Archdiocesan "excepting the towns of Marion, Mattapoisetts and Wareham" from Plymouth County, MA. This involved using the 2011 population of the five Archdiocesan counties and the aforementioned three excepted towns. Population for these entities were derived from <http://www.bea.gov/bea/regional/bearfacts/> and <http://www.massbenchmarks.org/statedata/data/census2011/Appendix%20A.xlsx>, the latter, for towns in Plymouth County, MA, downloaded from <http://www.massbenchmarks.org/statedata/news.htm>, both accessed 5/22/2013.

[42] The source for the estimate employed for current Catholic giving as 1.2% of income is as follows: " '[W]e know that the national statistics are that Catholics give to the church about 1.2 percent of their income' [Tim Dockery, director of development services for the Chicago archdiocese] said" (Cathleen Falsani, Religion Reporter, "Archdiocese May Ask for 10%: Cardinal George Considers Program That Includes Tithing," *Chicago Sun-Times*, Sunday, February 1, 2004, pp. 1A, and 6A).

[43] John Ronsvalle and Sylvia Ronsvalle, "An Exploration of Roman Catholic Giving Patterns," *The State of Church Giving through 1993* (Champaign, Ill.: empty tomb, inc., 1995), pp. 59-78. The article is also available at: < http://www.emptytomb.org/cathgiv.html>.

[44] A 2010 survey was conducted by the Center for Applied Research in the Apostolate (CARA), as a collaborative "work of five Catholic national ministerial organizations," (Mark M. Gray, Mary L. Gautier, and Melissa Cidade; "The Changing Face of U.S. Catholic Parishes"; National Association of May Ministry (Washington, D.C.); 2011; <www.emergingmodels.org/doc/Emerging Models Phase One report.pdf>; pp. 1, 2, 6 of 7/28/2011 printout). The survey found the "total average weekly offering in U.S. parishes" was $9,200. Multiplying that number by the 2010 number of parishes, 17,784, yielded a total annual offering calculation of $8,507,865,600. Using the *Official Catholic Directory* figure for membership, which was 68,503,456 in 2010, a per member total average weekly offering calculation of $124.20. The estimated 2010 U.S. per capita Disposable Person Income figure was $36,697. The $124.20 per member total average weekly offering amount represented 0.3% of 2010 income.

[45] Sharon Otterman; "New York Archdiocese to Close 24 Schools"; The New York Times; 1/22/2013; <http://www.nytimes.com/2013/01/23/nyregion/new-york-archdiocese-to-close-24-schools.html>; p. 1 of 8/11/2013 3:33 PM printout.

[46] Samuel G. Freedman; "As Catholic Schools Close in Major Cities, the Need Only Grows"; The New York Times; June 3, 2011; <http://www.nytimes.com/201/06/04/us/04religion.html>; pp. 2, 3 of 7/25/2011 4:42 PM printout.

[47] Associated Press; "More Catholic Schools Closing Across U.S."; msnbc; 4/12/2008; <http://www.msnbc.msn.com/id/24082482/ns/us_news-pope_in_america/t/more-catholic-schools-closing-across-us/>; p. 1, 2 of 7/25/2011 4:42 PM printout.

[48] *The Index of Global Philanthropy and Remittances 2012*; Hudson Institute Center for Global Prosperity; Created 4/3/2012; Modified 4/3/2012; downloaded 5/30/2012; <http://www.hudson.org/files/publications/2012IndexofGlobal PhilanthropyandRemittances.pdf>; 5/30/2012 printout.

[49] *The Index of Global Philanthropy and Remittances 2012*, p. 8.

[50] The native-born church member figure was calculated by multiplying the native-born population figure of 271,214,059 by 59.45%, the estimated percent of the U.S. population that has membership in historically Christian churches. The result was 161,236,758. The 271,214,059 figure for the native-born population was from U.S. Census Bureau; 2011 American Community Survey Dataset: 2011 American Community Survey 1-Year Estimates: Selected Social Characteristics in the United States: ID DP02; Accessed 7/10/2013; <http://factfinder2.census.gov/faces/tableservices/jsf/pages/ productview.xhtml?pid=ACS_11_1YR_DP02&prod Type=table>; p. 2 of 7/10/2013 10:12 AM printout.

The figure of 59.45% is an empty tomb analysis of data in George H. Gallup, Jr., *Religion in America 2002* (Princeton, NJ: Princeton Religion Research Center [2002?]), pp. 28, 40.

The Gross Domestic Product figures of Data Year 2009, $13,973.7, to Data Year 2011, $15,075.7, were obtained from: U.S. Bureau of Economic Analysis, "Table 1.1.5. Gross Domestic Product," Line 1: "Gross domestic product"; National Income and Product Accounts Tables; Hist data published July 27, 2012; 1969 - Present data published on March 28, 2013; 1969-2012: Tab "10105 Ann" of "Section1All_xls_1.1.9_1.1.5.xlsx" downloaded as xls file "Section1All_xls.xls" on 3/28/2013 from <http://www.bea.gov//national/nipaweb//SS_Data/Section1All_xls.xls>. [from <http://www.bea.gov//national/nipaweb/DownSS2.asp>].

[51] Yulya Spantchak; "2011 remittance data from DAC donor countries to developing countries"; prepublication email to research@emptytomb.org; 7/2/2013 10:46 AM.

[52] *The Index of Global Philanthropy and Remittances 2011*, pp. 9, 10, 16.

[53] *The Index of Global Philanthropy and Remittances 2012*, p. 20.

[54] U.S. Census Bureau; 2011 American Community Survey; p. 3.

chapter 7

Why and How Much Do Americans Give?

Before moving to a general discussion in chapter 8 of the church giving and membership data presented in previous chapters of this volume, there is one more analysis that may lend insight to the discussion. That is, religious giving can be considered in the context of total charitable giving in the United States.

Overview of Why and How Much Americans Give

Why Do Americans Give? The reasons for donating money vary by individual, and for the individual, may vary by circumstance.

Even so, some evidence exists regarding the broad motivation for the active participation among Americans in the practice of donating to charity.

A key source of information is the United States Government Department of Labor, Bureau of Labor Statistics (BLS) that takes a regular survey of Americans' spending patterns. In the Consumer Expenditure Survey (CE), the respondents are asked to categorize their "cash contributions" among four categories relevant to the present inquiry: (1) "charities and other organizations"; (2) "church, religious organizations"; (3) "educational institutions"; (4) "gifts to non-CU [consumer unit] members of stocks, bonds, and mutual funds."

In 2011, the category of gifts to "church, religious organizations" represented 69 percent of the charitable donations reported by Americans.

This percentage differs from other sources that report a lower percent directed to the category of "religion." A major difference may be due to the fact that, in other surveys, the frame of reference has been defined by the professional practitioners interested in certain end-use categories, rather than either by the perception of the donors or by the self-understanding and governance of the recipient organizations themselves.

Various well-known surveys of giving emphasize the end-use of the contributions. The much higher percent of giving categorized as "church, religious organizations" by donors in the CE is therefore of interest in that it may provide insight as to the motivation of donors. For example, while practitioner surveys might categorize a gift to Catholic Social Services or the Salvation Army under "human services," the donor may view the contribution as a gift to "church, religious organizations." Again, professional fundraiser surveys may label gifts to Lutheran World Relief and World Vision as "international" while donors would identify the gifts as being directed to "church, religious organizations." The net effect is that the category of "religion" is underreported in many surveys of charitable giving.

As can be seen from the analysis of CE data that follows, donors in every age group, in 11 of 12 income groups, and in three of four regions of the country identified gifts to "church, religious organizations" as the primary focus of their charitable activity.

Consider the analysis by Age. The Under-25 group gave the smallest portion of income to charity. However, of the amount given, 84% was categorized as gifts to "church, religious organizations." This observation suggests that young people learn their philanthropic values first in religious settings. As can be seen from Table 34, the categories of "charities and other organizations" and "educational institutions" were added as people aged, although gifts to "church, religious organizations" remained a large portion of total giving.

> An accurate understanding of the role of religion in the practice of philanthropy in the U.S. could benefit academics, practitioners, and the general population in the U.S., as well.

If, as observed in earlier chapters of this volume, giving to church is weakening, over time the observed trends could have a negative impact on the entire charitable sector in the U.S. An accurate understanding of the role of religion in the practice of philanthropy in the U.S. could benefit academics, practitioners, and the general population in the U.S., as well.

One suggestion for improving this categorization process is a revision of the nonprofit Form 990 reporting document. Before selecting one of the ten core definition categories, the reporting nonprofit organization could first indicate its form of governance as either "faith-based" or "secular."

How Much Do Americans Give? Various surveys provide different answers to the question of how much Americans give. The source that serves as a benchmark is the Consumer Expenditure Survey.

The Consumer Expenditure Survey. The U.S. Government Bureau of Labor Statistics, Consumer Expenditure Survey (CE) is a sophisticated research instrument that affects many aspects of American life through the Consumer Price Index.

The Consumer Expenditure Survey serves as a benchmark for understanding charitable giving patterns. The data series provides information about Americans' giving patterns by age, region of residence, and income levels.

In 2011, the CE figure for charitable giving by living individuals was $936.50 per household. Given that there were 122.287 million households in the U.S. in 2011, the aggregate amount of charitable giving from living individuals in 2011 was calculated to be $114.52 billion.

Other Sources of Giving Estimates. Another source of information about charitable giving is found in the U.S. Internal Revenue Service Form 990. The Form 990 series must be filled out by charitable organizations with at least $25,000 in income, and by foundations. Data for the Form 990 series was obtained for the period 1989 through 2009, the latest year for which Form 990 data was listed on the IRS Web site.

A third major source of philanthropic information is the *Giving USA* series. A major component of this series is based on deductions claimed on IRS Individual Tax returns. The series is "researched and written" on behalf of professional fundraisers by a university-based philanthropy center.

By adjusting both the Form 990 and the *Giving USA* series to yield cash contributions by living donors, the CE, the Form 990, and the *Giving USA* series were compared for 1989 through 2009. The resulting estimates of these two sources differed by as much as $52 billion from the CE.

Details of How Much Americans Give

Details of the Consumer Expenditure Survey, 2011. The U.S. Department of Labor, Bureau of Labor Statistics, Consumer Expenditure Survey (CE) provides a benchmark measure of Americans' charitable cash contributions. The CE provides the U.S. Government data designed to measure Americans' charitable contributions.

The CE presents data per "consumer unit." The definition reads:

A consumer unit consists of any of the following: (1) All members of a particular household who are related by blood, marriage, adoption, or other legal arrangements; (2) a person living alone or sharing a household with others or living as a roomer in a private home or lodging house or in permanent living quarters in a hotel or motel, but who is financially independent; or (3) two or more persons living together who use their incomes to make joint expenditure decisions. Financial independence is determined by spending behavior with regard to the three major expense categories: Housing, food, and other living expenses. To be considered financially independent, the respondent must provide at least two of the three major expenditure categories, either entirely or in part.

The terms consumer unit, family, and household are often used interchangeably for convenience. However, the proper technical term for purposes of the Consumer Expenditure Survey is consumer unit.[1]

The CE data for 2011 was aggregated, conflated, and analyzed by empty tomb, inc. Table 31 shows the result, that Americans gave $114.5 billion in cash contributions to charitable causes in 2011, the latest year for which data was available.

Table 31: **U.S. Bureau of Labor Statistics, Consumer Expenditure Survey, Cash Contributions: Americans' Charitable Giving (Aggregated) 2011**

Item	Average Annual Expenditures Multiplied by 122.287 Million Consumer Units: Aggregated (billions $)	Item as % of Total
Annual Expenditures		
Cash Contributions for Charitable Giving		
Cash contributions to:		
charities and other organizations	$26.38	23.0%
church, religious organizations	79.39	69.3%
educational institutions	3.10	2.7%
Gifts to non-CU members of stocks, bonds, and mutual funds	5.66	4.9%
Total	$114.52	100.0%

Details in the above table may not compute to the numbers shown due to rounding.
Source: empty tomb analysis; U.S. BLS CE, 2011   empty tomb, inc., 2013

The CE categories include "Cash contributions to: charities and other organizations; church, religious organizations; and educational institutions" as well as "Gifts to non-CU [Consumer Unit] members of stocks, bonds, and mutual funds."[2] An analysis of the CE data resulted in the finding that Americans contributed 69% of their charitable contributions to "church, religious organizations" in 2011.

Further detail regarding this analysis of U.S. Department of Labor, Bureau of Labor Statistics, Consumer Expenditure Survey charitable giving data is presented in Table 31.[3]

Cash Contributions by Income Level, 2011. The CE measured Americans' cash contributions to charitable causes by income levels, as displayed in Tables 32 and 33.[4]

An analysis was conducted for 12 income levels, ranging from "$5,000 to $9,999" up to both "$120,000 to $149,999" and the highest category of "$150,000 and more," with the average "Income after taxes" for the income levels ranging from $8,155 to $127,734 and $232,086, respectively.[5]

A comparison of cash contributions among different income brackets may be of interest.

However, it should be noted that CE lower income brackets, which for purposes of this analysis ranged from $5,000 through $39,999, reported higher expenses than income before taxes in 2011.[6] The CE observes:

> Data users may notice that average annual expenditures presented in the income tables sometimes exceed income before taxes for the lower income groups. The primary reason for that is believed to be the underreporting of income by respondents, a problem common to most household surveys …

Table 32: U.S. Bureau of Labor Statistics, Consumer Expenditure Survey, Cash Contributions for Charitable Giving by Income Level, 2011

Item	All consumer units	$5,000 to $9,999	$10,000 to $14,999	$15,000 to $19,999	$20,000 to $29,999	$30,000 to $39,999	$40,000 to $49,999	$50,000 to $69,999
Number of consumer units (in thousands)	122,287	5,449	8,170	7,745	14,460	13,328	11,347	17,376
Consumer unit characteristics:								
Income after taxes	$61,673	$8,155	$12,803	$17,955	$25,136	$34,750	$44,196	$58,070
Average Annual Expenditures								
Cash Contributions for Charitable Giving								
Cash contributions to:								
charities and other organizations	$215.69	$35.12	$40.55	$54.08	$70.27	$81.78	$94.84	$132.60
church, religious organizations	649.17	245.54	255.18	313.15	341.46	489.82	504.12	619.16
educational institutions	25.37	8.75	1.96	4.45	4.26	5.83	16.03	27.80
Gifts to non-CU members of stocks, bonds, and mutual funds	46.27	0.54	0.09	333.02	0.34	1.36	19.47	2.39
Total (calculated)	$936.50	$289.95	$297.78	$704.70	$416.33	$578.79	$634.46	$781.95
Calculated:								
% of Income after Taxes								
Cash contributions to:								
charities and other organizations	0.35%	0.43%	0.32%	0.30%	0.28%	0.24%	0.21%	0.23%
church, religious organizations	1.05%	3.01%	1.99%	1.74%	1.36%	1.41%	1.14%	1.07%
educational institutions	0.04%	0.11%	0.02%	0.02%	0.02%	0.02%	0.04%	0.05%
Gifts to non-CU members of stocks, bonds, and mutual funds	0.08%	0.01%	0.00%	1.85%	0.00%	0.00%	0.04%	0.00%
Total	1.5%	3.6%	2.3%	3.9%	1.7%	1.7%	1.4%	1.3%

Details in table may not compute to numbers shown due to rounding.   empty tomb, inc., 2013
Source: empty tomb analysis of U.S. BLS CE, 2011

There are other reasons why expenditures exceed income for the lower income groups. Consumer units whose members experience a spell of unemployment may draw on their savings to maintain their expenditures. Self-employed consumers may experience business losses that result in low or even negative incomes, but are able to maintain their expenditures by borrowing or relying on savings. Students may get by on loans while they are in school, and retirees may rely on savings and investments.[7]

To the extent that income is proportionately underreported across all income levels, but is more evident in lower income brackets, comparisons across income brackets may be informative on an exploratory basis.

Having noted this caveat, it is still of interest to observe that consumer units in the "$5,000 to $9,999" through the double category of "$30,000 to $39,999" income brackets reported charitable cash contributions that represented a higher portion of after-tax income than the next seven income brackets.

It may be observed that 2011 giving as a percent of income after taxes to "church, religious organizations" was higher in 11 of the 12 income levels, than to either "charities and other organizations," "educational institutions," or "Gifts to non-CU members of stocks, bonds, and mutual funds." The exception was the $15,000 to $19,999 bracket, in which "Gifts to non-CU members of stocks, bonds, and mutual funds" measured 47% of total charitable cash contributions, with "Gifts to churches, religious organizations" measuring 44%.

In the other 11 brackets, "charities and other organizations" received the second largest dollar donation per consumer unit, after "church, religious organizations" and before "educational institutions."

Table 33: U.S. Bureau of Labor Statistics, Consumer Expenditure Survey, Cash Contributions for Charitable Giving by Higher Income Level, 2011

Item	All consumer units	$70,000 to $79,999	$80,000 to $99,999	$100,000 to $119,999	$120,000 to $149,999	$150,000 and more
Number of consumer units (in thousands)	122,287	7,385	10,456	7,045	6,107	8,440
Consumer unit characteristics:						
Income after taxes	$61,673	$72,895	$86,417	$105,125	$127,734	$232,086
Average Annual Expenditures						
Cash Contributions for Charitable Giving						
Cash contributions to:						
charities and other organizations	$215.69	$240.68	$214.36	$222.43	$428.39	$1,347.48
church, religious organizations	649.17	803.27	956.43	983.98	1,236.16	1,672.17
educational institutions	25.37	8.78	18.70	49.22	44.20	150.72
Gifts to non-CU members of stocks, bonds, and mutual funds	46.27	3.99	21.49	0.91	37.27	270.99
Total (calculated)	$936.50	$1,056.72	$1,210.98	$1,256.54	$1,746.02	$3,441.36
Calculated						
% of Income after Taxes						
Cash contributions to:						
charities and other organizations	0.35%	0.33%	0.25%	0.21%	0.34%	0.58%
church, religious organizations	1.05%	1.10%	1.11%	0.94%	0.97%	0.72%
educational institutions	0.04%	0.01%	0.02%	0.05%	0.03%	0.06%
Gifts to non-CU members of stocks, bonds, and mutual funds	0.08%	0.01%	0.02%	0.00%	0.03%	0.12%
Total	1.5%	1.4%	1.4%	1.2%	1.4%	1.5%

Details in table may not compute to numbers shown due to rounding.   empty tomb, inc. 2013
Source: empty tomb analysis of U.S. BLS CE, 2011

In each income bracket, the dollars given to "church, religious organizations" was greater than the sum of the dollars given to "charities and other organizations" and "educational institutions."

Cash Contributions by Age, 2011. The CE also measured Americans' cash contributions to charitable causes by age of contributor.[8] Table 34 presents the data in tabular form.

The seven age categories under consideration started with the "Under 25 years" grouping, proceeded with "25-34 years" as the first of five 10-year periods, and culminated with the "75 years and older" cohort.

In 2011, giving as a percent of income after taxes to "church, religious organizations" grew as a portion of income in each bracket as age advanced, with the exception of the 35-44 years bracket. The 55-64 years bracket posted a lower income than the 45-54 years group did, and yet gave more dollars to "church, religious organizations," and "charities and other organizations." As a result, the portion of income given to those categories increased from the previous bracket.

Income for the 65-74 years bracket was 29% less than the 55-64 years cohort. Yet, the dollars given to "church, religious organizations" were larger in the 65-74 years bracket compared to the 55-64 years bracket. Again, the dynamic of decreased income and increased giving resulted in an increase in the percent of income given from the previous bracket.

Although the 75 years and older cohort had the lowest dollar income of any except the Under-25 years bracket, giving to the category of cash contributions to church, religious organizations as a percent of income was highest in the 75 years and older bracket, and third highest in the average numbers of dollars given to that category.

Table 34: U.S. Bureau of Labor Statistics, Consumer Expenditure Survey, Cash Contributions for Charitable Giving by Age, 2011

Item	All consumer units	Under 25 years	25-34 years	35-44 years	45-54 years	55-64 years	65-74 years	75 years and older
Number of consumer units (in thousands)	122,287	7,743	20,463	21,699	24,821	21,688	14,079	11,794
Consumer unit characteristics:								
Income after taxes	$61,673	$27,495	$56,851	$75,537	$75,234	$72,115	$51,161	$31,779
Average Annual Expenditures								
Cash Contributions for Charitable Giving								
Cash contributions to:								
charities and other organizations	$215.69	$27.10	$74.34	$166.70	$165.45	$363.17	$427.59	$256.51
church, religious organizations	649.17	147.21	465.17	588.41	670.80	769.87	963.72	766.72
educational institutions	25.37	0.97	5.64	18.61	22.99	48.20	39.53	34.23
Gifts to non-CU members of stocks, bonds, and mutual funds	46.27	NA	0.78	15.48	12.20	103.26	8.89	223.73
Total (calculated)	$936.50	$175.28	$545.93	$789.20	$871.44	$1,284.50	$1,439.73	$1,281.19
Calculated								
% of Income after Taxes								
Cash contributions to:								
charities and other organizations	0.35%	0.10%	0.13%	0.22%	0.22%	0.50%	0.84%	0.81%
church, religious organizations	1.05%	0.54%	0.82%	0.78%	0.89%	1.07%	1.88%	2.41%
educational institutions	0.04%	0.00%	0.01%	0.02%	0.03%	0.07%	0.08%	0.11%
Gifts to non-CU members of stocks, bonds, and mutual funds	0.08%	NA	0.00%	0.02%	0.02%	0.14%	0.02%	0.70%
Total	1.5%	0.6%	1.0%	1.0%	1.2%	1.8%	2.8%	4.0%

Details in table may not compute to numbers shown due to rounding.   empty tomb, inc. 2013
Source: empty tomb analysis of U.S. BLS CE, 2011

Contributions to "educational institutions" as a portion of income were highest in the 75 years and older age bracket. The second highest level of donations was posted by those in the 65-74 age bracket.

Contributions to "charities, and other organizations" as a portion of income increased from each cohort to the next, with the exception of the 45-54 years bracket. The highest amount to this category, both in dollars and as a percent of income, was given in the 65-74 years bracket.

The fact that members of the "Under 25 years" cohort directed 84% of their giving as a percent of after-tax income to the "church, religious organizations" category provides support for the view that religion serves as the seedbed of philanthropic giving in America. The portion of income given to that category among this group was considerably higher at 0.54% than to "charities and other organizations" at 0.10%. Contributions to "educational institutions" in this age bracket rounded to 0.00%.

The age bracket in which total charitable giving as a portion of income was highest was the 75 years and older cohort.

One factor that all age brackets had in common was that giving as a portion of income to "church, religious organizations" was the largest category. Further, in all cohorts, giving to "church, religious organizations" as a portion of income was greater than the sum of the two categories of "charities and other organizations" plus "educational institutions."

Cash Contributions by Region, 2011. In addition, as shown in Table 35, the CE also measured Americans' cash contributions to charitable causes by region.[9]

The four region categories for which information was presented in the CE data were Northeast, Midwest, South, and West. Regional charitable giving data and regional income figures were available for the comparison.

Analysis of the 2011 data showed that contributions to charitable causes were highest in the Midwest, at 1.7% of income after taxes. The South and West followed at 1.6%, with the South slightly higher in the unrounded percentages. The Northeast measured 1.1%.

Table 35: **U.S. Bureau of Labor Statistics, Consumer Expenditure Survey, Cash Contributions for Charitable Giving by Region of Residence, 2011**

Item	All consumer units	Northeast	Midwest	South	West
Number of consumer units (in thousands)	122,287	22,538	27,107	44,901	27,741
Consumer unit characteristics:					
Income after taxes	$61,673	$69,334	$59,394	$57,205	$64,909
Average Annual Expenditures					
Cash Contributions for Charitable Giving					
Cash contributions to:					
charities and other organizations	$215.69	$388.84	$195.19	$133.66	$227.82
church, religious organizations	649.17	351.64	657.25	770.66	686.35
educational institutions	25.37	23.38	20.80	17.80	43.73
Gifts to non-CU members of stocks, bonds, and mutual funds	46.27	2.85	107.66	10.97	78.69
Total (calculated)	$936.50	$766.71	$980.90	$933.09	$1,036.59
Calculated					
% of Income after Taxes					
Cash contributions to:					
charities and other organizations	0.35%	0.56%	0.33%	0.23%	0.35%
church, religious organizations	1.05%	0.51%	1.11%	1.35%	1.06%
educational institutions	0.04%	0.03%	0.04%	0.03%	0.07%
Gifts to non-CU members of stocks, bonds, and mutual funds	0.08%	0.00%	0.18%	0.02%	0.12%
Total	1.5%	1.1%	1.7%	1.6%	1.6%

Details in table may not compute to numbers shown due to rounding.   empty tomb, inc. 2013
Source: empty tomb analysis of U.S. BLS CE, 2011

In three of the four regions, contributions to "church, religious organizations" were higher than the sum of contributions to "charities and other organizations" and "educational institutions." In the Northeast, gifts to "charities and other organizations" were highest, with gifts to "church, religious organizations" second.

The differences in 2011 giving to the category of "church, religious organizations" were significant at the 0.05 level between the Northeast and each of the other three regions. The differences in the level of giving to "educational institutions" were significant at the 0.05 level between the West and the South, and the West and the Midwest. The differences in the level of giving to "charities and other organizations" between the South and the West, and the South and the Midwest, were significant at the 0.05 level.[10]

The charitable giving patterns, particularly to "church, religious organizations" correspond to the results of a 2009 Gallup poll that found states in the Northeast were "least religious" while those in the South were "most religious."[11] The title of an Associated Press article on church initiatives in the Northeast referred to the area as "spiritually cold."[12] Given the implications of charitable giving in the Under-25 years bracket with giving to "church, religious organizations"—that young people first learn philanthropy in the context of religion—the reported lack of religious fervor in the Northeast could be associated with the level of charitable giving.

Records were available back to 1987 from the Bureau of Labor Statistics, Consumer Expenditure Survey. The specific category of "Gifts to non-CU members of stocks, bonds, and mutual funds," however, was not available before the second quarter of 2001. Therefore, in the historical series for 1987–2011, comparing Charitable Giving as a portion of after-tax income, Charitable Giving included the three categories of "charities and other organizations," "church, religious organizations," and "educational institutions." Consequently, the 2011 numbers in Table 36, which does not include the category of "Gifts to non-CU members of stocks, bonds, and mutual funds," differ slightly from the figures in Table 35, which does include that category.

As can be seen in Table 36, the regional pattern indicates the South had the highest average percent of after-tax income in the "cash contributions for charitable giving" category in the 1987–2011 period. The Midwest and the West were next, and then the Northeast.

Table 36: U.S. Bureau of Labor Statistics, Consumer Expenditure Survey, Expenditures for Charitable Giving by Region of Residence, 1987-2011

Year	All consumer units	Northeast	Midwest	South	West
1987	1.46%	0.86%	1.53%	1.76%	1.56%
1988	1.40%	0.83%	1.43%	1.68%	1.52%
1989	1.56%	1.04%	1.55%	2.01%	1.47%
1990	1.43%	1.03%	1.40%	1.69%	1.50%
1991	1.58%	1.11%	1.69%	1.74%	1.72%
1992	1.58%	1.26%	1.78%	1.78%	1.42%
1993	1.46%	0.98%	1.57%	1.57%	1.68%
1994	1.44%	1.30%	1.42%	1.73%	1.20%
1995	1.50%	1.06%	1.41%	1.66%	1.79%
1996	1.42%	0.93%	1.57%	1.75%	1.23%
1997	1.39%	0.88%	1.41%	1.70%	1.41%
1998	1.41%	0.89%	1.42%	1.68%	1.50%
1999	1.58%	1.03%	1.59%	1.83%	1.75%
2000	1.46%	0.95%	1.93%	1.42%	1.50%
2001	1.53%	1.14%	1.66%	1.72%	1.48%
2002	1.55%	1.14%	1.69%	1.64%	1.65%
2003	1.57%	0.99%	1.75%	1.82%	1.57%
2004	1.47%	0.84%	1.93%	1.53%	1.52%
2005	1.68%	1.13%	1.94%	1.99%	1.49%
2006	1.82%	1.19%	1.91%	1.81%	2.28%
2007	1.66%	1.02%	1.60%	1.67%	2.25%
2008	1.55%	1.00%	1.55%	1.71%	1.81%
2009	1.59%	0.99%	1.64%	1.80%	1.76%
2010	1.41%	0.95%	1.51%	1.61%	1.41%
2011	1.44%	1.10%	1.47%	1.61%	1.48%
Average for the 1987-2011 Period	1.5%	1.0%	1.6%	1.7%	1.6%

Source: empty tomb analysis of U.S. BLS CE, 1987-2011

empty tomb, inc. 2013

The South's overall average was 1.7% of income given to charity during the 1987–2011 period. The Northeast posted the lowest portion of income donated for charitable purposes consistently throughout the 1987 through 2011 period, with the exception of 1994, when the Northeast was third and the West was the lowest in the comparison. In unrounded numbers, the Midwest's 1987–2011 average of 1.61% was slightly larger than the West's average of 1.60%.

The question may be asked whether regional differences in spending on other expenditure categories influence or limit charitable giving levels in the four regions. Table 37 presents expenditure data by region of residence for 2011.[13] The category of "Cash Contributions for Charitable Giving" was subtracted from the expenditures total. The reason for this adjustment was to calculate the portion of income remaining after expenditures other than charitable giving. The adjusted total expenditures figure was then divided by the region's after-tax income. The resulting percentage is shown in Table 37.

It was instructive to note that variations in giving to charity by region did not seem to be a function of regional expenditures in comparison to regional income differentials. The West had the highest expenditures as a percent of after-tax income, and a level of charitable giving as a percent of income in 2011 that was similar to that of the South. The Northeast had the highest income and a level of expenditures similar to the West, in terms of dollars, while it posted the lowest percent of income spent for cash contributions in 2011.

Table 37: U.S. Bureau of Labor Statistics, Consumer Expenditure Survey, Expenditures as a Percent of Income after Taxes, by Region of Residence, 2011

Item	All consumer units	Northeast	Midwest	South	West
Number of consumer units (in thousands)	122,287	22,538	27,107	44,901	27,741
Consumer unit characteristics:					
Income after taxes	$61,673	$69,334	$59,394	$57,205	$64,909
Average Annual Expenditures					
Seven Major Categories					
Food	$6,457.65	$6,799.02	$6,235.60	$5,979.54	$7,188.05
Housing	16,803.03	19,557.15	14,925.78	14,968.44	19,372.69
Apparel and services	1,739.79	1,905.37	1,623.83	1,614.62	1,925.73
Transportation	8,292.79	8,434.59	8,113.81	8,264.36	8,399.34
Health care	3,312.92	3,368.32	3,620.08	3,160.10	3,215.93
Entertainment	2,571.95	2,631.98	2,505.12	2,349.79	2,950.33
Personal insurance and pensions	5,423.57	5,960.59	5,178.40	4,935.82	6,016.29
Other Expenses*	5,103.18	5,890.42	4,988.91	4,425.91	5,677.07
Total Expenditures (calculated)	$49,704.88	$54,547.45	$47,191.54	$45,698.60	$54,745.43
Charitable Giving	$936.50	$766.71	$980.90	$933.09	$1,036.59
Total Expenditures Less Charitable Giving	$48,768.38	$53,780.74	$46,210.64	$44,765.51	$53,708.84
Calculated: **Average Annual Expenditures** **Less Charitable Giving as** **% Income after Taxes**	79%	78%	78%	78%	83%

Details in table may not compute to numbers shown due to rounding.   empty tomb, inc. 2013
*Other expenses include: "Alcoholic beverages; Personal care products and services; Reading; Education; Tobacco products and smoking supplies; Miscellaneous; Cash contributions."
"Cash contributions" includes: "Support for college students; Alimony expenditures; Child support expenditures; 'Charitable giving' (Cash contributions to charities and other organizations; Cash contributions to church, religious organizations; Cash contributions to educational institutions; Gift to non-CU members of stocks, bonds, and mutual funds); Cash contribution to political organizations."
Source: empty tomb analysis of U.S. BLS CE, 2011

General Information regarding the Consumer Expenditure Survey. One benefit of the CE is its unbiased data. The Mission Statement of the U.S. Department of Labor, Bureau of Labor Statistics reads:

> The **Bureau of Labor Statistics (BLS)** is the principal fact-finding agency for the Federal Government in the broad field of labor economics and statistics. The BLS is an independent national statistical agency that collects, processes, analyzes, and disseminates essential statistical data to the American public, the U.S. Congress, other Federal agencies, State and local governments, business, and labor. The BLS also serves as a statistical resource to the Department of Labor.

> BLS data must satisfy a number of criteria, including relevance to current social and economic issues, timeliness in reflecting today's rapidly changing economic conditions, accuracy and consistently high statistical quality, and impartiality in both subject matter and presentation.[14]

The BLS, among its various activities, is the source for the following indexes:

> **Producer price index (PPI)**—This index, dating from 1890, is the oldest continuous statistical series published by BLS. It is designed to measure average changes in prices received by producers of all commodities, at all stages of processing, produced in the United States ...

> **Consumer price indexes (CPI)**—The CPI is a measure of the average change in prices over time in a "market basket" of goods and services purchased either by urban wage earners and clerical workers or by all urban consumers. In 1919, BLS began to publish complete indexes at semiannual intervals, using a weighting structure based on data collected in the expenditure survey of wage-earner and clerical-worker families in 1917–19 (BLS Bulletin 357, 1924) ...

> **International price indexes**—The BLS International Price Program produces export and import price indexes for nonmilitary goods traded between the United States and the rest of the world.[15]

Among the numerous applications of the BLS Consumer Expenditure Survey, the Survey is used for periodic revision of the Consumer Price Index (CPI). Following are excerpted comments from a "Brief Description of the Consumer Expenditure Survey."

> The current CE program was begun in 1980. Its principal objective is to collect information on the buying habits of U.S. consumers. Consumer expenditure data are used in a variety of research endeavors by government, business, labor, and academic analysts. In addition, the data are required for periodic revision of the CPI.

> The survey, which is conducted by the U.S. Census Bureau for the Bureau of Labor Statistics, consists of two components: A diary or recordkeeping, survey ... and an interview survey, in which expenditures of consumer units are obtained in five interviews conducted at 3-month intervals ...

> Each component of the survey queries an independent sample of consumer units that is representative of the U.S. population ... The Interview sample, selected on a rotating panel basis, surveys about 7,500 consumer units each quarter. Each consumer unit is interviewed once per quarter, for 5 consecutive quarters. Data are collected on an ongoing basis in 105 areas of the United States.[16]

The BLS, in commenting on the various functions of the Consumer Expenditure Survey, observed that, "Researchers use the data in a variety of studies, including those that focus on the spending behavior of different family types, trends in expenditures on various expenditure components including new types of goods and services, gift-giving behavior, consumption studies, and historical spending trends."[17]

Writing in the mid-1980s with reference to the then forthcoming Consumer Expenditure Survey-based revisions in the CPI, eminent business columnist Sylvia Porter remarked that the CPI is "the most closely watched, widely publicized and influential government statistic we have ..."[18]

In addition to the fact that the "CPI is used to adjust federal tax brackets for inflation,"[19] a glimpse into the wide-ranging, Consumer Expenditure Survey-based network of CPI usage in American culture is gained from the following information:

> The CPI is the most widely used measure of inflation and is sometimes viewed as an indicator of the effectiveness of government economic policy. It provides information about price changes in the Nation's economy to government, business, labor, and private citizens and is used by them as a guide to making economic decisions. In addition, the President, Congress, and the Federal Reserve Board use trends in the CPI to aid in formulating fiscal and monetary policies.

> The CPI and its components are used to adjust other economic series for price changes and to translate these series into inflation-free dollars. Examples of series adjusted by the CPI include retail sales, hourly and weekly earnings, and components of the National Income and Product Accounts ...

> The CPI is often used to adjust consumers' income payments (for example, Social Security) to adjust income eligibility levels for government assistance and to automatically provide cost-of-living wage adjustments to millions of American workers. As a result of statutory action the CPI affects the income of about 80 million persons: the 51.6 million Social Security beneficiaries, about 21.3 million food stamp recipients, and about 4.6 million military and Federal Civil Service retirees and survivors. Changes in the CPI also affect the cost of lunches for 28.4 million children who eat lunch at school, while collective bargaining agreements that tie wages to the CPI cover over 2 million workers. Another example of how dollar values may be adjusted is the use of the CPI to adjust the Federal income tax structure. These adjustments prevent inflation-induced increases in tax rates, an effect called *bracket creep* ...

> Data from the Consumer Expenditure Survey conducted in 2001 and 2002, involving a national sample of more than 30,000 information families, provided detailed information on respondents' spending habits. This enabled BLS to construct the CPI market basket of goods and services and to assign each item in the market basket a weight, or importance, based on total family expenditures ...[20]

How Much Do Americans Give? An Estimate of Aggregate Giving to Religion, 1968–2011.
An estimate of Americans' giving to religion was calculated for the 1968 to 2011 period. This estimate employed a 1974 benchmark estimate of $11.7 billion for giving to religion provided by the watershed Commission on Private Philanthropy and Public Needs of the 1970s, commonly referred to as the Filer Commission.[21]

The amount of change from year to year, calculated for 1968 to 1973 and also 1975 to 2011, was the annual percent change in the composite denomination set analyzed in other chapters of this report.[22] This calculation yielded a total of

Table 38: **Giving to Religion, Based on the Commission on Private Philanthropy and Public Needs (Filer Commission) Benchmark Data for the Year of 1974, and Annual Changes in the Composite Denomination-Based Series, Aggregate Billions of Dollars and Per Capita Dollars as Percent of Disposable Personal Income, 1968-2011**

Year	Denomination-Based Series Keyed to 1974 Filer Estimate	
	Billions, Dollars	Per Capita Dollars as % of DPI
1968	$8.04	1.29%
1969	$8.35	1.24%
1970	$8.68	1.18%
1971	$9.14	1.14%
1972	$9.79	1.13%
1973	$10.72	1.10%
1974	$11.70	1.09%
1975	$12.74	1.07%
1976	$13.85	1.06%
1977	$14.99	1.04%
1978	$16.37	1.02%
1979	$18.09	1.01%
1980	$20.04	1.00%
1981	$22.10	0.99%
1982	$23.94	0.99%
1983	$25.60	0.98%
1984	$27.71	0.96%
1985	$29.40	0.95%
1986	$31.10	0.95%
1987	$32.31	0.94%
1988	$33.54	0.90%
1989	$35.33	0.89%
1990	$36.80	0.87%
1991	$38.20	0.86%
1992	$39.26	0.83%
1993	$40.32	0.82%
1994	$43.24	0.83%
1995	$44.03	0.81%
1996	$47.54	0.83%
1997	$49.24	0.81%
1998	$52.08	0.80%
1999	$54.81	0.81%
2000	$59.01	0.81%
2001	$61.48	0.80%
2002	$63.46	0.79%
2003	$64.13	0.77%
2004	$66.45	0.75%
2005	$68.81	0.74%
2006	$71.63	0.72%
2007	$74.48	0.71%
2008	$74.30	0.67%
2009	$73.06	0.68%
2010	$70.28	0.63%
2011	$70.45	0.61%

Source: empty tomb analysis; Commission on Private Philanthropy and Public Needs; *YACC* adjusted series; U.S. BEA   empty tomb, inc. 2013

$8.0 billion given to religion in 1968 and $70.5 billion in 2011. Table 38 presents this data both in aggregate form and as adjusted for population and income.

A Comparison of Three Sources

Estimates of charitable giving vary by substantial margins. Three sources of information can be described and compared in an attempt to develop an overview of aggregate charitable giving patterns among Americans. In this comparison series, data was available for 1989 through 2009 for all three sources of charitable giving information.

Consumer Expenditure Survey, 2009. As noted earlier, the U.S. Government Bureau of Labor Statistics, Consumer Expenditure Survey (CE) is a sophisticated research instrument that affects many aspects of American life. The CE is used to inform the Consumer Price Index which, in turn, is used, among other purposes, to adjust federal tax brackets, Social Security benefits, and military retirement benefits for inflation. The CE's figure for charitable giving serves as a benchmark for the level of philanthropy in the U.S.

As discussed earlier, the CE data included the categories of: "Cash contributions to charities and other organizations"; "Cash contributions to church, religious organizations"; "Cash contributions to educational institutions"; and "Gifts to non-CU [Consumer Unit] members of stocks, bonds, and mutual funds." The annual average expenditure for the four categories in 2009 was $975.86 per consumer unit. In 2009, there were 120.847 million consumer units in the United States. The average annual expenditure amount of $975.86 multiplied by the number of consumer units, resulted in a 2009 estimate of total charitable giving of $117.9 billion.

The CE charitable giving series is also available for the 1989–2009 period. However, the CE category of "Gifts to non-CU members of stocks, bonds, and mutual funds" was not available before the year 2000. Also, both the Form 990 series and the *Giving USA* series were adjusted to remove noncash donations; that category includes gifts of stocks, bonds and mutual funds. Therefore, the CE series for 1989–2009 used in Table 39 does not include the category of "Gifts to non-CU members of stocks, bonds, and mutual funds." In contrast, the category of "Gifts to non-CU members of stocks, bonds, and mutual funds" is included in the earlier discussion of charitable giving data elsewhere in this chapter. The revised 2009 CE figure, to exclude that category, was \$116.41 billion, with an average annual expenditure per consumer unit of \$963.32. Table 39 presents CE data for the year 2009, excluding gifts of stocks, bonds, and mutual funds, in both "consumer unit" and aggregate values.[23]

Form 990 Series. A second source of information about charitable giving is found in the U.S. Internal Revenue Service Form 990 series. The Form 990 series must be filled

Table 39: Living Individual Charitable Giving in the United States, Consumer Expenditure Survey, Not Including "Gifts of stocks, bonds, and mutual funds," 2009

Item	Average Annual Expenditure: All Consumer Units	Average Annual Expenditures Multiplied by 120,770 Consumer Units in 000's: Aggregated 000's of $	Item as % of Total
"Cash contributions to charities and other organizations"	$208.20	$25,160,345	21.6%
"Cash contributions to church, religious organizations"	$724.60	$87,565,736	75.2%
"Cash contributions to educational institutions"	$30.52	$3,688,250	3.2%
Total	$963.32	$116,414,332	100%

Details in table may not compute to numbers shown due to rounding.   empty tomb, inc., 2013
Source: empty tomb analysis of U.S. BLS CE, 2009

out by charitable organizations with at least \$25,000 in income, and by foundations. Form 990 data was obtained for the years 1989–2009, the latest year listed on the IRS Web site.[24]

The IRS changed the Form 990 category labels in 2008. Table 40 presents Form 990 data for the year 2009. The category of "All other contributions, gifts, etc." introduced in 2008 appears to be the equivalent of the previously used category of "Direct Public Support." As of the 2008 data, the combined categories of "Federated campaigns," "Fundraising events," and "Related organizations" appear to fall within the previous "Indirect Public Support" category that included receipts from parent charitable organizations or groups like the United Way. A third category introduced in the 2007 Form 990, support from Donor-Advised Funds, was not cited separately in 2008 or 2009. The sources of support detailed on the 2009 Form 990 totaled \$172.5 billion. Organizations with at least \$25,000 but less than \$100,000 in gross receipts were able to use Form 990-EZ to report receipts of \$9.4 billion in 2009, for a Form 990 and Form 990-EZ contributions total of \$181.9 billion.

A figure of \$32.4 billion was added to the Public Support figure to account for giving in 2009 to private foundations.[25] Private foundations are required to file the IRS Form 990-PF. An adjusted total for giving to foundations was published in *Giving USA 2013*.

Based on the Form 990 series data, the combined total of \$214.3 billion is the amount that charitable organizations received in 2009.

Form 990 could, but does not, request data for cash contributions by living individuals. One recommendation to improve the usefulness of information in the Form 990 is that charitable organizations be required to report cash contributions from living individuals on a separate line of the form.

In order to compare the Form 990 series data with the CE data for cash contributions from living individuals for a 1989 to 2009 series, the Form 990 series information was adjusted. To obtain a figure for contributions from living individuals, estimates for giving by corporations and foundations, and receipts from bequests,[26] were subtracted from the "Gifts to charities and foundations" figure in Table 40. Giving by Living Individuals was thus estimated to be $140.3 billion in 2009.

The Form 990 data also includes "Other than cash contributions." Therefore, the value of "Other than cash contributions" was subtracted from the Form 990 data to allow a comparison of charitable cash contributions. As shown in Table 40, the IRS estimated that Americans deducted $31.8 billion in "Other than cash contributions" in 2009.[27] This amount was subtracted from the Giving by Living Individuals figure of $140.3 billion, resulting in a subtotal of $108.5 billion in 2009.

To develop an estimate of Form 990 organizational receipts that could be compared with the CE figure of what people gave required one additional step. Churches are not required to file Form 990. The CE estimate, however, included a measure for charitable contributions to churches and religious organizations. The following procedure was followed to develop an estimate for church giving to be added to the Form 990 Living Individuals contributions figure. The CE figure for 2009 "Cash contributions to church, religious organizations" was $87.6 billion. The present analysis employs a working estimate that giving to church represents about 90% of giving to religion, based in part on the work of two publications in this area.[28] Charitable organizations that combine religion with international or human services activities would be expected to file Form 990, and therefore these figures would already be included in the 2009 Form 990 Living Individual figure of $108.5 billion. Subtracting 10% from the 2009 CE figure for "church, religious organizations" of $87.6 billion resulted in an estimate of $78.8 billion given to churches in 2009. When this "giving to church" estimate was added to the estimated 2009 Form 990 "Living Individual Giving in cash, not including giving to church" figure of $108.5 billion, Total Cash Giving by Living Donors was calculated to be $187.3 billion in 2009, based on the Form 990 series information.

Table 40 presents the procedure and results in tabular form for 2009. A similar procedure was followed to calculate the Form 990 series figures for 1989–2008,[29] to compare with the CE series for those years.

Table 40: Living Individual Charitable Giving in the United States, Form 990 Series, 2009

	000's of $
Form 990	
Federated campaigns	$3,070,589
Fundriaising events	$6,149,135
Related Organizations	$21,619,760
All other contributions, gifts, etc.	+ $141,663,143
Subtotal from Form 990	$172,502,627
Form 990-EZ contributions, gifts, and grants	+ $9,420,321
Form 990 and 990-EZ contributions	$181,922,948
Gifts to foundations	+ $32,390,000
Gifts to charities and foundations	$214,312,948
Less gifts from other than Living Individuals	
Giving by Corporations	- $13,790,000
Giving by Foundations	- $41,090,000
Giving by Bequests	- $19,120,000
Giving by Living Individuals	$140,312,948
Less Individual "Other than cash contributions"	- $31,816,050
Living Individuals Giving in cash, not including giving to church	$108,496,898
Church: Individual Giving to church, adjusted for religious organizations included in Form 990	+ $78,809,163
Total Cash Giving by Living Donors	$187,306,061

Data may not compute to numbers shown due to rounding.
Source: empty tomb analysis; IRS Form 990 series data, 2009; U.S. BLS CE 2009; *Giving USA 2013*   empty tomb, inc. 2013

Giving USA *Series.* A third source of charitable giving information, which is the most widely reported in the popular media, is from *Giving USA*, a series begun in the 1950s as an industry information compilation by a former vice president for public relations of a major professional fundraising firm.[30] The series has continued, and is currently prepared by a university-based philanthropy program, with active oversight by professional fundraisers. A major component of this series is based on deductions claimed on the IRS Individual Tax Returns. It may also be noted that the *Giving USA* series most recent estimates of philanthropy are built on the pre-academic measurements in the historical series. The involvement of the fundraising industry in the report series is reflected in the *Giving USA 2013* Editorial Board. Of the 15 individuals serving on the 2013 Editorial Board, 13 were principals or representatives of 13 of the 40 "member firms" that make up the "Giving Institute: Member Firms."[31] Eleven members of the Editorial Review Board contributed various "Good to Know!" points included in sections of *Giving USA 2013*, providing fundraising tips for nonprofits that want to increase donations.[32]

In order to compare a *Giving USA* estimate for individual giving with the CE data for the 1989–2009 period, the category of "Other than cash contributions" was subtracted from the *Giving USA* numbers. For the 2009 data, for example, the IRS $31.8 billion figure for "Other than cash contributions" that was subtracted from the Form 990 series data in the analysis above also was subtracted from the *Giving USA* figure. The *Giving USA* estimate for individual giving in 2009 was $200.37 billion.[33] When the $31.8 billion figure for "Other than cash contributions" was subtracted from that number, the result was a Total Individual Cash Giving figure of $168.6 billion.

Table 41 presents the development of the *Giving USA* figure for 2009 to be used in a comparison with the CE and Form 990 series data. A similar procedure was used to calculate comparable *Giving USA* figures for 1989 through 2008.

Table 41: Living Individual Charitable Cash Giving in the United States, *Giving USA*, 2009

Data Year 2009	000's of $
Giving by Individuals	$200,370,000
Less Individual "Other than cash contributions"	- $31,816,050
Total Individual Cash Giving	$168,553,950

Source: empty tomb analysis; *Giving USA 2013*, IRS Form 990

empty tomb, inc. 2013

A Comparison of Three Charitable Giving Estimates, 1989–2009.

Two of the sources of information on Total Charitable Giving in the U.S. differed from the CE by up to $52 billion in 2009. The differences between the CE series and the Form 990 expanded over time. In 1989, the CE aggregated total measured as 85% of the Form 990 adjusted total. In 2011, the CE measured 62% of the Form 990 figure. The CE measurement for Total Individual Contributions in 2009 was calculated to be $116 billion dollars. Data from the Form 990 series reports filed by recipient organizations, with an estimate of giving to religion added and other-than-cash contributions subtracted, resulted in a calculation of $187 billion received by nonprofits and foundations in 2009. Meanwhile, a *Giving USA* number for financial giving by living individuals in 2009, with other-than-cash contributions subtracted, was $169 billion, exceeding the benchmark CE figure by 31 percent.

The CE is a detailed U.S. BLS survey carried out on a quarterly basis.

The Form 990 series reports are completed by charitable organizations and foundations, based on their accounting records. Because the Form 990 does not presently ask for cash contributions from living individuals, only a calculated

Table 42: Living Individual Charitable Cash Giving in the United States, A Comparison of the Consumer Expenditure Survey, Form 990 Series, and *Giving USA*, 1989-2009

Year	U.S. BLS, CE Survey (Calculated) millions of $	Form 990 Series (Adjusted) millions of $	*Giving USA* (Adjusted) millions of $
1989	$42,631	$49,875	$71,899
1990	$40,052	$52,558	*$71,506*
1991	$47,601	$55,614	*$72,248*
1992	$48,721	$56,842	*$77,567*
1993	$46,695	$57,680	*$79,441*
1994	$48,593	$56,032	*$77,541*
1995	$52,239	$77,101	*$81,258*
1996	$51,674	$75,578	*$86,051*
1997	$53,747	$70,895	*$95,709*
1998	$57,864	*$89,257*	*$108,424*
1999	$69,861	*$92,333*	$116,343
2000	$66,217	*$85,463*	$126,834
2001	$75,330	*$103,946*	$135,062
2002	$81,652	*$101,287*	$139,497
2003	$88,159	*$116,523*	$143,429
2004	$89,384	*$120,709*	$158,587
2005	$110,846	*$142,889*	$172,763
2006	$125,659	*$171,845*	$172,129
2007	$121,589	*$175,752*	$174,303
2008	$115,803	*$170,698*	$173,339
2009	$116,414	$187,306	$168,554

Source: empty tomb analysis; IRS Form 990 series data, 2009; U.S. BLS CE 2009; *Giving USA 2013*   empty tomb, inc., 2013

estimate for cash contributions by living individuals can be developed. If for any reason the estimates for giving by corporations, foundations, or bequests—the categories that are used to calculate a Form 990 cash donations from living individuals figure—are not sound, that degree of error will impact the calculation. In this regard, it may be of interest to note that in 2007 the *Akron Beacon Journal* posted a short item with the lead sentence: "Warning: Analyzing trends in corporate philanthropy is far from a perfect science." Citing The Foundation Center, the Committee Encouraging Corporate Philanthropy, and *Giving USA*, the article noted corporate philanthropy in 2006 either increased 2.7% or 4.7%, or decreased 7.6%.[34]

The *Giving USA* series is based largely on deductions taken by Americans on their IRS Individual Income Tax Returns.

Table 42 shows the comparison of the three charitable giving estimates.

A CNN report on an annual poll conducted by the IRS Oversight Board found the number of Americans who indicated they cheated on their taxes had increased from 2008 to 2009, to 13% who thought it was acceptable, and to four percent for those who cheat "as much as possible." "Inflating the value of charitable donations and claiming personal expenses as business expenses" were both regarded as "common cheating tactics."[35]

A discussion of problems of noncash contributions estimates was presented in some detail in a previous edition in *The State of Church Giving* series.[36] Two comments may be relevant.

When he was Internal Revenue Service Commissioner, Mark W. Everson, in written testimony submitted to a Congressional hearing, in a section titled "Over-stated Deductions" wrote that, "A common problem occurs when a taxpayer takes an improper or overstated charitable contribution deduction. This happens most frequently when the donation is of something other than cash or readily marketable securities."[37] In a Chronicle of Philanthropy article, Mr. Everson was quoted as suggesting that noncash deductions may be overstated by as much as $15 to $18 billion a year.[38]

A 2008 *Chronicle of Philanthropy* item reported:

The misuse of nonprofit organizations to shield income or provide fake tax breaks has once again appeared on the Internal Revenue service's "dirty dozen," the agency's annual list of the top 12 tax scams in the United States. Most of the abuse stems from people giving money or property to charities but retaining too much control over the donations, or from people overestimating the value of donated property. In addition, the IRS says that an old scam—claiming private tuition payments as charitable donations—continues to grow.[39]

Scott Burns, business writer for *The Dallas Morning News* and Universal Press Syndicate columnist, considered the topic of "over-statement" of deductions in a 2010 column. A reader wrote in to say that a consultant had told the reader how he "can claim up to 10 percent of the total income as a write-off without proof or receipts." The reader wrote that he was pleased to be getting money back from the IRS, instead of paying taxes. He went on, "Our total income for 2005 was $101,083. My consultant has entered $9,224 for charities, $12,253 for job expenses and certain miscellaneous deductions, and $3,825 for meals and entertainment. I can tell you, those figures are exaggerated. But is it legal?"

Scott Burns began his reply with the comment, "Excuse me if I sound like a close relative of Goody Two Shoes, but do you really want to be a lying freeloader just because others are?" Burns also noted that, "The IRS has estimated unpaid taxes exceed $290 billion a year. The Treasury inspector general for tax administration thinks the IRS is low-balling the number." Burns advised the man to keep good records and deduct appropriately.[40]

The exchange in Scott Burns' column highlights some of the difficulties with using deductions from IRS Individual Income Tax Returns as a basis for calculating charitable giving in the U.S.

The results of this comparison of three estimates of individual giving suggest that the area of philanthropy measurement needs quality attention.

The results of this comparison of three estimates of individual giving suggest that the area of philanthropy measurement needs quality attention.

Recommendations for Improving the Measurements. Past editions in *The State of Church Giving* series have presented recommendations for improving the measurement of philanthropy in the United States.[41]

A Standing Commission on Nonprofits. One recent development has the potential for contributing to the objective reporting of philanthropy measurement. A 2010 news article indicated proposed legislation "would create a bi-partisan, 16-member U.S. Council on Nonprofit Organizations and Community Solutions, headed up by an executive director, as well as the Interagency Working Group on Nonprofit Organizations and the Federal Government." According to a news report on the legislation, in addition to providing the means to improve communication between the nonprofit sector and the Federal Government regarding policies affecting the sector, the proposed bill provides that an "existing federal agency would be tasked to compile data on nonprofits and develop metrics for performance, establish reporting requirements, and expand information to better inform Congress on the impacts of nonprofit organizations."[42] This proposal hearkens back to the 1975 Filer Commission report, which recommended that the original United States Commission on Private Philanthropy and Public Needs become a standing commission.[43] Such a commission could, among other activities, help improve the measurement and reporting of philanthropic data.

Consumer Expenditure Survey as a Benchmark. Presently, the CE data has become an important source of information on the giving patterns of Americans. The CE, by reporting only cash contributions, avoids the problems inherent in using tax

109

records, including cash and noncash deductions. It is recommended that the U.S. Department of Labor, Bureau of Labor Statistics, Consumer Expenditure Survey be utilized as the unbiased, broad-gauge benchmark of living Americans' aggregate cash giving to charity, until such time as the U.S. Internal Revenue Service makes summary Form 990 living individual giving data available on an annual basis.

Form 990 Living Donor Category. With some adjustments, the Form 990 information could also provide a sound basis on which to answer the question of how much Americans give. The Form 990 would be improved by obtaining a measure of giving by living donors. As can be seen in Table 40, currently a variety of adjustments need to be made in order to obtain a working estimate of this number.

Faith-based or Secular Governance Choice. An important refinement would provide a more complete picture of philanthropy in America. Before selecting one of the ten core definition categories, the nonprofit organization could first indicate its form of governance as either "faith-based" or "secular." This identification could provide valuable information to help clarify the role of religion in the area of giving. Form 990 could also require that the organization define itself, first by selecting either faith-based or secular as the category of governance, and then the specific activity described by one or more of the National Taxonomy of Exempt Organizations core codes.

The importance of being able to classify giving by both faith-based or secular categories, as well as by specific activity codes can be seen from an observation in *Giving USA 1990*'s discussion of "Giving to Religion." That issue of *Giving USA*, edited by Nathan Weber, noted, "Further, among many religious groups, giving to religion is considered identical with giving to human services, health care, etc., when such services are administered by organizations founded by the religious groups" (p. 187). An analysis of the CE data for 2011 found that donors identified 69% of their charitable donations as given to churches and religious organizations. That figure compares to an estimate of *Giving USA 2013* giving to religion as a percent of individual giving of 46% in 2011.[44] The extent of this variation suggests that the definitions of what constitutes a religious organization differ broadly among the charitable giving estimate sources.

In their book on the Unified Chart of Accounts, Russy D. Sumariwalla and Wilson C. Levis reproduced a graphic originally prepared by United Way of America that depicts how the account classification would appear

Figure 20: Account Classification Application with Faith-based/ Secular Governance Option Included

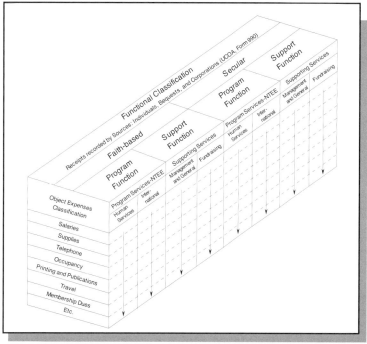

Source: Adaptation of graphic in Sumariwalla and Levis   empty tomb, inc. graphic 2001

in practical application.[45] For purposes of the present discussion, that graphic was adapted to include a statement about receipts classification, and to describe at what point the choice of faith-based or secular governance would be included in the accounting hierarchy (see Figure 20).

Associated Press and Other Media Reports on Philanthropy.

The power of the press in influencing the opinions of Americans was noted as a factor in a discussion of the "illusion of potential" in a 2010 book, *The Invisible Gorilla, And Other Ways Our Intuitions Deceive Us*. The authors, Christopher Chabris and Daniel Simons, state that the "*illusion of potential* leads us to think that vast reservoirs of untapped mental ability exist in our brains, just waiting to be accessed."[46] They give two examples of myths that became quickly accepted by the general public enamored with the illusion of potential. The media's role in popularizing myths was considered, and the following observation was made: "The media gives tremendous weight and coverage to the *first* study published on a research question, and essentially ignores all of those that come later"[47] (emphases in original).

Consider that other researchers could not reproduce the initial finding that listening to certain types of music makes one more intelligent, popularly known as the "Mozart Effect." Wide media reports of the initial research helped establish the legend, but less attention was given to the follow-up studies that contradicted the initial findings. Further, although the research was conducted on adult subjects, the idea that music could affect infants was also reported in the media. Chabris and Simons note, "Until we each had our first child, we didn't realize the extent to which the Mozart-for-babies myth has permeated the child-care industry. Intelligent, highly educated friends sent us toys that included — as a matter of routine, not a special feature — a 'Mozart' setting that played classical music."[48]

... the media's initial treatment of a topic may define that topic for the public, independent of the relevant facts.

Chabris and Simons also regard as a myth subliminal messages on movie screens impacting concessions purchases. They use as an example an "experiment" in the 1950s. The researcher reported that flashing subliminal messages in a movie theater increased popcorn and soft drink sales, helping to establish in the public's mind the idea of subliminal marketing. However, years later the "researcher" confessed that the "research" was fabricated as a way to increase business for his advertising firm. Yet a survey by Chabris and Simons found that 76 percent of respondents believed in subliminal marketing.[49]

These examples indicate that the media's presentation of information to the public can have an important role in how the public views an issue. The examples also demonstrate the media's initial treatment of a topic may define that topic for the public, independent of the relevant facts.

Aspects of the Associated Press's past presentation of philanthropy giving in the United States, from 2002 through 2011, may be regarded as helping to define the media's treatment of the topic. The Associated Press's reports over these years may have set the standard for how other media, for example Reuters wire service, reported findings from the new edition of *Giving USA* in 2012 and 2013.

A review of reporting on each new edition of the annual *Giving USA* edition from 2002 through 2011 found the Associated Press routinely led its article with information about the gross aggregate total of charitable donations. This aggregate number includes not only giving by individuals, but also includes corporate donations, bequests from dead people, and gifts to foundations. The Associated Press then routinely noted the change in this aggregate number from the previous year. This comparison across years did not take into account changes in either population or income.

Rarely does the media provide numbers to the public without placing those numbers in a larger context of population and/or the economy. Consider that the press routinely reports the crime rate, the unemployment rate, the savings rate, the poverty rate, the on-time flight rate, the unpaid mortgage rate, and the Consumer Confidence Index. In each case, numbers are not reported as aggregates, but rather are put into context of the larger population so that the reader has some basis to evaluate the meaning. For example, a major factor in the economic recovery is the creation of new jobs. When discussing job creation and the economic recovery, the media has routinely connected the number of jobs needed to changes of the population, as indicated by the formulation that it takes 125,000 new jobs a month to keep up with growth in the work force.[50]

Researchers considering the status of religion in the world offered another example of the importance of changes in population:

> An interesting overall comment is that virtually all activities of Christian churches, missions, denominations, and communions are growing numerically and expanding. This is usually interpreted as showing the success of church programs. In fact, however, everybody's programs are all expanding fast because since AD 1800 populations everywhere have been expanding rapidly and now stand at 372,000 births a day.

> In fact, the key to understanding religious trends is the ability to compare growth rates of religious variables with secular ones. This is the only way to know if a religion is growing faster or slower than the general population.[51]

Good reporting seems to include the responsibility of placing numbers in the larger context so the reader will understand the importance of the figures being quoted.

Yet the media emphasize aggregate charitable giving numbers that are independent of either population or the economy.

For example, once again in 2011, the Associated Press article that appeared on the release of the new *Giving USA* report reflected the *Giving USA* press release focus on the aggregate billions of dollars raised in 2010. Further, the lead emphasized the percent change in those aggregate billions of dollars from the previous year: "Total contributions from individuals, corporations and foundations were estimated at $290.9 billion, up from $280.3 billion in 2009, the Giving USA Foundation reported. That represented growth of 3.8 percent incurrent dollars and 2.1 percent in inflation-adjusted dollars."[52]

In fact, when population and changes in the economy were taken into account, individual giving as a percent of Disposable Personal Income declined 0.4% and total giving as a percent of the Gross Domestic Product declined 0.1%.

Nevertheless, other media, such as *The Washington Post*, *The New York Times*, and *The Wall Street Journal* also popularized the idea that charitable giving had increased in 2010, by leading their stories with the report on aggregate giving. *The Washington Post* suggested the increase was a sign of economic rebound.[53]

With the exception of coverage in 2008, different Associated Press reporters' lead focus did not adjust the announced aggregate data for population and economy changes. As a result, the articles announced, in 2002 through 2007, an increase in aggregate current dollars, even though a decrease has occurred when population and the economy were taken into account. For the 2009 and 2010 coverage, the lead focus was on aggregate decrease. The focus again returned to aggregate increase in the 2011 news report.

Consider that the change from 2003–2004 in total contributions was reported as an increase of 5.0 percent. When those billions of dollars were adjusted to a percent of Gross Domestic Product (GDP), there was actually a decline of 1.6%. Individual giving that year, as a percent of Disposable (after-tax) Personal Income (DPI), also declined 1.6%

The change in total contributions aggregate billions of dollars from 2007–2008 was reported as -2%. When those billions were adjusted to a percent of GDP, the decline was -5.2%. Individual giving that year, adjusted to a percent of DPI, was -7%.

The change from 2008–2009 was reported as a decline of 3.6%. When adjusted for GDP, the decline in total contributions was actually less, at 2.3%, and also less in individual giving adjusted for DPI, at 1.4%.

An Internet search indicated that the Associated Press apparently did not report on the release of *Giving USA 2012* or *Giving USA 2013*. A wire service that did publicize the findings of both editions was Reuters. Perhaps influenced by the standard set by AP's past approach, the wire service's stories emphasized aggregate totals both years. The wire story's title in 2013 was, "Giving USA Report: 2012 Charitable Giving Grew Almost 4%, Corporate Donations Grew 12%." The first mention of the percent change from the previous year again referred to the aggregate total: "Overall, U.S. donations to bolster the arts, health, religion, and other activities totaled $316.2 billion in 2012, a 3.5 percent increase from the $305.5 billion donated in 2011 ..."[54] In contrast to the headline, when the aggregate total cited in the Reuters story was put in context of the total economy, considered as a percent of Gross Domestic Product, the total decreased from 2011 to 2012 by -0.5%.

According to the Urban Institute, the nonprofit sector accounts for "5 percent of GDP, 8 percent of the economy's wages, and nearly 10 percent of jobs."[55]

Yet reporting about philanthropy in the U.S. is not put into context of the giving rate, but rather is left as the total amount of aggregate dollars.

The American people have a right to know how their charitable giving rates are changing from year to year. The measure that validly conveys that information is the category of individual giving as a percent of income, which adjusts the aggregate numbers for changes in both population and income. As illustrated in earlier chapters in this volume, church giving appears different when considered in aggregate form, and when giving is considered per member and as a portion of an after-tax income.

The American people have a right to know how their charitable giving rates are changing from year to year.

Table 43: Associated Press, 2001-2010, and Other Media, 2011-2012, Reported Giving Changes; Calculated Changes from Previous Year's Base, Adjusted for U.S. Population and Economy, Using *Giving USA* 2002-2013 Editions' Individual and Total Giving Data, 2001-2012

Giving USA Edition	*Giving USA* Data Year Interval	AP: First Percent Change from Previous Year Listed in AP Story: Aggregate Bil. $[56]	Per Capita Individual Giving as % of Per Capita DPI: % Change from Base Year[57]	Total Giving as % of GDP: % Change from Base Year[58]	AP Headline and AP First Mention of Percent Change	AP Byline and AP Dateline
2002	2000-01	0.5%	-2.6%	-2.8%	"2001 Charitable Giving Same As 2000" "Total giving by individuals, corporations and other groups amounted to $212 billion, up 0.5 percent from 2000 before inflation is figured in ..."	Helena Payne, Associated Press Writer, New York
2003	2001-02	1.0%	-4.7%	-2.5%	"Donations Held Steady in 2002" "Giving rose 1 percent last year to $240.92 billion from $238.46 billion in 2001 ..."	Mark Jewell, The Associated Press, Indianapolis
2004	2002-03	2.8%	-2.0%	-1.9%	"Charitable Giving Rises in 2003" "the survey showed a 2.8 percent increase over 2002, when giving amounted to $234.1 billion"	Kendra Locke, The Associated Press, New York
2005	2003-04	5.0%	-1.6%	-1.6%	"Charitable Giving Among Americans Rises" "Americans increased donations to charity by 5 percent in 2004 ..."	Adam Geller, AP Business Writer, New York
2006	2004-05	6.1%	2.0%	-0.3%	"Charitable Giving in U.S. Nears Record Set at End of Tech Boom" "The report released Monday by the Giving USA Foundation estimates that in 2005 Americans gave $260.28 billion, a rise of 6.1 percent ..."	Vinnee Tong, AP Business Writer, New York
2007	2005-06	1.0%	-0.9%	-2.0%	"Americans Give Nearly $300 Billion to Charities in 2006, Set a New Record" "Donors contributed an estimated $295.02 billion in 2006, a 1 percent increase when adjusted for inflation, up from $283.05 billion in 2005."	Vinnee Tong, AP Business Writer, New York
2008	2006-07	"remained at..." [0.0% implied]	-2.8%	-1.0%	"Americans Are Steady in Donations to Charity" "Donations by Americans to charities remained at 2.2 percent of gross domestic product in 2007 ..."	Vinnee Tong, AP Business Writer, New York
2009	2007-08	-2.0%	-7.0%	-5.2%	"Amid Meltdown, Charitable Gifts in US Fell in 2008" "Charitable giving by Americans fell by 2 percent in 2008 as the recession took root ..."	David Crary, AP National Writer [AP National Reporting Team: Family and Relationships], New York
2010	2008-09	-3.6%	-1.4%	-2.3%	"2009 Charitable Giving Falls 3.6 Percent in US" "Charitable giving fell by 3.6 percent last year as Americans continued to struggle with the recession ..."	Caryn Rousseau, Associated Press Writer, Chicago
2011	2009-10	3.8%	-0.4%	-0.1%	"Charitable Giving in US Rebounds a Bit after Drop" "That represented growth of 3.8 percent in current dollars and 2.1 percent in inflation-adjusted dollars."	David Crary, AP National Writer, New York
2012	2010-11	4.0%	0.1%	0.1%	"U.S. Charitable Giving Approaches $300 Billion in 2011" "Giving by Americans increased 4 percent in 2011 compared with 2010 ..."	Michelle Nichols, Reuters, New York
2013	2011-12	3.5%	0.6%	-0.5%	"Giving USA Report: 2012 Charitable Giving Grew Almost 4%, Corporate Donations Grew 12%" "Overall, U.S. donations to bolster the arts, health, religion and other activities totaled $316.2 billion in 2012, a 3.5 percent increase from the $305.5 billion donated in 2011 ..."	Susan Heavey, Reuters, Washington

Source: empty tomb analysis; Associated Press; Reuters; U.S. BEA; *Giving USA*

empty tomb, inc., 2013

Table 44: *Giving USA* **Executive Statement or Foreword First Mention of Percent Change and** *Giving USA* **Attribution from** *Giving USA* **2002-2013 Editions**

Giving USA Executive Statement or Foreword First Mention of Percent Change	*Giving USA* Attribution
"The 0.5 percent increase in giving for 2001 is more attributable to the economy than to crisis."	(Indianapolis, Ind.: AAFRC Trust for Philanthropy, 2002), p. 1 Executive Statements: Statement of Chair, AAFRC Trust for Philanthropy: Leo P. Arnoult, CFRE, Chair, AAFRC Trust for Philanthropy
"Giving in 2002 is estimated to be $240.92 billion, growing one percent over the new estimate for 2001 of $238.46 billion."	(Indianapolis, Ind.: AAFRC Trust for Philanthropy, 2003), p. ii Foreword: Leo P. Arnoult, CFRE, Chair, AAFRC Trust for Philanthropy John J. Glier, Chair, AAFRC Eugene R. Tempel, Ed.D., CFRE, Executive Director, The Center on Philanthropy at Indiana University
"Giving in 2003 grew 2.8 percent over the revised estimate for 2002 of $234.09 billion."	(Glenview, Ill.: AAFRC Trust for Philanthropy, 2004), p. ii Foreword: Henry (Hank) Goldstein, CFRE, Chair, Giving USA Foundation John J. Glier, Chair, AAFRC Eugene R. Tempel, Ed.D., CFRE, Executive Director, The Center on Philanthropy at Indiana University
"Giving grew at the highest rate since 2000, 5.0 percent over a revised estimate of $236.73 billion for 2003 (2.3 percent adjusted for inflation)."	(Glenview, Ill.: AAFRC Trust for Philanthropy, 2005), p. ii Foreword: Henry (Hank) Goldstein, CFRE, Chair, Giving USA Foundation™, President, The Oram Group, Inc., New York, New York C. Ray Clements, Chair, American Association of Fundraising Counsel, CEO and Managing Member, Clements Group, Salt Lake City, Utah Eugene R. Tempel, Ed.D., CFRE, Executive Director, The Center on Philanthropy at Indiana University
"The combined result is that charitable giving rose to $260.28 billion, showing growth of 6.1 percent (2.7 percent adjusted for inflation)."	(Glenview, Ill.: Giving USA Foundation, 2006), p. ii Foreword: Richard T. Jolly, Chair, Giving USA Foundation™, George C. Ruotolo, Jr., CFRE, Acting Chair, Giving Institute: Leading Consultants to Non-Profits Eugene R. Tempel, Ed.D., CFRE, Executive Director, The Center on Philanthropy at Indiana University
"In constant [*sic*] dollars, the increase was 4.2 percent over 2005; in inflation-adjusted numbers, the increase was 1.0 percent."	(Glenview, Ill.: Giving USA Foundation, 2007), p. ii Foreword: Richard T. Jolly, Chair, Giving USA Foundation™, George C. Ruotolo, Jr., CFRE, Chair, Giving Institute: Leading Consultants to Non-Profits Eugene R. Tempel, Ed.D., CFRE, Executive Director, The Center on Philanthropy at Indiana University
"The estimates for 2007 indicate that giving rose by 3.9 percent over the previous year (1 percent adjusted for inflation), to reach a record $306.39 billion."	(Glenview, Ill.: Giving USA Foundation, 2008), p. ii Foreword: Del Martin, CFRE, Chair, Giving USA Foundation™, George C. Ruotolo, Jr., CFRE, Chair, Giving Institute: Leading Consultants to Non-Profits Eugene R. Tempel, Ed.D., CFRE, Executive Director, The Center on Philanthropy at Indiana University
"This is a drop of 2 percent in current dollars (-5.7 percent adjusted for inflation), compared to 2007."	(Glenview, Ill.: Giving USA Foundation, 2009), p. ii Foreword: Del Martin, CFRE, Chair, Giving USA Foundation™, publisher of *Giving USA* Nancy L. Raybin, Chair, Giving Institute: Leading Consultants to Non-Profits Patrick M. Rooney, Ph.D., Executive Director, The Center on Philanthropy at Indiana University
"Total charitable giving fell 3.6 percent (-3.2 percent adjusted for inflation) in 2009, to an estimated $303.75 billion."	*Giving USA 2010;* Created: 6/8/10; published by Giving USA Foundation, Glenview, Ill.; <www.givingusa2010.org/downloads.php>; p. ii of 6/9/2010 printout. Foreword: Edith H. Falk, Chair, Giving USA Foundation Nancy L. Raybin, Chair, Giving Institute: Leading Consultants to Non-Profits Patrick M. Rooney, Ph.D., Executive Director, The Center on Philanthropy at Indiana University
"It is promising to see the 2010 inflation-adjusted increase of 2.1 percent after two years of such steep declines."	*Giving USA 2011;* Created: 6/20/11; published by Giving USA Foundation, Chicago, Ill.; <www.givingusareports.org/downloads.php>; p. i of 6/20/2011 printout. Foreword: Edith H. Falk, Chair, Giving USA Foundation Thomas W. Mesaros, CFRE, Chair, Giving Institute: Leading Consultants to Non-Profits Patrick M. Rooney, Ph.D., Executive Director, The Center on Philanthropy at Indiana University
"Total giving grew 4.0 percent in 2011."	*Giving USA 2012;* Created: 6/18/12; published by Giving USA Foundation, Chicago, Ill.; accessed via <store.givingusareports.org/Default.aspx>; p. 1 of 6/27/2012 printout. Foreword: James D. Yunker, Ed.D., Chair, Giving USA Foundation Thomas W. Mesaros, CFRE, Chair, Giving Institute Patrick M. Rooney, Ph.D., Executive Director, The Center on Philanthropy at Indiana University
"Our data reveal that American households and individuals gave 3.9 percent more in 2012 than in 2011."	*Giving USA 2013;* Created: 6/18/13; published by Giving USA Foundation, Chicago, IL; accessed via <store.givingusareports.org>; p. 1 of 6/26/2013 printout. Foreword: L. Gregg Carlson, Chair, Giving USA Foundation David H. King, CFRE, Chair, The Giving Institute Gene Tempel, Ed.D., CFRE, Founding Dean, Indiana University Lilly Family School of Philanthropy

Source: empty tomb analysis; *Giving USA* series

empty tomb, inc., 2013

Tables and Chart regarding the Disparity between Associated Press and Other Media Reports on Aggregate Charitable Giving Levels, and Giving Adjusted for Population and Income. As pointed out above, the Associated Press charitable giving articles' coverage of the annual release of new *Giving USA* charitable giving data frequently led with an emphasis on the generally upbeat tone of the *Giving USA* press releases in terms of aggregate billions of dollars raised, unadjusted for population and income.

An analysis of AP reporting of *Giving USA* releases for the past ten years found the following. In seven years, 2002, 2003, 2004, 2005, 2006, 2007, and 2011, the AP article released nationally and internationally led with a percent change that indicated an increase in total charitable giving from the previous year. Yet, when a basic adjustment for changes in U.S. population and economic growth was made to the *Giving USA* aggregate numbers, individual giving as a percent of DPI declined rather than increased in six of the seven years, and total giving as a percent of U.S. GDP declined in all seven years.

This pattern of disparity between AP reports on aggregate billions of dollars raised and the complete picture of changes in charitable giving patterns can be observed in Table 43, which also includes the text from the related AP release. This AP text can be compared with the first mention of percent change included in the related editions in the *Giving USA* series, also presented in Table 44.

The titles and first number reference text in the Reuters articles on the release of *Giving USA 2012* and *2013* are also included in Table 43. For each edition in the *Giving USA* series, the media reporting can be compared to the statement from the *Giving USA* Foreword in Table 44.

Figure 21: Associated Press, 2001-2010, and Other Media, 2011-2012, Reported Aggregate Changes; Calculated Changes from Previous Year's Base, Adjusted for U.S. Population and Economy, Using *Giving USA* 2002-2013 Editions' Individual and Total Giving Data, 2001-2012

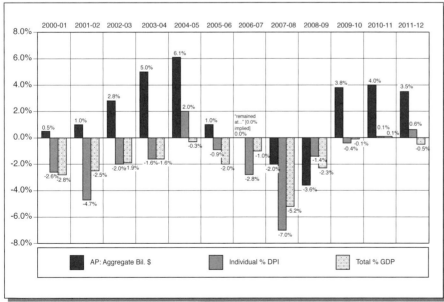

Source: Associated Press; Reuters; *Giving USA* data; U.S. BEA data; empty tomb analysis   empty tomb, inc. 2013

Figure 21 illustrates the disparity in the category of percent changes in aggregate total charitable giving reported by the AP, and most recently Reuters, and the cited Total Contributions aggregate billions adjusted to a percent of GDP. In addition, the percent change from one year to the next for each *Giving USA* edition's Individual giving figure is presented as a portion of DPI.

The observation may be made that the media, specifically the Associated Press and Reuters, apparently chose to highlight an industry's interpretation of its own work in a relatively uncritical fashion that de-emphasizes essential elements of the whole truth.

Total current dollar philanthropy as presented by *Giving USA*, unadjusted by population and income, has increased, that is, "set a new record" each year for 53 years from the first edition in 1955 through the 2008 edition, with qualification obtaining only for the year 1987.[59] This consistent pattern of growth is not surprising in light of the fact that both U.S. population and U.S. per capita DPI in current dollars increased each year from 1955 through 2007, the period under consideration.[60]

When correspondence was sent to then-Associated Press Vice President and Senior Managing Editor Mike Silverman, describing this topic, he responded in a May 8, 2010, letter: "You make some interesting points about how we might put these reports into better perspective for our readers." Note in Table 43 that Associated Press business writer Vinnee Tong led in the 2008 article on the release of *Giving USA 2008* with the aggregate billions of charitable dollars as a percent of GDP, which accounted for changes in population. This perspective was an improvement in the reported information provided to the public, even though the percent change in Total Giving as a percent of GDP between 2006 and 2007 was actually -1.0%.

However, the 2009 Associated Press article on the release of *Giving USA 2009* was written by someone listed on the AP Web site as reporting on Family and Relationships, and the lead returned to the standard aggregate current dollar change. It may be reasonable that the writer focused on the decrease in aggregate current dollars of -2% as newsworthy, given that only in 1987 did such a decline also occur. In the fifteenth paragraph of a 16-paragraph story, the AP writer did note that when adjusted for inflation, aggregate total charitable giving was down 5.7%. However, in the sixteenth paragraph, when discussing individual giving, the writer again referred to aggregate dollars declining 2.7%, and did not present individual giving as a percent of DPI, which measure was down 7%. Also, there was no discussion of the fact that total charitable giving, as a percent of GDP, was down 5.2% from 2007 to 2008. Both of the latter measures would have placed the charitable giving numbers into the broader context of the economy, including changes in population, and helped the reader understand rates of giving rather than only gross amounts.

In 2010, an AP writer from Chicago emphasized a decline in aggregate dollars of -3.6% from 2008–2009, which, as noted above, was more than the decline measured when adjusted for population and changes in the economy.

As noted, the 2011 AP story emphasized an aggregate increase of 3.8%, which was in fact a decline in both individual and total giving when population and change in the economy were taken into account.

The 2013 Reuters story announced an increase of "Almost 4%," which measured 0.6% for individual giving, and -0.5% for total giving, when population and change in the economy were taken into account.

The nonprofit area constitutes a large enough sector of the American economy that the philanthropy practices supporting it deserve the quality of reporting applied to other economic sectors, including adjustment for population and income to provide information about changes in the rate of giving.

The nonprofit area constitutes a large enough sector of the American economy that the philanthropy practices supporting it deserve the quality of reporting applied to other economic sectors …

Summary

Individuals give to charity for a variety of reasons. When given the opportunity to categorize their own donations in 2011, Americans indicated that 69% of their giving was to "churches, religious organizations." This finding suggests that religion plays a vital role in the practice of philanthropy in the United States.

The comparison of various estimates of giving in the U.S. suggests that the measurement of philanthropy could be improved. Currently, the U.S. Bureau of Labor Statistics, Consumer Expenditure Survey serves as a benchmark in providing unbiased information about giving levels in the United States.

Notes for Chapter 7

[1] U.S. Department of Labor, Bureau of Labor Statistics; "Frequently Asked Questions"; n.d.; <http://www.bls.gov/cex/csxfaqs.htm>; p. 2 of 5/28/2005 10:32 AM printout.

[2] The estimate of $105 billion is likely a high measure of charitable giving insofar as it includes all of the $1.28 billion in the category, "Gift[s] to non-CU members of stocks, bonds, and mutual funds." This attribution thus assumes that all of the $1.28 billion given in this category went to charitable organizations, although the CE does not allocate the funds of this category between charitable and non-charitable recipients.

[3] Americans' charitable giving was calculated by multiplying the 122,287,000 "Number of consumer units" by each of the average annual consumer unit contributions for 2011, the components of which were $215.69 ("charities and other organizations"), $649.17 ("church, religious organizations"), $25.37 ("educational institutions"), and $46.27 ("Gifts to non-CU members of stocks, bonds, and mutual funds"). The resultant sum of the aggregated components, $936.50, yielded a total giving amount of $114.5 billion. The "Cash contributions to church, religious organizations" amount, therefore, was calculated by multiplying the number of consumer units by $649.17 yielding an amount of $79.4 billion for 2011. Religion as a percent of the total was calculated by dividing $79.4 billion by $114.5 billion, yielding 69%. "Cash contributions" items not included in the above calculations for charitable contributions were "Support for college students (Sec.19); Alimony expenditures (Sec. 19); Child support expenditures (Sec. 19); Cash contribution to political organizations; Other cash gifts." Data source: U.S. Department of Labor, U.S. Bureau of Labor Statistics, "Table 1800. Region of residence: Average annual expenditures and characteristics, Consumer Expenditure Survey, 2011" [Item detail]; StTable1800Region2011. pdf; Created 11/6/2012 12:39 PM; unnumbered pp. 1, 17 & 28 of 4/30/2013 printout.

[4] Data sources: U.S. Department of Labor, U.S. Bureau of Labor Statistics, "Table 1202. Income before taxes: Average annual expenditures and characteristics, Consumer Expenditure Survey, 2011" [Item detail]; StTable1202Income2011.txt; Created NA; unnumbered pp. 1, 11, & 18 of 4/30/2013 printout; and "Table 2301. Higher Income before taxes: Average annual expenditures and characteristics, Consumer Expenditure Survey, 2011" [Item detail]; StTable2301HiInc2011. pdf; Created 11/6/2012 12:46 PM; unnumbered pp. 1, 18, & 30 of 4/30/2013 printout.

[5] Information from the outlier "Less than $5,000" bracket, while part of the "All consumer units" data, was not otherwise included in the present analysis.

[6] U.S. Department of Labor, U.S. Bureau of Labor Statistics, Table 1202, p. 1.

[7] Consumer Expenditure Survey "Frequently Asked Questions"; U.S. Department of Labor, U.S. Bureau of Labor Statistics, Consumer Expenditure Surveys, Branch of Information and Analysis; Last Modified Date: March 17, 2005; <http://www.bls.gov/cex/csxfaqs.htm>; p. 7 of 5/28/05 10:32 AM printout.

[8] Data source: U.S. Department of Labor, U.S. Bureau of Labor Statistics, "Table 1300. Age of reference person: Average annual expenditures and characteristics, Consumer Expenditure

Interview Survey, 2011" [Item detail]; StTable1300Age%RepItw2011.pdf; Created 9/17/2012 10:24 AM; unnumbered pp. 1, 18 & 30 of 4/30/2013 printout.

[9] Data source: U.S. Department of Labor, U.S. Bureau of Labor Statistics, "Table 1800. Region of residence: Average annual expenditures and characteristics, Consumer Expenditure Survey, 2011" [Item detail]; StTable1800Region.2011.pdf; Created 11/6/2012 12:39 PM; unnumbered pp. 1, 17 & 28 of 4/30/2013 printout.

[10] The significance levels noted in the text reflected a z statistic having an absolute value greater than 2.

[11] See Adelle M. Banks, RNS, "God Big in South, Not So Much in New England and Pacific Northwest," *Christian Century*, March 20, 2009, p. 15. Also, Jennifer Riley; "Report: Top 10 Most Religious States in America"; Christian Post; 2/2/2009; <http://www.christianpost.com/Society/Polls_reports/2010/02/report-top-10-most-religious-states-in-america-02/index.html>; pp. 1-2 of 2/3/2009 8:16 AM printout.

[12] An Associated Press article titled "Denominations Target Spiritually Cold Region," appearing in *Champaign (Ill.) News-Gazette*, October 30, 2009, p. B-7.

[13] Data source: U.S. Department of Labor, Bureau of Labor Statistics, Table 1800, unnumbered pp. 1, 5, 10, 12-14, 16-17, & 28 of 4/30/2013 printout.

[14] "Mission Statement"; U.S. Department of Labor, Bureau of Labor Statistics; Last Modified Date: October 16, 2001; <http://www.bls.gov/bls/blsmissn.htm>; p. 1 of 8/15/05 4:59 PM printout.

[15] U.S. Census Bureau, *Statistical Abstract of the United States: 2006*, 125th edition; published 2005; <http://www.census.gov/prod/2005pubs/06statab/prices.pdf>; pp. 479, 481 of 5/31/06 printout.

[16] "Consumer Expenditures in 2004"; Report 992; U.S. Department of Labor, U.S. Bureau of Labor Statistics; April 2006; <http://www.bls.gov/cex/csxann04.pdf>; pp. 4-5 of 5/30/06 printout.

[17] Consumer Expenditure Survey "Frequently Asked Questions"; U.S. Department of Labor, U.S. Bureau of Labor Statistics, Consumer Expenditure Surveys, Branch of Information and Analysis; Last Modified Date: March 17, 2005; <http://www.bls.gov/cex/csxfaqs.htm>; p. 2 of 5/28/05 10:32 AM printout.

[18] Sylvia Porter, "Out-of-Date Consumer Price Index to Be Revised in '87," a "Money's Worth" column appearing in *Champaign (Ill.) News-Gazette*, January 9, 1985, p. D-3.

[19] "Price Index Undergoes Statistical Adjustment," an Associated Press (Washington) article appearing in the *Champaign (Ill.) News-Gazette*, April 19, 1998, p. D-1.

[20] Consumer Price Indexes "Addendum to Frequently Asked Questions"; U.S. Department of Labor, Bureau of Labor Statistics, Division of Consumer Prices and Price Indexes; Last Modified Date: March 28, 2005; <http://www.bls.gov/cpi/cpiadd.htm#2_1>; pp. 1-2 of 5/31/06 10:54 AM printout.

[21] Gabriel Rudney, "The Scope of the Private Voluntary Charitable Sector," Research Papers Sponsored by The Commission on Private Philanthropy and Public Needs, Vol. 1, History, Trends, and Current Magnitudes, (Washington, DC: Department of the Treasury, 1977), p. 136. The nature of these numbers, specifically whether they are for giving to church only or combine giving to church and religious organizations, would benefit from a review in light of the relatively recent CE introduction of the "church, religious organizations" category.

[22] For this comparison, the composite data set of denominations was adjusted for missing data.

[23] U.S. Department of Labor, Bureau of Labor Statistics; "Table 1800. Region of Residence: Average annual expenditures and characteristics, Consumer Expenditure Survey, 2009"; StTable1800Region2009.pdf; Created 8/31/2010 7:04 AM; unnumbered pp. 1, 17.

[24] See Appendix B-6 for sources of Form 990 series detail.

[25] Giving USA Foundation (2013); *Giving USA 2013*; Created: 6/18/13; published by Giving USA Foundation, Chicago, Ill.; accessed via <store.givingusareports.org>; p. 251 of 6/26/2013 printout.

[26] *Giving USA 2013*, p. 248.

[27] Individual Income Tax Returns: Other than cash contributions: "Table 3. Returns with Itemized Deductions: Itemized Deductions by Type and by Size of Adjusted Gross Income, Tax Year 2009"; IRS; download 09in03id.xls; <http://www.irs.gov/pub/irs-soi/09in03id.xls>; p. 3 of 4/9/2012 5:05 PM printout.

[28] See Appendix B-6 for 2009 CE data source. "church represents 90% of giving to religion": Dean R. Hoge, Charles Zech, Patrick McNamara, Michael J. Donahue, *Money Matters: Personal Giving in American Churches* (Louisville: Westminster John Knox Press, 1996), p. 49; Jerry White, *The Church & the Parachurch* (Portland, OR: Multnomah Press, 1983), p. 104.

[29] See Appendix B-6 for the data used and sources.

[30] *Giving USA 1980 Annual Report* (New York: American Association of Fund-Raising Counsel, Inc., 1980), p. 9.

[31] *Giving USA 2013*, pp. 274, 277.

[32] See for example, *Giving USA 2013*, pp. 126, 131, 140, 146, 160, 202, 224.

[33] *Giving USA 2013*, p. 248.

[34] Paula Schleis; "Ups and Downs"; Akron Beacon Journal; posted 8/13/07; <http://www.ohio.com/business/9119806.html>; p. 1 of 8/15/07 11:45 AM printout.

[35] Blake Ellis; "Are You A Tax Cheat?"; CNNMoney.com; 2/19/2010; <http://money.cnn.com/2010/02/19/news/economy/tax_cheating/>; p. 1 of 2/26/10 11:13 AM printout.

[36] John Ronsvalle and Sylvia Ronsvalle, *The State of Church Giving through 2003* (Champaign, IL: empty tomb, inc., 2005), pp. 91-93. The chapter is also available at: <http://www.emptytomb.org/scg03chap7.pdf>.

[37] Mark W. Everson; "Written Statement of Mark W. Everson, Commissioner of Internal Revenue, Before The Committee on Finance, United States Senate, Hearing On Exempt Organizations: Enforcement Problems, Accomplishments, and Future Direction"; April 5, 2005; <http://finance.senate.gov/hearings/testimony/2005test/metest040505.pdf>; p. 9 of 4/27/05 printout.

[38] Brad Wolverton (Washington), "Taking Aim at Charity," *Chronicle of Philanthropy*, published by The Chronicle of Higher Education, Inc., Washington, D.C., April 14, 2005, p. 27.

[39] Sam Kean, Peter Panepento, and Grant Williams, "Tax Watch: Write-Offs," *The Chronicle of Philanthropy*, April 3, 2008, p. 42.

[40] Scott Burns, "No, It's Not OK to Lie on Return," *Champaign (Ill.) News-Gazette,* May 10, 2006, p. B-8.

[41] For the complete discussion of these recommendations, see Ronsvalle and Ronsvalle, *The State of Church Giving through 2003*, pp. 93-100. The chapter is also available at: <http://www.emptytomb.org/scg03chap7.pdf>.

[42] "Legislation Seeks New Federal Agency for Nonprofits"; The NonProfit Times; 7/12/2010; <http://www.nptimes.com/10July/weekly-100712.html?tr=y&auid=6612712>; p. 1 of 7/12/2010 1:27 PM printout.

[43] Commission on Private Philanthropy and Public Needs, *Giving in America: Toward a Stronger Voluntary Sector: Report of the Commission on Private Philanthropy and Public Needs* (n.p.: Commission on Private Philanthropy and Public Needs, 1975), pp. 191-193.

[44] *Giving USA 2013*, pp. 248, 250. Calculated by attributing 100% of 2011 Religion, $101.78 billion, to 2011 Individuals, $220.26 billion.

[45] Russy D. Sumariwalla and Wilson C. Levis, *Unified Financial Reporting System for Not-for-Profit Organizations: A Comprehensive Guide to Unifying GAAP, IRS Form 990, and Other Financial Reports Using a Unified Chart of Accounts* (San Francisco: Jossey-Bass, 2000), p. 41.

[46] Christopher Chabris and Daniel Simons, *The Invisible Gorilla, And Other Ways Our Intuitions Deceive Us*, (New York, Crown, 2010), p. 186.

[47] Chabris and Simons, p. 190.

[48] Chabris and Simons, pp. 186-197, especially pp. 191, 194-195.

[49] Chabris and Simons, pp. 200-203.

[50] An Associated Press article appearing as "Job Growth Weak in November," *Champaign (Ill.) News-Gazette*, December 4, 2010, p. A-4, col. 2. See also the transcript: "Dismal Unemployment Report Suggests Recovery May Be Stalling"; PBS Newshour; 7/8/2011; <http://www.pbs.org/newshour/bb/business/july-dec11/jobs_07-08.html>; p. 1 of 7/9/2011 2:35 PM printout.

[51] David B. Barrett, Todd M. Johnson, and Peter F. Crossing, "Missiometrics 2008: Reality Checks for Christian World Communions," *International Bulletin of Missionary Research*, Vol. 32, No. 1, January 2008, p. 27.

[52] David Crary, Associated Press; "Charitable Giving in US Rebounds a Bit after Drop"; Yahoo.com; 6/20/2011; <http://news.yahoo.com/s/ap/20110620/ap_on_re_us/us_charitable_giving>; p. 1 of 6/22/2011 4:31 PM printout.

[53] Annie Gowen; "Rise in Giving Signals Economic Rebound"; Washington Post; 6/19/2011; <http://www.washingtonpost.com/local/rise-in-giving-signals-economic-rebound/2011/06/16/AGX8nKcH_story.html>; p. 1 of 6/20/2011 4:22 PM printout.

Stephanie Strom; "Charitable Giving Rose Last Year for First Time Since 2007"; New York Times; 6/19/2011; <http://www.nytimes.com/2011/06/20/business/20charity.html?_r=1>; p. 2 of 6/20/2011 4:18 PM printout.

Melanie Grayce West; "Charitable Giving Rose Last Year, Still Below Peak"; Wall Street Journal Online; 6/19/2011; <http://online.wsj.com/article/SB10001424052702304070104576395800746718570.html>; p. 1 of 6/22/2011 4:44 PM printout.

[54] Susan Heavey, Reuters; "Giving USA Report: 2012 Charitable Giving Grew Almost 4%, Corporate Donations Grew 12%"; published June 18, 2013 12:00 AM EDT, updated 6/18/2013 10:00 AM EDT; <http://www.huffingtonpost.com/2013/06/18/giving-usa-report-_n_3457244.html>; p. 1 of 6/18/2013 9:08 AM printout.

[55] The Urban Institute; "Nonprofits"; 2010; <http://www.urban.org/nonprofits/index.cfm>; p. 1 of 8/16/2010 12:56 PM printout.

[56] The references for the Associated Press stories listed are as follows:

• Helena Payne, Associated Press Writer; "2001 Charitable Giving Same As 2000"; published June 20, 2002, 12:20 PM; <http://www.washingtonpost.com/ac2/wp-dyn/A17534-2002Jun20?language=printer>; p. 1 of 6/27/02 9:09 PM printout.

• Mark Jewell; "Donations Held Steady in 2002"; published June 23, 2003, 4:23 PM; <http://www.washingtonpost.com/ wp-dyn/A23604-2003Jun23.html>; p. 1 of 6/26/03 8:49 AM printout.

• Kendra Locke; "Charitable Giving Rises in 2003"; published June 21, 2004, 12:24 AM; <http://www.washingtonpost.com/wp-dyn/articles/A56830-2004Jun21.html>; p. 1 of 6/25/04 4:56 PM printout.

• Adam Geller, AP Business Writer; "Charitable Giving Among Americans Rises"; published June 14, 2005 10:16 AM; <http://www.guardian.co.uk/worldlateststory/0,1280,-5073041,00.html>; p. 1 of 6/15/2005 9:42 AM printout.

• Vinnee Tong, AP Business Writer; "Charitable Giving in U.S. Nears Record Set at End of Tech Boom"; The Associated Press, New York, published June 18, 2006 11:10 PM GMT; <http://web.lexis.com[…extended URL]>; p. 1 of 6/20/2006 8:51 AM printout.

• Vinnee Tong, AP Business Writer; "Americans Give Nearly $300 Billion to Charities in 2006, Set a New Record"; published June 25, 2007 4:58 GMT; <http://web.lexis.com…>; p. 1 of 6/25/07 5:01 PM printout.

• Vinnee Tong, AP Business Writer; "Americans Are Steady in Donations to Charity"; published June 23, 2008; 11:43 AM GMT; <http://web.lexis.com…>; p. 1 of 6/23/2008 5:23 PM printout.

• David Crary, AP National Writer; "Amid Meltdown, Charitable Gifts in US Fell in 2008"; published June 10, 2010; 04:01 AM GMT; <http://web.lexis.com…>; p. 1 of 6/10/2010 5:11 PM printout.

• Caryn Rousseau, Associated Press Writer; "2010 Charitable Giving Falls 3.6 Percent in US"; published June 9, 2010; 04:01 AM GMT; <http://web.lexis.com…>; p. 1 of 6/9/2010 3:56 PM printout.

• David Crary, AP National Writer, New York; "Charitable Giving in US Rebounds a Bit After Drop"; published June 20 12:01 am ET [2011]; <http://news.yahoo.com/s/ap/20110620/ap_on_re_us/us_charitable_giving>; p. 1 of 6/22/2011 4:31 PM printout.

• Michelle Nichols, Reuters; "U.S. Charitable Giving Approaches $300 Billion in 2011"; published June 19, 2012 12:02 am EDT; <http://www.reuters.com/article/2012/06/19/us-usa-charity-idUSBRE85I05T20120619>; p. 1 of 6/19/2012 5:13 PM printout.

• Susan Heavey, Reuters, June 6/18/2013.

[57] See Appendix C for the source of data on which the calculation of "Per Capita Individual Giving as % of Per Capita Disposable Personal Income: % Change from Base Year" figures by empty tomb, inc. was based.

[58] The calculation of "Total Giving as % of Gross Domestic Product: % Change from Base Year" figures by empty tomb, inc. was based on the following data. The aggregate Total Giving sources for the 2000-01, 2001-02, 2002-03, 2003-04, 2004-05, 2005-06, 2006-2007, 2007-2008, 2008-2009, and 2009-2010 intervals were the 2002 (p. 177), 2003 (p. 194), 2004 (p. 218), 2005 (p. 194), 2006 (p. 204), 2007 (p. 212), 2008 (p. 210), 2010 (p. 210), 2010 (p. 50), 2011 (p. 53), 2012 (p. 264), and 2013 (p. 248) Giving USA editions, respectively. The source of Gross Domestic Product (GDP) data in current dollars: U.S. Bureau of Economic Analysis; "Table 1.1.5. Gross Domestic Product"; Line 1: "Gross domestic product"; National Income and Product Accounts Tables; Hist data published July 27, 2012; 1969-Present data published on March 28, 2013; 1969-2012: Tab "10105 Ann" of Section1All_xls_1.1.9_1.1.5.xls" downloaded as xls file "Section1All_xls.xls";

<http://www.bea.gov/national/nipaweb/SS_Data/Section1All_xls.xls>; downloaded 3/28/2013 [from <http://bea.gov//national/nipaweb/DownSS2.asp>]

[59] For the years 1955 through 1979, see *Giving USA, 1980 Annual Report, 25th Anniversary Issue* (New York: American Association of Fund-Raising Counsel, Inc., 1980), p. 22. For a revised, overlapping series covering the years 1970 through 2010, see *Giving USA 2011* (p. 53).

In the 1988 edition of *Giving USA: The Annual Report for the Year 1987* (New York: American Association of Fund-Raising Counsel Trust for Philanthropy, 1988), Total Contributions increased from 1986 to 1987 (p. 11). Although the 1987 figure was later revised to show a decrease from 1986 (see *Giving USA 1998: The Annual Report on Philanthropy for the Year 1997*, p. 156), any media reports at the time of the release of the 1988 *Giving USA* edition would have had access only to the information that giving increased in 1987.

The 1988 edition of *Giving USA* Foreword, coauthored by Maurice G. Gurin, Chairman, AAFRC Trust for Philanthropy, and George A. Brakeley III, Chairman, American Association of Fund-Raising Counsel, opened with the following paragraph. "The stock market crash of October 19 and the loss of the charitable deduction gave rise to predictions that philanthropic giving last year would suffer significantly. Quite the opposite occurred: total giving increased significantly. Indeed it achieved an impressive new high" (p. 5).

The "State of the Philanthropic Sector, 1987" section, located a number of pages further in the same volume, opens with the heading in bold type and closing punctuation of "$93.68 Billion!" The complete first two paragraphs of that section including the ellipsis follow. "Stock market crash. End of the charitable tax deduction for non-itemizers. Decline in the economy's competitiveness. Well-publicized hijinks of televangelists using much of the money donated for 'religion' to create their own heavens on earth.... In the face of it all, estimated giving in the United States reached an all-time high in 1987 — $93.68 billion.

"That amount represents an increase of 6.45 percent over the estimated amount donated a year earlier. The yearly increase marks the continuation of a decades-long trend" (p. 16). Yet, as noted above, subsequent corrections to the initial estimate so enthusiastically announced and reported found that giving actually declined rather than increased from 1986 to 1987.

[60] See Appendix C for U.S. population, 1955 through 2011. For Gross Domestic Product, see U.S. Bureau of Economic Analysis; "Table 1.1.5.Gross domestic product"; Line 1 (see End Note 58 for full citation). 1969-2011: Tab "10105 Ann" of Section1All_xls_1.1.9_1.1.5 downloaded as xls file "Section1All_xls.xls."

1955-1968: Tab "10105 Ann" of "Section1All_Hist_1.1.9_1.1.5.xls" downloaded as xls file "Section1All_Hist.xls"; <http://www.bea.gov/national/nipaweb/SS_Data/Section1All_Hist.xls>; on 3/28/2013 [from <http://www.bea.gov//national/nipaweb/DownSS2.asp>].

chapter 8

The Kingdom of God, Church Leaders & Institutions, Global Triage Needs, and the Promises of Jesus

"Why be like the pagans who are so deeply concerned about these things? Your heavenly Father already knows all your needs, and he will give you all you need from day to day if you live for him and make the Kingdom of God your primary concern."
> —Jesus Christ quoted in Matthew 6:32-33 (New Living Translation)

"For whoever wishes to save his life will lose it, but whoever loses his life for my sake will find it."
> —Jesus Christ quoted in Matthew 16:25 (New American Bible)

"I tell you the truth, anyone who has faith in me will do what I have been doing. He will do even greater things than these, because I am going to the Father."
> —Jesus Christ quoted in John 14:12 (New International Version)

The Kingdom of God

Luke 9:1-2 reads, "When Jesus had called the Twelve together, he gave them power and authority to drive out all demons and to cure diseases, and he sent them out to preach the kingdom of God and to heal the sick" (NIV).

Jesus was given works to do by the Father: "The works that the Father has given me to complete, the very works that I am doing, testify on my behalf that the Father has sent me" (John 5:36, NRSV). These works were miraculous. Many focused on healing people: "Many followed him and he healed all their sick" (Matt. 12:15b, NIV). Jesus raised three people from the dead, one of whom was a child (Mark 5:21-43; Luke 11:17; John 11:1-44). When Jesus sent out the Twelve to preach the kingdom of God, he gave them power to heal the sick.

The kingdom of God needs to be revisited today. Despite the analyses and interpretations of the concept that have occurred since Bible times, the implications that the present age of affluence have for the kingdom of God have not been seriously explored and therefore understood.

Jesus' miraculous works of healing showed love to people, and gained their interest in what Jesus had to say about the kingdom of God. Jesus was then able to point them to the ultimate healing of an eternal relationship with God.

What works has the Father given Jesus now, to be carried out by the body of Christ?

Jesus anticipated that the church would come into being after his earthly ministry. The longest recorded encounter of Jesus talking to the Father is in John 17:1-26. In verse 20, Jesus states that he is not just praying for the first disciples, but also for "those who will believe in me through their message." His prayer for those who follow is that they would be one in order to "let the world know that you sent me and have loved them even as you have loved me" (v. 23, both NIV).

Earlier, Jesus promised in John 14:12-14, that those who believe in him will do even greater works than Jesus did.

So, key elements of the kingdom of God include oneness among believers, and doing works in the pattern of Jesus. Additional factors that are unique at this point in time, in the U.S., in the 21st century, are: many who identify themselves as Christians; the massive amount of information about the world and the needs faced by people in it; and the post-World War II widespread affluence at a level never seen before in history.

Jesus, when in a corporeal body, was given the power to heal by a word or a touch. Jesus, in the corporate body of Christ, has been given the organization of the church. The works of the kingdom of God for this time likely include the mobilizing of voluntary church member giving through the miracle of oneness among church people for which Jesus prayed. This increased church member giving can be applied on a global scale and, because of the information about desperate needs and the amount of resources available, be launched with the full expectation that the needs can be met.

As Jesus healed the sick and raised Jairus' daughter from the dead, restoring her to her parents, the church in the U.S. can prevent children from dying, and restore them to their grieving parents, through networks of church delivery channels already in place. As Jesus gained the interest of people and could then talk to them about how to be healed for eternity, so the works of the kingdom of God in this time can gain people's interest in what the church has to say about this good news.

In light of the vast information available about global need and the broad distribution of resources among so many who identify with Christianity, now is the time to revisit the works of the kingdom of God. As the apostle Paul wrote, "For the kingdom of God is not a matter of talk but of power" (1 Cor. 4:20, NIV).

Yet, the giving and membership trends analyzed in the first five chapters of this volume do not suggest that the kingdom of God is currently being pursued at the level of power evident in the miracles that Jesus did while on earth, and the miracles he asked his disciples to do when he sent them out. In the past recent decades, church leaders have not worked through their institutions to build on the great amount of information

Jesus' miraculous works of healing showed love to people, and gained their interest in what Jesus had to say about the kingdom of God.

available about global need, and to mobilize more of the resources resulting from increasing incomes through voluntary giving, to address global needs at a scale to solve, rather than cope with them. Instead, the internal expenses of the congregation have been increasingly emphasized. The portion of the church budget directed to Benevolences, what might be termed the larger mission of the church, decreased rather than increasing dramatically. Perhaps as a consequence, since it was Jesus' works that attracted attention to his message, membership as a percent of population has been shrinking in the U.S. in the absence of works greater than Jesus did.

It may be observed that neither theology—conservative or liberal—has been a strong enough influence to stem the declines in giving and membership. As of 2011, as shown in Table 10 in chapter 3, both the National Association of Evangelicals (NAE)-affiliated denominations and the National Council of the Churches of Christ in the U.S.A. (NCC)-affiliated denominations in the analysis declined by 53% from the 1968 base, in per member giving as a percent of income to Benevolences. The NAE-affiliated denominations began from a higher base, and continued to give a larger portion of income, but the trends are similar.

In regard to membership, a larger group of conservative denominations than those analyzed in Table 10 grew as a percent of U.S. population up to the mid-1980s, when the group, as a whole, began to decline, as seen in Figure 11 in chapter 5.

If conservative theology were a determining factor, in and of itself, one might expect that a large group of evangelical denominations would be increasing, perhaps at a level that counterbalanced the decline observed in the mainline denominations. However, that trend is not evident in either the membership or giving patterns.

The lack of recovery of giving as a percent of income in the post-recession years of 2010 and 2011, as can be seen in Table 1 in chapter 1, may suggest that the 2008–09 recession provided a stress point on giving that exposed a weakness in church members' commitment to their churches. Given the emphasis within churches on Congregational Finances in the allocation of donations, the data may suggest that church members do not see the maintenance of institutions as a compelling reason to divert income from other areas of their lifestyle activities.

Church members may suspect that the pursuit of the kingdom of God should be less like only supporting and maintaining church structures, and more like being a football fan. Consider the couple who, as Alabama football fans, only missed one game—away or at home—in 31 years, and that one was seen on television while the mother/mother-in-law living with them was dying (she died 15 minutes after the game ended). An author of five books on college football stated, "The game matters more to people in the South ... It's more ingrained in the culture — it's part of your identity. Being an Alabama fan is the prism through which you view your entire life. That identification is your context for the outside world."[1]

The following discussion explores aspects of the observed gap described by church member giving and membership trends and the potential to carry out, in Jesus' name, the works of the kingdom of God at unprecedented levels, out of love for God and love for neighbor. Through an exploration of these ideas, perhaps the possibilities inherent in the kingdom of God can be better understood in this age of affluence.

Church members may suspect that the pursuit of the kingdom of God should be less like only supporting and maintaining church structures, and more like being a football fan.

Church Leaders and Institutions

Pastors of congregations are on the front lines of interactions with church members. When negative trends are evident in giving and membership, the pastor as leader is often seen as having the first line of responsibility. That puts the pastor in a difficult spot.

Surveys in the two largest Protestant communions found that many pastors are struggling. The United Methodist Board of Pension and Health Benefits Center for Health 2012 online survey found that pastors who responded to the survey, "experienced obesity, high cholesterol, borderline hypertension, asthma and depression at significantly higher rates than do other demographically comparable U.S. adults."[2] The Southern Baptist Convention (SBC) LifeWay Research surveyed Protestant pastors nationally and found that 55% expressed discouragement, and an equal percent indicated that they were lonely.[3]

Other research found that issues of congregational control were a top reason a pastor may be fired.[4] Research by the American Guild of Organists found that "rivals may be the most prevalent description" between pastors and musicians in congregations.[5]

Sociologist-novelist-priest Andrew Greeley saw a difficulty facing the pastor in terms of challenge and comfort: "There's a tradition that emphasizes both comforting and challenging. We do a reasonably good job with comforting—marriage, death. The difficulty is challenging. To challenge, stir up excitement, recapture the energy that is so clear in St. Mark's Gospel. This is a frantically busy culture, overcommitted. In the midst of that the church should be stirring up religious excitement so it would transform everything they do. That's the biggest challenge."[6]

A reason pastors may not emphasize challenge is because it is no easy task to inspire the congregation to transform. Jeffrey Bullock, canon theologian for the Episcopal Diocese of Arizona, applied psychologist Daniel Kahneman's Nobel Memorial Prize-winning theories to congregations' approaches to change. Kahneman described his "loss aversion" theory as follows: "Many of the options we face in life are 'mixed': there is a risk of loss and an opportunity for gain, and we must decide whether to accept the gamble or reject it."[7] Jeffrey Bullock wrote that Kahneman states that, "traditional theories ignore the fact that the fear of disadvantage far outweighs the prospect of advantage."[8] Bullock then considers how that theory is evident in churches: "Why, we wonder, do churches react so negatively to membership decline and yet even when they're in decline cling to the status quo?" Based on Kahneman's theories, Bullock suggests, "Churches don't cling to the status quo just because they're recalcitrant; they cling to the status quo because change feels disadvantageous. The fear of losing something trumps any expectation of new benefits."[9]

An observation by Frank S. Page, president of the Southern Baptist Convention's Executive Committee, speaks to the pattern described by "loss aversion":

> Our 21st century churches to a great extent have become ease loving churches. Such being the case, too often churches are not willing to pay the price that revival costs. It is true for individuals as well. At times we hate our deadness, our lack of spiritual vitality, but we hate still more to be bothered into action. That may sound

"To challenge, stir up excitement, recapture the energy that is so clear in St. Mark's Gospel ... the church should be stirring up religious excitement so it would transform everything they do."
—Andrew Greeley

126

a bit pessimistic and unkind, but I am confident that this is the reality in which we live. There are many, no doubt, who would like to have a true revival, but many would also ask that revival come without much serious alteration of behavior and priority. We must understand today that revival is costly. It always has been. It always will be.[10]

Church leaders appear to struggle in a similar way as do municipal leaders who hesitate to build a barrier against the rising tides experienced, for example, in New York. An engineer evaluated the November 2012 Storm Sandy damage to New York City and observed, "Unfortunately, they probably won't do anything until something bad happens … and I don't know if this will be considered bad enough." That same attitude also meant that the Dutch did not build a sturdy enough barrier until dikes collapsed in 1953, drowning more than 1,800 people and displacing 100,000 others.[11]

One may wonder what might be "bad enough" for church institutions in the U.S. to engender strong efforts at transformation. The Call to Action Interim Operations Team, formed in 2010 to help The United Methodist Church (UMC) "reorder the life of the church," issued a report in 2012. The report concluded that "The United Methodist Church's way of doing business remains 'unsustainable.' " The report further concluded, "Dramatically different and new behaviors, not incremental changes, are required … We have not yet seen the degree of shared sense of urgency or commitment to systemic adaptations with the redirection of leadership expectations and sufficient resources that our situation requires."[12]

In 2011, the Southern Baptist Convention reported declining membership for five years in a row, while the number of baptisms saw a 20% decrease since 1999. Ed Stetzer of SBC LifeWay Research noted that "the ratio of attendance to membership did not shift" suggesting that attendees were not countering declining membership.[13] A year later, data for 2012 indicated the declines continued.[14]

The Roman Catholic Church has also experienced a decline in membership as a percent of population from 1968–2011. Timothy Cardinal Dolan commented on the cultural development of "believing without belonging" that is occurring. "We hear that more and more people have absolutely no problem with faith, but they do with religion … While more and more people have no problem at all with Jesus Christ, they love him and accept him as their Lord and saviour, they do have problems with the church … More and more people don't see the need for the church."[15]

The venerable National Council of the Churches of Christ in the U.S.A. cut staff and moved from its headquarters at 475 Riverside Drive, New York, to offices in the Washington, DC, United Methodist Building. When the groundbreaking for the 475 Riverside Drive building took place on October 12, 1958, then-President Dwight D. Eisenhower laid the cornerstone.[16] The building was constructed with land and funds from John D. Rockefeller, Jr., and others. The New York building came to be known as the "God Box," housing the NCC and several denominational headquarters.[17] As of 2012, the NCC had 16 people on staff, 12 of whom were fulltime, down from the 1960s when 400 were employed, and down from the year 2000 when fulltime staff measured 59.[18]

David Hollinger, University of California-Berkeley history professor, credited ecumenical [mainline] Protestant leaders with urging their constituencies to "follow

One may wonder what might be "bad enough" for church institutions in the U.S. to engender strong efforts at transformation.

them in antiracist, anti-imperialist, feminist and multicultural directions." Allowing that the churches lost numbers due to these cultural stands taken by the leadership, even while they "simultaneously failed to persuade many of their own progeny that churches remained essential institutions in the advancement of these values," he nevertheless asserted a positive outcome. "Ecumenists yielded much of the symbolic capital of Christianity to evangelicals, which is a significant loss. But ecumenists won much of the U.S. There are trade-offs."[19]

The decline in membership as a percent of population and giving as a percent of income observed across the theological spectrum is one consideration that raises the possibility that there may be other explanations for the statistical patterns of the mainline churches.

Meanwhile, 77% of Americans felt that religion was losing influence in the U.S., a higher level than the previous peak of 75% in 1970.[20]

Another view was offered by David A. Roozen, director of the Hartford Institute for Religion Research, as he reflected on the status of those same "oldline" [mainline] Protestant churches: "I don't think that the liberal theologians and church leaders have made the case for why religion adds anything to a liberal lifestyle ... Why do you need the church to do Habitat for Humanity?"[21]

Comments from Richard Land, for many years the head of the SBC Ethics and Liberty Commission, indicate that the problem of who is influencing whom is not limited to any single part of the body of Christ. He was quoted in a chapel address as saying that Christians "have got to decide whether we're going to be thermometers or thermostats. Thermometers reflect the spiritual temperature; thermostats set the spiritual temperature ... Make no mistake about it, our churches are either going to have their temperature changed by those who are seeking ... to be spiritual change agents who are going to change the temperature, or we'll just be thermometers and reflect the temperature."[22]

To date, although a variety of strategies to address the patterns of decline have been attempted, the data trends discussed in earlier chapters have not shown a reversal. Further, the much talked about October 2012 Pew Research study found, "The number of Americans who do not identify with any religion continues to grow at a rapid pace." The study also found that between 2007 and 2012, those who identify as "Christian" decreased from 78% of the population to 73%. Of interest in that number, "White evangelicals," "White mainline," and "Catholic" all showed decreases, while the percent of "Black Protestant" and "Orthodox" remained the same. Meanwhile, "Unaffiliated" grew from 15% to 20% of the population.[23]

The declining church member giving as a portion of income and the accompanying decline in membership as a percent of population may be the result of the factors that are similar to a submerged iceberg. The symptoms appear as peaks. Denominations and congregations try a variety of creative programs to address these symptoms. However, the factors themselves, the submerged mass producing the peak symptoms, are not addressed.

In another context, John Kenneth Galbraith, Harvard economist, identified a helpful concept that may be useful in describing the submerged mass that is impacting the church. Whatever one thinks of his economic theories, Galbraith's construction

The declining church member giving as a portion of income and the accompanying decline in membership as a percent of population may be the result of the factors that are similar to a submerged iceberg. The symptoms appear as peaks.

of "uncorrected obsolescence,"[24] in his book *The Affluent Society*, is most useful in describing the difference between current economic reality and the mindset of those making decisions.

Church leaders seem to function in a state of uncorrected obsolescence, as if they are unaware of the practical potential of the affluence that has spread through U.S. society since World War II. Christians in the U.S. have been living in widespread affluence that has not ever before been typical of an entire society.

In these new circumstances, the analyses in chapter 6 of the present volume demonstrate that this affluence can help move institutions from being the central focus of a maintenance agenda into structures that are vital to the service of God's agenda to impact global triage needs. And yet church leaders live as though no such economic change has flooded American culture in the last 60 years. Old Testament professor and theologian Walter Brueggemann described the dichotomy as "The Liturgy of Abundance, The Myth of Scarcity," reviewing the Biblical narrative of a generous God because, "Our abundance and the poverty of others need to be brought into a new balance."[25]

As the spread of affluence throughout the U.S. went unappreciated, an accompanying tendency was for church members to turn into consumers of church services, as opposed to joining in order to learn about discipleship.[26] To the degree that church members resemble consumers more than disciples, their view of Jesus' promises, for example in John 14:12-14, may resemble a pagan response rather than a faith-based response. In that passage, Jesus promises that someone with faith will do greater things than Jesus did. Sociologist Rodney Stark described the pagan mindset, "that the gods can be induced to exchange services for sacrifices." Stark asserts that Christianity introduced the new view that the relationship with God was more than "self-interested exchange." That God loved those who loved him and wanted those who loved God to show it by loving one another was "alien to pagan beliefs."[27] A pagan mindset would limit a person's ability to believe Jesus when Jesus points to the possibilities that Jesus promises to his followers (John 14:12-14).

Jesus' promise that in losing one's life, one will find it (Matt. 16:25) makes no sense standing on Mammon's playing field, where the rules are the gratification of self. Yet, when standing on the field of Jesus' commands, the view opens onto a completely different world. Ross Douthat contrasted orthodoxy with heresy, giving as one example the church's traditional view that Jesus was both God and man, not one or the other. He wrote,

> The boast of Christian orthodoxy, as codified by the councils of the early Church and expounded in the Creeds, has always been its fidelity to *the whole of* Jesus. Its dogmas and definitions seek to encompass the seeming contradictions in the gospel narratives rather than evading them.
>
> The goal of the great heresies, on the other hand, has often been to extract from the tensions of the gospel narratives a more consistent, streamlined, and noncontradictory Jesus[28] [emphasis in original].

This tension in the whole of Jesus is difficult for church members to embrace when they are being recruited for Mammon's team, and it is up to church leaders to guide those members onto God's playing field and toward the kingdom of God.

Church leaders seem to function in a state of uncorrected obsolescence, as if they are unaware of the practical potential of the affluence that has spread through U.S. society since World War II.

Jesus presented a choice to his first followers between serving God or Mammon (Matt. 6:24), a choice still keenly relevant for those who would follow him in the 21st century U.S. In light of this choice, it is of interest that John Milton described the fallen angel Mammon, as "the least erected spirit that fell / From heaven, for even in heaven his looks and thoughts / Were always downward bent, admiring more / The riches of heaven's pavement, trodden gold / Than aught divine or holy else enjoyed / In vision beatific ..." It is this Mammon who is the builder, first in heaven but then in hell, constructing "Pandaemonium, the high capital / Of Satan and his peers ..."[29] The turning inward of the church, emphasizing Congregational Finances while not at the same time expanding Benevolences as members' incomes grew, may be a function of spiritual dynamics as much as practical ones. The 1968–2011 trend to decrease the portion of income given to the church was accompanied by a decreasing emphasis on the larger mission of the church represented by Benevolences, as seen in Table 1 in chapter 1, even as incomes increased, 131% in inflation-adjusted dollars between 1968 and 2011.

That weakening of the church's prophetic emphasis on the use of money comes at a time when the need for a higher vision in that area is being expressed. Consider comments made by Elisabeth Murdoch, daughter of Rupert Murdoch, whose New Corp went through the scandal of hacking private citizens' phone lines in an attempt to ferret out sensational news. At an August 2012 conference, Elisabeth Murdoch countered her brother's assertion that profit was the most important way for media to remain independent:

> The reason his statement sat so uncomfortably is that profit without purpose is a recipe for disaster.
>
> Profit must be our servant, not our master ... It's increasingly apparent that the absence of purpose – or a moral language – within government, media or business, could become one of the most dangerous own [*sic*] goals for capitalism and for freedom.[30]

Had church leaders recognized the inherent potential in members' increasing incomes, they could have developed that positive agenda for affluence, that "purpose for profits" called for by Elisabeth Murdoch. An exploration of such an agenda is presented in chapter 8 of *The State of Church Giving through 2010*.[31]

The church is the natural entity to have helped the culture at large navigate the potentially treacherous waters of the affluence flooding society. Journalist and scholar Os Guinness considered the dynamic that allows a society such as America to function: "Freedom requires virtue, which requires faith, which requires freedom — ad infinitum, a recycling triangle, a brilliant, daring suggestion as to how freedom can be sustained."[32] The church is the steward of God's wisdom on these topics, and can have a positive impact on the culture at large.

If the church does not develop and strengthen its unique perspective, there will be pressure to conform to the world's standards in the area of money. Consider a suggestion in *Giving USA 2013*, the nationally reported analysis of Americans' charitable giving patterns. The 2013 Editorial Board was made up of representatives from national fundraising companies. The Editorial Board provided "Good to Know!" information items in each of the charitable giving category sections. Under "Religion," the Editorial Board writers declared, "As other types of nonprofit organizations develop more sophisticated approaches to reaching constituents who become donors, houses of worship tend to remain 'old school' in their approaches." The observations about Religion giving continued, noting, for example, that few houses of worship have "in-house professional development officers."[33] That comment ignores the traditional role of the stewardship officials at all levels of denominational structures who have spent years integrating Christian beliefs with the practice of philanthropy. Nor does that "Good to Know!" suggestion take into account the various extra-denominational groups that provide services to the denominations and congregations, through annual stewardship campaigns and other fundraising services. Of more import, no credit was given to the fact that, even by *Giving USA*'s measurement system, which produces a lower estimate for religion as a percent of total charitable giving than the Consumer Expenditure Survey (CE), religion has received the highest portion of total charitable contributions of any category since the beginning of the survey series. Further, the analysis of the CE data by age, presented in chapter 7 of this volume, found once again that those in the Under-25 age bracket reported the vast majority of their donations being directed to "church, religious organizations," suggesting that Americans learn their initial practice of philanthropy in a religious setting.

The Editorial Board offered another suggestion in the same "Good to Know!" item: churches should increase their "knowledge about giving preferences and priorities of congregants" much like educational institutions and hospitals strive to do.[34] This suggestion sounds dangerously close to the seeker-friendly theories popularized in the mid-1980s. The Willow Creek congregation in South Barrington, Illinois, was one of the key proponents of the theory. The word "dangerously" is used in this context because, in a 2008 survey, Willow Creek found a level of dissatisfaction among some of its members that were "stalled" in their spiritual growth. As a result, the congregation was reported to be planning a change in focus toward more discipleship and less of the seeker emphasis implied in the fundraising tip in the *Giving USA 2013* Religion section.[35]

If the church is not developing and strengthening its own authentic approach to the area of money through discipleship, integrating faith and practice, the secular culture will be all too happy to fill the void, and to lead in ways that may not be in the church's best interests.

It may be noted that an authentic approach to the area of money through discipleship is not something that can be led by church stewardship or mission personnel without the involved commitment of the top denominational leaders whether in formal or informal roles.

What may be less obvious about the impact of declining trends in churches is that the entire culture has been impacted by the absence of the church's contribution of a unique view from within Jesus' frame of reference. For example, writer Paul Elie, in *The New York Times*, lamented a "post-Christian fiction" lacking authors such as Flannery O'Connor or John Updike whose contributions to literature were widely recognized.[36]

Or consider that, in the absence of a strong moral culture, rooted in the past in church teachings that grew out of a high level of commitment to church by the many, fathers have disappeared from households with increasing frequency. The percent

... an authentic approach to the area of money through discipleship is not something that can be led by church stewardship or mission personnel without the involved commitment of the top denominational leaders ...

of households headed by single mothers grew from 11 percent of U.S. population in 1960, compared to about a third in 2012. A consequence is more children living in poverty, as incomes of single mothers average $24,000, compared to average incomes of $80,000 for married couples.[37]

Without a strong alternative view impacting the culture, one that emphasizes the importance of the community of faith as a base for service, technology can feed self-preoccupation. For example, the '#me' hashtag appears on 25 million photos on one photo Web site.[38] One overview of the Millennials age cohort described the members of that generation as "earnest and optimistic" who "embrace the system" while being "pragmatic idealists." Yet they're "not going to church, even though they believe in God, because they don't identify with big institutions; one-third of adults under 30, the highest percentage ever, are religiously unaffiliated."[39] Of course, it may be something other than the size of the institution preventing Millennials from being engaged in church, since sales numbers suggest they and a large portion of the U.S. population have no trouble patronizing Apple, with its iPhones and iPads, even though Apple is a large institution as evidenced by its market capitalization.[40]

The absence of traditional values does not leave a neutral zone.

Changes in values reflect an absence of traditional church perspectives. For example, a review noted multiple movies "choose to linger on glitzy stuff" because that is what more viewers want. The article cites one psychologist who found "teenagers have become more materialistic in their attitudes. Fewer than half of the 12th-graders surveyed in the late 1970s said it was important to have a lot of money, but 62% of seniors polled in 2005–2007 answered that it was."[41]

The absence of traditional values does not leave a neutral zone. The movies present fictional young people who steal to obtain what they want, based on young people who really did steal to obtain what they wanted.[42] Other young people form gangs and riot. British Prime Minister David Cameron responded to riots that included looting and violence in a variety of English cities during August 2011: "These riots were not about race ... These riots were not about government cuts ... And these riots were not about poverty. No, this was about behavior ... people showing indifference to right and wrong; people with a twisted moral code; people with a complete absence of self-restraint."[43]

Youth are not the only ones revising moral codes. A story in the *International Business Times* reported that the Belgian Federal Parliament was considering adding children to its laws allowing the choice of euthanasia, presently limited to those 18 and above, so "gravely ill children" could consult with doctors about deciding whether to end their lives. "The bill would also likely allow euthanasia for patients suffering from Alzheimer's and other diseases leading to advanced dementia, who may otherwise be deemed incompetent to make the decision to die."[44]

The growing flexibility toward morals led one Slate article to propose the legalization of polygamy, arguing that, "The definition of marriage is plastic ... All marriages deserve access to the support and resources needed to build happy, healthy lives, no matter how many partners are involved."[45]

Even as the church emphasizes its internal operations, traditional Christian values have increasingly come under hostile scrutiny. A widely reported view of a U.S. Army training instructor made news, when he warned in a briefing that Evangelical

Christianity and Roman Catholicism should be included in a list of "extremist" groups.[46] Meanwhile, a neurosurgeon at the University of Oxford proposed that science may be able to "identify religious fundamentalism as a 'mental illness' and cure it."[47]

The institutions of the church have also increasingly come under attack. Reports continue to surface of Christian groups on university campuses that are not allowed to function.[48]

The 2012 debate about limiting charitable deductions[49] caught up religious institutions in its wide net.[50] According to a report on a University of Tampa study the federal government "gives up at least $71-billion in annual revenue by offering tax exemptions to religious institutions."[51] The phrase "gives up" suggests a shift in the debate to the cost to government and away from the value that religious institutions contribute to society, thereby justifying their unique status.

A report on a presentation by an Alliance Defending Freedom (ADF) attorney quoted the attorney as stating that the organization is filing suits against city laws and zoning ordinances that discriminate against churches building new sanctuaries, and renting schools for public meetings. According to the report, "Cities increasingly are viewing churches as a financial drain, writing laws that make it difficult—and expensive—for congregations to build new properties ..."[52]

Increasing limitations on religion have also been reported in regard to the presence of religious views on the Internet. The National Religious Broadcasters drafted a proposal that Internet services such as Facebook, Google and Apple "should voluntarily abide by the First Amendment's free speech requirement" according to one report, which continued, "NRB's report included many examples of religious censorship throughout the Internet."[53]

Bishop Daniel R. Jenky wrote a letter to the Peoria Diocese Catholic parishes that was also published in a local newspaper. The letter began, "Since the foundation of the American Republic and the adoption of the Bill of Rights, I do not think there has ever been a time more threatening to our religious liberty than the present."[54]

The Stanford Law School opened the first legal clinic in the United States that is "devoted exclusively to religious freedom cases." The new clinic's director, James Sonne, was quoted as saying, "As our culture diversifies, people might look at religious liberty as a historical accident ... And we're trying to show that's not the case. It's a natural human right that affects us all."[55]

In a country where about three-quarters of the population identify with Christianity, any infringement on religious liberty will impact the practice of that tradition. However, the problems facing Christianity may not be only external. Leaders within the church have raised questions about the practice of Christianity in the U.S.

Tom Elliff, president of the Southern Baptist Convention International Mission Board (IMB), wrote a letter to other leaders in the denomination. He affirmed the theological direction that accompanied the "Conservative Resurgence" that the denomination dated from 1979,[56] but grieved over the difference between the teaching and practice: "We are in danger of becoming theoretical conservatives but

In a country where about three-quarters of the population identify with Christianity, any infringement on religious liberty will impact the practice of that tradition.

practicing liberals, arising each day with little sense of urgency to fulfill the Great Commission."[57]

An economist who is also a layman in the UMC, the second largest Protestant communion in the U.S., asserted in an interview, "The United Methodist Church in the United States has been in decline since the 1960s. In 2002, the rate of decline markedly increased and has persisted. If this ten-year trend continues, the denomination will cease to exist as we know it in 37 years." [58]

Table 45 presents comments from additional church leaders on the status of the church in the U.S.

The case can be, and is being, made that there is still great value in the present church structures, including denominations. For example, Andy Crouch, executive editor of *Christianity Today*, observed, "For cultural change to grow and persist, it has to be institutionalized, meaning it must become part of the fabric of human life through a set of learnable and repeatable patterns. It must be transmitted beyond its founding generation to generations yet unborn."[66]

On a blog site hosted by *Christian Century*, Ken Carter, a United Methodist District Superintendent, wrote of the need for denominations to complement the work of the congregation: "A denomination, at its best, provides a framework for the protection of the clergy in a workplace and supervision of even the most powerful clergy leaders. In addition, a denomination works out the implications of a missional strategy in an area that is more nuanced than simply whatever the market can bear."[67]

Ed Stetzer of the SBC LifeWay Research described networks springing up among unaffiliated congregations as "proto-denominations" and "missional networks" that he suggests will become denominational in form in a few years, noting the Methodist movement followed that pattern. Stetzer also noted the continuity that denominations offer, and the experience that can prevent congregations from repeating mistakes. Further, while affirming start-ups, he wrote, "But make no mistake: The vast majority of world missions, church planting, discipleship, and other forms of ministry are done through denominational partnerships."[68]

The key factor seems to be not that denominations are bad, or that congregations are no longer useful for the practice of religion. Rather, the problems may develop when national or local leaders are tempted to make necessary and inherently good structures the goal, rather than a tool to help members pursue a larger vision. For example, consider the unified budget. The unified budgets became the trend in the 1920s. Denominations refer to the expected per member support contributions by names such as "apportionments," "cooperative program," "per capita," and "assessments." The tension between support for international missions and the other functions of the church was discussed in some length in a previous edition in *The State of Church Giving* series chapter titled, "Abolition of the Institutional Enslavement of Overseas Missions."[69]

To be successfully implemented, the unified budget must be subservient to the higher aspirations of the denominations. Nationally promoted specialized offerings could provide the extraordinary income needed to pursue the larger visionary mission goals of the denominations, in a way that is freed from the departmental balance designed to be maintained through the unified budgets. In these circumstances, the

> Rather, the problems may develop when national or local leaders are tempted to make necessary and inherently good structures the goal, rather than a tool to help members pursue a larger vision.

Table 45: Church Leaders Comment on the Lukewarm Church in the U.S.

"Although pastors and members of the declining congregations attribute the decline in membership and attendance primarily to external social change over which they have no control, such an attribution is not supported by the data. The decline of these congregations is not characterized by a decline only in the frequency of attendance, which Gruber and Hungerman show to be the effect of Sunday retail activity. The decline in these congregations is mainly characterized instead by the loss of many members, including most of their younger members, and an inability to attract any new members." Steve McMullin, Arcadia Divinity College, Nova Scotia, on a study of 16 declining congregations in Canada and the U.S., and the effect of the secularization of Sundays[59]
"No account of Christian origins is more authoritative than any other, 'cafeteria' Christianity is more intellectually serious than the orthodox attempt to grapple with the entire New Testament buffet, and the only Jesus who really matters is the one you invent for yourself." Ross Douthat, author of *Bad Religion: How We Became a Nation of Heretics*, on the currently dominant Christian premises in the U.S.[60]
"So, in my view, when we look at a violent and suffering world, and we all watch the news every night, I think we have a decision to make on where to lay the blame … Should we lay the blame at the feet of a compassionate God, who has been sending life-enhancing visions to millions of leaders all over the world? Or should we lay the blame at the feet of a large number of gutless, cowardly leaders who aborted the misery-alleviating visions that God could have blessed wildly had there been the leadership courage to give them birth?" Bill Hybels, at the 2013 Willow Creek Global Leadership Summit[61]
"Have we exhibited the faithfulness that would attract people to our church? Have we demonstrated a missionary zeal on behalf of others? Have we as a church lost our spiritual, biblical and theological literacy so that we can no longer speak and act in faith with confidence?" Jeffrey Bullock, theological canon of the Episcopal Dioceses of Arizona, on the "larger questions" that churches may need to ask themselves about declining membership[62]
"I have a great fear that a [Western] church in decline, reacting to its decline, will bring us a theology that does not suit a church in springtime." Ajith Fernando, Sri Lankan Bible teacher, on his concern about Western influence on the growing Asian churches[63]
"The world was asking, 'Where was God?' I was asking, 'Where were God's people?' " Gary Haugen, president and CEO of International Justice Mission, reflecting in 2013 on the horrors of the 1994 Rwandan genocide[64]
"Now we focus on raising funds, not raising stewards … In America today, the most prevalent sin among Christians is our materialism and greed. Preachers are afraid to confront it as a core problem and offer the training needed to correct poor stewardship." Jeff Iorg, president of Southern Baptist Convention Golden Gate Seminary, on the need for discipleship in the church[65]

unified budget becomes the base framework on which church members can stand in order to accomplish some of the "greater things" that Jesus promised in John 14:12.

And denominations do have special campaigns, although not commensurate with the potential resources of the entire body of Christ in the U.S. Two of these, The United Methodist Imagine No Malaria five-year campaign, and the ongoing Southern Baptist Lottie Moon Christmas Offering, are discussed below.

When the unified budget becomes the primary concern of national denominational officials, separating the denominational structure from aspirational goals that capture the imaginations of the members, the denomination can move to a regulatory agency model, focusing on tasks including "the development of procedures and policies for adjudicating the distribution of dwindling resources."[70] Denominations could be reduced to functioning largely as trade associations, providing, among other services, pastor referrals, health insurance, and pensions. The regulatory nature of denominations might be evident in the use of the term "taxes" by pastors describing the expected unified budget contribution.[71]

In light of the tension faced by denominations in relationship to their congregations, two articles by syndicated history professor Bruce Kauffman illustrate the difference in how the role of institutions can be implemented.

In an April 2013 column, Kauffmann wrote about Alexis de Tocqueville's 1859 description of despotic government, which, apparently de Tocqueville warned, could develop from a democracy in America as well as from other government systems. Kauffmann quoted de Tocqueville's description of such a despotic government, a description that could apply to any institutional structure, not just secular government.

> After having thus taken each individual one by one into its powerful hands, and having molded him as it pleases, the sovereign power (government) extends its arms over the entire society; it covers the surface of society with a network of small, complicated, minute, and uniform rules, which the most original minds and the most vigorous souls cannot break through to go beyond the crowd; it does not break wills, but it softens them, bends them and directs them; it rarely forces action, but it constantly opposes your acting; it does not destroy, it prevents birth; it does not tyrannize, it hinders, it represses, it enervates, it extinguishes, it stupefies, and finally it reduces each nation to being nothing more than a flock of timid and industrious animals, of which the government is the shepherd.[72]

In contrast, in a January 2008 column, Kauffmann reviewed the creative use of administrative structure by George C. Marshall, U.S. Army chief of staff in the 1940s. Marshall was recommending to President Franklin Delano Roosevelt the generals who would have command of the D-Day invasion of Normandy. He put himself forward, but FDR said "I can't spare him" and so Marshall recommended General Dwight D. Eisenhower. It was Marshall's "genius" to understand "that an army's logistics and support infrastructure—its ability to manufacture equipment and supplies, and transport them to the battlefield—was as crucial to victory as battle-hardened soldiers." After the war, the Marshall Plan reconstruction and economic recovery of Europe "would be the most successful economic assistance program in history, and—fittingly—it earned the man who never received a combat command the Nobel Peace Prize, making him the only professional soldier to be so honored."[73]

Denominations, properly used, can be a support structure through which individual Christians are able to assemble in their congregations in order to engage in the great works that Jesus foresaw for the body of Christ. However, such a scenario requires both the implied risk found in Jesus' promise in Matthew 16:25, that in losing life it

Denominations, properly used, can be a support structure through which individual Christians are able to assemble in their congregations in order to engage in the great works that Jesus foresaw for the body of Christ.

can be found, and also the faith that the promise can apply to institutions comprised of individuals as well as to individuals themselves.

Many people in the United States continue to identify with Christianity, which suggests that the church has great opportunities to explore. For example, a December 2011 Gallup poll found that 76% of Americans identify with the historically Christian religion.[74] However, those opportunities will require new approaches since many in the U.S. are not interested in the church as it presently practices the faith.

Larry Alex Taunton conducted an interview survey through his foundation, Fixed Point Foundation. Talking to students active in atheist, humanist and secular campus organizations, he asked simply, "What led you to become an atheist?" In an article about his survey, Taunton wrote that he was surprised to find that many of the college people interviewed had been in church and left, often during high school: "these students were, above all else, idealists who longed for authenticity, and having failed to find it in their churches, they settled for a non-belief that, while less grand in its promises, felt more genuine and attainable." Taunton went on to quote one of the interviewees: "Christianity is something that if you *really* believed it, it would change your life and you would want to change [the lives] of others. I haven't seen too much of that"[75] [emphasis in the original].

The student's approach-avoidance was reflected by a broader segment of the population in another survey. As noted above, a May 2013 Gallup Poll found that 77% of Americans felt religion was losing influence on American society (the "most negative evaluations of the impact of religion since 1970"). At the same time, 75% of Americans answered "Positive" to the statement, "If more Americans were religious, would that be positive or negative for American society?"[76]

It would have been imminently reasonable that the great spread of affluence in the U.S. after World War II could have resulted in Christians using these resources to increase their efforts to implement God's plan for word and deed witness throughout the world, on a scale that reflected the increasing resources available, and the level of the global need that existed. It did not. Instead, the data points to churches turning inward and emphasizing the needs of current members more than the larger mission of the church.

The remittances analysis in chapter 6 of this volume demonstrates that this level of increased giving is in the realm of possibility. The level of remittances from foreign-born residents in the U.S., largely "immigrants and migrant workers," was, on average, over $2,000 a year per person. Remittances are frequently sent to developing countries in Latin America and the Caribbean, with Mexico receiving over half that amount, as well as Asia and the Pacific, predominantly China, India and the Philippines.[77] Those sending the remittances maintain their own households in the U.S. even while sending this amount to their countries of origin. The amount of over $2,000 compares to less than $100 per native-born church member sent to international ministries. If native-born church members gave on an equivalent scale of over $2,000 per church member, the additional money for overseas ministries would be $385 billion a year.

The fact that those foreign-born residents sending remittances respond to affluence differently than native-born church members have, suggests that the problem is not

The fact that those foreign-born residents sending remittances respond to affluence differently than native-born church members have, suggests that the problem is not ability but desire.

ability but desire. This potential giving increase among church members is irrelevant unless church leadership is more concerned with kingdom of God goals at a scale that can address global needs in Jesus' name, rather than primarily with individual institution sustenance.

At-scale goals would require cross-institutional action as a function of the John 17 oneness for which Jesus prayed.

Instead of manifesting this oneness, the church might be described as resembling the various interest groups in J.R.R. Tolkien's *Lord of the Rings* trilogy. The Shire folk feel it is only necessary to preserve The Shire; the king of Rohan does not see the needs beyond his kingdom as of relevance; the Steward of Gondor feels that as long as Gondor survives, the rest of the world will be all right. What becomes clear throughout the trilogy is that none of these communities will continue unless they also recognize their common purpose.

The steward of Gondor, in fact, resists the returning king, much like tenants in Jesus' parable in Matthew 21:33-44. Although he dutifully sits on the lower step of the throne, never presuming to occupy the role of king, the steward ultimately would rather die than yield his steward role to the rightful heir.

Richard Stearns, president of World Vision U.S., wrote about another parable of Jesus, this one in Matthew 22:1-7. In that parable, Jesus describes a king who invites a variety of people to his son's wedding banquet, only to have the invitations refused. In his quotation of the parable, Richard Stearns adds emphasis to the words in verse 7: "*The king was enraged.*" He summarizes the implications of the parable as follows:

> While these religious leaders did not yet grasp Jesus' true identify, today, two thousand years later, we have no excuse for failing to RSVP. We have the benefit of knowing who Jesus is, that he rose from the dead to forgive our sins and that he has invited us to join him in his great mission to invite people from all nations to the wedding banquet of the King. But even with our greater understanding, we still insult the King, going off instead to pursue our own priorities—our careers, our lifestyles, our social lives, and our happiness—even as the King beckons us. I have no doubt that our King is also enraged ... and heartbroken.[78]

Although these verses are generally applied to individual discipleship, they also apply to church leaders and their institutions. Church leaders at the congregational, regional, and national levels face the difficult task of raising the sights of church members who live in a culture preaching self-indulgence. Deciding that the best that can be expected is to leave the institution in the same shape it was received might be regarded as an acceptable alternative to risking one's career and resisting the pressure to keep the institution secure as the primary goal. However, this shortsighted approach is not the way to foster the longer-term goals of the kingdom of God. Rather, it is succumbing to a perspective that the emergency manager of Detroit used to describe the culture he found in the bankrupt city's employees: IBG-YBG, that is, "I'll be gone and you'll be gone when the reckoning arrives."[79]

That attitude ended in the bankruptcy of Detroit. The church giving and membership trends of the past decades may point to the truth that church leaders need to consider the larger and long-term goals of the structures for which they are responsible. Taking a shorter-term view, limited to the term of office, may not work any better for church structures than it did for Detroit.

Taking a shorter-term view, limited to the term of office, may not work any better for church structures than it did for Detroit.

The idea of a broad multi-denominational campaign to raise the voluntary church member giving to fund work, along coordinated though parallel paths through existing church delivery channels, to address agreed-upon global triage goals at the scale needed to solve, rather than cope with, those needs could be tried as an antidote to declining trends in the church. Instead, the more common practice is to hold conferences and publish books that talk about claims of discipleship.

For example, a cover story in the March 2013 *Christianity Today* featured recent books on "radical" approaches to Christian discipleship.[80] The May 2013 issue of *Christianity Today* contained a letter about the article from Howard Snyder, whose own book, *The Problem of Wineskins*, was widely discussed in the mid-1970s for its evaluation of the church. Howard Snyder's letter read as follows:

> " 'Here Come the Radicals!' was informative but also odd. It talks about a 'radical movement' but gives little evidence any such movement exists. What we have, rather, is another string of hot-selling books critiquing popular Christianity."[81]

That is not to say that what is going on through church institutions is not commendable. It is. The issue is that it is not sufficient.

The SBC LifeWay's Ed Stetzer noted above that the vast majority of global missions through the church are being conducted through "denominational partnerships." Still, the question should be asked whether these efforts are adequate in light of both the potential giving that could be raised for missions, and the need that results in millions of children dying unnecessarily from preventable causes, and millions of people with no opportunity to hear of God's love for them through Jesus Christ. Nothing dictates that this level of need must exist. As Richard Stearns has stated, "The body of Christ in the twenty-first century has everything required to finish the job: the knowledge, the scale, the gifts and skills, the resources, and the mandate ... All we lack is the will."[82] In fact, the job not being finished is the result of the contentment among church leaders that accompanies present levels of activity.

The State of Church Giving through 2010 presented a more detailed discussion of the efforts of the two largest Protestant denominations in the U.S. to pursue identified mission goals.[83] A brief review of these two examples will be included here as a means to consider not the value but the adequacy of the level of current church mission activities in light of the level of the needs and the potential for increased giving.

1. The United Methodist Church set a goal of raising the modest equivalent of $1.97 per member per year, from 2010 through June 2014, for a total of $75 million. The purpose was to apply the funds to eliminate malaria in Africa by 2015. As of December 2012, more than halfway to the goal in terms of the amount of time that had passed, United Methodists had given or pledged $32.9 million.[84] Those numbers mean, with 67% of the timeframe passed, 44% of the goal donations had been received or pledged.

2. A primary purpose of the Southern Baptist Convention since its founding in 1845 has been its global evangelization efforts. The SBC leadership has repeatedly initiated campaigns that would complete the task. However, Tom Elliff, president of the SBC International Mission Board stated at a May 2013 IMB trustees meeting that the number of missionaries the SBC IMB is able to field has dropped. A report of the meeting said, "But the drop isn't for lack of qualified applicants, Elliff said, noting

That is not to say that what is going on through church institutions is not commendable. It is. The issue is that it is not sufficient.

Figure 22: SBC Lottie Moon Christmas Offering, Per Member Giving as a Percent of Income, and U.S. Per Capita Disposable Personal Income, Inflation-Adjusted 2005 Dollars, 1921-2011

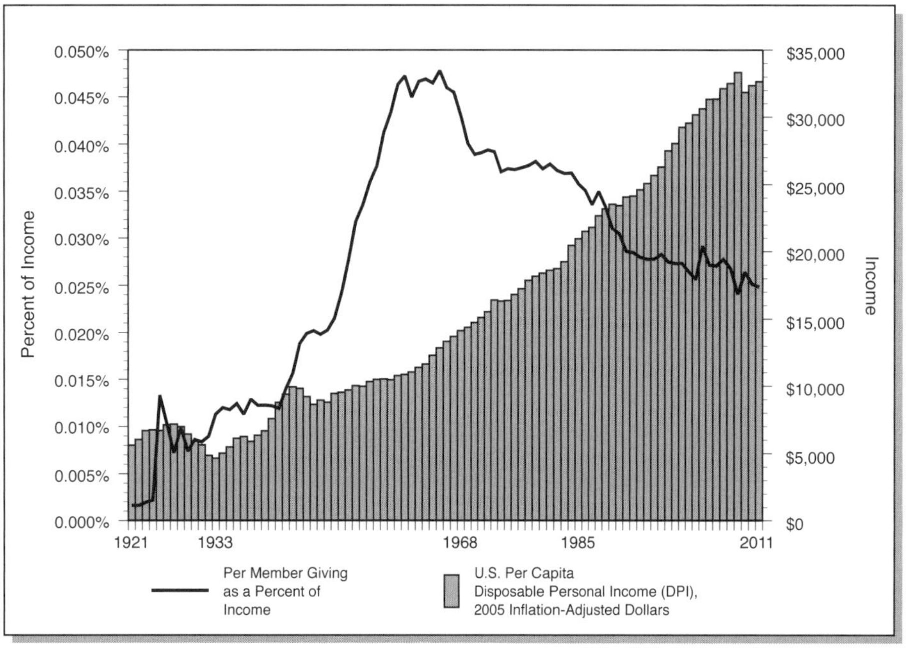

Source: empty tomb analysis; SBC IMB; U.S. BEA   empty tomb, inc., 2013

that many missionary candidates must be put on hold until a position becomes vacant or additional funding is secured." Nor, according to the article on the meeting, is the delay in fielding missionaries due to a lack of feasibility: "Elliff contrasted a time of unprecedented lostness with unprecedented access, resources and manpower willing to combat that lostness ..."[85]

In addition to an allocation of the unified budget called the Cooperative Program in the SBC, a special once-a-year offering, the Lottie Moon Christmas Offering, is a primary source of funds for the SBC IMB's activities. As a portion of income, per member donations to this effort peaked in 1965. By 2011, per member donations to the campaign, measured as a percent of income, were down by 48% from the 1965 base, from 0.048% in 1965, to 0.025% in 2011. This decline occurred even though Americans' incomes had increased 154% in inflation-adjusted dollars from 1965–2011.[86] See Figure 22.

The fact that the leadership of both The United Methodist Church and the Southern Baptist Convention set goals is commendable. However, neither goal is commensurate with the resources available to church members, nor with the global triagic need. Neither approach takes seriously the prayer of Jesus that believers would be one by mobilizing beyond their own traditions. These two denominations, or any of the others, could provide the type of leadership that could begin a movement at a scale that could be labeled "greater works" of the kingdom of God.

One fear that may be present at all levels of the church is that there will not be enough money to maintain the institutions while pursuing the larger goals. In a multi-denominational survey, at the congregational level, 60% of pastors surveyed agreed or strongly agreed with the statement: "To some extent, pastors perceive denominationally-affiliated entities as competitors for the congregation members' money." Interestingly, 89% of the regional and 85% of the national denominational representatives agreed with the statement.[87]

Within this framework, institutions can become silos that insulate leaders from each other, even within the same denomination. These fortresses begin to appear as territories to be protected that prevent progress toward the larger common goal. It is possible for a tool, as creative and as helpful as the unified budget, to become a fortress to be protected at all costs, rather than an enabling platform that allows church members to participate in the glorious task of continuing the great works of Jesus as the body of Christ.

The consequence of these defenses is reductionism. With the primary goal the sustenance of the structure, the potential to do all that God has designed for the church is ignored. Jesus' prayer that all those who believe will be one so that the world will believe that the Father sent Jesus is ignored.

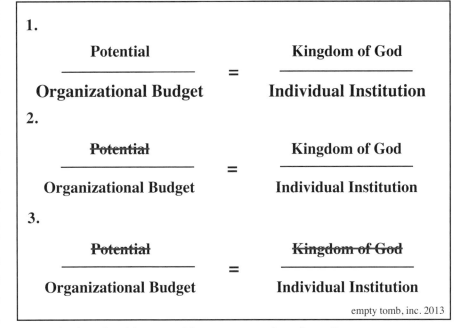

Figure 23: Three Steps of Reductionism in the Purpose of the Church

empty tomb, inc. 2013

The need for congregation members to be involved in something great as a function of their faith is ignored. And those who have no access to the Bible, or who are watching their young children die from what should be preventable causes are ignored.

Figure 23 provides an illustration of the reductionism that too often takes place in the church.

Initially, the organizational budget is the base, and potential giving could be tapped through special campaigns. The plan would be for the individual institution both to keep basic operations going, and also to carry out efforts to accomplish larger kingdom of God goals.

In fact, the potential of increased giving through special campaigns for kingdom of God goals is ignored out of fear that it will compete with efforts to secure the basic organizational budget. At this point, the individual institution continues to declare the kingdom of God goals in theory, while operating on the base organizational budget that is now the primary priority.

Inevitably, reducing the primary financial goal to funding the organizational budget, ignoring the potential for increased giving that could be recruited for at-scale missional purposes, stresses the individual institution's ability to function, while its vision is reduced to maintaining operations, with the proclamation of the kingdom of God goals sounding increasingly like empty rhetoric.

In summary, when the potential for increased giving for missions goals at a scale designed to meet those global mission needs is ignored, the organizational budget of the individual institution becomes the priority, and the kingdom of God goals fade in importance.

In the presence of this reductionism, wealthy donors have not seen religion as an important recipient of their extraordinary giving. Of the largest twelve gifts or pledges in 2011, ranging in size from $60 million to $498.8 million, not one was donated to a religious cause.[88] Of course, Religion remains the largest single recipient category of donations by any measure. However, it may be a comment about the size of the church's vision that wealthy donors are not attracted enough to help fund the plans outlined by the church.

Instead, the vagueness of an Illinois ethics law may seem uncomfortably similar to the way denominational mission efforts are defined. A newspaper editorial criticized the government ethics law that provided the illusion of oversight when none exists. The law does not clearly define what is meant by ethical violations, provides no penalties if a violation is determined to be present, and prohibits public disclosure: "That pretty much constitutes the hat trick of non-enforcement—no specificity for what constitutes wrongdoing, no penalties and no publicity."[89]

Denominational missions funded through unified budgets, and denominational missions funded through special campaigns, which to this point in time have not been at a scale commensurate with either the needs or the potential resources, may both be treated in a similar way. Rather than serving as a base to give church members a significant task to do, while meeting needs that devastate global neighbors, "On an unconscious (or conscious) level, overseas missions might be regarded in the same way as a trained animal, kept in a cage and trotted out at convenient times. Animals, such as elephants, often also provide practical services in the setup and breakdown of a circus, for example, but the animal is given limited freedom to function."[90]

Even as church leaders reduce their vision to maintain their institutions, they may be blinded to the path that could lead to strengthening their structures.

Jonathan Haidt, a moral psychologist, observed that, "Believing, doing, and belonging are three complementary yet distinct aspects of religiosity, according to many scholars." He proposes a model of religion that "says that the function of those beliefs and practices is ultimately to create a community."[91]

Sociologist Rodney Stark asked and answered a question that is most relevant to the present discussion: "How do religions 'revitalize'? Primarily by effectively mobilizing people to attempt collective action."[92]

To date, in general, church leaders have not, as a group across denominational platforms, identified basic clear kingdom of God goals, which include timeframes, to address global triage needs around which all Christians could organize in a parallel fashion through their own, unique denominational structures. Such an approach would provide a very broad common purpose while maximizing each denomination's unique place in the body of Christ. For example, although there has been discussion about engaging unreached people groups, there has been no general agreement, even among a subset of denominations, to accomplish the task in a given timeframe using a specified amount of needed dollars that would allow individual denominations to pursue the goal in a parallel and yet coordinated fashion alongside, although not necessarily formally linked to, their counterparts. The exception of Wycliffe Bible Translators, and the more recent plans of the Issachar Initiative, are discussed below. On the suffering side of global need, although world leaders, in the year 1990, and again in the year 2000, set a goal to reduce the number of global under-age-five child deaths to specified measurable levels, within a specified timeframe, church leaders have not presented members with the goal, and the related amount of needed giving.

> "How do religions 'revitalize'? Primarily by effectively mobilizing people to attempt collective action."
> —Rodney Stark

Yet if Haidt and Stark are correct, organizing for such basic goals may be a key element of a healthy church.

Courage is needed to follow through on God's visions. "Every significant vision that God births in you is going to put your courage to the test—you can count on this," said Bill Hybels at the 2013 Willow Creek Global Leadership Summit.[93]

Choosing to act as the body of Christ, which necessarily includes a broad mix of Christians, to pursue a basic set of priorities as a function of God's agenda, would indeed take courage on the part of leaders.

Global Triage Needs

A prescription for what ails the church may be developing a common goal to meet two significant global triage needs. If there is to be any mobilization of church members in what Rodney Stark terms "collective action," church leaders will be key to such mobilization. As one pastor observed, "A pastor cannot do anything single-handedly in a congregation, but a pastor can stop anything single-handedly in a congregation."[94] Just as likely, a pastor will not be emboldened to take the risks attendant with mobilization efforts without strong backing from those in the denominational structure.

Mobilization could result from church leaders giving people something significant to do, other than live for themselves. Whole industries exist to provide ways for the great resources in this culture to absorb people's focus and energy as they seek to satisfy themselves. If the church is not providing a vital alternative, the church loses the hearts and minds of church members by default. As a result, church members suffer. Consider the comments from one returned soldier. He described the tasks on the battlefront in contrast to life after deployment:

> Just on a functional level of going from an experience where you knew exactly what you had to do … And it may be the most difficult thing you ever had to do in your life, but you knew what you were supposed to do. And then coming home, [you have] essentially no direction. I think 'rudderless' is probably an appropriate way of describing it. You see the world; you see all these directions that you could go. How do you possibly begin to decide? Particularly if you're feeling emotionally numbed.[95]

A comment from two missionaries returning to the U.S. sounded similar: "Everything there was black and white. Here everything seems gray."[96]

The spiritual battle that the apostle Paul described in Ephesians 6 is being waged no less in the U.S. than in other countries. However, as Juvenal remarked as he watched the decline of the Roman Empire, "Luxury is more deadly than war, broods over the city, and avenges a conquered world."[97] The responsibility to provide meaning for church members who are otherwise trapped in the throes of the most affluent culture in history sits squarely on the shoulders of church leaders.

The key question is how to change patterns that have developed slowly over time, to go beyond rhetoric that merely flavors business as usual. Here is a more specific question: How can church leaders organize with other leaders in the denominational structures and other Christian organizations, and then in 300,000 congregations that represent the largest identity group in the U.S.?

"Luxury is more deadly than war, broods over the city, and avenges a conquered world."
—Juvenal, watching the decline of the Roman Empire

The solution to obeying the "enraged" and "heartbroken" king, as described by Richard Stearns, is to identify one or two core issues that grow out of the common confession of the Christian faith, and then mobilize church members to address those needs at a scale commensurate with our resources (knowledge, ability, and money) and with the needs.

After describing the strategic advantages the church has for helping to impact global need, Scott Todd wrote, "The ultimate reason why the Church is critical to the work of ending poverty is the promise of Jesus." Noting that Jesus did not choose to work through government or create a business, Todd states, "Instead he established the Church and promised that 'the gates of hell shall not prevail against it' (Matthew 16:18, KJV) ... No other organization was founded by Christ or carries the promise of victory against the forces of hell."[98]

Jesus Christ promised that nothing is impossible with God (Matt. 17:20; and Matt. 19:26, Mark 10:27, and Luke 18:27). Walter Brueggemann went so far as to extend that idea even to church member giving: "Sharing our abundance may, as Jesus says, be impossible for mortals, but nothing is impossible for God."[99]

Once leaders agree that the time is ripe for mobilizing church members for common goals identified as core Biblical needs, the specific goals need to be identified. Here it might be helpful to reflect on comments from jazz great Dave Brubeck, who died in December 2012. In an article reviewing his career, Dave Brubeck was quoted from a 2005 interview: "Jazz is about freedom within discipline ... Many people don't understand how disciplined you have to be to play jazz ... You don't just get out there and do anything you want."[100]

That combination of freedom within discipline produces great jazz, as one soloist after another brings individual insight to a common theme. It can produce a seamless and visually spontaneous dance display in *Swing Time* by Fred Astaire and Ginger Rogers produced from over 40 takes that left Ginger Rogers' feet bleeding.[101] And the individual strengths of the various denominational structures can work in parallel paths in joyful obedience in pursuit of achieving a work of the kingdom of God, at a scale that matches both what it takes to address the need and at the level of available resources, by inspiring individual churches to work through their own delivery channels, each bringing their unique gifts to achieve a common purpose. Although Christians are free to choose to go in any direction to pursue their calling, they can also recognize the power that results from the voluntary oneness that Jesus prayed for on their behalf.

In a previous edition in *The State of Church Giving* series, two key global triage issues were identified as (1) engaging the unengaged, unreached people groups with a presentation of the gospel of Jesus Christ, and (2) the reduction of global child deaths.[102] Therefore, only a brief review will be offered here.

The topic of engaging the unengaged unreached people groups is a direct response to the command that Jesus gave to the disciples in Matthew 28:18-20. Often referred to as the Great Commission, the direction is to go into the whole world, making disciples and teaching those disciples to obey Jesus' commands. The idea that every group of people should have enough information, in order to decide about the claims of Jesus Christ, is commonly agreed upon by most Christians, in theory. However, after 2,000 years, that task has yet to be completed. Therefore, providing a practical way for all Christians to act on this goal is to help those Christians be faithful to one of the most elemental mandates of the faith.

With regard to the second global triage goal, it may be observed that not only have churches not mobilized around a common goal as a manifestation of the body of Christ on earth, but they have also encouraged many, many priorities with little distinction made among them. For example, one denomination in the early 1990s held a convocation to identify the mission priorities of that communion. The result was a 256-page document summarizing the priorities in 143 reports, each from a separate subgroup.[103] Given this experience, it would not be surprising if there were many different priorities clamoring for congregations' and denominations' attention.

However, the goal here is to identify a basic priority that is large enough to call for participation by the vast majority of all church members, and that all church members can embrace *in addition to* the broad range of ongoing priorities currently being pursued. Reducing global child deaths seems to meet that need for a number of reasons.

First, Jesus asked the blind men, "What do you want me to do for you?" (Matt. 20:32). As Christ's body we continue the works that God has prepared: "For we are his handiwork, created in Christ Jesus for the good works that God has prepared in advance, that we should live in them" (Eph. 2:10, NAB). As Jesus asked the blind men, the church can ask the world, "What do you want us as Christ's body to do for you?"

> As Jesus asked the blind men, the church can ask the world, "What do you want us as Christ's body to do for you?"

And the world has already announced its priority: Reduce child deaths (Millennium Development Goal [MDG] 4). This goal first became a priority when "71 heads of State and Government — presidents, prime ministers, royal personages" as well as "senior representatives of 88 other countries" convened in 1990, the largest such gathering to that point in time.[104] Out of that summit came 10 priorities to further child survival during 1990–2000. The first priority listed read: "A one-third reduction in 1990 under-five death rates (or to 70 per 1,000 live births, whichever is less)." The other goals supported that priority.[105] That effort failed to meet its goal. World leaders then reconvened in 2000 and came up with eight MDGs. Reducing child deaths was now number 4 of eight goals focused on a number of development needs,[106] rather than the top priority as it had been from 1990–2000.

A UNICEF report stated that, as of 2012, the world has made progress on reducing the rate of global child deaths. The report went on, "However, this progress has not been enough, and the target risks being missed at the global level."[107]

In a foreword to The Millennium Development Goals Report 2013, United Nations General Secretary Ban Ki-moon wrote, "We are now less than 1,000 days to the 2015 target date for achieving the MDGs ... Through accelerated action, the world can achieve the MDGs and generate momentum for an ambitious and inspiring post-2015 development framework. Now is the time to step up our efforts to build a more just, secure and sustainable future for all."[108]

In a radio interview, Mr. Ban stated, "We must intensify our efforts, particularly to tackle the disparities across regions and between different social groups. Greater progress toward the MDGs will fuel confidence and mobilize support for an ambitious post-2015 development agenda. And our post-2015 efforts should build on the work begun and the lessons learned through the MDGs."[109]

Thus, the issue of reducing child deaths is a key stated need of the world as represented by global leaders, with a clear statement that additional intervention is needed immediately.

There is already support among Christians for increased initiative in the area of addressing global poverty, and more specifically reducing child deaths. A press release about a 2011 study by The Barna Group for Compassion International found that 93% of church-attending Christians "say they are concerned about global poverty." Further, "45% of younger Christians believe their churches should be more involved in helping the poor, compared to 23% of older Christians, and 37% said they would donate more to their church if their church increased its involvement."[110]

In 2001, empty tomb, inc. conducted a survey of national denominational leaders, asking them to respond to one statement: "Church members in the United States should increase giving through their churches in an effort to stop the millions of annual preventable global child deaths in Jesus' name." The questionnaire was sent to 453 national leaders in 198 denominations. Of these, 105 of the leaders, or 24%, returned the form. These leaders represented 81 denominations. A total of 83 of the leaders in 66 of the denominations, that is, 79%, chose "Yes" to affirm the statement. Those affirming the statement were from African American, Anabaptist, Baptist, Evangelical, Fundamental, Mainline Protestant, Orthodox, Other Catholic, Pentecostal, and Roman Catholic communions.[111]

To date, that survey has remained at the "in principle" level. In order to achieve the goal of reducing child deaths, Christians can be encouraged to increase their financial support through their own church delivery channels. These delivery channels are already delivering some of the most effective services to those in need globally. Each denomination could use the increased donations received from church members to expand the amount of services delivered through their networks already in place.

To succeed in communicating one goal across the broad combination of traditions that make up the historically Christian church in the U.S., the task is to define the issue in its most basic terms. *The State of the World's Children* series provides a useful perspective at this point: "The under-five mortality rate (U5MR) is used as the principal indicator of progress in child well-being ... U5MR has several advantages as a gauge of child well-being: First, U5MR measures an end result of the development process rather than an 'input' such as school enrollment level, per capita calorie availability or number of doctors per thousand population—all of which are means to an end."[112]

In 2003, *The Lancet* medical journal published an article titled "How Many Child Deaths Can We Prevent This Year?" The authors represented UNICEF, the Centers for Disease Control and Prevention, and Johns Hopkins Bloomberg School of Public Health, among other institutions. The paper concluded that as many as 63% of the under-five child deaths could be prevented by health interventions such as insecticide-treated materials, providing zinc and Vitamin A, and vaccines, as well as antibiotics for pneumonia and measles. Educating mothers about the simple intervention of oral rehydration therapy, a mixture of salt, sugar and clean water, administered to children with diarrhea, could prevent as many as 15% of all deaths.[113] Table 47 outlines the causes of death by country.

Thus, the issue of reducing child deaths is a key stated need of the world as represented by global leaders, with a clear statement that additional intervention is needed immediately.

Another metric was described by Melinda French Gates of the Gates Foundation. In a September 2010 presentation, she stated that in her travels to the most remote areas of the world, she always found Coca-Cola to be available. She then listed the strategies that Coke used to reach these areas, and applied them to efforts to improve the living conditions of desperately poor people. One key strategy of Coke, she noted, was "aspirational" marketing. The company researches what makes people happy in a culture, and then pitches their product to that value. For example, in Latin America "happiness is associated with family life" while in South Africa it is "community respect." Melinda Gates ended her presentation by saying that if Coke marketers ever asked her to define happiness, "I'd say my vision of happiness is a mother holding a healthy baby in her arms. To me, that is deep happiness … that happiness can be just as ubiquitous as Coca Cola."[114]

Church members of all ages who sing, "Jesus loves the little children, all the children of the world," probably could embrace an effort to reduce, in Jesus' name, global child deaths, if church leaders were to make such a special campaign a top priority. The denominations could deliver the specific health interventions to reduce the impact of the causes of death in Table 47 in a parallel way, coordinated with many denominations and Christian organizations working through their own delivery channels. What the common goal would accomplish is to marshal the resources of the church in the U.S. in a way designed to impact the critical need to reduce global child deaths at a level that will also need participation from many Christians, who can have the expectation that they are making a significant difference by donating a relatively small amount of money.

It should be emphasized that this common goal, designed to increase mission participation on the part of more Christians and church members who are presently involved to only a limited degree, is in addition to current activities. Leaders would need to emphasize the value of expanding the mission involvement of church members contributing through their delivery channels and not, as is too often the case, merely refocus attention from one need to another. Thus, important issues such as ending human trafficking, or increasing literacy, should in no way be reduced by the pursuit of a common-goal effort.

> It should be emphasized that this common goal, designed to increase mission participation on the part of more Christians … is in addition to current activities.

However, the reduction of child deaths is a primary life-and-death issue. Expanding quality of life concerns will definitely need to be continued and addressed afresh once it is established that there will, in fact, be life at all for these children. The critical nature of the Under-5 Mortality Rate reduction effort can be seen in Figure 24. The difference that can be made with simple interventions is shown in the two photos of this young child, the second taken only 11 days after the first. The chart in the figure contrasts the MDG 4 progress targets with the actual progress figures. As indicated in Figure 24,[115] although the goal for 2011 was an estimated reduction to 35 under-5 child deaths per 1,000 live births, the actual 2011 number was 51, well behind the goal.

Based on *The State of Church Giving through 2011* analysis, if all were on track, the world ought to be 90% towards the goal of achieving MDG 4, with 10% farther to go by 2015. Instead, this analysis of *The State of the World's Children* series data found that the world was, on average, about 62% toward meeting the MDG 4 target, leaving 38% of the goal to be achieved before 2015.[116]

Because of this lack of progress since 1990, an estimated 2,226,982 children under the age of five died in 2011, children who would not have died if the world had kept its promises to help them.

As indicated in Figure 24, if the rate evident in the 2011 reported data continues at its present pace, in 2014 there will be mothers and fathers helplessly watching an estimated 2,297,991 children under the age of five die from preventable causes. These parents would not have to grieve the loss of their children if world leaders

Figure 24: Exponential Interpolation of MDG 4 Under-5 Child Deaths Per 1,000 Live Births, Based on Reported 1990 Data and 2015 Goal; Reported Data, 1995, 2000, 2005, 2010, and 2011; Projected 2014 Data

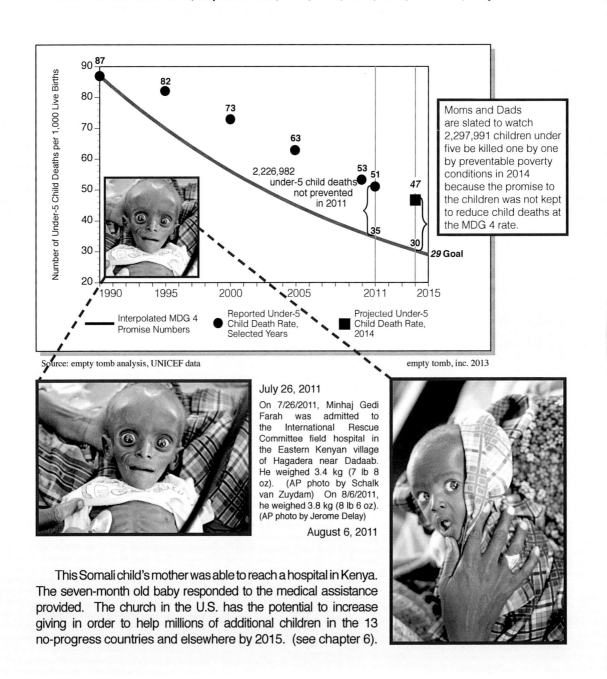

Source: empty tomb analysis, UNICEF data   empty tomb, inc. 2013

July 26, 2011

On 7/26/2011, Minhaj Gedi Farah was admitted to the International Rescue Committee field hospital in the Eastern Kenyan village of Hagadera near Dadaab. He weighed 3.4 kg (7 lb 8 oz). (AP photo by Schalk van Zuydam) On 8/6/2011, he weighed 3.8 kg (8 lb 6 oz). (AP photo by Jerome Delay)

August 6, 2011

This Somali child's mother was able to reach a hospital in Kenya. The seven-month old baby responded to the medical assistance provided. The church in the U.S. has the potential to increase giving in order to help millions of additional children in the 13 no-progress countries and elsewhere by 2015. (see chapter 6).

kept their promise to the children to reduce child deaths at a rate that would achieve the goal by 2015, as indicated in Figure 24.

It may be of interest that many of the child deaths occur in countries in which people also identify themselves as Christians. Table 46 provides an overview of 13 countries making "no progress" on reducing the rate of child deaths. It is notable that nine of these countries have populations with a large percent of Christians.

Table 46: Thirteen Countries Making "No Progress" in Reducing Under-5 Child Deaths, Number of Under-5 Child Deaths, 2010; Country Population, 2010; Christian Percent of Country, Mid-2000; and Four Christian Traditions Affiliated Adherents Percent of Country, Mid-2000

Country	Number of Under-5 Child Deaths, 2010	Population 2010	Christian Percent of Country, Mid-2000	Four Christian Traditions, Affiliated Adherents Percent of Country, Mid-2000			
				Roman Catholic	Protestant	Anglican	Orthodox
Burkina Faso	120,000	16,469,000					
Cameroon	93,000	19,599,000	54.2%	26.5%	20.7%		
Central African Republic	23,000	4,401,000	67.8%	18.4%	14.4%		
Chad	80,000	11,227,000					
Democratic Republic of the Congo	465,000	65,966,000	95.4%	50.9%	20.3%	0.9%	
Haiti	45,000	9,993,000	95.8%	79.3%	17.5%	1.3%	
Kenya	122,000	40,513,000	79.3%	23.3%	21.2%	10.0%	2.5%
Lesotho	5,000	2,171,000	91.0%	37.5%	13.0%	4.7%	
Mauritania	13,000	3,460,000					
Sao Tome and Principe	80	165,000	95.8%	75.3%	3.7%		
Somalia	70,000	9,331,000					
South Africa	58,000	50,133,000	83.1%	8.3%	30.7%	6.6%	0.4%
Zimbabwe	29,000	12,571,000	67.5%	9.60%	12.3%	2.7%	0.1%
Total Under-5 Child Deaths	1,123,000						

Note: The *World Christian Encyclopedia* Christian Percent of Country figure shown reflects additional traditions present in the country and may include an adjustment for "doubly-affiliated."   empty tomb, inc., 2012
Source: empty tomb analysis; *The State of the World's Children, 2010*; *Countdown to 2015 Decade Report (2000–2010)*; *World Christian Encyclopedia* (2001)

The church has a great advantage in the amount of information that has been made available on the causes of child deaths. Tables 47 through 48 develop a mathematical model to estimate the cost to address various causes of death impacting children around the globe.

In Table 47, a summed dollar figure for all Neonatal causes is presented.

Table 48 presents the Neonatal detail.

The results presented in Tables 47 and 48 provide dollar-cost estimates for the causes of under-5 deaths in each of the 74 countries included in the tables.[117] The rows presenting data for the 13 no-progress countries are in bold-italics. The model suggests the type of information that can be developed to foster initiatives to eliminate conditions that result in needless child deaths.

Two valuable sources of information served as the basis of the analysis. The United Nations Children's Fund (UNICEF) 2012 edition of the annual *State of the World's Children* report with data for 2010 provided detailed information on "Basic Indicators," including the number of under-5 child deaths by country.[118]

Table 47: Country-Specific Dollar-Cost Estimates for Causes of Under-5 Child Deaths, 74 Countries, with 13 No-Progress Countries Highlighted, 2010

	Nation	Under-5 Mortality Rank	Annual no. of Under-5 Deaths (000s) 2010	Country Total as % of Total Annual No. of Under-5 Deaths (000s) 2010	Country Total$ Need, Based on $5 Billion Total Estimate
	Africa: 46 Nations		3,766	52%	$2,589,338,503
1	Angola	8	121	1.66%	$83,185,524
2	Benin	20	39	0.54%	26,811,863
3	Botswana	61	2	0.03%	1,374,967
4	*Burkina Faso*	*3*	*120*	*1.65%*	*82,498,041*
5	Burundi	14	38	0.52%	26,124,380
6	*Cameroon*	*15*	*93*	*1.28%*	*63,935,982*
7	*Central African Republic*	*9*	*23*	*0.32%*	*15,812,124*
8	*Chad*	*5*	*80*	*1.10%*	*54,998,694*
9	Comoros	34	2	0.03%	1,374,967
10	Congo	29	13	0.18%	8,937,288
11	Côte d'Ivoire	18	80	1.10%	54,998,694
12	*Democratic Republic of the Congo*	*6*	*465*	*6.39%*	*319,679,908*
13	Djibouti	31	2	0.03%	1,374,967
14	Egypt	91	41	0.56%	28,186,831
15	Equatorial Guinea	19	3	0.04%	2,062,451
16	Eritrea	49	11	0.15%	7,562,320
17	Ethiopia	23	271	3.73%	186,308,075
18	Gabon	43	3	0.04%	2,062,451
19	Gambia	28	6	0.08%	4,124,902
20	Ghana	43	57	0.78%	39,186,569
21	Guinea	17	48	0.66%	32,999,216
22	Guinea-Bissau	10	8	0.11%	5,499,869
23	*Kenya*	*35*	*122*	*1.68%*	*83,873,008*
24	*Lesotho*	*35*	*5*	*0.07%*	*3,437,418*
25	Liberia	24	15	0.21%	10,312,255
26	Madagascar	48	44	0.60%	30,249,282
27	Malawi	30	56	0.77%	38,499,086
28	Mali	2	120	1.65%	82,498,041
29	*Mauritania*	*21*	*13*	*0.18%*	*8,937,288*
30	Morocco	69	23	0.32%	15,812,124
31	Mozambique	16	114	1.57%	78,373,139
32	Niger	12	100	1.37%	68,748,367
33	Nigeria	12	861	11.84%	591,923,442
34	Rwanda	31	38	0.52%	26,124,380
35	*Sao Tome and Principe*	*37*	*0.4*	*0.01%*	*274,993*
36	Senegal	42	34	0.47%	23,374,445
37	Sierra Leone	4	39	0.54%	26,811,863
38	*Somalia*	*1*	*70*	*0.96%*	*48,123,857*
39	*South Africa*	*51*	*58*	*0.80%*	*39,874,053*
40	Sudan and South Sudan	24	143	1.97%	98,310,165
41	Swaziland	39	3	0.04%	2,062,451
42	Togo	24	19	0.26%	13,062,190
43	Uganda	27	141	1.94%	96,935,198
44	United Republic of Tanzania	41	133	1.83%	91,435,328
45	Zambia	21	60	0.82%	41,249,020
46	*Zimbabwe*	*37*	*29*	*0.40%*	*19,937,026*

Details in table may not compute to numbers shown due to rounding.

empty tomb, inc., 2012

Sources: empty tomb analysis, UNICEF data

	Pneumonia	Diarrhoea	Measles	Meningitis	Injuries	Malaria	HIV/AIDS	Other	Neonatal (Total)
Africa	$359,874,328	$284,421,620	$26,120,255	$60,590,686	$117,092,219	$372,606,526	$101,060,100	$478,463,886	$790,765,719
1	$12,477,829	$12,477,829	$0	$2,495,566	$3,327,421	$8,318,552	$1,663,710	$20,796,381	$22,460,092
2	3,217,424	2,681,186	0	268,119	804,356	6,166,729	268,119	5,630,491	7,507,322
3	151,246	82,498	0	13,750	54,999	0	206,245	302,493	549,987
4	*10,724,745*	*9,899,765*	*2,474,941*	*1,649,961*	*2,474,941*	*19,799,530*	*824,980*	*17,324,589*	*18,149,569*
5	4,441,145	3,657,413	0	783,731	1,306,219	1,044,975	1,567,463	5,224,876	8,098,558
6	*8,311,678*	*8,311,678*	*0*	*1,278,720*	*1,918,079*	*10,229,757*	*3,196,799*	*14,065,916*	*16,623,355*
7	*2,055,576*	*1,581,212*	*0*	*316,242*	*474,364*	*4,111,152*	*474,364*	*2,371,819*	*4,427,395*
8	*8,799,791*	*7,699,817*	*0*	*1,649,961*	*1,649,961*	*10,999,739*	*1,649,961*	*8,249,804*	*14,299,660*
9	164,996	109,997	0	13,750	54,999	192,495	0	302,493	536,237
10	714,983	625,610	0	89,373	268,119	2,323,695	446,864	1,608,712	2,859,932
11	5,499,869	4,399,896	0	549,987	1,649,961	13,749,673	1,649,961	8,249,804	18,699,556
12	*44,755,187*	*38,361,589*	*0*	*3,196,799*	*9,590,397*	*57,542,383*	*3,196,799*	*70,329,580*	*92,707,173*
13	164,996	137,497	13,750	13,750	54,999	13,750	54,999	384,991	536,237
14	2,818,683	1,973,078	0	281,868	563,737	0	0	10,147,259	12,402,205
15	206,245	123,747	0	20,625	41,249	433,115	164,996	412,490	659,984
16	1,361,218	831,855	151,246	302,493	604,986	75,623	151,246	1,739,334	2,344,319
17	33,535,454	24,220,050	7,452,323	11,178,485	11,178,485	3,726,162	3,726,162	31,672,373	61,481,665
18	164,996	123,747	61,874	20,625	61,874	309,368	164,996	391,866	742,482
19	453,739	371,241	0	82,498	123,747	824,980	123,747	742,482	1,402,467
20	3,918,657	2,743,060	391,866	783,731	1,567,463	7,053,582	1,175,597	7,053,582	14,890,896
21	3,959,906	2,969,929	0	659,984	989,976	8,909,788	329,992	4,949,882	10,229,757
22	769,982	659,984	0	109,997	164,996	989,976	164,996	1,044,975	1,539,963
23	*12,580,951*	*7,548,571*	*0*	*1,677,460*	*4,193,650*	*2,516,190*	*5,871,111*	*20,129,522*	*29,355,553*
24	*378,116*	*240,619*	*34,374*	*34,374*	*137,497*	*0*	*618,735*	*584,361*	*1,443,716*
25	1,237,471	824,980	1,031,226	206,245	309,368	1,856,206	206,245	1,546,838	3,196,799
26	4,839,885	3,024,928	302,493	604,986	2,117,450	1,814,957	0	6,352,349	11,192,234
27	4,234,899	2,694,936	769,982	769,982	1,539,963	5,004,881	5,004,881	6,544,845	11,934,717
28	11,549,726	11,549,726	2,474,941	1,649,961	2,474,941	13,199,687	0	16,499,608	22,274,471
29	*1,161,847*	*893,729*	*625,610*	*178,746*	*357,492*	*536,237*	*0*	*1,966,203*	*3,038,678*
30	1,581,212	948,727	0	158,121	948,727	0	0	3,636,789	8,380,426
31	8,621,045	7,053,582	783,731	783,731	2,351,194	14,890,896	7,837,314	11,755,971	23,511,942
32	12,374,706	9,624,771	0	2,062,451	2,749,935	10,312,255	687,484	13,749,673	16,499,608
33	82,869,282	65,111,579	5,919,234	17,757,703	17,757,703	118,384,688	23,676,938	88,788,516	171,657,798
34	4,441,145	3,134,926	0	522,488	1,567,463	522,488	522,488	6,531,095	8,882,289
35	*38,499*	*30,249*	*2,750*	*2,750*	*13,750*	*11,000*	*0*	*85,248*	*90,748*
36	2,804,933	1,869,956	467,489	467,489	934,978	3,272,422	233,744	4,441,145	8,648,545
37	3,753,661	3,217,424	0	536,237	804,356	6,166,729	268,119	5,094,254	6,971,084
38	*9,143,533*	*7,218,579*	*0*	*1,924,954*	*1,443,716*	*3,368,670*	*481,239*	*8,662,294*	*16,843,350*
39	*3,588,665*	*1,993,703*	*398,741*	*398,741*	*1,594,962*	*0*	*11,164,735*	*8,373,551*	*12,759,697*
40	9,831,017	9,831,017	0	0	24,577,541	1,966,203	2,949,305	12,780,321	37,357,863
41	268,119	144,372	0	41,249	103,123	0	474,364	453,739	598,111
42	1,567,463	1,306,219	0	261,244	522,488	2,351,194	391,866	2,612,438	4,179,901
43	15,509,632	9,693,520	0	1,938,704	4,846,760	12,601,576	6,785,464	18,417,688	27,141,855
44	11,886,593	7,314,826	914,353	1,828,707	4,571,766	10,057,886	4,571,766	16,458,359	32,916,718
45	4,949,882	3,712,412	1,649,961	824,980	1,649,961	5,362,373	4,124,902	7,012,333	11,962,216
46	*1,993,703*	*1,395,592*	*199,370*	*199,370*	*598,111*	*1,594,962*	*3,987,405*	*2,990,554*	*6,778,589*

Details in table may not compute to numbers shown due to rounding.

Sources: empty tomb analysis, UNICEF data

empty tomb, inc., 2012

Table 47: Country-Specific Dollar-Cost Estimates for Causes of Under-5 Child Deaths, 74 Countries, with 13 No-Progress Countries Highlighted, 2010 (continued)

Nation		Under-5 Mortality Rank	Annual no. of Under-5 Deaths (000s) 2010	Country Total as % of Total Annual No. of Under-5 Deaths (000s) 2010	Country Total$ Need, Based on $5 Billion Total Estimate
Asia: 20 Nations			3,318	46%	$2,281,070,825
1	Afghanistan	11	191	2.63%	$131,309,381
2	Azerbaijan	63	9	0.12%	6,187,353
3	Bangladesh	61	140	1.92%	96,247,714
4	Cambodia	58	16	0.22%	10,999,739
5	China	108	315	4.33%	216,557,357
6	Democratic People's Rep. of Korea	73	12	0.16%	8,249,804
7	India	46	1,696	23.32%	1,165,972,308
8	Indonesia	72	151	2.08%	103,810,035
9	Iraq	67	43	0.59%	29,561,798
10	Kyrgyzstan	68	5	0.07%	3,437,418
11	Lao People's Democratic Republic	55	8	0.11%	5,499,869
12	Myanmar	45	56	0.77%	38,499,086
13	Nepal	59	35	0.48%	24,061,929
14	Pakistan	33	423	5.82%	290,805,593
15	Philippines	80	66	0.91%	45,373,922
16	Tajikistan	46	12	0.16%	8,249,804
17	Turkmenistan	52	6	0.08%	4,124,902
18	Uzbekistan	57	31	0.43%	21,311,994
19	Viet Nam	90	34	0.47%	23,374,445
20	Yemen	40	69	0.95%	47,436,373

Nation		Under-5 Mortality Rank	Annual no. of Under-5 Deaths (000s) 2010	Country Total as % of Total Annual No. of Under-5 Deaths (000s) 2010	Country Total$ Need, Based on $5 Billion Total Estimate
Latin America/Caribbean: 6 Nations			176	2%	$120,997,126
1	Bolivia (Plurinational State of)	55	14	0.19%	$9,624,771
2	Brazil	103	55	0.76%	37,811,602
3	Guatemala	76	14	0.19%	9,624,771
4	*Haiti*	*7*	*45*	*0.62%*	*30,936,765*
5	Mexico	113	37	0.51%	25,436,896
6	Peru	103	11	0.15%	7,562,320

Nation		Under-5 Mortality Rank	Annual no. of Under-5 Deaths (000s) 2010	Country Total as % of Total Annual No. of Under-5 Deaths (000s) 2010	Country Total$ Need, Based on $5 Billion Total Estimate
Oceania: 2 Nations			13	0.20%	$8,593,546
1	Papua New Guinea	49	12	0.16%	$8,249,804
2	Solomon Islands	81	0.5	0.01%	$343,742

Nation		Under-5 Mortality Rank	Annual no. of Under-5 Deaths (000s) 2010	Country Total as % of Total Annual No. of Under-5 Deaths (000s) 2010	Country Total$ Need, Based on $5 Billion Total Estimate
Total for 74 Nations			7,273	100%	$5,000,000,000

Details in table may not compute to numbers shown due to rounding. empty tomb, inc., 2012
Sources: empty tomb analysis, UNICEF data

	Pneumonia	Diarrhoea	Measles	Meningitis	Injuries	Malaria	HIV/AIDS	Other	Neonatal (Total)
Asia	$338,716,330	$213,271,185	$48,220,105	$53,059,990	$113,448,556	$4,173,026	$783,731	$355,848,424	$1,145,423,421
1	$26,261,876	$19,696,407	$2,626,188	$5,252,375	$6,565,469	$0	$0	$27,574,970	$42,019,002
2	866,229	433,115	0	61,874	371,241	0	0	1,856,206	2,536,815
3	10,587,249	5,774,863	962,477	2,887,431	5,774,863	962,477	0	13,474,680	56,786,151
4	1,539,963	879,979	0	219,995	769,982	219,995	109,997	2,529,940	4,619,890
5	32,483,604	4,331,147	0	4,331,147	17,324,589	0	0	32,483,604	125,603,267
6	1,072,475	412,490	0	164,996	494,988	0	0	1,814,957	4,289,898
7	174,895,846	128,256,954	34,979,169	23,319,446	46,638,892	0	0	139,916,677	606,305,600
8	12,457,204	5,190,502	5,190,502	2,076,201	6,228,602	2,076,201	0	20,762,007	49,828,817
9	3,547,416	1,478,090	0	295,618	1,773,708	0	0	6,799,214	15,667,753
10	378,116	206,245	0	34,374	240,619	0	0	962,477	1,581,212
11	989,976	549,987	0	219,995	439,990	54,999	54,999	1,154,973	2,144,949
12	6,159,854	2,694,936	384,991	1,154,973	1,924,954	384,991	384,991	7,699,817	18,094,570
13	3,368,670	1,443,716	0	962,477	1,203,096	0	0	3,128,051	13,955,919
14	43,620,839	29,080,559	2,908,056	8,724,168	14,540,280	0	0	61,069,175	133,770,573
15	6,352,349	2,722,435	0	1,361,218	3,629,914	0	0	9,982,263	21,779,483
16	1,154,973	742,482	0	82,498	494,988	0	0	2,392,443	3,382,420
17	494,988	329,992	0	41,249	206,245	0	0	1,237,471	1,814,957
18	2,557,439	1,491,840	0	213,120	1,278,720	0	0	6,606,718	9,164,157
19	2,337,444	2,337,444	1,168,722	233,744	701,233	0	233,744	4,441,145	12,154,711
20	7,589,820	5,218,001	0	1,423,091	2,846,182	474,364	0	9,961,638	19,923,277

	Pneumonia	Diarrhoea	Measles	Meningitis	Injuries	Malaria	HIV/AIDS	Other	Neonatal (Total)
LA/C	$10,277,881	$6,159,854	$0	$1,615,587	$22,590,713	$0	$577,486	$25,457,520	$53,279,985
1	$1,251,220	$866,229	$0	$96,248	$577,486	$0	$0	$2,502,441	$4,234,899
2	2,268,696	1,134,348	0	378,116	1,512,464	0	0	7,562,320	24,577,541
3	1,154,973	673,734	0	192,495	769,982	0	192,495	2,021,202	4,619,890
4	*2,784,309*	*2,165,574*	*0*	*618,735*	*17,015,221*	*0*	*309,368*	*2,784,309*	*4,949,882*
5	2,289,321	1,017,476	0	254,369	2,034,952	0	0	8,394,176	11,192,234
6	529,362	302,493	0	75,623	680,609	0	75,623	2,193,073	3,705,537

	Pneumonia	Diarrhoea	Measles	Meningitis	Injuries	Malaria	HIV/AIDS	Other	Neonatal (Total)
Oceania	$1,192,784	$673,734	$0	$168,433	$522,488	$859,355	$164,996	$1,632,774	$3,378,982
1	$1,154,973	$659,984	$0	$164,996	$494,988	$824,980	$164,996	$1,567,463	$3,217,424
2	$37,812	$13,750	$0	$3,437	$27,499	$34,374	$0	$65,311	$161,559

	Pneumonia	Diarrhoea	Measles	Meningitis	Injuries	Malaria	HIV/AIDS	Other	Neonatal (Total)
Total	$710,061,324	$504,526,392	$74,340,359	$115,434,696	$253,653,976	$377,638,906	$102,586,314	$861,402,604	$1,992,848,107

Details in table may not compute to numbers shown due to rounding.
Sources: empty tomb analysis, UNICEF data

empty tomb, inc., 2012

153

Table 48: Country-Specific Dollar-Cost Estimates Detail for Causes of Neonatal Deaths, 74 Countries, with 13 No-Progress Countries Highlighted, 2010

Nation		Country Total Neonatal Need ($s)	Neonatal Pneumonia ($s)	Neonatal Preterm ($s)	Neonatal Asphyxia ($s)	Neonatal Sepsis ($s)	Neonatal Other ($s)	Neonatal Congenital ($s)	Neonatal Diarrhoea ($s)
Africa: 46 Nations		$790,765,719	$78,168,269	$279,316,366	$207,692,942	$133,898,445	$31,306,631	$44,165,326	$16,513,358
1	Angola	$22,460,092	$1,663,710	$7,486,697	$5,822,987	$4,991,131	$831,855	$831,855	$831,855
2	Benin	7,507,322	1,340,593	2,681,186	2,144,949	536,237	268,119	536,237	0
3	Botswana	549,987	41,249	206,245	123,747	54,999	27,499	82,498	0
4	*Burkina Faso*	*18,149,569*	*3,299,922*	*5,774,863*	*4,949,882*	*1,649,961*	*824,980*	*824,980*	*0*
5	Burundi	8,098,558	522,488	2,873,682	2,089,950	2,089,950	261,244	261,244	0
6	*Cameroon*	*16,623,355*	*1,278,720*	*5,754,238*	*4,475,519*	*3,196,799*	*639,360*	*639,360*	*0*
7	*Central African Republic*	*4,427,395*	*474,364*	*1,423,091*	*1,106,849*	*790,606*	*158,121*	*158,121*	*158,121*
8	*Chad*	*14,299,660*	*1,649,961*	*4,949,882*	*3,849,909*	*2,199,948*	*549,987*	*549,987*	*0*
9	Comoros	536,237	82,498	178,746	151,246	54,999	27,499	41,249	0
10	Congo	2,859,932	536,237	983,102	804,356	178,746	178,746	178,746	0
11	Côte d'Ivoire	18,699,556	2,749,935	6,049,856	4,949,882	2,749,935	549,987	1,099,974	549,987
12	*Democratic Republic of the Congo*	*92,707,173*	*12,787,196*	*28,771,192*	*22,377,594*	*12,787,196*	*3,196,799*	*6,393,598*	*3,196,799*
13	Djibouti	536,237	109,997	192,495	137,497	13,750	27,499	54,999	0
14	Egypt	12,402,205	281,868	5,637,366	1,973,078	563,737	845,605	2,818,683	0
15	Equatorial Guinea	659,984	82,498	206,245	164,996	103,123	41,249	61,874	20,625
16	Eritrea	2,344,319	75,623	831,855	680,609	378,116	75,623	151,246	0
17	Ethiopia	61,481,665	5,589,242	22,356,969	16,767,727	11,178,485	1,863,081	3,726,162	1,863,081
18	Gabon	742,482	61,874	268,119	185,621	103,123	41,249	61,874	20,625
19	Gambia	1,402,467	206,245	494,988	412,490	164,996	41,249	82,498	0
20	Ghana	14,890,896	1,175,597	5,486,120	4,310,523	2,351,194	783,731	1,175,597	0
21	Guinea	10,229,757	1,319,969	3,299,922	2,639,937	1,649,961	329,992	329,992	329,992
22	Guinea-Bissau	1,539,963	219,995	494,988	439,990	274,993	54,999	54,999	54,999
23	*Kenya*	*29,355,553*	*838,730*	*10,064,761*	*8,387,301*	*5,871,111*	*1,677,460*	*1,677,460*	*0*
24	*Lesotho*	*1,443,716*	*68,748*	*515,613*	*378,116*	*309,368*	*68,748*	*68,748*	*34,374*
25	Liberia	3,196,799	206,245	1,031,226	928,103	618,735	103,123	206,245	103,123
26	Madagascar	11,192,234	604,986	3,932,407	3,327,421	1,814,957	302,493	907,478	0
27	Malawi	11,934,717	1,154,973	4,234,899	3,464,918	1,924,954	769,982	769,982	0
28	Mali	22,274,471	4,124,902	7,424,824	5,774,863	2,474,941	824,980	824,980	824,980
29	*Mauritania*	*3,038,678*	*268,119*	*983,102*	*804,356*	*536,237*	*178,746*	*178,746*	*89,373*
30	Morocco	8,380,426	790,606	3,794,910	1,897,455	474,364	316,242	1,106,849	0
31	Mozambique	23,511,942	3,134,926	7,837,314	6,269,851	3,134,926	783,731	783,731	783,731
32	Niger	16,499,608	2,749,935	6,874,837	4,124,902	2,062,451	687,484	687,484	0
33	Nigeria	171,657,798	17,757,703	59,192,344	47,353,875	35,515,407	5,919,234	5,919,234	5,919,234
34	Rwanda	8,882,289	522,488	3,134,926	2,612,438	1,567,463	522,488	522,488	0
35	*Sao Tome and Principe*	*90,748*	*8,250*	*32,999*	*24,749*	*11,000*	*5,500*	*8,250*	*0*
36	Senegal	8,648,545	934,978	3,038,678	2,571,189	1,168,722	233,744	701,233	0
37	Sierra Leone	6,971,084	804,356	2,144,949	1,876,830	1,340,593	268,119	268,119	268,119
38	*Somalia*	*16,843,350*	*2,887,431*	*5,293,624*	*4,331,147*	*2,406,193*	*481,239*	*962,477*	*481,239*
39	*South Africa*	*12,759,697*	*1,196,222*	*5,183,627*	*2,791,184*	*1,196,222*	*797,481*	*1,594,962*	*0*
40	Sudan and South Sudan	37,357,863	0	17,695,830	6,881,712	7,864,813	1,966,203	2,949,305	983,102
41	Swaziland	598,111	20,625	226,870	164,996	103,123	41,249	41,249	0
42	Togo	4,179,901	522,488	1,567,463	1,175,597	522,488	130,622	261,244	0
43	Uganda	27,141,855	969,352	9,693,520	7,754,816	4,846,760	969,352	969,352	0
44	United Republic of Tanzania	32,916,718	1,828,707	11,886,593	9,143,533	6,400,473	1,828,707	1,828,707	0
45	Zambia	11,962,216	824,980	4,537,392	3,299,922	2,474,941	412,490	412,490	0
46	*Zimbabwe*	*6,778,589*	*398,741*	*2,591,813*	*1,794,332*	*1,196,222*	*398,741*	*398,741*	*0*

Nation		Country Total Neonatal Need ($s)	Neonatal Pneumonia ($s)	Neonatal Preterm ($s)	Neonatal Asphyxia ($s)	Neonatal Sepsis ($s)	Neonatal Other ($s)	Neonatal Congenital ($s)	Neonatal Diarrhoea ($s)
Asia: 20 Nations		$1,145,423,421	$129,996,288	$403,002,929	$250,959,040	$158,409,988	$74,227,612	$106,993,084	$18,816,428
1	Afghanistan	$42,019,002	$6,565,469	$14,444,032	$10,504,751	$6,565,469	$1,313,094	$1,313,094	$1,313,094
2	Azerbaijan	2,536,815	185,621	1,051,850	494,988	185620.592	247,494	309,368	0
3	Bangladesh	56,786,151	2,887,431	25,024,406	13,474,680	8,662,294	1,924,954	4,812,386	0
4	Cambodia	4,619,890	219,995	1,979,953	1,099,974	659,984	109,997	439,990	0
5	China	125,603,267	4,331,147	30,318,030	34,649,177	2,165,574	34,649,177	15,159,015	2,165,574
6	Democratic People's Rep. of Korea	4,289,898	164,996	1,897,455	742,482	412,490	329,992	659,984	0
7	India	606,305,600	93,277,785	209,875,015	116,597,231	93,277,785	23,319,446	58,298,615	11,659,723
8	Indonesia	49,828,817	2,076,201	21,800,107	10,381,003	5,190,502	3,114,301	6,228,602	0
9	Iraq	15,667,753	1,773,708	5,025,506	4,138,652	1,478,090	591,236	2,660,562	295,618
10	Kyrgyzstan	1,581,212	103,123	549,987	343,742	137,497	206,245	240,619	0
11	Lao People's Democratic Republic	2,144,949	54,999	934,978	549,987	329,992	54,999	164,996	0
12	Myanmar	18,094,570	769,982	8,469,799	3,849,909	2,694,936	1,154,973	1,154,973	0
13	Nepal	13,955,919	721,858	7,218,579	2,646,812	1,924,954	481,239	962,477	0
14	Pakistan	133,770,573	11,632,224	49,436,951	34,896,671	26,172,503	2,908,056	5,816,112	2,908,056
15	Philippines	21,779,483	907,478	8,621,045	5,444,871	2,722,435	453,739	3,176,175	0
16	Tajikistan	3,382,420	247,494	1,154,973	824,980	329,992	412,490	329,992	0
17	Turkmenistan	1,814,957	123,747	701,233	371,241	164,996	247,494	206,245	0
18	Uzbekistan	9,164,157	639,360	3,409,919	1,918,079	852,480	1,065,600	1,065,600	0
19	Viet Nam	12,154,711	467,489	3,973,656	2,337,444	1,636,211	1,168,722	2,571,189	0
20	Yemen	19,923,277	2,846,182	7,115,456	5,692,365	2,846,182	474,364	1,423,091	474,364
Latin America/Caribbean: 6 Nations		$53,279,985	$1,808,082	$18,397,063	$9,308,529	$7,727,316	$6,503,596	$8,827,290	$0
1	Bolivia (Plurinational State of)	$4,234,899	$192,495	$1,636,211	$1,058,725	$673,734	$192,495	$384,991	$0
2	Brazil	24,577,541	378,116	7,940,436	3,781,160	3,781,160	4,159,276	4,159,276	0
3	Guatemala	4,619,890	192,495	1,636,211	1,251,220	673,734	192,495	673,734	0
4	*Haiti*	*4,949,882*	*309,368*	*1,856,206*	*1,237,471*	*618,735*	*309,368*	*309,368*	*0*
5	Mexico	11,192,234	508737.918	3,815,534	1,526,214	1526213.752	1,271,845	2,543,690	0
6	Peru	3,705,537	226,870	1,512,464	453,739	453,739	378,116	756,232	0
Oceania: 2 Nations		$3,378,982	$268,119	$1,209,971	$952,165	$505,300	$89,373	$274,993	$0
1	Papua New Guinea	$3,217,424	$247,494	$1,154,973	$907,478	$494,988	$82,498	$247,494	$0
2	Solomon Islands	161,559	20,625	54,999	44,686	10,312	6,875	27,499	0
Total for 74 Nations		$1,992,848,107	$210,240,757	$701,926,329	$468,912,676	$300,541,050	$112,127,212	$160,260,694	$35,329,786

Details in above table may not compute to numbers shown due to rounding. empty tomb, inc., 2012
Sources: empty tomb analysis, UNICEF data

The second source was the *Countdown to 2015 Decade Report, The 2012 Report*.[119] This report included data for 2010, for 75 countries and territories, on eight "Causes of under-5 deaths," one of which was "Neonatal," which also had a breakout of seven "Causes of neonatal deaths."[120]

The number of under-5 child deaths in the 74 countries listed in the Tables 47 and 48 accounted for 96% of the under-5 child deaths in the world.

This model, a first approximation for estimating country-specific costs to prevent child deaths, was based on the assumption that the cost of the disease or other cause of death remedies was equal for each disease. A second working assumption was that the cost of a package of disease remedies per child was the same across the different countries. While this model could be refined by disease (or other cause of death)-specific and country-specific pricing factors plus rate of progress information, this first approximation may be useful for exploring how to address, and mobilize for meeting, specific country goals.

Reasonableness of the Goals. An article on changes in the level of confidence in religious leaders over the period 1973–2010 found a loss of confidence in the age brackets born in 1945–1970, rather than in those older or younger. The article observed that a church must not only have a committed member base but also, if it wants to grow, it must "maintain a general aura of trust and confidence that they are doing good work and making a positive difference for people and the community." The article concluded:

> Assuming a rise in skepticism, individualism, and disenchantment with various types of organizations and institutions, religious and other groups share many of the same challenges. Therefore, religious leaders need to find better ways to show how their organizations differ from secular institutions and can be counted on to provide distinctive services that cannot be obtained by alternative or individualistic means.[121]

Engaging individual Christians in a corporate effort pursuing strategic goals that are consistent with Biblical priorities may not only meet global triage needs, but it may also provide the basis for revitalization for church members and church structures. Of course, the main goal of the mobilization effort would be to help Christians love God and their neighbors as themselves. However, it could well fall within the Great Physician's prescription that, as church leaders are willing to risk their structures in order to improve the health of children around the world, that those leaders may also find their structures restored to better health.

Further, the cost per church member for the implementation of each of these goals means that church leaders who began immediately to mobilize these additional resources might find it reasonable to hope for success.

As noted in chapter 6, an increase of an estimated $5 billion a year has been estimated as the amount needed to reduce global child deaths. Were 100 million church members each to contribute $50 in 2013, 2014, and 2015, church delivery channels could provide the $5 billion in extra resources to improve the rate of progress to the MDG 4 goal trajectory. Further, the voluntary campaign—which it should be noted once again, would be in addition to the unified budget support—would be conducted through church channels, thus enabling the assistance to be provided in Jesus' name. Church members might increase their appreciation for the structures delivering the services and, as a result, better understand the need for the base support of the unified budget.

Also noted in chapter 6 is an estimate for global evangelization. The estimate of $200 million would require an additional $10 per year from each of 20 million Christians.

There is no single denomination that encompasses 100 million church members in the U.S. However, together, it is estimated that over 237 million Americans identified with historic Christianity in 2011.[122]

However, it could well fall within the Great Physician's prescription that, as church leaders are willing to risk their structures in order to improve the health of children around the world, that those leaders may also find their structures restored to better health.

Most of these Christians will not be called to frontline service, and therefore the church needs to provide significant opportunities for the majority to be faithful. One writer suggested that the emphasis on "radical" service among younger evangelical national leaders, means that "many young adults feel ashamed if they 'settle' into ordinary jobs, get married early, and start families, live in small towns, or as 1 Thessalonians 4:13 says, 'aspire to live quietly, and to mind [their] affairs and to work with [their] hands' "[123] [brackets in original]. A campaign to engage all the unengaged unreached people groups in a limited, specified timeframe, and to improve the progress on meeting MDG 4 so that the reduction in global child deaths is back on the goal trajectory for the year 2015, is a significant activity that can challenge Christians who are otherwise abandoned to an agenda of self-gratification preached by the larger society.

It would be ideal if some denominations are able to move quickly on such a mobilization. Others may not choose to move unless they first see a populist movement developing among individuals in the more than 300,000 historically Christian congregations in the U.S.

Another stream of activity may come through the networks of congregations, referred to by Ed Stetzer as proto-denominations or missional networks. These communication systems could provide the initiating base upon which a larger movement could build in the rest of 2013, and in 2014 and 2015. However, to reach 100 million Christians will ultimately require the participation of a variety of denominations.

The response of church leaders in the U.S. should be as urgent as if ... it were their children or their sibling confronting these threatening conditions.

The idea might also form among individuals, and then spread into the denominational structures that will then help not only mobilize the money, but also play a key role through the delivery channels to distribute the assistance provided in Jesus' name where it is most needed.

The urgency of the task is not only due to the external deadline of 2015. The urgency is that each child dying from preventable conditions, and each person dying without a chance to hear of God's love through Jesus Christ, is as precious to God as those in the church in the U.S. The response of church leaders in the U.S. should be as urgent as if they themselves were being confronted with that challenge, as if it were their children or their sibling confronting these threatening conditions. That response could make the timeframe of 2013, 2014, and 2015 workable. As Dr. Ransom in C.S. Lewis' *Out of the Silent Planet* found, "It was necessary and the necessary was always possible."[124]

As suggested in chapter 6, wealthy Christians could play a catalyzing role by providing matching money. Those with high incomes might also be able to popularize the idea of a mobilization initiative for the two triage needs, perhaps through creative ads.

A review of the Forbes 400 "Rich Listers" for 2012[125] found that those on the list are dispersed throughout the U.S., with the West having the most, the South second, followed by the Northeast and the Midwest. Table 49 locates those listed in the 2012 Forbes 400 list by U.S. region. Ten of the individuals on the list reside abroad. Given the church population of the United States, it is possible that as many as 238 of the 400 individuals on the list, or 60%, may be members of historically Christian churches.

Table 49: Forbes 400 "Rich Listers" 2012, Region of Residence Summary

Region of U.S.	Northeast	Midwest	South	West	Subtotal	Abroad	Total
Number of Rich Listers	94	53	121	122	390	10	400
Aggregate Wealth ($ Billions)	$382.95	$216.07	$441.50	$617.85	$1,658.37	$36.95	$1,695.32

Source: empty tomb analysis   empty tomb, inc., 2013

There are two key dynamics to be avoided in pursuing a mobilization effort, one of general concern, and one that those with wealth may be more prone to experience.

The first dynamic is what is called "equalization." That is, if a congregation or denomination receives designated money for an expense, that congregation or denomination may be tempted to reduce the amount of undesignated funds that would otherwise have been allocated to that expense. The end result is that the designated funds did not *expand* the amount of money available for the expense, but rather *replaced* undesignated money that would otherwise have gone to that expense. Donors at all levels of income need to be sure that any church structure receiving money through a mobilization campaign to engage unengaged unreached people groups, and to accelerate the reduction of global child death rates, will use the designated funds to expand the delivery channel distributions, rather than maintain those activities at their present levels with no net gain for the two global triage needs.

The other dynamic that may affect primarily the wealthy is a control dynamic that leads the wealthy to prefer to limit their participation to what they themselves can do to meet the needs, rather than providing seed capital to mobilize small donations from vast numbers of church members. The wealthy may feel they do not have, or in fact do not want to give, enough money to meet the two global triage needs identified, and so such an approach will not actually provide the scale of solutions required to address the needs. Nor should the wealthy prevent other Christians from having a meaningful role in meeting such needs. A finding from a study of congregational dynamics regarding money illustrates the problem.

> It also appears that many congregations are limited by what the biggest givers are able or willing to do. A national official described a congregation where one wealthy member always made up the balance of the budget at the end of the year. As a result, this individual had an important veto on what goals were set by the congregation. A new pastor came to the congregation and enthusiastically urged the congregation to broaden its mission. In the congregational meeting, the key individual hesitated but could not resist the pastor's enthusiasm, and so, with his approval, the budget was set for a higher amount that year. The same dialogue happened the next year, with more hesitation on the part of the wealthy individual, yet the budget goal was again raised. In the third year, the large donor protested and said, "Wait, we can't do that! I can't afford to make up that much money." The pastor smiled and said, "Good, because we don't want you to. We've reached a place where we need everyone, including you."[126]

The task of the wealthy person in a mobilization campaign would not be to meet the need him- or herself, but rather to mobilize many other Christians who can make smaller donations as well. In this way, the larger amounts that wealthy donors give will multiply the effect, as seed capital, and in this way encourage a burgeoning reality of the body of Christ at work.

The Promises of Jesus.

Isaiah 59:15b-16 reads in the New Living Translation: "The LORD looked and was displeased to find that there was no justice. He was amazed to see that no one intervened to help the oppressed. So he himself stepped in to save them with his mighty power and justice."

Ultimately, the Father helped the oppressed, and the entire world, by sending Jesus. The focus on those in need was also at the heart of Jesus' announcement of his ministry, based on Isaiah 61:1-2 as recorded in his announcement of his ministry in Luke 4:18-19: " 'The Spirit of the Lord is on me, because he has anointed me to preach good news to the poor. He has sent me to proclaim freedom for the prisoners and recovery of sight for the blind, to release the oppressed, to proclaim the year of the Lord's favor' " (NIV). After Jesus healed the sick and cast out demons, the people in Capernaum wanted him to stay, but he told them, "I must preach the good news of the kingdom of God to the other towns also, because that is why I was sent" (Luke 4:43, NIV).

God helped the world through Jesus who demonstrated God's power with miracles on a person-to-person basis. Now, the church has been empowered as Christ's body, to continue Jesus' miraculous outreach, the works of the kingdom of God, on a broader scale.

> "The LORD looked and was displeased to find that there was no justice. He was amazed to see that no one intervened to help the oppressed."
> —Isaiah 59

The previous chapters in this book document a church that has posted declining giving as a percent of income and membership as a percent of population over a period of decades. Those numbers describe but do not determine the church's condition. The promises of Jesus can be taken and acted on by church leaders to help encourage a movement that could give new energy and vitality to the church in the U.S. As believers living in the 21st century U.S. embrace the miracle of oneness that Jesus prayed for on their behalf in John 17:20-23, the result can be God working in the church, giving church members "the desire to obey him and the power to do what pleases him" (Phil. 2:13, New Living Translation).

Indeed, there are signs that a movement of God's Spirit in some quarters of the church has already led to action.

Signs of Hope: The Word Component of the Task. The task of global evangelization has been discussed for some 2,000 years. Jesus told the disciples they would be his witnesses in the whole world (Acts 1:8) and then ascended into heaven (v. 9). When the disciples stood there looking up (v.10), two angels sent them on their way: " 'Men of Galilee,' they said, 'why do you stand here looking into the sky?' " (NIV). In other words, "Church, get busy!"

Various movements have pursued the goal of global evangelism in the two millennia that followed. As an example, in the year 2000, a group of organizations built on an initial conversation at a conference, while seated at Table 71, to begin coordinating their activities focused on reaching the remaining unreached people groups. Some time later, the National Christian Foundation began to talk to the Table 71 participants about how business leaders could assist. In 2010, the Issachar Initiative was formed as "an independent advocacy group of men and women, not tied to any particular ministry, who would serve the Church."[127] At a January 16, 2012, meeting of the Issachar Initiative, "over 187 made commitments to personally give and/or mobilize over \$4.6 billion between now and 2025 toward the completion of the Great Commission."[128] According to the Web site, the intention is to "constantly be asking where the church is not present, and will seek to find organizations and donors who will begin making disciples and planting the church in the most neglected people groups or areas of the world."[129] Two of the group's objectives include: (1) "To serve the body of Christ by bring[ing] clarity and focus to the unmet needs of the Great Commission"; and, (2) "To influence denominations and mission organizations to focus and align their strategies toward the least-reached."[130]

This activity is in addition to the initiative shown by Wycliffe Bible Translators. Wycliffe identified a specific task—to start a Bible translation in the last language that does not have one—by 2025. The announced financial target was \$1.15 billion, beginning in 2008.[131] The Wycliffe Last Languages Campaign has three key components: a vision for making an important contribution to one of the two global triage needs that is designed to address the need on a scale to solve it, a timeframe in which to meet the need, and a stated financial goal for the effort.

Signs of Hope: The Deed Component of the Task. An information mailing from the National Christian Foundation celebrated the fact that the fund's donors had made \$4 billion in grants to charities since the Fund's founding. The headline read, "Zero meant nothing ... until now." The brochure included global progress statistics on reductions in children dying from measles (down 71% since 2003), 22 countries halving their malaria rate, global poverty being cut in half, reduction in AIDS infections in 25 low- and middle-income countries, reduction in the rate of global under-5 child deaths, reduction in the number of unreached people groups, and the fact that the Fund distributed 70% of the new contributions to the fund in 2012, that is, \$605 million of \$871 million received. A summary statement read, "We're celebrating 4,000,000,000 but our goal is ZERO." The brochure stated, "We're excited because the ministries and churches we support are working to bring the numbers of lost and suffering down to nothing."[132]

Pursuing the Potential. The mindset evident in the Issachar Initiative, Wycliffe Bible Translators, and the National Christian Foundation mailing are as significant as the content they convey. Their focus is on the potential for increased activity within the body of Christ, on pursuing ideas at a previously unheard of scale, out of a desire to love God and neighbor.

The statistics in the first five chapters of this volume indicate that the church in the U.S. has been weakening over decades in terms of member giving and membership. That information can lead to lament or be seen as a wake-up call for action to change those trends. Chapter 6 builds on the information in the first five chapters to demonstrate the increased giving potential that exists among church members that could be mobilized by church structures in the U.S. That mobilization will likely require leadership.

For a mobilization initiative to succeed, God's selection of the leadership will be essential. However, to prime the pump, so to speak, a list of potential mobilizers—one might even use the term "dream team"—follows. These leaders, or others, could facilitate a movement of church members and structures in the pursuit of expanded

God's selection of the leadership will be essential. However, to prime the pump, so to speak, a list of potential mobilizers—one might even use the term "dream team"—follows.

works of the kingdom of God. The movement's initiators might include one or more of the following people.

—Bill Hybels, pastor of Willow Creek, South Barrington, Illinois, sponsors the annual Global Leadership Summit, and also has a network in the Willow Creek Association.

—Franklin Graham, president of Samaritan's Purse and also the Billy Graham Association, combines two key elements of word and deed mission, bringing national stature to the tasks.

—Richard Stearns, president of World Vision U.S., has focused on the potential and need to complete the "Unfinished" tasks related to global word and deed need.[133]

—Timothy Cardinal Dolan, current president of the National Conference of Catholic Bishops and archbishop of New York,[134] served as chair of the board of Catholic Relief service, until he "stepped down from the post reluctantly when his election as president of the U.S. Conference of Catholic Bishops required it."[135]

—Wesley Granberg-Michaelson, former general secretary and currently serving as associate for ecumenical relations, of the Reformed Church in America, and a founding energy in Christian Churches Together,[136] has long experience in the broader church and experience in encouraging dialogue among various parts of the body of Christ.

—Eileen Lindner, who has served as Associate General Secretary for Christian Unity in the office of the National Council of the Churches of Christ in the U.S.A. General Secretary, and the Deputy General Secretary and Director of Research and Planning for the NCC, and continues in her role as editor of the *Yearbook of American and Canadian Churches*,[137] has broad experience in facilitating interaction among Christians from varying backgrounds.

—Samuel Rodriquez, president of the National Hispanic Christian Leadership Conference, has become nationally visible as a writer and leader.

—Rick Warren, pastor of Saddleback Church in Orange County, CA, wrote about the "five giants" of global need, and has demonstrated what one congregation can do by encouraging members of Saddleback to visit every country in the world, as part of developing a global evangelization effort, with the final country visited on November 18, 2010.[138]

Two components within the body of Christ in the U.S. that maintained the same percent of U.S. population between 2007 and 2012, according to Pew Research,[139] are:

—African-American Protestants. One nationally visible leader is T.D. Jakes. Another possibility would be a representative from the Conference of National Black Churches.

—The Orthodox Church. Because of its structure, it may be appropriate to contact His All Holiness Bartholomew, Archbishop of Constantinople, for a recommendation, if it is not clear from other ecumenical settings who would be a likely leader located in the U.S.

Of course, denominational officials or other church leaders not on this list might self-identify in response to God's leading, to help develop an interchange with

Of course, denominational officials or other church leaders not on this list might self-identify in response to God's leading, to help develop an interchange with other leaders focused on mobilizing 100 million Christians in collective action on a common goal.

other leaders focused on mobilizing 100 million Christians in collective action on a common goal. Anything is possible.

Which is exactly what Jesus promised. The potential, rather than decline, should be the focus of church leaders. It is important to use the statistics to take the temperature of the church. However, the next step is to evaluate how to get well, not hide under the covers.

Three of Jesus' promises were highlighted at the beginning of this chapter. It seems reasonable to believe that the promises hold true for church leaders and institutions as well as for individuals. Each was chosen for what it seemed to convey about church giving and membership patterns.

> "Why be like the pagans who are so deeply concerned about these things? Your heavenly Father already knows all your needs, and he will give you all you need from day to day if you live for him and make the Kingdom of God your primary concern."
> —Jesus Christ quoted in Matthew 6:32-33 (New Living Translation)

> "For whoever wishes to save his life will lose it, but whoever loses his life for my sake will find it."
> —Jesus Christ quoted in Matthew 16:25 (New American Bible)

> "I tell you the truth, anyone who has faith in me will do what I have been doing. He will do even greater things than these, because I am going to the Father."
> —Jesus Christ quoted in John 14:12 (New International Version)

Will the church say, "Amen!"?

Anything is possible. Which is exactly what Jesus promised.

Notes for Chapter 8

[1] Blair Kerkhoff, "Y'all Ready for This?" a Kansas City Star article appearing in *Champaign (Ill.) News-Gazette*, August 17, 2012, p. C-5.

[2] Heather Hahn, "Stress Biggest Health Risk to United Methodist Clergy," *The Current* of The United Methodist Illinois Great Rivers Conference, April 2013, p. 4.

[3] Thom S. Rainer; "Pastors Are Hurting"; Christian Post; 9/10/2012; <http://www.christianpost.com/news/pastors-are-hurting-81347/print.html>; p. 1 of 9/11/2012 8:03 AM printout.

[4] Chris Turner, "Control Issues Head List for Pastoral Terminations," *SBC Life*, Fall 2012, p. 9.

[5] Adelle M. Banks, "Ministers and Musicians: Allies or Adversaries?" a Religion News Service article appearing in *Christian Century*, November 14, 2012, p. 18.

[6] John Ronsvalle and Sylvia Ronsvalle, *Behind the Stained Glass Windows: Money Dynamics in the Church* (Grand Rapids, MI: Baker Books, 1996), p. 179.

[7] Daniel Kahneman, *Thinking Fast and Slow* (New York: Farrar, Straus and Giroux, 2011), p. 283.

[8] Jeffrey Bullock, "How We Make Choices," *Christian Century*, June 12, 2013, p. 12.

[9] Jeffrey Bullock, "How We Make Choices," p. 13.

[10] Frank S. Page; "First-Person: The Need for Spiritual Revival in the SBC"; Baptist Press; 7/18/2012; <http://www.bpnews.net/printerfriendly.asp?ID=38291>; pp. 1-2 of 7/19/2012 7:58 AM printout.

[11] Jeff Donn, "Putting Up Barriers?" an Associated Press article appearing in *Champaign (Ill.) News-Gazette*, 11/26/2012, pp. A-1, A-10.

[12] Heather Hahn; "Final Report: Church Path 'Unsustainable' "; United Methodist Church; 10/1/2012; <http://www.umc.org/site/apps/nlnet/content3.aspx?c=lwL4KnN1LtH&b=2789393&ct=12212387&notoc=1>; p. 1 of 10/8/2012 3:47 PM printout.

[13] Ed Stetzer; "SBC 2011 Statistical Realities—Facts Are Our Friends But These Are Not Very Friendly Facts"; edstetzer.com; 6/13/2012; <http://www.edstetzer.com/2012/06/sbc-2011-statistical-realities.html; pp. 2, 8 of 5/13/2013 4:54 PM printout.

[14] Bob Allen, "Southern Baptist Numbers Drop for Baptisms, Membership," an Associated Baptist Press story appearing in *Christian Century*, July 10, 2013, p. 15.

[15] Tom Heneghan; " 'Believing without Belonging' Challenges Catholicism – Dolan"; Reuters; 3/1/2013; <http://www.globalpost.com/dispatch/news/Thomson-Reuters/130301/believing-without-belonging-challenges-catholicism-dolan>; p. 1, 2 of 8/17/2013 11:00 AM printout.

[16] "History: The Founding Years"; The Interchurch Center; 2008; <http://www.interchurch-center.org/history.html>; p. 1 of 3/20/2013 10:19 AM printout.

[17] John Dart, "From Gotham City to Capitol Hill," *Christian Century*, March 20, 2013, p. 14.

[18] "NCC Envisions Itself as Smaller, More Agile," *Christian Century*, October 31, 2012, p. 15.

[19] Amy Frykholm, "Culture Changers," *Christian Century*, July 11, 2012, p. 26.

[20] Frank Newport; "Most Americans Say Religion Is Losing Influence in U.S."; Gallup; 5/29/2013; <http://www.gallup.com/poll/162803/americans-say-religion-losing-influence.aspx>; pp. 1-3 of 8/2/2013 10:48 AM printout.

[21] John Dart, "UCC Has Been Progressive Pacesetter," *Christian Century*, 8/7/2013, p. 15.

[22] Diane Chandler; "2nd View: ERLC's Land Delivers Farewell Chapel Message"; Baptist Press; 4/30/2013; <http://www.bpnews.net/printerfriendly.asp?ID-40193; p. 2 of 4/30/2013 6:26 PM printout.

[23] Pew Research; " 'Nones' on the Rise"; Religion & Public Life Project; 10/9/2012; <http://www.pewforum.org/2012/10/09/nones-on-the-rise/>; pp. 1, 5 of 8/15/2013 2:33 PM printout.

[24] John Kenneth Galbraith, *The Affluent Society*, Third Edition, Revised (New York: Mentor Books, 1976), p. 3.

[25] Walter Brueggemann;; "The Liturgy of Abundance, the Myth of Scarcity"; Christian Century; 3/24/1999; <http://www.eee.christiancentury.org/article/2012-01/liturgy-abundance-myth-scarcity>; p. 4 of 8/19/2013 1:24 PM printout.

[26] Ronsvalle, *Behind the Stained Glass Windows: Money Dynamics in the Church*, p. 31.

[27] Rodney Stark, *The History of Christianity* (New York: HarperOne, 1996), p. 86.

[28] Ross Douthat, *Bad Religion: How We Became a Nation of Heretics* (New York: Free Press, 2012), p. 153.

[29] John Milton, *Paradise Lost* (New York: Oxford University Press, 2008), p. 26, lines 679-84, and p. 28, lines 756-57.

[30] Paul Sandle; "Elisabeth Murdoch Takes Aim at Brother on Media Morality"; Reuters; 8/23/2012; <http://www.reuters.com/article/2012/08/23/us-britain-murdoch-idUSBRE87MOUC20120823>; p. 2 of 8/23/2012 5:58 PM printout.

[31] John Ronsvalle and Sylvia Ronsvalle, *The State of Church Giving through 2010: Who's in Charge Here? A Case for a Positive Agenda for Affluence* (Champaign, IL: empty tomb, inc., 2012), pp. 123-174.

[32] Marvin Olasky, "Aliens and Strangers," *World* magazine, June 29, 2013, p. 38.

[33] Giving USA Foundation (2013); *Giving USA 2013*; Created: 6/18/13; published by Giving USA Foundation, Chicago, Ill.; accessed via <store.givingusareports.org>; p. 126 of 6/26/2013 printout.

[34] *Giving USA 2013*, p. 126.

[35] Matt Branaugh; "Willow Creek's 'Huge Shift' "; Christianity Today; 5/15/2008; <http://www.christianitytoday.com/ct/2008/june/5.13.html>; p. 1 of 8/16/2013 2:39 PM printout.

[36] "Fiction Without Faith?" A *New York Times* 12/19/2012 item noted in *Christian Century*, January 23, 2013, p. 9.

[37] Luke Rosiak; "Fathers Disappear from Households Across America"; Washington Times; 12/25/2012; <http://www.washingtontimes.com/news/2012/dec/25/fathers-disappear-from-households-across-america/print/>; p. 1 of 12/28/2012 8:48 AM printout.

[38] Dispatches>Quotables, "#me," *World* magazine, June 1, 2013, p. 12.

[39] Joel Stein, "The New Greatest Generation, Why Millennials Will Save Us All," *Time* magazine, May 20, 2013, p. 34.

[40] "List of Corporations by Market Capitalization"; Wikipedia; n.d.; <http://en.wikipedia.org/wiki/List_of_corporations_by_market_capitalization>; p. 2 of 8/24/2013 12:32 AM printout.

[41] Lily Rothman, "The New Cinema of Stuff, Materialism Just the Way You Like It," *Time* magazine, June 10, 2013, p. 62.

[42] Rothman, p. 61.

[43] Christian Today; "Moral Relativism Won't Cut It Anymore, Says UK Prime Minister"; Christian Post; 8/15/2011; <http://www.christianpost.com/news/moral-relativism-wont-cut-it-anymore-says-uk-prime-minister-53930/>; p. 1 of 8/15/2011 10:58 AM printout.

[44] Connor Adams Sheets; "Belgian Parliament Posed to Approve Child Euthanasia Law"; International Business Times; 6/11/2013; <http://www.ibtimes.com/Belgian-parliament-posed-approve-child-euthanasia-law-1301825#>; pp. 1, 2 of 6/11/2013 5:23 PM printout.

[45] Dispatches>Quotables, "The definition of marriage is plastic."; *World* magazine; May 18, 2013, p. 18.

[46] AWR Hawkins; "U.S. Army Instructor: Beware Religious Extremism of Evangelicals, Roman Catholics"; Breitbart; 4/7/2013; <http://www.breitbart.com/Big-Peace/2013/04/07/U-S-Army-Instructor-Beware-Religious-Extremism-of-Evangelicals-and-Roman-Catholics>; p. 1 of 4/8/2011 9:56 AM printout.

[47] David Edwards; "Leading Neuroscientist: Religious Fundamentalism May Be a 'Mental Illness' that Can Be 'Cured' "; The Raw Story; 5/30/2013; <http://www.rawstory.com/rs/2013/05/30/leading-neuroscientist-religious-fundamentalism-may-be-mental-illness-that-can-be-cured/>; p. 1 of 5/31/2013 5:56 PM printout.

[48] Anugrah Kumar; "Michigan University Denies It Removed InterVarsity from Campus"; Christian Post; 2/3/2013; <http://www.christianpost.com/news/michigan-university-denies-it-removed-intervarsity-from-campus-89365/print.html#>; p. 1 of 3/1/2013 2:28 PM printout.

[49] Jerry Markon and Peter Wallsten; "White House, Nonprofit Groups Battle over Charitable Deductions"; Washington Post; 12/13/2012; <http://www.washingtonpost.com/politics/white-house-nonprofit-groups-battle-over-charitable-deductions/2012/12/13/80e67400-43f2-11e2-9648-a2c323a991d6_print.html>; pp. 1-4 of 12/13/2012 4:09 PM printout.

[50] Tom Strode; "Charitable Deduction Cap Would Be 'Devastating' "; Baptist Press; 11/29/2012; <http://www.bpnews.net/printerfriendly.asp?asp?ID=39250>; pp. 1-2 of 11/30/2012 8:32 AM printout.

[51] What's New News Briefing; "Religious Tax Exemptions Cost U.S. at Least $71-Billion," *Chronicle of Philanthropy*, June 28, 2012, p. 3.

[52] Michael Foust; "Attorney: City Laws Against Churches on Rise"; Baptist Press; 12/17/2012; <http://www.bpnews.net/printerfriendly.asp?ID=39380>; p. 1 of 12/18/2012 8:14 AM printout.

[53] Anne Reiner; "Facebook, Others, Urged to Allow Free Speech"; Baptist Press; 9/13/2012; <http://www.bpnews/net/printerfriendly.asp?ID=38711>; p. 1 of 9/13/2012 4:17 PM printout.

[54] Bishop Daniel R. Jenky, "Religious Liberty Faces Grave Threat," *Champaign (Ill.) News-Gazette*, November 4, 2012, p. C-3.

[55] Emily Belz; "Stanford Opens 'Religious Liberty Clinic' "; Baptist Press; 1/30/2013; <http://www.bpnews.net/printerfriendly.asp?ID-39613>; p. 1-2 of 1/30/2013 4:49 PM printout.

[56] SBC Resolutions; "On Twenty-Five Years of the Conservative Resurgence"; SBC; June 2004; <http://www.sbc.net/resolutions/amResolution.asp?ID=1138>; p. 1 of 8/26/2013 3:51 PM printout.

[57] John Yeats; "First-Person: The Need for Cooperative Missions"; Baptist Press; 8/22/2012; <http://www.bpnews.net/printerfriendly.asp?ID=38558>; p. 1 of 8/22/2012 3:53 PM printout.

[58] Michael Gryboski; "Economist Pitches Plan to Reverse Decline of UMC Before It 'Ceases to Exist As We Know It' "; Christian Post; 7/31/2013; <http://www.christianpost.com/news/economist-pitches-plan-to-reverse-decline-of-umc-before-it-cease-to-exist-as-we-know-it-101262/print.html>; p. 2 of 8/1/2013 8:14 AM printout.

[59] Steve McMullin, "The Secularization of Sunday: Real or Perceived Competition for Churches," *Review of Religious Research*, March 2013, Vol. 55, No. 1, p.58.

[60] Ross Douthat, *Bad Religion: How We Became a Nation of Heretics*, p. 181.

[61] Jeff Schapiro; "Bill Hybels: Leadership Takes Courage to Carry Out God's Big Visions"; Christian Post; 8/9/2013; <http://www.christianpost.com/news/bill-hybels-leadership-takes-courage-to-carry-out-gods-big-visions-101874/print.html>; p. 2 of 8/9/2013 9:04 AM printout.

[62] Jeffrey Bullock, "How We Make Choices," p. 13.

[63] Tim Stafford, "The Choice," *Christianity Today*, October 2012, p. 44.

[64] Ruth Malhotra; "Gary Haugen at Passion 2013: You Can Be the Generation That Ends Slavery in the World"; Christian Post; 1/3/2013; <http://www.christianpost.com/news/gary-haugen-at-passion-2013-you-can-be-the-generation-that-ends-slavery-in-the-world-87615/>; p. 1 of 1/3/2013 5:23 PM printout.

[65] Jeff Iorg, " 'Learning Outcomes' and Discipleship: A Sermon on the Church at Antioch," *SBC Life*, Spring 2013, p. 17.

[66] Andy Crouch, "Planting Deep Roots," *Christianity Today*, June 2013, p. 61.

[67] Ken Carter; "Why Congregations Need Denominations"; CC Blogs; 10/5/2011; <http://revkencarter.blogspot.com/2011/10/why=congregations-need-denominations.html>; p. 2 of 10/18/2011 3:42 PM printout.

[68] Ed Stetzer, "Life in Those Old Bones," *Christianity Today*, June 2010, pp. 26, 27.

[69] John Ronsvalle and Sylvia Ronsvalle; "Abolition of the Institutional Enslavement of Overseas Missions, *The State of Church Giving through 2005*; empty tomb, inc.; 2007; < http://www.emptytomb.org/SCG05.ch8excerpt.pdf>; pp. 105-131.

[70] Craig Dykstra and James Hudnut-Beumler, "The National Organizational Structures of Protestant Denominations: An Invitation to a Conversation," in Milton J Coalter, John M. Mulder and Louis B. Weeks, eds., *The Organizational Revolution: Presbyterians and American Denominationalism* (Louisville, KY: Westminster/John Knox Press, 1992), p. 321.

[71] Ronsvalle, *Behind the Stained Glass Windows: Money Dynamics in the Church*, p. 75.

[72] Bruce Kauffmann, "Alexis de Tocqueville's Democracy in America," *Champaign (Ill.) News-Gazette*, 4/21/2013, p. C-6.

[73] Bruce Kauffmann, "Marshall: The Architect of Victory," *Champaign (Ill.) News-Gazette*, 1/6/2008, p. B-5.

[74] Frank Newport; "Christianity Remains Dominant Religion in the United States"; Gallup; 12/23/2011; <http://www.gallup.com/poll/151760/Christianity-Remains-Dominant-Religion-United-States.aspx?version=print>; p. 1 of 1/5/2012 4:00 PM printout.

[75] Larry Alex Taunton; "Listening to Young Atheists: Lessons for a Strong Christianity"; The Atlantic; 6/6/2013; <http://www.theatlantic.com/national/archive/2013/06/listening-to-young-atheists-lessons-for-a-stronger-christianity/276584/>; p. 5 of 8/2/2013 10?46 AM printout.

[76] Frank Newport; "Most Americans Say Religion Is Losing Influence in U.S."; pp. 1-3.

[77] *The Index of Global Philanthropy and Remittances 2012*; Hudson Institute Center for Global Prosperity; Created 4/3/2012; Modified 4/3/2012; downloaded 5/30/2012; <http://www.hudson.org/files/publications/2012IndexofGlobalPhilanthropyandRemittances.pdf>; p. 18, 20 of 5/30/2012 printout

[78] Richard Stearns, *Unfinished* (Nashville: Thomas Nelson, 2013), p. 86.

[79] George Will, "Hard to Rebuild City When the Money All but Runs Out," *Champaign (Ill.) News-Gazette*, August 4, 2013, p. C-2.

[80] Matthew Lee Anderson, "Here Come the Radicals," *Christianity Today*, March 2013, pp. 20-25.

[81] Howard Snyder, "Viewpoints" letter to the editor, *Christianity Today*, May 2013, p. 59.

[82] Richard Stearns, *Unfinished*, p. 215.

[83] Ronsvalle, *The State of Church Giving through 2010: Who's in Charge Here? A Case for a Positive Agenda for Affluence*, pp. 138-143.

[84] Sandra Long Weaver; "Imagine No Malaria Fundraising Campaign Both Saves and Changes Lives"; The United Methodist Church Board of Global Ministries; March-April 2013; <http://www.umcmission.org/Find-Resources/New-World-Outlook-Magazine/2013/March-April-2013/Imagine-No-Malaria-Campaign>; p. 1 of 8/18/2013 1:36 PM printout.

[85] Don Graham; "Great Commission Moment is Now, IMB's Elliff Tells Trustees"; Baptist Press; 5/17/2013; <http://bpnews.net/printerfriendly.asp?ID=40330>; p. 1 of 5/20/2013 8:17 AM printout.

[86] SBC Lottie Moon Sources:

1921–2009: "Lottie Moon Christmas Offering from its Beginning in 1888"; International Mission Board, SBC; LMCO Historical Campaign Year.xls, attachment to e-mail from David Steverson, IMB; June 9, 2010 6:54 AM; p. 1 of 6/9/2010 11:53 AM printout. 2010: "Lottie Moon Christmas Offering," *SBC Life*, Dec. 2011-Feb. 2012, p. 2. 2011: Don Graham; "IMB int'l missions offering: $146.8M in 2011, up $1.1M"; Baptist Press; 6/11/2012; <http://www.bpnews.net/printerfriendly.asp?ID=40461>; p. 1 of 6/13/2012 12:15 PM printout.

1921–1952 SBC Membership: *Historical Statistics of the United States: Colonial*

Table 50: SBC Lottie Moon Christmas Offerings, 1921–2011, and SBC Membership, 1921–1967

Table 50 Year	Lottie Moon Christmas Offering $	SBC Membership	Year	Lottie Moon Christmas Offering $	SBC Membership	Year	Lottie Moon Christmas Offering $	Year	Lottie Moon Christmas Offering $
1921	28,615.78	3,220,000	1945	1,201,962.24	5,866,000	1968	15,159,206.92	1990	79,358,610.87
1922	29,583.67	3,366,000	1946	1,381,048.76	6,079,000	1969	15,297,558.63	1991	81,358,723.00
1923	42,206.37	3,494,000	1947	1,503,010.12	6,271,000	1970	16,220,104.99	1992	80,980,881.11
1924	48,677.00	3,575,000	1948	1,669,683.38	6,489,000	1971	17,833,810.22	1993	82,899,291.40
1925	306,376.21	3,649,000	1949	1,745,682.81	6,761,000	1972	19,664,972.53	1994	85,932,597.88
1926	246,152.84	3,617,000	1950	2,110,019.07	7,080,000	1973	22,232,757.09	1995	89,019,719.75
1927	172,457.36	3,674,000	1951	2,668,051.30	7,373,000	1974	23,234,093.89	1996	93,089,179.27
1928	235,274.31	3,706,000	1952	3,280,372.79	7,634,000	1975	26,169,421.12	1997	100,064,318.10
1929	190,130.81	3,771,000	1953	3,602,554.86	6,999,275	1976	28,763,809.71	1998	101,713,066.69
1930	200,799.84	3,850,000	1954	3,957,821.00	7,246,233	1977	31,938,553.04	1999	105,443,786.95
1931	170,724.87	3,945,000	1955	4,628,691.03	7,517,653	1978	35,919,605.40	2000	113,175,191.96
1932	143,331.24	4,066,000	1956	5,240,745.39	7,725,486	1979	40,597,113.02	2001	113,709,471.17
1933	172,512.86	4,174,000	1957	6,121,585.14	7,952,397	1980	44,700,339.76	2002	115,015,216.49
1934	213,925.81	4,277,000	1958	6,762,448.63	8,221,384	1981	50,784,173.38	2003	136,204,648.17
1935	240,455.12	4,389,000	1959	7,706,847.29	8,413,859	1982	54,077,464.49	2004	133,886,221.58
1936	292,401.57	4,482,000	1960	8,238,471.07	8,631,627	1983	58,025,336.79	2005	137,939,677.59
1937	290,219.74	4,596,000	1961	9,315,754.78	9,978,139	1984	64,775,763.83	2006	150,178,098.06
1938	315,000.40	4,770,000	1962	10,323,591.69	10,192,451	1985	66,862,113.65	2007	150,409,653.86
1939	330,424.70	4,949,000	1963	10,949,857.35	10,395,226	1986	69,412,195.09	2008	141,315,110.24
1940	363,746.30	5,104,000	1964	11,870,649.35	10,601,935	1987	69,912,637.50	2009	148,984,819.41
1941	449,162.48	5,238,000	1965	13,194,357.32	10,770,573	1988	78,787,726.26	2010	145,662,925.00
1942	562,609.30	5,367,000	1966	13,760,146.80	10,947,389	1989	80,197,870.78	2011	146,828,116.00
1943	761,269.79	5,493,000	1967	14,664,679.30	11,140,486				
1944	949,844.17	5,668,000						empty tomb, inc., 2013	

Times to 1970, Bicentennial Edition, Part 1 (Washington Bureau of the Census, 1975), series H 805, pp. 391-392. 1953–1967: *YACC* series. 1968–2011, see Appendix B-1.

87 Ronsvalle, *Behind the Stained Glass Windows: Money Dynamics in the Church*, p. 332.

88 "Biggest Gifts Announced by Individuals in 2011," *Chronicle of Philanthropy*, January 17, 2013, p. 36.

89 "Toothless Legislative Ethics Law," *Champaign (Ill.) News-Gazette*, August 6, 2013, p. A-4.

90 Ronsvalle, *The State of Church Giving through 2005: Abolition of the Enslavement of Overseas Missions*, p. 107.

91 Jonathan Haidt, *The Righteous Mind: Why Good People Are Divided by Politics and Religion* (New York: Pantheon Books, 2012), pp. 250-251.

92 Rodney Stark, *The Rise of Christianity*, p. 78.

93 Jeff Schapiro; "Bill Hybels: Leadership Takes Courage to Carry Out God's Big Visions"; p. 1.

94 Ronsvalle, *Behind the Stained Glass Windows: Money Dynamics in the Church*, p. 56.

95 Lynn Sherr, "Coming Home," *Parade* magazine, October 21, 2012, p. 11.

96 A comment made to the authors in an informal conversation by a couple when they had recently returned from the mission field.

97 Justin Kaplan, General Editor, *Bartlett's Familiar Quotations*, 16th edition (Boston: Little, Brown and Company, 1982), p. 108.

98 Scott C. Todd, *Fast Living: How the Church Will End Extreme Poverty* (Colorado Springs, CO: Compassion International, 2011), p. 151.

99 Walter Brueggemann; "The Liturgy of Abundance, the Myth of Scarcity"; p. 4.

100 Charles J. Gans, "Jazz Master Redefined, Popularized His Genre," an Associated Press article appearing in *Champaign (Ill.) News-Gazette*, December 6, 2012, p. A-3.

101 "Swing Time," Ginger Rogers and Fred Astaire; Reel Classics; 12/16/2008; <http://www.reelclassics.com/Teams/Fred&Ginger/fred&ginger6.htm>; p. 4 of 8/19/2013 7:20 PM printout.

102 John Ronsvalle and Sylvia Ronsvalle; *The State of Church Giving through 2006*, "Global Triage, MDG 4, and Unreached People Groups"; empty tomb, inc.; 2008; <http://www.emptytomb.org/SCG06.ch8excerpt.pdf>.

103 Ronsvalle, *Behind the Stained Glass Windows: Money Dynamics in the Church*, pp. 74-75.

104 "The Promise a Year Later," *First Call for Children*, UNICEF, No. 2 (n.d., approximately 1991).

105 James P. Grant, *The State of the World's Children 1995* (New York: Oxford University Press, 1995), p. 10.

106 "unstats / Millennium Indicators"; Millennium Development Goals, United Nations; n.d.; <http://mdgs.un.org/unsd/mdg/Host.aspex?Content=Data/Trends.htm>; p. 1-22 of 4/20/2007 4:46 PM printout.

107 Danzhen You, Jin Rou New, and Tessa Wardlaw; "Introduction," *Levels & Trends in Child Mortality Report 2012*; UNICEF; 2012; <apromiserenewed.org/files/UNICEF_2012_child_mortality_for_web_0904.pdf>; p. 2.

108 Ban Ki-moon, "Foreword," *The Millennium Development Goals Report 2013*; United Nations; 6/26/2013; <reliefweb.int/sites/reliefweb.int/files/resources/The%20Millennium%20Development%20Goals%20Report%202013.pdf>; p. 3 of 7/1/2013 3:09 PM printout.

109 Patrick Maigua; "More Millennium Development Goals Achievable by 2015"; United Nations Radio, Geneva; 7/1/2013; <http://www.unmultimedia.org/radio/English/2013/07/more-millennium-development-goals-achievable-by-2015/>; p. 1 of 7/1/2013 9:46 AM printout.

110 Scott C. Todd, Ph.D.; "Barna Study Reveals 93% of Christians Are Concerned About Global Poverty"; Religion Press Release Services, Religion News Service; 10/17/2011; <http://campaign.r20.constantcontact.com/rener?llr=8rmq6mcab&v=001p...6yYAehUnXBMMZYjUnpEGAwiGrljDpEubd6nSXH1ThCfUSUxD8HyinUhC66jJbyGVB>; p. 1 of 10/17/2011 9:10 AM printout.

111 John Ronsvalle and Sylvia Ronsvalle; "National Church Leaders Response Form," *The State of Church Giving through 1999*; empty tomb, inc.; 2001; <http://www.emptytomb.org/ResponseForm.html>. It should be noted that a few of the respondents requested that the sentence be revised to read: "Church members in the United States should increase giving through their churches in an effort to stop in Jesus' name the millions of annual preventable global child deaths."

112 For example, see Abid Aslam, editor, *The State of the World's Children 2013* (New York: UNICEF, 2013), p. 97.

113 Gareth Jones, et al.; "How Many Child Deaths Can We Prevent This Year?"; *The Lancet*, vol. 362; 7/5/2003; <http://www.thelancet.com/journal/vol1362/iss9377/full/llan.362.9377.child_survival.26292.1>; pp. 1, 4 of 7/7/03 2:06 PM printout.

[114] Melinda French Gates; "What Nonprofits Can Learn from Coca Cola"; TED; 09-2010, uploaded (YouTube), 10/12/2010; <http://www.youtube.com/watch?annotation_id=annotation_238169&feature=iv&src_vid=bfAzi6D5 FpM&v=GIUS6KE67Vs>; transcribed at minutes 7:40 of 8/22/2013 viewing, and 15:40 of 8/14/13 viewing.

[115] empty tomb, inc. licensed use of the photos illustrating Figure 24 from the Associated Press.

[116] *The State of the World's Children 2013*, pp. 95, 103, 139.

[117] The information was analyzed as follows. The annual number of under-5 child deaths for each country was entered on that country's row of a spreadsheet. The sum of the under-5 child deaths in these 74 countries totaled 7,272,900 in 2010. With a UNICEF figure of 7,606,900 under-5 deaths in 2010, it was calculated that these 74 countries accounted for 96% of the under-5 child deaths in 2010.

Next, the percent of the under-5 deaths due to each cause was entered in the spreadsheet row for each of the 74 nations. Each country's percent of the total number of child deaths was then calculated.

Having calculated a percent of the total under-5 child deaths for each country, that individual percent was used as a multiplier for $5 billion, which served as a base cost figure for preventing the 7.2729 million annual under-5 child deaths. The result was the cost-per-country dollar figure that would be needed to address causes of under-5 mortality in that country.

The cost estimate of $5 billion is the same figure used to develop a cost-per-child death figure cited in chapter 6. The *Bulletin of the World Health Organization* cited a figure of $52.4 billion that would be needed over the ten years, from 2006 through 2015, to "address the major causes of mortality among children aged < 5 years." [Karin Stenberg, Benjamin Johns, Robert W. Scherpbier, & Tessa Tan-Torres Edejer; "A Financial Road Map to Scaling Up Essential Child Health Interventions in 75 Countries"; Bulletin of the World Health Organization; April 2007, 85 (4); <http://www.who.int/bulletin/volumes/85/4/06-032052.pdf>; p. 1 of 8/8/2009 printout.]

The annual average for that estimate was $5.2 billion a year, thus providing support for the use of $5 billion for the present purpose.

Once a dollar figure was developed for each country, that dollar figure was multiplied by the percent of each cause of under-5 child deaths within that country. The result was a dollar-cost estimate by country per cause of death for each of the measured categories. Those categories included: Pneumonia; Diarrhea; Measles; Meningitis; Injuries; Malaria; HIV/AIDS; Other; and Neonatal.

Similarly, a dollar-cost estimate was calculated for each of the seven "Causes of neonatal deaths." The "Neonatal" categories included: Pneumonia; Preterm; Asphyxia; Sepsis; Other; Congenital; Diarrhea.

[118] Abid Aslam and Julia Szczuka, *The State of the World's Children 2012* (New York: UNICEF, 2012), p. 88-91.

[119] Jennifer Requejo, Jennifer Bryce, and Cesar Victora, *Countdown to 2015, Maternal, Newborn & Child Survival: The 2012 Report* (New York: World Health Organization and UNICEF, 2012).

[120] See Countdown to 2015 Coordinating Committee; *Countdown to 2015 Decade Report (2000–2010): Taking Stock of Maternal, Newborn and Child Survival*; World Health Organization and UNICEF; created 5/21/2010; modified 6/3/2010; <http://www.countdown2015mnch.org/documents/2010report/CountdownReportAndProfiles. pdf>; pp. 158-159 (unnumbered). Data that included a percentage enumeration for nine "Causes of under-5 deaths," one of which was the summary category, "Neonatal," was provided for 73. Additionally, detail data for seven "Causes of neonatal deaths" was provided for the same 73 countries and territories.

It may be noted that Tables 47-48 include information for 74 countries. In the case of Sudan and the new nation of South Sudan, 2010 information on the causes of death was not listed for either country. The 2010 pre-cession data was used as a combined figure for Sudan and South Sudan for the rate of under-5 child deaths. Since 2010 data for causes of death was not listed for either country, the 2008 figures for Sudan were used in the analysis.

Eight of the nine Data Year 2008 "Causes of Under-5 Deaths" fit into the nine DY 2010 "Causes of Under-5 Deaths" labels without the need for adjustment. One DY 2010 label, Meningitis, was new. The seven DY 2008 "Causes of Neonatal Deaths" labels did not fit into the seven DY 2010 "Causes of Neonatal Deaths" labels without the need for adjustment. Five labels are the same: Preterm, Asphyxia, Other, Congenital, and Diarrhoea. Two DY 2010 new labels were Pneumonia and Sepsis, the latter of which is noted as "Sepsis/meningitis/tetanus." Two DY 2008 labels not used for DY 2010 are Tetanus and Infection, which were combined with Sepsis. The DY 2008 percent amounts were then adjusted to the DY 2010 percent amounts.

[121] John P. Hoffman, "Declining Religious Authority? Confidence in the Leaders of Religious Organizations, 1973–2010," *Review of Religious Research*, March 2013, Vol. 55, No. 1, pp. 1, 23.

[122] Gallup estimate of 76.1% Americans self-identifying as Christian multiplied by a 2011 U.S. population figure of 312,036,000. Gallup figure from Frank Newport; "Christianity Remains Dominant Religion in the United States";

Gallup; 12/23/2011; <http://www.gallup.com/poll/151760/Christianity-Remains-Dominant-Religion-United-States. aspx?version=print>; p. 1 of 1/5/2012 4:00 PM printout.

[123] Anthony Bradley; "The 'New Legalism' "; World; 5/4/2013 12:54 PM; <http://www.worldmag.com/ 2013/05/the_new_legalism>; p. 1 of 8/16/2013 10:54 AM printout.

[124] C. S. Lewis, *Out of the Silent Planet* (New York: Scribner Paperback Fiction, 1996), p. 77.

[125] Luisa Kroll, Forbes Staff; "The Forbes 400: The Richest People in America"; Forbes.com; 9/19/2012; <http:// www.forbes.com/sites/luisakroll/2012/09/19/the-forbes=400-the-richest-people-in-america/print>; p. 3 of 9/19/2012 11:30 AM printout.

[126] Ronsvalle, *Behind the Stained Glass Windows: Money Dynamics in the Church*, p. 225.

[127] "About the Movement: History of Issachar"; Issachar Initiative; 2012; <http://issacharinitiative.org/about-issachar/ about-the-movement/>; pp. 1-3 of 7/18/2013 8:43AM printout.

[128] "What Happened in Costa Mesa"; Issachar Initiative; 2012; <http://issacharinitiative.org/what-happened-in-costa-mesa/>; p. 2 of 7/18/2013 printout.

[129] "Why Issachar?"; Issachar Initiative; 2012; <http://issacharinitiative.org/about-issachar/why-issachar/>; p. 2 of 7/18/2013 8:49 AM printout.

[130] "Objectives"; Issachar Initiative; 2012; <http://issacharinitiative.org/about-issachar/objectives/>; p. 1 of 7/18/2013 8:51 AM printout.

[131] Last Languages Campaign: Great Support; "More is Needed"; Wycliffe Bible Translators; 2009; <http://www. wycliffe.org/LLC_old/LLCMain/GreatSupport.aspx>; p. 2 of 8/25/2012 6:31 PM printout. "The Last Languages Campaign"; Wycliffe; n.d.; <http://www.lastlanguagescampaign.org/LLC.aspx>; p. 1 of 8/18/2012 11:14 AM printout.

[132] "We're celebrating 4,000,000,000 but our goal is ZERO," National Christian Foundation, Alpharetta, GA, brochure mailing received 7/17/2013.

[133] Richard Stearns, *Unfinished*, p. 56.

[134] "USCCB Officers"; U.S. Conference of Catholic Bishops; 2013; <http://www.usccb.org/about/leaderhip/usccb-officers.cfm>; p. 1 of 8/22/2013 7:00 PM printout.

[135] Francis X. Rocca, "Pope Names 22 New Cardinals, 2 from U.S.; Ceremony Feb. 16," a Catholic News Service article appearing in *Peoria (Ill.) Catholic Post*, January 22, 2012, p. 10.

[136] Wesley Granberg-Michaelson, "Neighbors in Christ," *Christian Century*, August 21, 2013, p. 28, and "Staff Directory and Contact Information"; Reformed Church in America; 2013; <https://www.rca.org/sslpage. aspx?pid=224>; p. 1 of 8/22/2013 2:13 PM printout.

[137] Eileen Lindner, ed., *Yearbook of American and Canadian Churches 2000: Religious Pluralism in the New* Millennium (Nashville: Abingdon Press, 2002), back cover, and Eileen Lindner, ed., *Yearbook of American and Canadian Churches 2012: Can the Church Log in with the "Connected Generation"?* (Nashville: Abingdon, 2012), back cover.

[138] Timothy C. Morgan, "Rick Warren's Final Frontier," *Christianity Today*, April 2013, p. 36.

[139] Pew Research; " 'Nones' on the Rise"; p. 5.

APPENDIXES

APPENDIX A: *List of Denominations*

Church Member Giving, 1968-2011, Composite Set

American Baptist Churches in the U.S.A.
The American Lutheran Church (through 1986)
Associate Reformed Presbyterian Church
   (General Synod)
Brethren in Christ Church
Christian Church (Disciples of Christ)
Church of God (Anderson, Ind.) (through 1997)
Church of God General Conference (McDonough,
   Ga.; formerly of Oregon, Ill., and Morrow, Ga.)
Church of the Brethren
Church of the Nazarene
Conservative Congregational Christian Conference
Cumberland Presbyterian Church
Evangelical Congregational Church
Evangelical Covenant Church (through 2007)
Evangelical Lutheran Church in America
   The American Lutheran Church (merged 1987)
   Lutheran Church in America (merged 1987)
Evangelical Lutheran Synod
Fellowship of Evangelical Bible Churches
Fellowship of Evangelical Churches (formerly
   Evangelical Mennonite Church)
Free Methodist Church-USA (formerly
   of North America)
Friends United Meeting (through 1990)
General Association of General Baptists
Lutheran Church in America (through 1986)
Lutheran Church-Missouri Synod
Mennonite Church USA (1999)
   Mennonite Church (merged 1999)
   Mennonite Church, General Conference
      (merged 1999)
Moravian Church in America, Northern Province
North American Baptist Conference (through 2006)
The Orthodox Presbyterian Church
Presbyterian Church (U.S.A.)
Reformed Church in America
Seventh-day Adventist Church, North American
   Division of
Southern Baptist Convention
United Church of Christ
Wisconsin Evangelical Lutheran Synod

Church Member Giving, 2010–2011

The Composite Set Denominations included in the
   1968-2011 analysis with data available for both
   years, plus the following:
Allegheny Wesleyan Methodist Connection
Baptist Missionary Association of America
Bible Fellowship Church
Christ Community Church (Evangelical-Protestant)
Christian and Missionary Alliance
Church of Christ (Holiness) U.S.A.
Church of the Lutheran Brethren of America
Church of the Lutheran Confession
Churches of God General Conference
The Episcopal Church
The Missionary Church
Presbyterian Church in America
Primitive Methodist Church in the U.S.A.
The United Methodist Church
The Wesleyan Church

By Organizational Affiliation: NAE, 1968-2011

Church of the Nazarene
Conservative Congregational Christian Conference
Evangelical Congregational Church
Fellowship of Evangelical Churches
   (formerly Evangelical Mennonite Church)
Free Methodist Church-USA (formerly
   of North America)
General Association of General Baptists

By Organizational Affiliation: NCC, 1968-2011

American Baptist Churches in the U.S.A.
Christian Church (Disciples of Christ)
Church of the Brethren
Evangelical Lutheran Church in America
Moravian Church in America, Northern Province
Presbyterian Church (U.S.A.)
Reformed Church in America
United Church of Christ

11 Denominations, 1921-2011

American Baptist (Northern)
Christian Church (Disciples of Christ)
Church of the Brethren
The Episcopal Church
Evangelical Lutheran Church in America
   The American Lutheran Church
      American Lutheran Church
      The Evangelical Lutheran Church
      United Evangelical Lutheran Church
      Lutheran Free Church
   Evangelical Lutheran Churches, Assn. of
   Lutheran Church in America
      United Lutheran Church
         General Council Evangelical Lutheran Ch.
         General Synod of Evangelical Lutheran Ch.
         United Synod Evangelical Lutheran South
      American Evangelical Lutheran Church
      Augustana Lutheran Church
      Finnish Lutheran Church (Suomi Synod)
Moravian Church in America, Northern Province
Presbyterian Church (U.S.A.)
   United Presbyterian Church in the U.S.A.
      Presbyterian Church in the U.S.A.
      United Presbyterian Church in North America
   Presbyterian Church in the U.S.
Reformed Church in America
Southern Baptist Convention
United Church of Christ
   Congregational Christian
      Congregational
   Evangelical and Reformed
      Evangelical Synod of North America/German
      Reformed Church in the U.S.
The United Methodist Church
   The Evangelical United Brethren
   The Methodist Church
      Methodist Episcopal Church
      Methodist Episcopal Church South
      Methodist Protestant Church

Trends in Membership, 11 Mainline Protestant Denominations, 1968-2011

American Baptist Churches in the U.S.A.
Christian Church (Disciples of Christ)
Church of the Brethren
The Episcopal Church
Evangelical Lutheran Church in America
Friends United Meeting

Moravian Church in America, Northern Province
Presbyterian Church (U.S.A.)
Reformed Church in America
United Church of Christ
The United Methodist Church

Trends in Membership, 15 Evangelical Denominations, 1968-2011

Assemblies of God
Brethren in Christ Church
Christian and Missionary Alliance
Church of God (Cleveland, Tenn.)
Church of the Nazarene
Conservative Congregational Christian Conference
Converge Worldwide (formerly Baptist General
   Conference)
Evangelical Congregational Church
Fellowship of Evangelical Bible Churches
Fellowship of Evangelical Churches
   (formerly Evangelical Mennonite Church)
Free Methodist Church-USA (formerly
   of North America)
General Association of General Baptists
Lutheran Church-Missouri Synod
Salvation Army
Southern Baptist Convention

Trends in Membership, 35 Protestant Denominations and the Roman Catholic Church, 1968-2011

11 Mainline Protestant Denominations (above)
15 Evangelical Denominations (above)
The Roman Catholic Church
Nine Additional Composite Denominations:
   Associate Reformed Presbyterian Church
      (General Synod)
   Church of God (Anderson, Ind.)
   Church of God General Conference (McDonough,
      Ga.; formerly of Oregon, Ill. and Morrow, Ga.)
   Cumberland Presbyterian Church
   Evangelical Lutheran Synod
   Mennonite Church USA
   The Orthodox Presbyterian Church
   Seventh-day Adventist Church, North American
      Division of
   Wisconsin Evangelical Lutheran Synod

APPENDIX B SERIES: *Denominational Data Tables*

Introduction

The data in the following tables is from the *Yearbook of American and Canadian Churches* (*YACC*) series unless otherwise noted. The series title was *Yearbook of American Churches* (*YAC*) from 1933 to 1972. Financial data is presented in current dollars.

Data in italics indicates a change from the previous edition in *The State of Church Giving* (SCG) series.

The Appendix B tables are described below.

Appendix B-1, Church Member Giving, 1968-2011: This table presents aggregate data for the denominations which comprise the data set analyzed for the 1968 through 2011 period.

Elements of this data are also used for the analyses in chapters two through seven.

In Appendix B-1, the data for the Presbyterian Church (U.S.A.) combined data for the United Presbyterian Church in the U.S.A. and the Presbyterian Church in the United States for the period 1968 through 1982. These two communions merged to become the Presbyterian Church (U.S.A.) in 1983, data for which is presented for 1983 through 2011.

Also in Appendix B-1, data for the Evangelical Lutheran Church in America (ELCA) appears beginning in 1987. Before that, the two major component communions that merged into the ELCA—the American Lutheran Church and the Lutheran Church in America—are listed as individual denominations from 1968 through 1986.

In the Appendix B series, the denomination listed as the Fellowship of Evangelical Bible Churches was named the Evangelical Mennonite Brethren Church prior to July 1987.

For 1999, the Mennonite Church (Elkhart, IN) provided information for the Mennonite Church USA. This communion is the result of a merger passed at a national convention in July 2001 between the Mennonite Church and the Mennonite Church, General Conference. The latter's 1968-1998 data has been added to the composite set series. The Mennonite Church USA dollar figures for 1999, and membership through 2001, combine data for the two predecessor communions.

The 1999, 2000, 2001, and 2002 data for the Southern Baptist Convention used in the 1968-2011 analysis includes data only for those State Conventions that provided a breakdown of total contributions between Congregational Finances and Benevolences for that year. For the 11 Denominations 1921-2011 analysis, 1999, 2000, 2001, and 2002, Southern Baptist Convention Total Contributions is $7,772,452,961, $8,437,177,940, $8,935,013,659, and $9,461,603,271 respectively. For the 11 Denominations 1921-2011 analysis, and the Membership Trends analysis, 1999, 2000, 2001, and 2002, Southern Baptist Convention Membership is 15,581,756, 15,960,308, 16,052,920, and 16,137,736 respectively.

The 2006, 2007, 2008, 2009, 2010, and 2011 data for the Southern Baptist Convention used in the 1968-2011 analysis also includes data only for those State Conventions that provided a breakdown of total contributions between Congregational Finances and Benevolences for that year. For the Membership analysis, the data is: 2006: 16,306,246; 2007: 16,266,920; 2008: 16,228,438; 2009: 16,160,088; 2010: 16,136,044; 2011: 15,978,112.

Data for the American Baptist Churches in the U.S.A. has been obtained directly from the denominational office as follows. In discussions with the American Baptist Churches Office of Planning Resources, it became apparent that there had been no distinction made between the membership of congregations reporting financial data, and total membership for the denomination, when reporting data to the *YACC*. Records were obtained from the denomination for a smaller membership figure that reflected only those congregations reporting financial data. While this revised membership data provided a more useful per member giving figure for Congregational Finances, the total Benevolences figure reported to the *YACC*, while included in the present data set, does reflect contributions to some Benevolences categories from 100% of the American Baptist membership. The membership reported in Appendix B-1 for the American Baptist Churches is the membership for congregations reporting financial data, rather than the total membership figure provided in editions of the *YACC*. However, in the sections that consider membership as a percentage of population, the Total Membership figure for the American Baptist Churches, shown in Appendix B-4, is used.

The Church of God General Conference (Oregon, IL and Morrow, GA) changed its name to Church of God General Conference (McDonough, GA).

The Free Methodist Church of North America changed its name to Free Methodist Church-USA.

Appendix B-2, Church Member Giving for 38 Denominations, 2010-2011: Appendix B-2 presents the Full or Confirmed Membership, Congregational Finances and Benevolences data for the 15 additional denominations included in the 2010-2011 comparison.

Appendix B-3, Church Member Giving for 11 Denominations, In Current Dollars, 1921-2011: This appendix presents additional data that is not included in Appendix B-1 for the 11 Denominations.

The data from 1921 through 1928 in Appendix B-3.1 is taken from summary information contained in the *YACC*, 1949 Edition, George F. Ketcham, ed. (Lebanon, PA: Sowers Printing Company, 1949, p. 162). The summary membership data provided is for Inclusive Membership. Therefore, giving as a percentage of income for the years 1921 through 1928 may have been somewhat higher had Full or Confirmed Membership been used. The list of denominations that are summarized for this period is presented in the *YAC*, 1953 Edition, Benson Y. Landis, ed. (New York: National Council of the Churches of Christ in the U.S.A., 1953, p. 274).

The data from 1929 through 1952 is taken from summary information presented in the *YAC*, Edition for 1955, Benson Y. Landis, ed. (New York: National Council of the Churches of Christ in the U.S.A., 1954, pp. 286-287). A description of the list of denominations included in the 1929 through 1952 data summary on page 275 of the *YAC* Edition for 1955 indicated that the Moravian Church, Northern Province is not included in the 1929 through 1952 data.

The data in Appendix B-3.2 for 1953 through 1964 was obtained for the indicated denominations from the relevant edition of the *YAC* series. Giving as a percentage of income was derived for these years by dividing the published Total Contributions figure by the published Per Capita figure to produce a membership figure for each denomination. The Total Contributions figures for the denominations were added to produce an aggregated Total Contributions figure. The calculated membership figures were also added to produce an aggregated membership figure. The aggregated Total Contributions figure was then divided by the aggregated membership figure to yield a per member giving figure which was used in calculating giving as a percentage of income.

Data for the years 1965 through 1967 was not available in a form that could be readily analyzed for the present purposes, and therefore data for these three years was estimated by dividing the change in per capita Total Contributions from 1964 to 1968 by four, the number of years in this interval, and cumulatively adding the result to the base year of 1964 and the succeeding years of 1965 and 1966 to obtain estimates for the years 1965 through 1967.

In most cases, this procedure was also applied to individual denominations to avoid an artificially low total due to missing data. If data was not available for a specific year, the otherwise blank entry was filled in with a calculation based on surrounding years for the denomination. For example, this procedure was used for the American Baptist Churches for the years 1955 and 1996, the Christian Church (Disciples of Christ) for the years 1955 and 1959, and the Evangelical United Brethren, later to merge into The United Methodist Church, for the years 1957, 1958 and 1959. Data for the Methodist Church was changed for 1957 in a similar manner.

Available Total Contributions and Full or Confirmed Members data for The Episcopal Church and The United Methodist Church for 1968 through 2011 is presented in Appendix B-3.3. These two communions are included in the 11 Denominations. The United Methodist Church was created in 1968 when the Methodist Church and the Evangelical United Brethren Church merged. While the Methodist Church filed summary data for the year 1968, the Evangelical United Brethren Church did not. Data for these denominations was calculated as noted in the appendix. However, since the 1968 data for The Methodist Church would not have been comparable to the 1985 and 2011 data for The United Methodist Church, this communion was not included in the more focused 1969-2011 composite analysis. The United Methodist Church Connectional Clergy Support 1968-2008 data used in Chapter 5 was obtained directly from the denominational source and is also presented in this appendix.

Appendix B-4, Membership for Seven Denominations, 1968-2011: This appendix presents denominational membership data used in the membership analyses presented in chapter five that is not available in the other appendixes. Unless otherwise indicated, the data is from the *YACC* series. The Baptist General Conference changed its name to Converge Worldwide.

Appendix B-5, Overseas Missions Income, 2003, 2004, 2005, 2006, 2007, 2008, 2009, 2010, and 2011: This appendix presents numbers provided on the four lines of the Overseas Missions Income form completed by the respective denominations. Also provided is Overseas Missions Income for denominations that are not otherwise included in one or more years of the analyses (see chapter 6, note 9).

Appendix B-6, Estimates of Giving: This appendix provides the data used in the comparison presented in chapter 7 of the Consumer Expenditure Survey, the Form 990 series, and the Giving USA series, for 1989-2009.

APPENDIX B-1: *Church Member Giving, 1968-2011*

Key to Denominational Abbreviations: Data Years 1968-2011

Abbreviation	Denomination
abc	American Baptist Churches in the U.S.A.
alc	The American Lutheran Church
arp	Associate Reformed Presbyterian Church (General Synod)
bcc	Brethren in Christ Church
ccd	Christian Church (Disciples of Christ)
cga	Church of God (Anderson, IN)
cgg	Church of God General Conference (McDonough, GA; formerly of Oregon, IL and Morrow, GA)
chb	Church of the Brethren
chn	Church of the Nazarene
cccc	Conservative Congregational Christian Conference
cpc	Cumberland Presbyterian Church
ecc	Evangelical Congregational Church
ecv	Evangelical Covenant Church
elc	Evangelical Lutheran Church in America
els	Evangelical Lutheran Synod
emc	Evangelical Mennonite Church
feb	Fellowship of Evangelical Bible Churches
fec	Fellowship of Evangelical Churches
fmc	Free Methodist Church-USA (formerly of North America)
fum	Friends United Meeting
ggb	General Association of General Baptists
lca	Lutheran Church in America
lms	Lutheran Church-Missouri Synod
mch	Mennonite Church
mgc	Mennonite Church, General Conference
mus	Mennonite Church USA
mca	Moravian Church in America, Northern Province
nab	North American Baptist Conference
opc	The Orthodox Presbyterian Church
pch	Presbyterian Church (U.S.A.)
rca	Reformed Church in America
sda	Seventh-day Adventist, North American Division of
sbc	Southern Baptist Convention
ucc	United Church of Christ
wel	Wisconsin Evangelical Lutheran Synod

Appendix B-1: Church Member Giving, in Current Dollars, 1968-2011

	Data Year 1968			Data Year 1969			Data Year 1970		
	Full/Confirmed Members	Congregational Finances	Benevolences	Full/Confirmed Members	Congregational Finances	Benevolences	Full/Confirmed Members	Congregational Finances	Benevolences
abc	1,179,848	95,878,267 [a]	21,674,924 [a]	1,153,785 [a]	104,084,322 [a]	21,111,333	1,231,944 [a]	112,668,310	19,655,391
alc	1,767,618	137,260,390	32,862,410 [a]	1,771,999	143,917,440	34,394,570	1,775,573	146,268,320	30,750,030
arp	28,312 [a]	2,211,002 [a]	898,430 [a]	28,273	2,436,936 [a]	824,628 [a]	28,427	2,585,974 [a]	806,071 [a]
bcc	8,954	1,645,256	633,200 [a]	9,145	1,795,859	817,445	9,300	2,037,330 [a]	771,940 [a]
ccd	994,683	105,803,222	21,703,947	936,931	91,169,842	18,946,815 [a]	911,964	98,671,692	17,386,032
cga	146,807	23,310,682	4,168,580	147,752	24,828,448	4,531,678	150,198	26,962,037	4,886,223
cgg	6,600	805,000	103,000	6,700	805,000	104,000	6,800	810,000	107,000
chb	187,957	12,975,829	4,889,727	185,198	13,964,158	4,921,991	182,614	14,327,896	4,891,618
chn	364,789	59,943,750 [a]	14,163,761 [a]	372,943	64,487,669 [a]	15,220,339 [a]	383,284	68,877,922 [a]	16,221,123 [a]
cccc	15,127	1,867,978	753,686 [a]	16,219	1,382,195	801,534	17,328	1,736,818	779,696
cpc	87,044 [a]	6,247,447 [a]	901,974 [a]	86,435 [a]	7,724,405 [a]	926,317 [a]	86,683 [a]	7,735,906 [a]	1,011,911 [a]
ecc	29,582 [a]	3,369,308 [a]	627,731 [a]	29,652 [a]	3,521,074 [a]	646,187 [a]	29,437 [a]	3,786,288 [a]	692,428 [a]
ecv	66,021	14,374,162 [a]	3,072,848 [a]	67,522	14,952,302 [a]	3,312,306 [a]	67,441	15,874,265 [a]	3,578,876 [a]
elc	ALC & LCA	ALC & LCA	ALC & LCA	ALC & LCA	ALC & LCA	ALC & LCA	ALC & LCA	ALC & LCA	ALC & LCA
els	10,886 [a]	844,235 [a]	241,949 [a]	11,079 [a]	1,003,746 [a]	315,325 [a]	11,030 [a]	969,625	242,831 [a]
emc	2,870 [a]	447,397 [a]	232,331	NA	NA	NA	NA	NA	NA
feb	1,712 [a]	156,789 [a]	129,818 [a]	3,324	389,000	328,000	3,698	381,877	706,398
fec	see EMC	see EMC	see EMC	see EMC	see EMC	see EMC	see EMC	see EMC	see EMC
fmc	47,831	12,032,016 [a]	2,269,677 [a]	47,954	13,187,506 [a]	2,438,351 [a]	64,901	9,641,202	7,985,264
fum	55,469	3,564,793 [a]	1,256,192 [a]	55,257	3,509,509 [a]	1,289,026	53,970	3,973,802	1,167,183
ggb	65,000	4,303,183 [a]	269,921 [a]	NA	NA	NA	NA	NA	NA
lca	2,279,383	166,337,149 [a]	39,981,858 [a]	2,193,321	161,958,669 [a]	46,902,225	2,187,015	169,795,380	42,118,870
lms	1,877,799	178,042,762 [a]	47,415,800 [a]	1,900,708	185,827,626 [a]	49,402,590	1,922,569	193,352,322	47,810,664
mch	85,682	7,078,164 [a]	5,576,305 [a]	85,343	7,398,182 [a]	6,038,730 [a]	83,747 [a]	7,980,917 [a]	6,519,476 [a]
mgc	36,337	2,859,340 [a]	2,668,138 [a]	35,613	2,860,555 [a]	2,587,079 [a]	35,536	3,091,670	2,550,208
mus	MCH & MGC	MCH & MGC	MCH & MGC	MCH & MGC	MCH & MGC	MCH & MGC	MCH & MGC	MCH & MGC	MCH & MGC
mca	27,772 [b]	2,583,354	444,910 [a]	27,617	2,642,529 [b]	456,182	27,173	2,704,105	463,219
nab	42,371	5,176,669 [a]	1,383,964 [a]	55,100	6,681,410	2,111,588	55,080	6,586,929	2,368,288
opc	9,197	1,638,437 [a]	418,102 [a]	9,276	1,761,242 [a]	464,660	9,401	1,853,627 [a]	503,572 [a]
pch	4,180,093	375,248,474 [b]	102,622,450 [a]	4,118,664	388,268,169 [b]	97,897,522 [a]	4,041,813	401,785,731	93,927,852
rca	226,819 [b]	25,410,489 [b]	9,197,642 [b]	224,992 [b]	27,139,579 [b]	9,173,312 [b]	223,353 [b]	29,421,849 [b]	9,479,503 [b]
sda	395,159	36,976,280 [a]	95,178,335 [a]	407,766	40,378,426 [a]	102,730,594	420,419	45,280,059	109,569,241
sbc	11,332,229	666,924,020 [a]	128,023,731 [a]	11,487,708	709,246,590 [a]	133,203,885	11,628,032	753,510,973	138,480,329
ucc	2,032,648	152,301,536 [a]	18,869,136 [a]	1,997,898	152,791,512 [a]	27,338,543 [a]	1,960,608	155,248,767	26,934,289
wel	259,649	18,982,244 [a]	6,572,250 [a]	264,710	20,761,838 [a]	6,414,099 [a]	270,073	22,525,244 [a]	6,781,600 [a]
Total	27,852,248	2,126,599,624	569,206,727	27,738,884	2,200,875,738	595,650,854	27,879,411	2,310,446,837	599,147,126

[a] Data obtained from denominational source.
[b] empty tomb review of RCA directory data.

Appendix B-1: Church Member Giving, in Current Dollars, 1968-2011 (continued)

	Data Year 1971			Data Year 1972			Data Year 1973		
	Full/Confirmed Members	Congregational Finances	Benevolences	Full/Confirmed Members	Congregational Finances	Benevolences	Full/Confirmed Members	Congregational Finances	Benevolences
abc	1,223,735 [a]	114,673,805	18,878,769	1,176,092 [a]	118,446,573	18,993,440	1,190,455 [a]	139,357,611 [a]	20,537,388 [a]
alc	1,775,774 [a]	146,324,460	28,321,740	1,773,414	154,786,570	30,133,850	1,770,119 [a]	168,194,730 [a]	35,211,440 [a]
arp	28,443	2,942,577 [a]	814,703 [a]	28,711	3,329,446 [a]	847,665 [a]	28,763 [a]	3,742,773 [a]	750,387 [a]
bcc	9,550	2,357,786	851,725	9,730	2,440,400	978,957	9,877 [a]	2,894,622 [a]	1,089,879 [a]
ccd	884,929	94,091,862	17,770,799	881,467	105,763,511	18,323,685	868,895	112,526,538	19,800,843
cga	152,787	28,343,604	5,062,282	155,920	31,580,751	5,550,487	157,828	34,649,592	6,349,695
cgg	7,200	860,000	120,000	7,400	900,000	120,000	7,440	940,000	120,000
chb	181,183	14,535,274	5,184,768	179,641	14,622,319 [c]	5,337,277 [c]	179,333	16,474,758	6,868,927
chn	394,197	75,107,918 [a]	17,859,332 [a]	404,732	82,891,903 [a]	20,119,679 [a]	417,200 [a]	91,318,469 [a]	22,661,140 [a]
cccc	19,279 [a]	1,875,010 [a]	930,485 [a]	20,081	1,950,865 [a]	994,453 [a]	20,712 [a]	2,080,038 [a]	1,057,869 [a]
cpc	86,945 [a]	7,729,131 [a]	1,009,657 [a]	88,200	8,387,762 [a]	1,064,831 [a]	88,203 [a]	9,611,201 [a]	1,220,768 [a]
ecc	29,682 [a]	4,076,576 [a]	742,293 [a]	29,434	4,303,406 [a]	798,968 [a]	29,331 [a]	4,913,214 [a]	943,619 [a]
ecv	68,428	17,066,051	3,841,887	69,815	18,021,767 [a]	4,169,053	69,922	18,948,864 [a]	4,259,950
elc	ALC & LCA	ALC & LCA	ALC & LCA	ALC & LCA	ALC & LCA	ALC & LCA	ALC & LCA	ALC & LCA	ALC & LCA
els	11,426 [a]	1,067,650 [a]	314,335 [a]	11,532	1,138,953	295,941 [a]	12,525	1,296,326 [a]	330,052 [a]
emc	NA	NA	NA	NA	NA	NA	3,131	593,070	408,440
feb	NA	NA	NA	NA	NA	NA	NA	NA	NA
fec	see EMC	see EMC	see EMC	see EMC	see EMC	see EMC	see EMC	see EMC	see EMC
fmc	47,933 [a]	13,116,414 [a]	2,960,525 [a]	48,400	14,311,395 [a]	3,287,000 [a]	48,763 [a]	15,768,216 [a]	3,474,555 [a]
fum	54,522	3,888,064	1,208,062	54,927	4,515,463	1,297,088	57,690	5,037,848	1,327,439
ggb	NA	NA	NA	NA	NA	NA	NA	NA	NA
lca	2,175,378	179,570,467	43,599,913	2,165,591	188,387,949	45,587,481	2,169,341	200,278,486	34,627,978
lms	1,945,889	203,619,804	48,891,368	1,963,262	216,756,345	50,777,670	1,983,114	230,435,598	54,438,074
mch	88,522	8,171,316	7,035,750	89,505	9,913,176	7,168,664	90,967	9,072,858	6,159,740
mgc	36,314	3,368,100	2,833,491	36,129	3,378,372	3,219,439	36,483	3,635,418	3,392,844
mus	MCH & MGC	MCH & MGC	MCH & MGC	MCH & MGC	MCH & MGC	MCH & MGC	MCH & MGC	MCH & MGC	MCH & MGC
mca	26,101	2,576,172	459,447	25,500	2,909,252	465,316	25,468	3,020,667	512,424
nab	54,997	7,114,457	2,293,692	54,441	7,519,558	2,253,158	41,516	6,030,352	1,712,092
opc	9,536 [a]	2,054,448 [a]	533,324 [a]	9,741	2,248,969 [a]	602,328	9,940 [a]	2,364,079 [a]	658,534 [a]
pch	3,963,665	420,865,807	93,164,548	3,855,494	436,042,890	92,691,469	3,730,312 [d]	480,735,088 [d]	95,462,247 [d]
rca	219,915 [b]	32,217,319 [b]	9,449,655 [b]	217,583	34,569,874 [b]	9,508,818 [b]	212,906 [b]	39,524,443 [b]	10,388,619 [b]
sda	433,906	49,208,043	119,913,879	449,188	54,988,781	132,411,980	464,276	60,643,602	149,994,942
sbc	11,824,676	814,406,626	160,510,775	12,065,333	896,427,208	174,711,648	12,295,400	1,011,467,569	193,511,983
ucc	1,928,674	158,924,956	26,409,521	1,895,016	165,556,364	27,793,561	1,867,810	168,602,602	28,471,058
wel	274,635 [a]	24,315,801 [a]	7,456,829 [a]	277,628	26,585,530 [a]	8,204,262 [a]	282,355 [a]	29,377,447 [a]	8,623,460 [a]
Total	27,958,221	2,434,469,498	628,423,554	28,043,907	2,612,675,352	667,708,168	28,170,075	2,873,536,079	714,366,386

a Data obtained from denominational source.
b empty tomb review of RCA directory data.
c YACC Church of the Brethren figures reported for 15 months due to fiscal year change: adjusted here to 12/15ths.
d The Presbyterian Church (USA) data for 1973 combines United Presbyterian Church in the U.S.A. data for 1973 (see YACC 1975) and an average of Presbyterian Church in the United States data for 1972 and 1974, since 1973 data was not reported in the YACC series.

Appendix B-1: Church Member Giving, in Current Dollars, 1968-2011 (continued)

	Data Year 1974			Data Year 1975			Data Year 1976		
	Full/Confirmed Members	Congregational Finances	Benevolences	Full/Confirmed Members	Congregational Finances	Benevolences	Full/Confirmed Members	Congregational Finances	Benevolences
abc	1,176,989 a	147,022,280	21,847,285	1,180,793 a	153,697,091	23,638,372	1,142,773 a	163,134,092 a	25,792,357
alc	1,764,186	173,318,574	38,921,546	1,764,810	198,863,519	75,666,809	1,768,758	215,527,544	76,478,278
arp	28,570	3,935,533 a	868,284	28,589	4,820,846 a	929,880	28,581	5,034,270 a	1,018,913 a
bcc	10,255	3,002,218	1,078,576	10,784	3,495,152	955,845	11,375	4,088,492	1,038,484
ccd	854,844	119,434,435	20,818,434 a	859,885	126,553,931	22,126,459 a	845,058	135,008,269	23,812,274
cga	161,401	39,189,287	7,343,123	166,259	42,077,029	7,880,559	170,285	47,191,302	8,854,295
cgg	7,455	975,000	105,000	7,485	990,000	105,000	7,620	1,100,000	105,000
chb	179,387	18,609,614	7,281,551	179,336	20,338,351	7,842,819	178,157	22,133,858	8,032,293
chn	430,128	104,774,391 a	25,534,267 a	441,093	115,400,881 a	28,186,392 a	448,658	128,294,499	32,278,187 a
cccc	21,661 a	2,452,254 a	1,181,655 a	22,065 a	2,639,472 a	1,750,364 a	21,703 a	3,073,413 a	1,494,355 a
cpc	87,875 a	9,830,198 a	1,336,847 a	86,903 a	11,268,297 a	1,445,793 a	85,541 a	10,735,854 a	1,540,692 a
ecc	29,636 a	4,901,100 a	1,009,726 a	28,886 a	5,503,484 a	1,068,134 a	28,840 a	6,006,621 a	1,139,209 a
ecv	69,960	21,235,204 a	5,131,124 a	71,808	23,440,265 a	6,353,422 a	73,458	25,686,916 a	6,898,871 a
elc	ALC & LCA	ALC & LCA	ALC & LCA	ALC & LCA	ALC & LCA	ALC & LCA	ALC & LCA	ALC & LCA	ALC & LCA
els	13,097	1,519,749	411,732 a	13,489	1,739,255	438,875 a	14,504	2,114,998	521,018 a
emc	3,123	644,548	548,000	NA	NA	NA	3,350	800,000	628,944
feb	NA	NA	NA	NA	NA	NA	NA	NA	NA
fec	see EMC	see EMC	see EMC	see EMC	see EMC	see EMC	see EMC	see EMC	see EMC
fmc	49,314 a	17,487,246 a	3,945,535 a	50,632	19,203,781 a	4,389,757 a	51,565	21,130,066 a	4,977,546 a
fum	NA	NA	NA	56,605	6,428,458	1,551,036	51,032	6,749,045	1,691,190
ggb	NA	NA	NA	NA	NA	NA	NA	NA	NA
lca	2,166,615	228,081,405	44,531,126	2,183,131	222,637,156	55,646,303	2,187,995	243,449,466	58,761,005
lms	2,010,456	249,150,470	55,076,955	2,018,530	266,546,758	55,896,061	2,026,336	287,098,403	56,831,860
mch	92,930 a	13,792,266	9,887,051	94,209	15,332,908	11,860,385	96,092	17,215,234	12,259,924
mgc	35,534	4,071,002 a	4,179,003 a	35,673	3,715,279 a	3,391,943 a	36,397	4,980,967 a	4,796,037 a
mus	MCH & MGC	MCH & MGC	MCH & MGC	MCH & MGC	MCH & MGC	MCH & MGC	MCH & MGC	MCH & MGC	MCH & MGC
mca	25,583	3,304,388	513,685	25,512	3,567,406	552,512	24,938	4,088,195	573,619
nab	41,437	6,604,693	2,142,148	42,122	7,781,298	2,470,317	42,277	8,902,540	3,302,348
opc	10,186 a	2,627,818	703,653	10,129	2,930,128	768,075	10,372	3,288,612 a	817,589
pch	3,619,768	502,237,350	100,966,089	3,535,825	529,327,006	111,027,318	3,484,985	563,106,353	125,035,379
rca	210,866 b	41,053,364 b	11,470,631 b	212,349 b	44,681,053 b	11,994,379 b	211,628 b	49,083,734 b	13,163,739 b
sda	479,799	67,241,956	166,166,766	495,699	72,060,121	184,689,250	509,792	81,577,130	184,648,454
sbc	12,513,378	1,123,264,849	219,214,770	12,733,124	1,237,594,037	237,452,055	12,917,992	1,382,794,494	262,144,889
ucc	1,841,312	184,292,017	30,243,223	1,818,762	193,524,114	32,125,332	1,801,241	207,486,324	33,862,658
wel	286,083 a	32,596,319 a	9,974,758 a	292,431 a	35,807,415 a	11,173,226 a	297,037	39,932,827 a	11,260,203 a
Total	28,221,828	3,126,649,528	792,432,543	28,466,918	3,371,964,491	903,376,672	28,578,340	3,690,813,518	963,759,610

a Data obtained from denominational source.
b empty tomb review of RCA directory data.

Appendix B-1: Church Member Giving, in Current Dollars, 1968-2011 (continued)

Data Year 1977

	Full/Confirmed Members	Congregational Finances	Benevolences
abc	1,146,084 [a]	172,710,063	27,765,800 [a]
alc	1,772,227	231,960,304	54,085,201
arp	28,371 [a]	5,705,295 [a]	1,061,285 [a]
bcc	11,915 [a]	4,633,334 [a]	957,239 [a]
ccd	817,288	148,880,340	25,698,856
cga	171,947	51,969,150	10,001,062
cgg	7,595	1,130,000	110,000
chb	177,534	23,722,817	8,228,903
chn	455,100	141,807,024 [a]	34,895,751 [a]
cccc	21,897 [a]	3,916,248 [a]	1,554,143 [a]
cpc	85,227 [a]	11,384,825 [a]	1,760,117 [a]
ecc	28,712 [a]	6,356,730 [a]	1,271,310 [a]
ecv	74,060	28,758,357 [a]	7,240,548 [a]
elc	ALC & LCA	ALC & LCA	ALC & LCA
els	14,652 [a]	2,290,697	546,899 [a]
emc	NA	NA	NA
feb	NA	NA	NA
fec	see EMC	see EMC	see EMC
fmc	52,563	23,303,722 [a]	5,505,538 [a]
fum	52,599	6,943,990	1,895,984
ggb	72,030	9,854,533	747,842
lca	2,191,942	251,083,883	62,076,894
lms	1,991,408	301,064,630	57,077,162
mch	96,609	18,540,237	12,980,502
mgc	35,575 [a]	5,051,708 [a]	4,619,590 [a]
mus	MCH & MGC	MCH & MGC	MCH & MGC
mca	25,323	4,583,616	581,200
nab	42,724	10,332,556	3,554,204
opc	10,683 [a]	3,514,172	931,935
pch	3,430,927	633,187,916	130,252,348
rca	210,637 [b]	53,999,791 [b]	14,210,966 [b]
sda	522,317	98,468,365	216,202,975
sbc	13,078,239	1,506,877,921	289,179,711
ucc	1,785,652	219,878,772	35,522,221
wel	301,125 [a]	44,378,032 [a]	11,600,902 [a]
Total	28,712,962	4,026,289,028	1,022,117,088

Data Year 1978

	Full/Confirmed Members	Congregational Finances	Benevolences
abc	1,008,495 [a]	184,716,172	31,937,862 [a]
alc	1,773,179	256,371,804	57,145,861
arp	28,644	6,209,447 [a]	1,031,469 [a]
bcc	12,430 [a]	4,913,311 [a]	1,089,346 [a]
ccd	791,633	166,249,455	25,790,367
cga	173,753	57,630,848	11,214,530
cgg	7,550	1,135,000	110,000
chb	175,335	25,397,531	9,476,220
chn	462,124	153,943,138 [a]	38,300,431 [a]
cccc	22,364 [a]	4,271,435 [a]	1,630,565 [a]
cpc	84,956 [a]	13,359,375 [a]	1,995,388 [a]
ecc	28,459 [a]	6,890,381 [a]	1,454,826 [a]
ecv	74,678	32,606,550 [a]	8,017,623 [a]
elc	ALC & LCA	ALC & LCA	ALC & LCA
els	14,833 [a]	2,629,719	833,543 [a]
emc	3,634	1,281,761	794,896
feb	3,956	970,960	745,059
fec	see EMC	see EMC	see EMC
fmc	52,698	25,505,294 [a]	5,869,970 [a]
fum	53,390	8,172,337	1,968,884
ggb	NA	NA	NA
lca	2,183,666	277,186,563	72,426,148
lms	1,969,279	329,134,237	59,030,753
mch	97,142	22,922,417	14,124,757
mgc	36,775 [a]	5,421,568 [a]	5,062,489 [a]
mus	MCH & MGC	MCH & MGC	MCH & MGC
mca	24,854	4,441,750	625,536
nab	42,499	11,629,309	3,559,983
opc	10,939	4,107,705	1,135,388
pch	3,382,783	692,872,811	128,194,954
rca	211,778 [b]	60,138,720 [b]	15,494,816 [b]
sda	535,705	104,044,989	226,692,736
sbc	13,191,394	1,668,120,760	316,462,385
ucc	1,769,104	232,593,033	37,789,958
wel	303,134 [a]	50,123,714 [a]	12,907,953 [a]
Total	28,531,163	4,414,992,094	1,092,914,696

Data Year 1979

	Full/Confirmed Members	Congregational Finances	Benevolences
abc	1,036,054 [a]	195,986,995 [a]	34,992,300
alc	1,768,071	284,019,905	63,903,906
arp	28,513	6,544,759 [a]	1,125,562 [a]
bcc	12,923	5,519,037	1,312,046
ccd	773,765	172,270,978	27,335,440
cga	175,113	65,974,517	12,434,621
cgg	7,620	1,170,000	105,000
chb	172,115	28,422,684	10,161,266
chn	473,726	170,515,940 [a]	42,087,862 [a]
cccc	23,481	4,969,610 [a]	1,871,754 [a]
cpc	85,932 [a]	13,928,957 [a]	2,192,562 [a]
ecc	27,995 [a]	7,552,495 [a]	1,547,857 [a]
ecv	76,092	37,118,906 [a]	9,400,074 [a]
elc	ALC & LCA	ALC & LCA	ALC & LCA
els	15,081 [a]	2,750,703	904,774 [a]
emc	3,704	1,380,806	828,264
feb	NA	NA	NA
fec	see EMC	see EMC	see EMC
fmc	52,900	27,516,302 [a]	6,614,732 [a]
fum	51,426	6,662,787	2,131,108
ggb	73,046	13,131,345	1,218,763
lca	2,177,231	301,605,382	71,325,097
lms	1,965,422	360,989,735	63,530,596
mch	98,027	24,505,346	15,116,762
mgc	36,736 [a]	6,254,850 [a]	5,660,477 [a]
mus	MCH & MGC	MCH & MGC	MCH & MGC
mca	24,782	4,600,331	689,070
nab	42,779	13,415,024	3,564,339
opc	11,306	4,683,302	1,147,191
pch	3,321,787	776,049,247	148,528,993
rca	210,700 [b]	62,997,526 [b]	16,750,408 [b]
sda	553,089	118,711,906	255,936,372
sbc	13,372,757	1,864,213,869	355,885,769
ucc	1,745,533	249,443,032	41,100,583
wel	305,454 [a]	54,789,339 [a]	14,178,008 [a]
Total	28,723,160	4,887,695,615	1,213,581,556

[a] Data obtained from denominational source.
[b] empty tomb review of RCA directory data.

Appendix B-1: Church Member Giving, in Current Dollars, 1968-2011 (continued)

	Data Year 1980			Data Year 1981			Data Year 1982		
	Full/Confirmed Members	Congregational Finances	Benevolences	Full/Confirmed Members	Congregational Finances	Benevolences	Full/Confirmed Members	Congregational Finances	Benevolences
abc	1,008,700 a	213,560,656	37,133,159	989,322 a	227,931,461	40,046,261	983,580 a	242,750,027	41,457,745
alc	1,763,067	312,592,610	65,235,739 a	1,758,452	330,155,588	96,102,638 a	1,758,239	359,848,865	77,010,444 a
arp	28,166 a	6,868,650 a	1,054,229 a	28,334	7,863,221 a	1,497,838	29,087	8,580,311 a	1,807,572 a
bcc	13,578 a	6,011,465 a	1,490,334 a	13,993	6,781,857	1,740,711	14,413	7,228,612 a	1,594,797 a
ccd	788,394	189,176,399	30,991,519	772,466	211,828,751	31,067,142	770,227	227,178,861	34,307,638
cga	176,429	67,367,485	13,414,112	178,581	78,322,907	14,907,277	184,685	84,896,806	17,171,600
cgg	NA	NA	NA	5,981	1,788,298	403,000	5,781	1,864,735	418,000 a
chb	170,839	29,813,265	11,663,976	170,267	31,641,019	12,929,076	168,844	35,064,568	12,844,415
chn	483,101	191,536,556	45,786,446 a	490,852	203,145,992	50,084,163 a	497,261	221,947,940	53,232,461 a
cccc	24,410 a	6,017,539 a	2,169,298 a	25,044 a	8,465,804	2,415,233	26,008	9,230,111	2,574,569
cpc	86,941 a	15,973,738 a	2,444,677 a	87,493 a	16,876,846 a	2,531,539 a	88,121 a	17,967,709 a	2,706,361 a
ecc	27,567 a	8,037,564 a	1,630,993 a	27,287 a	8,573,057 a	1,758,025 a	27,203 a	9,119,278 a	1,891,936 a
ecv	77,737	41,888,556 a	10,031,072 a	79,523	45,206,565 a	8,689,918	81,324	50,209,520 a	8,830,793
elc	ALC & LCA	ALC & LCA	ALC & LCA	ALC & LCA	ALC & LCA	ALC & LCA	ALC & LCA	ALC & LCA	ALC & LCA
els	14,968 a	3,154,804	876,929 a	14,904	3,461,387	716,624	15,165	3,767,977	804,822
emc	3,782	1,527,945	1,041,447	3,753	1,515,975	908,342	3,832	1,985,890	731,510
feb	4,329	1,250,466	627,536	NA	NA	NA	2,047	696,660	1,020,972
fec	see EMC	see EMC	see EMC	see EMC	see EMC	see EMC	see EMC	see EMC	see EMC
fmc	54,145 a	30,525,352	6,648,248 a	54,764	32,853,491	7,555,713 a	54,198	35,056,434	8,051,593
fum	51,691	9,437,724	2,328,137	51,248	9,551,765	2,449,731	50,601	10,334,180	2,597,215
ggb	74,159	14,967,312	1,547,038	75,028	15,816,060	1,473,070	NA	NA	NA
lca	2,176,991	371,981,816	87,439,137	2,173,558	404,300,509	82,862,299	2,176,265	435,564,519	83,217,264
lms	1,973,958	390,756,268	66,626,364	1,983,198	429,910,406	86,341,102	1,961,260	468,468,156	75,457,846
mch	99,511	28,846,931	16,437,738	99,651	31,304,278	17,448,024	101,501	33,583,338	17,981,274
mgc	36,644 a	6,796,330 a	5,976,652 a	36,609 a	7,857,792	7,203,240 a	37,007	8,438,680 a	7,705,419 a
mus	MCH & MGC	MCH & MGC	MCH & MGC	MCH & MGC	MCH & MGC	MCH & MGC	MCH & MGC	MCH & MGC	MCH & MGC
mca	24,863	5,178,444	860,399	24,500	5,675,495	831,177	24,669	6,049,857	812,015
nab	43,041	12,453,858	3,972,485	43,146	15,513,286	4,420,403	42,735	17,302,952	4,597,515
opc	11,553 a	5,235,294	1,235,849	11,884	5,939,983	1,382,451	11,956	6,512,125 a	1,430,061 a
pch	3,262,086	820,218,732	176,172,729	3,202,392	896,641,430	188,576,382	3,157,372	970,223,947	199,331,832
rca	210,762	70,733,297	17,313,239 b	210,312	77,044,709	18,193,793 b	211,168	82,656,050	19,418,165 b
sda	571,141	121,484,768	275,783,385	588,536	133,088,131	297,838,046	606,310	136,877,455	299,437,917
sbc	13,600,126	2,080,375,258	400,976,072	13,782,644	2,336,062,506	443,931,179	13,991,709	2,628,272,553	486,402,607
ucc	1,736,244	278,546,571	44,042,186	1,726,535	300,730,591	48,329,399	1,708,847	323,725,191	52,738,069
wel	307,810 a	60,458,213 a	15,989,577 a	310,553 a	67,830,319	18,198,804 a	311,364	71,611,865 a	18,608,914 a
Total	28,906,733	5,402,773,866	1,348,940,701	29,020,810	5,953,679,479	1,492,832,600	29,102,779	6,517,015,172	1,536,193,341

a Data obtained from denominational source.
b empty tomb review of RCA directory data.

Appendix B-1: Church Member Giving, in Current Dollars, 1968-2011 (continued)

	Data Year 1983			Data Year 1984			Data Year 1985		
	Full/Confirmed Members	Congregational Finances	Benevolences	Full/Confirmed Members	Congregational Finances	Benevolences	Full/Confirmed Members	Congregational Finances	Benevolences
abc	965,117 a	254,716,036	43,683,021 a	953,945 a	267,556,088	46,232,040 a	894,732 a	267,694,684	47,201,119
alc	1,756,420 a	375,500,188	84,633,617	1,756,558	413,876,101	86,601,067	1,751,649	428,861,660	87,152,699
arp	31,738	10,640,050 a	2,180,230 a	31,355	11,221,526 a	3,019,456 a	32,051	12,092,868 a	3,106,994 a
bcc	14,782	7,638,413	1,858,632	15,128	8,160,359	2,586,843	15,535	8,504,354	2,979,046 a
ccd	761,629	241,934,972	35,809,331	755,233	263,694,210	38,402,791	743,486	274,072,301	40,992,053
cga	182,190 a	81,309,323	13,896,753	185,404	86,611,269	14,347,570	185,593	91,078,512	15,308,954
cgg	5,759	1,981,300	412,000	4,711	2,211,800	504,200	4,575	2,428,730	582,411
chb	164,680	39,726,743	14,488,192	161,824	37,743,527	15,136,600	159,184	40,658,904	16,509,718
chn	506,439	237,220,642 a	57,267,073 a	514,937	253,566,280	60,909,810 a	520,741	267,134,078	65,627,515 a
cccc	26,691 a	9,189,221 a	2,980,636	28,383	10,018,982	3,051,425	28,624	11,729,365	3,350,021
cpc	87,186 a	19,252,942 a	3,028,953 a	86,995 a	20,998,768 a	3,331,065 a	85,346 a	22,361,332 a	3,227,932 a
ecc	26,769 a	9,505,479 a	2,019,373 a	26,375 a	10,302,554	2,220,852 a	26,016	8,134,641	1,777,172 a
ecv	82,943	53,279,350 a	10,615,909 a	84,185	60,295,634 a	11,243,908 a	85,150	63,590,735 a	13,828,030 a
elc	ALC & LCA	ALC & LCA	ALC & LCA	ALC & LCA	ALC & LCA	ALC & LCA	ALC & LCA	ALC & LCA	ALC & LCA
els	15,576	3,842,625	838,788	15,396	4,647,714	931,677 a	15,012	4,725,783	791,586
emc	3,857	1,930,689	738,194	3,908	2,017,565	862,350	3,813	2,128,019	1,058,040
feb	2,094	622,467	1,466,399	NA	NA	NA	2,107	1,069,851	402,611 a
fec	see EMC	see EMC	see EMC	see EMC	see EMC	see EMC	see EMC	see EMC	see EMC
fmc	56,442 a	36,402,355 a	8,334,248 a	56,667	39,766,087	8,788,189 a	56,242	42,046,626 a	9,461,369 a
fum	49,441	11,723,240	2,886,931	48,713	11,549,163	2,875,370	48,812	12,601,820	3,012,658
ggb	75,133	17,283,259	1,733,755	75,028	17,599,169	1,729,228	73,040	18,516,252	1,683,130
lca	2,176,772	457,239,780	88,909,363	2,168,594	496,228,216	99,833,067	2,161,216	539,142,069	103,534,375
lms	1,984,199	499,220,552	76,991,991 a	1,986,392	539,346,935	81,742,006 a	1,982,753	566,507,516	83,117,011 a
mch	103,350 a	34,153,628	17,581,878 a	90,347	37,333,306	16,944,094	91,167	34,015,200	25,593,500
mgc	36,318 a	8,702,849 a	7,661,415 a	35,951	9,217,458 a	7,795,680 a	35,356	9,217,964 a	7,070,700 a
mus	MCH & MGC	MCH & MGC	MCH & MGC	MCH & MGC	MCH & MGC	MCH & MGC	MCH & MGC	MCH & MGC	MCH & MGC
mca	24,913	6,618,339	911,787	24,269	7,723,611	1,183,741	24,396	8,698,949	1,170,349
nab	43,286	18,010,853	5,132,672	43,215	19,322,720	5,724,552	42,863	20,246,236	5,766,686
opc	12,045	6,874,722	1,755,169	12,278	7,555,006	2,079,924	12,593	8,291,483	2,204,998
pch	3,122,213	1,047,756,995	197,981,080	3,092,151	1,132,098,779	218,412,639	3,057,226	1,252,885,684	232,487,569 a
rca	211,660	92,071,986	20,632,574	209,968 b	100,378,778	21,794,880	209,395	103,428,950	22,233,299
sda	623,563	143,636,140	323,461,439	638,929	155,257,063	319,664,449	651,594	155,077,180	346,251,406
sbc	14,178,051	2,838,573,815	528,781,000	14,341,822	3,094,913,877	567,467,188	14,477,364	3,272,276,486	609,868,694
ucc	1,701,513	332,613,396	55,716,557	1,696,107	385,786,198	58,679,094	1,683,777	409,543,989	62,169,679 a
wel	312,974 a	75,825,104	24,037,480 a	314,559	82,507,020	22,845,856 a	315,374 a	86,879,662	22,275,822 a
Total	29,345,743	6,974,997,453	1,638,426,440	29,459,327	7,589,485,763	1,726,941,611	29,476,782	8,045,641,883	1,841,797,146

a Data obtained from denominational source.
b empty tomb review of RCA directory data.

Appendix B-1: Church Member Giving, in Current Dollars, 1968-2011 (continued)

	Data Year 1986			Data Year 1987			Data Year 1988		
	Full/Confirmed Members	Congregational Finances	Benevolences	Full/Confirmed Members	Congregational Finances	Benevolences	Full/Confirmed Members	Congregational Finances	Benevolences
abc	862,582 [a]	287,020,378 [a]	49,070,083 [a]	868,189 [a]	291,606,418 [a]	55,613,855	825,102 [a]	296,569,316 [a]	55,876,771
alc	1,740,439	434,641,736	96,147,129	See ELCA	See ELCA	See ELCA	See ELCA	See ELCA	See ELCA
arp	32,438 [a]	12,336,321 [a]	3,434,408 [a]	32,289	13,553,176	3,927,030	31,922	13,657,776	5,063,036 [a]
bcc	15,911	10,533,883	2,463,558	16,136	11,203,321	3,139,949	16,578	13,522,101	4,346,690 [a]
ccd	732,466	288,277,386	42,027,504	718,522	287,464,332	42,728,826	707,985	297,187,996	42,226,128
cga	188,662	91,768,855	16,136,647	198,552	124,376,413	20,261,687	198,842	132,384,232	19,781,941
cgg	NA	NA	NA	4,348	2,437,778	738,818	4,394	2,420,600	644,000 [a]
chb	155,967	43,531,293	17,859,101	154,067	45,201,732	19,342,402	151,169	48,008,657	19,701,942 [a]
chn	529,192	283,189,977	68,438,998 [a]	541,878	294,160,356	73,033,568 [a]	550,700	309,478,442	74,737,057 [a]
cccc	28,948	15,559,846 [a]	3,961,037	29,429	15,409,349	3,740,688	29,015	13,853,547	4,120,974
cpc	84,579 [a]	22,338,090 [a]	3,646,356 [a]	85,781	22,857,711	3,727,681	85,304	23,366,911 [e]	3,722,607 [e]
ecc	25,625 [a]	10,977,813 [a]	2,422,879 [a]	25,300	14,281,140	2,575,415	24,980	12,115,762	2,856,766 [a]
ecv	86,079	67,889,353 [a]	14,374,707	86,741	73,498,123 [a]	14,636,000	87,750	77,504,445	14,471,178 [a]
elc	ALC & LCA	ALC & LCA	ALC & LCA	3,952,663	1,083,293,684	169,685,942	3,931,878	1,150,483,034	169,580,472
els	15,083 [a]	4,996,111 [a]	1,050,715 [a]	15,892	5,298,882	1,082,198	15,518	5,713,773	1,043,612 [a]
emc	NA	NA	NA	3,841	2,332,216	1,326,711	3,879	2,522,533	1,438,459
feb	NA	NA	NA	NA	NA	NA	NA	NA	NA
fec	see EMC	see EMC	see EMC	see EMC	see EMC	see EMC	see EMC	see EMC	see EMC
fmc	56,243	46,150,881	9,446,120	57,262	47,743,298	9,938,096	57,432	48,788,041	9,952,103
fum	48,143	12,790,909	2,916,870	47,173	13,768,272	3,631,353	48,325	14,127,491	3,719,125
ggb	72,263	19,743,265	1,883,826	73,515	20,850,827	1,789,578	74,086	21,218,051	1,731,299
lca	2,157,701	569,250,519	111,871,174	See ELCA	See ELCA	See ELCA	See ELCA	See ELCA	See ELCA
lms	1,974,798	605,768,688	87,803,646 [a]	1,973,347	620,271,274	86,938,723 [a]	1,962,674	659,288,332	88,587,175 [a]
mch	91,467 [a]	40,097,500 [a]	24,404,200 [a]	92,673	43,295,100	25,033,600	92,682	47,771,200	27,043,900
mgc	35,170	10,101,306 [a]	7,717,998 [a]	34,889	11,560,998	8,478,414	34,693	11,399,995	9,638,417
mus	MCH & MGC	MCH & MGC	MCH & MGC	MCH & MGC	MCH & MGC	MCH & MGC	MCH & MGC	MCH & MGC	MCH & MGC
mca	24,260	8,133,127	1,155,350	24,440	9,590,658	1,174,593	23,526	9,221,646	1,210,476
nab	42,084	20,961,799	5,982,391	42,150	23,773,844 [a]	7,873,096	42,629	24,597,288	6,611,840
opc	12,919 [a]	9,333,328 [a]	2,347,928 [a]	13,013	9,884,288	2,425,480	13,108	10,797,786	2,648,375 [a]
pch	3,007,322	1,318,440,264	249,033,881	2,967,781	1,395,501,073	247,234,439	2,929,608	1,439,655,217	284,989,138
rca	207,993	114,231,429	22,954,596	203,581	114,652,192	24,043,270	200,631	127,409,263	25,496,802 [b]
sda	666,199	166,692,974	361,316,753	675,702	166,939,355	374,830,065	687,200	178,768,967	395,849,223
sbc	14,613,638	3,481,124,471	635,196,984	14,722,617	3,629,842,643	662,455,177	14,812,844	3,706,652,161	689,366,904
ucc	1,676,105	429,340,239	63,808,091	1,662,568	451,700,210	66,870,922	1,644,787	470,747,740	65,734,348
wel	315,510 [a]	92,309,279 [a]	22,354,781 [a]	316,393	97,179,349 [a]	22,112,031	316,098	101,545,536	22,323,451 [a]
Total	29,499,786	8,517,531,020	1,931,227,711	29,640,732	8,943,528,012	1,960,389,607	29,605,339	9,270,777,839	2,054,514,209

[a] Data obtained from denominational source.

[b] empty tomb review of RCA directory data.

[e] A *YACC* prepublication data table listed 23,366,911 for Congregational Finances which, added to Benevolences, equals the published Total of 27,089,518.

Appendix B-1: Church Member Giving, in Current Dollars, 1968-2011 (continued)

	Data Year 1989			Data Year 1990			Data Year 1991		
	Full/Confirmed Members	Congregational Finances	Benevolences	Full/Confirmed Members	Congregational Finances	Benevolences	Full/Confirmed Members	Congregational Finances	Benevolences
abc	789,730 [a]	305,212,094 [a]	55,951,539 [a]	764,890 [a]	315,777,005 [a]	54,740,278 [a]	773,838 [a]	318,150,548 [a]	52,330,924 [a]
alc	See ELCA	See ELCA	See ELCA	See ELCA	See ELCA	See ELCA	See ELCA	See ELCA	See ELCA
arp	32,600	16,053,762	4,367,314 [a]	32,817	17,313,355	5,031,504 [a]	33,494	17,585,273	5,254,738 [a]
bcc	16,842	12,840,038	3,370,306	17,277	13,327,414	3,336,580	17,456	14,491,918	3,294,169 [a]
ccd	690,115	310,043,826	42,015,246	678,750	321,569,909	42,607,007	663,336	331,629,009	43,339,307
cga	199,786	134,918,052	20,215,075	205,884	141,375,027	21,087,504	214,743	146,249,447	21,801,570 [a]
cgg	4,415	3,367,000	686,000	4,399	3,106,729	690,000	4,375	2,756,651	662,500
chb	149,681	51,921,820	19,737,714 [a]	148,253	54,832,226	18,384,483	147,954	55,035,355	19,694,919 [a]
chn	558,664	322,924,598	76,625,913 [a]	563,756	333,397,255	77,991,665 [a]	572,153	352,654,251	82,276,097 [a]
cccc	28,413	18,199,823	4,064,111	28,355	16,964,128	4,174,133	28,035	17,760,290	4,304,052
cpc	84,994 [a]	25,867,112 [a]	4,086,994 [a]	85,025 [a]	27,027,650 [a]	4,139,967 [a]	84,706 [a]	28,069,681 [a]	5,740,846 [a]
ecc	24,606	13,274,756 [a]	2,703,095 [a]	24,437	12,947,150 [a]	2,858,077 [a]	24,124	13,100,036 [a]	3,074,660 [a]
ecv	89,014	80,621,293 [a]	15,206,265	89,735	84,263,236 [a]	15,601,475	89,648	87,321,563 [a]	16,598,656
elc	3,909,302	1,239,433,257	182,386,940	3,898,478	1,318,884,279	184,174,554	3,890,947	1,375,439,787	186,016,168
els	15,740	6,186,648	1,342,321	16,181	6,527,076	1,193,789	16,004	6,657,338	1,030,445
emc	3,888	2,712,843	1,567,728	4,026	2,991,485	1,800,593	3,958	3,394,563	1,790,115
feb	NA	NA	NA	NA	NA	NA	2,008	1,398,968 [a]	500,092 [a]
fec	see EMC	see EMC	see EMC	see EMC	see EMC	see EMC	see EMC	see EMC	see EMC
fmc	59,418 [a]	50,114,090	10,311,535	58,084	55,229,181	10,118,505	57,794	57,880,464	9,876,739
fum	47,228	16,288,644	4,055,624	45,691	10,036,083	2,511,063	50,803 [f]	NA [f]	NA
ggb	73,738	23,127,835	1,768,804	74,156	23,127,835	1,737,011	71,119	22,362,874	1,408,262 [a]
lca	See ELCA	See ELCA	See ELCA	See ELCA	See ELCA	See ELCA	See ELCA	See ELCA	See ELCA
lms	1,961,114	701,701,168	90,974,340	1,954,350	712,235,204	96,308,765	1,952,845	741,823,412	94,094,637
mch	92,517	55,353,313	27,873,241	92,448	65,709,827	28,397,083	93,114	68,926,324	28,464,199
mgc	33,982	12,096,435	9,054,682	33,535	13,669,288	8,449,395	33,937	13,556,484	8,645,993
mus	MCH & MGC	MCH & MGC	MCH & MGC	MCH & MGC	MCH & MGC	MCH & MGC	MCH & MGC	MCH & MGC	MCH & MGC
mca	23,802	10,415,640	1,284,233	23,526	10,105,037	1,337,616	22,887	10,095,337	1,205,335
nab	42,629	28,076,077	3,890,017	44,493	31,103,672	7,700,119	43,187	27,335,239	7,792,876
opc	12,573 [a]	11,062,590	2,789,427	12,177	10,631,166	2,738,295	12,265	11,700,000	2,700,000
pch	2,886,482	1,528,450,805	295,365,032	2,847,437	1,530,341,707	294,990,441	2,805,548	1,636,407,042	311,905,934
rca	198,832	136,796,188 [b]	29,456,132 [b]	197,154	144,357,953 [b]	27,705,029 [b]	193,531	147,532,382 [b]	26,821,721 [b]
sda	701,781	196,204,538	415,752,350	717,446	195,054,218	433,035,080	733,026	201,411,183	456,242,995
sbc	14,907,826	3,873,300,782	712,738,838	15,038,409	4,146,285,561	718,174,874	15,232,347	4,283,283,059	731,812,766
ucc	1,625,969	496,825,160	72,300,698	1,599,212	527,378,397	71,984,897	1,583,830	543,803,752	73,149,887
wel	316,163 [a]	110,112,151	22,717,491 [a]	315,840 [a]	115,806,027	23,983,079 [a]	315,853	121,159,792	24,160,350 [a]
Total	29,581,844	9,793,502,338	2,134,659,005	29,616,221	10,261,375,080	2,166,982,861	29,718,062	10,658,972,022	2,225,990,952

[a] Data obtained from denominational source.

[b] empty tomb review of RCA directory data.

[f] Inclusive membership, obtained from the denomination and used only in Chapter 5 analysis; not included in the Total sum on this page.

Appendix B-1: Church Member Giving, in Current Dollars, 1968-2011 (continued)

	Data Year 1992			Data Year 1993			Data Year 1994		
	Full/Confirmed Members	Congregational Finances	Benevolences	Full/Confirmed Members	Congregational Finances	Benevolences	Full/Confirmed Members	Congregational Finances	Benevolences
abc	730,009 a	310,307,040 a	52,764,005 a	764,657 a	346,658,047 a	53,562,811 a	697,379 a	337,185,885 a	51,553,256 a
alc	See ELCA	See ELCA	See ELCA	See ELCA	See ELCA	See ELCA	See ELCA	See ELCA	See ELCA
arp	33,550	18,175,957 a	5,684,008 a	33,662 a	20,212,390 a	5,822,845 a	33,636	22,618,802 a	6,727,857
bcc	17,646 a	15,981,118 a	3,159,717 a	17,986	13,786,394	4,515,730	18,152	14,844,672	5,622,005
ccd	655,652	333,629,412	46,440,333	619,028	328,219,027	44,790,415	605,996	342,352,080	43,165,285
cga	214,743	150,115,497	23,500,213	216,117	158,454,703	23,620,177	221,346	160,694,760 a	26,262,049 a
cgg	4,085	2,648,085	509,398	4,239	2,793,000	587,705	3,996	2,934,843	475,799
chb	147,912	57,954,895	21,748,320	146,713	56,818,998	23,278,848	144,282	57,210,682	24,155,595
chn	582,804 a	361,555,793 a	84,118,580 a	589,398 a	369,896,767 a	87,416,378 a	595,303	387,385,034	89,721,860
cccc	30,387	22,979,946 a	4,311,234 a	36,864	24,997,736 a	5,272,184 a	37,996	23,758,101 a	5,240,805 a
cpc	85,080 a	27,813,626 a	4,339,933 a	84,336 a	27,462,623 a	4,574,550 a	83,733	29,212,802 a	4,547,149 a
ecc	24,150	13,451,827 a	3,120,351 a	23,889	13,546,159 a	3,258,595 a	23,504	13,931,409	3,269,986
ecv	90,985 a	93,071,869 a	16,732,701 a	89,511	93,765,006 a	16,482,315 a	90,919	101,746,341	17,874,955
elc	3,878,055	1,399,419,800 a	189,605,837 a	3,861,418	1,452,000,815 a	188,393,158 a	3,849,692	1,502,746,601	187,145,886
els	15,929 a	6,944,522 a	1,271,058 a	15,780	6,759,222 a	1,100,660 a	15,960	7,288,521	1,195,698
emc	4,059	3,839,838 a	1,403,001 a	4,130	4,260,307 a	1,406,682 a	4,225	4,597,730 a	1,533,157 a
feb	1,872 a	1,343,225 a	397,553 a	1,866 a	1,294,646 a	429,023 a	1,898 a	1,537,041 a	395,719 a
fec	see EMC	see EMC	see EMC	see EMC	see EMC	see EMC	see EMC	see EMC	see EMC
fmc	58,220 a	60,584,079 a	10,591,064 a	59,156	62,478,294	10,513,187	59,354	65,359,325	10,708,854
fum	50,005 f	NA	NA a	45,542 f	NA	NA a	44,711 f	NA	NA
ggb	72,388 a	21,561,432 a	1,402,330 a	73,129 a	22,376,970 a	1,440,342 a	71,140 a	19,651,624 a	2,052,409 a
lca	See ELCA	See ELCA	See ELCA	See ELCA	See ELCA	See ELCA	See ELCA	See ELCA	See ELCA
lms	1,953,248 a	777,467,488 a	97,275,934 a	1,945,077	789,821,559	96,355,945 a	1,944,905	817,412,113	96,048,560
mch	94,222 a	68,118,222 a	28,835,719 a	95,634	71,385,271	27,973,380	87,911	64,651,639	24,830,192
mgc	34,040	14,721,813 a	8,265,700 a	33,629	14,412,556	7,951,676	32,782	16,093,551	8,557,126
mus	MCH & MGC	MCH & MGC	MCH & MGC	MCH & MGC	MCH & MGC	MCH & MGC	MCH & MGC	MCH & MGC	MCH & MGC
mca	22,533	10,150,953 a	1,208,372 a	22,223	9,675,502	1,191,131	21,448	9,753,010	1,182,778
nab	43,446	28,375,947 a	7,327,594 a	43,045	30,676,902	7,454,087	43,236	32,800,560	7,515,707
opc	12,580 a	12,466,266 a	3,025,824 a	12,924 a	13,158,089 a	3,039,676 a	13,970	14,393,880	3,120,454
pch	2,780,406 a	1,696,092,968 a	309,069,530 a	2,742,192	1,700,918,712	310,375,024	2,698,262	1,800,008,292	307,158,749
rca	190,322 b	147,181,320 b	28,457,900 b	188,551 b	159,715,941 b	26,009,853 b	185,242	153,107,408	27,906,830
sda	748,687	191,362,737 a	476,902,779 a	761,703	209,524,570	473,769,831	775,349	229,596,444	503,347,816
sbc	15,358,866 a	4,462,915,112 a	751,366,698 a	15,398,642	4,621,157,751	761,298,249	15,614,060	5,263,421,764	815,360,696
ucc	1,555,382 a	521,190,413 a	73,906,372 a	1,530,178	550,847,702	71,046,517	1,501,310	556,540,722	67,269,762
wel	315,062 a	127,139,400 a	26,239,464 a	314,757 a	136,405,994 a	24,403,323 a	314,141 a	142,238,820 a	23,825,002 a
Total	29,756,320	10,958,560,600	2,282,981,522	29,730,434	11,313,481,653	2,287,334,297	29,791,127	12,195,074,456	2,367,771,996

a Data obtained from denominational source.
b empty tomb review of RCA directory data.
f Inclusive membership, obtained from the denomination and used only in Chapter 5 analysis; not included in the Total sum on this page.

Appendix B-1: Church Member Giving, in Current Dollars, 1968-2011 (continued)

	Data Year 1995			Data Year 1996			Data Year 1997		
	Full/Confirmed Members	Congregational Finances	Benevolences	Full/Confirmed Members	Congregational Finances	Benevolences	Full/Confirmed Members	Congregational Finances	Benevolences
abc	726,452 [a]	365,873,197 [a]	57,052,333 [a]	670,363 [a]	351,362,401 [a]	55,982,392 [a]	658,731 [a]	312,860,507 [a]	54,236,977 [a]
alc	See ELCA	See ELCA	See ELCA	See ELCA	See ELCA	See ELCA	See ELCA	See ELCA	See ELCA
arp	33,513	23,399,372 [a]	5,711,882 [a]	34,117	23,419,989 [a]	5,571,337 [a]	34,344	25,241,384	6,606,829
bcc	18,529	16,032,149	5,480,828	18,424	16,892,154	4,748,871	19,016	17,456,379	5,934,414
ccd	601,237	357,895,652	42,887,958	586,131	370,210,746	42,877,144	568,921	381,463,761	43,009,412
cga	224,061	160,897,147	26,192,559	229,240	180,581,111	26,983,385	229,302	194,438,623	29,054,047
cgg	3,877	2,722,766	486,661	3,920	2,926,516	491,348	3,877	2,987,337	515,247
chb	143,121	60,242,418	22,599,214	141,811	60,524,557	19,683,035	141,400	60,923,817	19,611,047
chn	598,946	396,698,137	93,440,095	608,008	419,450,850	95,358,352	615,632	433,821,462	99,075,440
cccc	38,853 [a]	24,250,819 [a]	5,483,659 [a]	38,469 [a]	25,834,363 [a]	4,989,062 [a]	38,956	28,204,355	5,167,644
cpc	81,094 [a]	31,072,697 [a]	4,711,934 [a]	80,122 [a]	31,875,061 [a]	5,035,451 [a]	79,576 [a]	32,152,971 [a]	5,152,129 [a]
ecc	23,422	14,830,454	3,301,060	23,091	14,692,608	3,273,685	22,957	15,658,454	3,460,999
ecv	91,458	109,776,363 [a]	17,565,085 [a]	91,823	115,693,329 [a]	18,726,756 [a]	93,414	127,642,950	20,462,435
elc	3,845,063	1,551,842,465 [a]	188,107,066 [a]	3,838,750	1,629,909,672 [a]	191,476,141 [a]	3,844,169	1,731,806,133	201,115,441
els	16,543 [a]	7,712,358	1,084,136	16,511	8,136,195	1,104,996	16,444	8,937,103	1,150,419
emc	4,284 [a]	5,321,079 [a]	1,603,548 [a]	4,201 [a]	5,361,912 [a]	1,793,267 [a]	4,348 [a]	7,017,588 [a]	2,039,740 [a]
feb	1,856 [a]	1,412,281 [a]	447,544 [a]	1,751 [a]	1,198,120 [a]	507,656 [a]	1,763 [a]	1,120,222 [a]	518,777 [a]
fec	see EMC	see EMC	see EMC	see EMC	see EMC	see EMC	see EMC	see EMC	see EMC
fmc	59,060	67,687,955	11,114,804	59,343	70,262,626	11,651,462	62,191	78,687,325	12,261,465
fum	43,440 [f]	NA	NA	42,918 [f]	NA	NA	41,040 [f]	NA	NA
ggb	70,886 [a]	24,385,956 [a]	1,722,662 [a]	70,562 [a]	27,763,966 [a]	1,832,909 [a]	72,326 [a]	28,093,944 [a]	1,780,851 [a]
lca	See ELCA	See ELCA	See ELCA	See ELCA	See ELCA	See ELCA	See ELCA	See ELCA	See ELCA
lms	1,943,281	832,701,255	98,139,835	1,951,730	855,461,015	104,076,876	1,951,391	887,928,255	110,520,917
mch	90,139	71,641,773	26,832,240	90,959	76,669,365	27,812,549	92,161	76,087,609	25,637,872
mgc	35,852	15,774,961 [a]	7,587,049	35,333	18,282,833	7,969,999	34,731	14,690,904	6,514,761
mus	MCH & MGC	MCH & MGC	MCH & MGC	MCH & MGC	MCH & MGC	MCH & MGC	MCH & MGC	MCH & MGC	MCH & MGC
mca	21,409	10,996,031	1,167,513	21,140	11,798,536	1,237,349	21,108	12,555,760	1,148,478
nab	43,928	37,078,473	7,480,331	43,744	37,172,560	7,957,860	43,850	37,401,175	7,986,099
opc	14,355	16,017,003	3,376,691	15,072	17,883,915	3,467,207	15,072	20,090,259	3,967,490
pch	2,665,276	1,855,684,719	309,978,224	2,631,466	1,930,179,808	322,336,258	2,609,191	2,064,789,378	344,757,186
rca	183,255	164,250,624	29,995,068	182,342	183,975,696	31,271,007	180,980	181,977,101	32,130,943
sda	790,731	240,565,576	503,334,129	809,159	242,316,834	524,977,061	825,654	249,591,109	552,633,569
sbc	15,663,296	5,209,748,503	858,635,435	15,691,249	5,987,033,115	891,149,403	15,891,514	6,098,933,137	930,176,909
ucc	1,472,213	578,042,965	67,806,448	1,452,565	615,727,028	69,013,791	1,438,181	651,176,773	70,180,193
wel	312,898 [a]	150,060,963	33,096,069	313,446 [a]	156,363,694	47,334,098	314,038	163,568,990	52,241,401
Total	29,818,888	12,404,616,111	2,436,422,060	29,754,842	13,488,960,575	2,530,690,707	29,925,238	13,947,304,765	2,649,049,131

[a] Data obtained from denominational source.
[f] Inclusive membership, obtained from the denomination and used only in Chapter 5 analysis; not included in the Total sum on this page.

Appendix B-1: Church Member Giving, in Current Dollars, 1968-2011 (continued)

	Data Year 1998			Data Year 1999			Data Year 2000		
	Full/Confirmed Members	Congregational Finances	Benevolences	Full/Confirmed Members	Congregational Finances	Benevolences	Full/Confirmed Members	Congregational Finances	Benevolences
abc	621,232 a	326,046,153 a	53,866,448 a	603,014 a	331,513,521 a	58,675,160 a	593,113 a	359,484,902 a	63,042,002 a
alc	See ELCA	See ELCA	See ELCA	See ELCA	See ELCA	See ELCA	See ELCA	See ELCA	See ELCA
arp	34,642 a	28,831,982 a	7,378,121 a	35,643 a	33,862,219 a	7,973,285 a	35,022 a	33,004,995 a	8,048,586 a
bcc	19,577	24,116,889	5,274,612	20,010	22,654,566	5,913,551	20,587	25,148,637	5,703,506
ccd	547,875 a	395,699,954 a	45,576,436 a	535,893	410,583,119	47,795,574	527,363	433,965,354	48,726,390
cga	234,311 f	NA	NA	235,849 f	NA	NA	238,891 f	NA	NA
cgg	3,824	3,087,000	689,756	4,083	3,357,300	503,365	4,037	3,232,160	610,113
chb	140,011 a	57,605,960 a	22,283,498 a	138,304 a	63,774,756 a	21,852,687 a	135,978	67,285,361	25,251,272
chn	623,028	460,776,715	104,925,922	626,033 a	487,437,668 a	110,818,743 a	633,264	516,708,125	122,284,083
cccc	38,996	28,976,122	5,194,733	40,414	31,165,218	5,931,456	40,974 a	33,537,589 a	6,360,912 a
cpc	80,829 a	33,623,232 a	5,412,917 a	79,452 a	36,303,752 a	5,879,014 a	86,519	39,533,829	6,591,617
ecc	22,868	15,956,209	3,599,440	22,349	16,574,783	3,587,877	21,939	17,656,789	1,982,328
ecv	96,552	140,823,872	20,134,436	98,526	161,361,490	23,237,513	101,317	181,127,526	25,983,315
elc	3,840,136	1,822,915,831	208,853,359	3,825,228	1,972,950,623	220,647,251	3,810,785	2,067,208,285	231,219,316
els	16,897	9,363,126	1,120,386	16,734	10,062,900	1,129,969	16,569	10,910,109	949,421
emc	4,646 a	6,472,868 a	1,854,222 a	4,511 a	7,528,256 a	1,982,985 a	4,929 a	8,289,743 a	2,085,475 a
feb	1,828 a	1,433,305 a	502,839 a	1,936 a	1,496,949 a	534,203 a	1,764 a	1,360,133 a	373,057 a
fec	see EMC	see EMC	see EMC	see EMC	see EMC	see EMC	see EMC	see EMC	see EMC
fmc	62,176	82,254,922	12,850,607	62,368	86,906,899	12,646,064	62,453	98,853,770	13,430,274
fum	33,908 f	NA	NA	34,863 f	NA	NA	41,297 f	NA	NA
ggb	67,314 a	28,533,439 a	2,594,098 a	55,549 a	22,857,097 a	2,331,087 a	66,296 a	30,470,298 a	2,950,915 a
lca	See ELCA	See ELCA	See ELCA	See ELCA	See ELCA	See ELCA	See ELCA	See ELCA	See ELCA
lms	1,952,020	975,113,229	121,536,226	1,945,846	986,295,136	123,632,549	1,934,057	1,101,690,594	127,554,235
mch	92,002	75,796,469	26,452,444	See MUS	See MUS	See MUS	See MUS	See MUS	See MUS
mgc	36,600	14,786,936	5,853,292	See MUS	See MUS	See MUS	See MUS	See MUS	See MUS
mus	MCH & MGC	MCH & MGC	MCH & MGC	123,404 a	95,843,112 a	34,821,702 a	120,381 l	NA	NA
mca	20,764	13,082,671	1,131,742	20,400	11,527,684	849,837	20,925	13,224,765	1,014,314
nab	43,844 a	41,939,978 a	7,731,550 a	45,738	47,207,867	9,055,128	47,097	54,866,431	9,845,352
opc	15,936	22,362,292	4,438,333	17,279	24,878,935	4,920,310	17,914	28,120,325	5,978,474
pch	2,587,674	2,173,483,227	355,628,625	2,560,201	2,326,583,688	384,445,608	2,525,330	2,517,278,130	398,602,204
rca	179,085	189,390,759	33,890,048	178,260	216,305,458	36,158,625	177,281	226,555,821	37,221,041
sda	839,915	269,679,595	588,227,010	861,860	301,221,572	629,944,965	880,921	316,562,375	675,000,508
sbc	15,729,356	6,498,607,390	953,491,003	14,001,690 g	6,001,443,051 g	795,207,316 g	15,221,959 g	7,037,516,273 g	936,520,388 g
ucc	1,421,088	678,251,694	74,861,463	1,401,682	700,645,114	76,550,398	1,377,320	744,991,925	78,525,195
wel	314,265 a	177,633,393 a	44,584,079 a	314,217 a	181,513,283 a	49,143,360 a	314,941 a	193,625,639 a	52,918,434 a
Total	29,454,980	14,596,645,212	2,719,937,645	27,640,624	14,593,856,016	2,676,169,582	28,680,654	16,162,209,883	2,888,772,727

a Data obtained from denominational source.

f Inclusive membership, obtained from the denomination and used only in Chapter 5 analysis; not included in the Total sum on this page.

g The 1999 and 2000 data for the Southern Baptist Convention used in the 1968-2011 analysis includes data only for those State Conventions that provided a breakdown of Total Contributions between Congregational Finances and Benevolences for that year. For the 11 Denominations 1921-2011 analysis, 1999 and 2000 Southern Baptist Convention Total Contributions are $7,772,452,961 and $8,437,177,940, respectively. For the 11 Denominations 1921-2011 analysis, and the Membership Trends analysis, 1999 and 2000 Southern Baptist Convention Membership is 15,851,756 and 15,960,308, respectively.

l Data obtained from denominational source and used only in Chapter 5 analysis; not included in Total sum on this page.

Appendix B-1: Church Member Giving, in Current Dollars, 1968-2011 (continued)

	Data Year 2001			Data Year 2002			Data Year 2003		
	Full/Confirmed Members	Congregational Finances	Benevolences	Full/Confirmed Members	Congregational Finances	Benevolences	Full/Confirmed Members	Congregational Finances	Benevolences
abc	631,771 [a]	381,080,930 [a]	74,228,212 [a]	617,034 [a]	396,380,200 [a]	65,103,943 [a]	572,218	391,456,166 [a]	60,965,853 [a]
alc	See ELCA	See ELCA	See ELCA	See ELCA	See ELCA	See ELCA	See ELCA	See ELCA	See ELCA
arp	35,181	36,976,653	7,707,456	35,556	37,394,125	8,091,930	35,418	36,664,331	7,615,661
bcc	20,739	29,566,287	6,864,936	20,579	29,069,369	5,619,911	21,538	30,219,066	6,090,287
ccd	518,434	437,447,942	48,609,107	504,118	438,378,385	46,708,737	491,085	456,513,192	45,243,300
cga	237,222 [l]	NA	NA	247,007 [k]	NA	NA	250,052 [l]	NA	NA
cgg	4,155	3,436,200	477,457	3,860 [k]	NA	NA	3,694	3,786,000	511,394
chb	134,828	68,790,933	22,869,690	134,844	70,524,998	22,730,417	132,481	73,120,173	20,756,646
chn	639,296 [a]	557,589,101 [a]	121,203,179 [a]	639,330	587,027,991	132,183,078	616,069	595,552,079	133,379,908
cccc	40,857	34,483,917	6,754,192	40,041	36,747,983	8,190,510	42,032	46,340,288	6,232,465
cpc	85,427	41,216,632	6,744,757	84,417	42,570,586	6,876,097	83,742	41,950,671	7,218,214
ecc	21,463	17,932,202	2,011,619	21,208	18,195,387	2,002,028	20,743	17,648,320	1,980,327
ecv	103,549 [a]	198,202,551 [a]	25,137,813 [a]	105,956 [a]	211,733,299 [a]	22,644,569 [a]	108,594	222,653,578	24,786,692
elc	3,791,986 [a]	2,166,061,437 [a]	239,796,502 [a]	3,757,723	2,238,773,875	233,875,597	3,724,321	2,285,110,767	231,916,904
els	16,815	11,361,255	1,246,189	16,849	11,787,432	1,010,416	16,674	12,018,180	995,710
emc	5,278 [a]	10,563,872 [a]	2,335,880 [a]	see FEC	see FEC	see FEC	see FEC	see FEC	see FEC
feb	1,271 [a]	1,086,582 [a]	246,296 [a]	1,896 [a]	1,651,056 [a]	512,269 [a]	1,861	1,723,143	673,694
fec	see EMC	see EMC	see EMC	5,686 [a]	10,457,231 [a]	1,811,985 [a]	5,780	11,862,813	2,275,726
fmc	61,202	111,415,741	14,595,290	62,742 [f]	106,896,098 [a]	12,628,325 [a]	64,726	111,701,313	13,167,275
fum	40,197 [f]	NA	NA	38,764 [f]	NA	NA	37,863 [f]	NA	NA
ggb	66,636 [a]	30,152,750 [a]	3,091,252 [a]	67,231 [a]	31,000,633 [a]	2,922,004 [a]	62,377 [a]	32,581,954 [a]	2,846,173 [a]
lca	See ELCA	See ELCA	See ELCA	See ELCA	See ELCA	See ELCA	See ELCA	See ELCA	See ELCA
lms	1,920,949	1,092,453,907	124,703,387	1,907,923	1,086,223,370	117,110,167	1,894,822	1,131,212,373	125,169,844
mch	See MUS	See MUS	See MUS	See MUS	See MUS	See MUS	See MUS	See MUS	See MUS
mgc	See MUS	See MUS	See MUS	See MUS	See MUS	See MUS	See MUS	See MUS	See MUS
mus	113,972 [l]	NA	NA	112,688 [k]	NA	NA	111,031 [l]	NA	NA
mca	21,319 [a]	13,237,006 [a]	1,054,515 [a]	20,583 [a]	13,037,136 [a]	971,527 [a]	19,456	16,939,268	925,302
nab	49,017	50,871,441	9,742,646	47,692	56,813,620	8,952,067	47,812	55,566,213	9,602,812
opc	18,414	30,012,219	6,077,752	18,746	29,251,600	5,216,600	19,725	30,972,500	5,671,600
pch	2,493,781	2,526,681,144	409,319,291	2,451,969	2,509,677,412	392,953,913	2,405,311	2,361,944,688	381,693,067
rca	173,463	228,677,098	39,313,564	171,361	229,560,092	39,393,056	168,801	235,422,160	39,932,078
sda	900,985	329,285,946	707,593,100	918,882	346,825,034	725,180,278	935,428	348,219,525	740,463,422
sbc	15,315,526 [g]	7,477,479,269 [g]	980,224,243	15,394,653 [g]	7,935,692,549 [g]	1,028,650,682 [g]	16,205,050	8,546,166,798 [g]	1,102,363,842
ucc	1,359,105	772,191,485	80,464,673	1,330,985	789,083,286	78,157,356	1,296,652	802,327,537	76,647,374
wel	314,360 [a]	203,334,779 [a]	53,455,670 [a]	313,690	211,121,810	49,035,869	313,330	227,521,597	50,687,438
Total	28,745,807	16,861,589,279	2,995,868,668	28,691,694	17,475,874,557	3,018,533,331	29,309,740	18,127,194,693	3,099,813,008

a Daa obtained from denominational source.

f Inclusive membership, obtained from the denomination and used only in Chapter 5 analysis; not included in the Total sum on this page.

g The 2001 and 2002 data for the Southern Baptist Convention used in the 1968-2011 analysis includes data only for those State Conventions that provided a breakdown of Total Contributions between Congregational Finances and Benevolences for that year. For the 11 Denominations 1921-2011 analysis 2001 and 2002 Southern Baptist Convention Total Contributions are $8,935,013,659 and $9,461,603,271, respectively. For the 11 Denominations 1921-2011 analysis, and the Membership Trends analysis, 2001 and 2002 Southern Baptist Convention Membership is 16,052,920 and 16,137,736, respectively.

k Data available in YACC series used only in Chapter 5 analysis; not included in Total sum on this page.

l Data obtained from denominational source and used only in Chapter 5 analysis; not included in Total sum on this page.

Appendix B-1: Church Member Giving, in Current Dollars, 1968-2011 (continued)

	Data Year 2004			Data Year 2005			Data Year 2006		
	Full/Confirmed Members	Congregational Finances	Benevolences	Full/Confirmed Members	Congregational Finances	Benevolences	Full/Confirmed Members	Congregational Finances	Benevolences
abc	498,407 a	372,241,219 a	60,493,722 a	375,917 a	277,122,001 a	59,772,842 a	343,301 a	261,159,450 a	51,325,563 a
alc	See ELCA	See ELCA	See ELCA	See ELCA	See ELCA	See ELCA	See ELCA	See ELCA	See ELCA
arp	35,640 a	43,324,132 a	5,965,950 a	35,209 a	41,256,621 a	9,664,612 a	34,939 a	40,305,680 a	8,286,494 a
bcc	22,818 a	27,218,450 a	5,016,990 a	23,498 a	34,920,636 a	4,879,420 a	22,168 a	37,146,168 a	5,211,550 a
ccd	479,075 a	447,535,858 a	45,841,497 a	431,365 a	453,623,467 a	49,421,931 a	450,057 a	489,840,866 a	49,271,591 a
cga	252,419 k	NA	NA	255,771 l	NA	NA	249,845 k	NA	NA
ogg	3,267 a	3,966,000 a	479,000 a	3,200 a	4,115,400 a	381,422 a	3,080 a	4,030,000 a	391,793
chb	131,201	71,402,128	19,038,122	128,820	73,982,601	23,958,373	126,994	72,676,903	20,157,405
chn	623,774	610,902,447	132,624,279	630,159	622,257,466	143,177,276	633,154	655,937,953	136,893,238
cccc	42,725	51,335,963	8,459,095	42,838 j	50,845,153 j	8,501,074 j	42,862	55,997,723	9,419,501 a
cpc	83,007 a	42,431,192 a	7,368,979	81,464 a	45,769,458 a	8,379,379 a	81,034 a	46,396,330 a	8,331,581
ecc	20,745 a	19,402,040 h	3,429,948 h	20,169 a	17,880,135 a	3,528,552 a	19,166 a	18,741,363 a	3,432,641
ecv	113,002 a	244,040,438 a	23,226,589	114,283 a	266,614,225 a	25,232,786 a	120,030 a	290,965,669 a	22,805,559
elc	3,685,987	2,329,793,744	238,220,062	3,636,948	2,348,010,569	256,787,436 a	3,580,402	2,413,738,345	250,408,865
els	16,407	11,808,028	1,118,456	15,917	12,581,651	1,250,120 a	16,319	15,105,802	1,306,478
emc	See FEC	See FEC	See FEC	See FEC	See FEC	See FEC	See FEC	See FEC	See FEC
feb	1,844 a	2,023,545 a	511,470 a	1,664 a	2,043,940 a	595,313 a	1,434 a	2,265,710 a	427,685
fec	6,496 a	13,855,056 a	2,670,733	6,694 a	15,751,410 a	2,675,422 a	6,786 a	16,301,682 a	2,729,537
fmc	65,272 a	120,200,104 a	14,200,169 a	65,816 a	125,761,586 a	15,928,702 a	65,802 a	131,152,830 a	15,397,433
fum	34,323 f	NA	NA	38,121 f	NA	NA	43,612 f	NA	NA
ggb	78,863 a	30,631,505 a	3,140,132 a	60,559 a	36,990,479 a	3,156,104 a	52,279 a	32,918,373 a	2,987,587
lca	See ELCA	See ELCA	See ELCA	See ELCA	See ELCA	See ELCA	See ELCA	See ELCA	See ELCA
lms	1,880,213	1,186,000,747	121,763,263	1,870,659	1,176,649,592	120,169,146	1,856,783	1,229,305,441	126,153,117
mch	See MUS	See MUS	See MUS	See MUS	See MUS	See MUS	See MUS	See MUS	See MUS
mgc	See MUS	See MUS	See MUS	See MUS	See MUS	See MUS	See MUS	See MUS	See MUS
mus	110,420 i	NA	NA	109,808 l	NA	NA	109,385 l	NA	NA
mca	19,021	17,545,228	969,697	18,529	16,738,701	1,096,554	17,955	16,729,153	1,051,451
nab	46,995 a	59,832,412 a	10,342,080 a	46,671 l	NA	NA	47,150	62,175,197	10,104,273
opc	19,993 a	32,760,800 a	5,899,500 a	19,965 a	34,520,600 a	6,215,800 a	20,850	38,642,300	7,241,000
pch	2,362,136	2,387,317,945	387,589,903	2,313,662	2,425,999,953	388,271,070	2,267,118	2,459,679,132	395,040,718
rca	166,761	256,915,687	39,941,147	164,697	267,082,267	43,827,424	163,160	286,075,445	42,718,072
sda	948,787 a	347,797,864 a	773,751,848 a	964,811	427,285,012	846,114,329	980,551	426,686,109	863,635,364
sbc	16,267,494	8,971,390,824	1,199,806,224	16,270,315	9,487,900,433	1,233,644,135	15,908,425 g	10,086,992,362	1,285,616,031
ucc	1,266,129 a	822,172,566 a	73,481,544 a	1,224,297	827,237,883	81,488,911	1,218,541 a	846,482,513 a	73,611,594 a
wel	313,088 a	245,098,070 a	51,692,943 a	311,950 a	244,718,123 a	54,606,362 a	310,338 a	250,589,183 a	63,427,503 a
Total	29,199,147	18,768,943,992	3,237,043,342	28,833,405	19,337,659,362	3,392,724,495	28,390,678	20,288,037,682	3,457,383,624

a Data obtained from denominational source.

f Inclusive membership, obtained from the denomination and used only in Chapter 5 analysis; not included in the Total sum on this page.

g The 2006 data for the Southern Baptist Convention used in the 1968-2011 analysis includes data only for those State Conventions that provided a breakdown of Toal Contributions between Congregational Finances and Benevolences for that year. For the 11 Denominations 1921-2011 analysis, and the Membership Trends analysis, 2006 Southern Baptist Convention Membership is 16,306,246.

h Data obtained from the denomination included the following note: "2004 figures differ substantially due to change in accounting procedures."

i 2004 membership data is an average of 2003 and 2005 data obtained from the denomination; used only in Chapter 5 analysis; not included in Total sum on this page.

j The denomination stated that the data appearing in *YACC* 2007 as 2004 data was actually for 2005.

k Data available in *YACC* series used only in Chapter 5 analysis; not included in Total sum on this page.

l Data obtained from denominational source and used only in Chapter 5 analysis; not included in Total sum on this page.

Appendix B-1: Church Member Giving, in Current Dollars, 1968-2011 (continued)

	Data Year 2007			Data Year 2008			Data Year 2009		
	Full/Confirmed Members	Congregational Finances	Benevolences	Full/Confirmed Members	Congregational Finances	Benevolences	Full/Confirmed Members	Congregational Finances	Benevolences
abc	345,588 a	272,304,732 a	53,636,473 a	331,262 a	268,264,419 a	49,073,811 a	305,486 a	241,316,884 a	47,522,456 a
alc	See ELCA	See ELCA	See ELCA	See ELCA	See ELCA	See ELCA	See ELCA	See ELCA	See ELCA
arp	34,954 a	40,442,600 a	8,981,600 a	34,911	32,784,800	14,163,289 a	34,977	43,677,370 a	11,123,351 a
bcc	22,732 a	38,797,921 a	5,138,646 a	22,967 a	39,993,609 a	4,678,366 a	23,014	35,229,064	5,141,733 a
ccd	447,340	473,677,625	45,405,339	434,008	479,485,251	44,728,431	417,068	453,043,802	42,944,443
cga	252,905 k	NA	NA	251,429 l	NA	NA	250,202 k	NA	NA
cgg	3,039 a	4,066,200 a	312,545 a	3,122 a	3,655,813 a	400,946 a	3,010	3,568,750	445,000
chb	125,418	68,434,534	20,233,969	123,855	69,331,885	18,163,083	121,781	72,679,289	16,952,618
chn	635,526	677,586,886	140,135,344	636,923	690,867,740	138,934,121	639,182	690,753,074	133,162,454
cccc	41,772 a	64,471,078	9,996,077	42,149	62,792,643	9,885,002	42,296	60,595,568	9,900,687
cpc	78,451	49,306,468	8,460,302	78,074	49,052,918	8,593,296	77,811 a	48,174,829 a	8,208,372
ecc	19,339 a	15,731,559	1,449,196	18,710	16,658,718	2,077,928	17,834	17,551,723	2,042,520
ecv	123,150 a	301,961,227	21,955,749 a	126,351 m	NA	NA	129,635 m	NA	NA
elc	3,533,956 a	2,470,777,573 a	254,571,455 a	3,483,336 a	2,507,117,689	256,892,032	3,444,041	2,474,851,188	241,234,666
els	15,734	14,738,808	1,365,828	15,672	14,565,105	1,070,176	15,672	14,271,293	1,648,567
emc	See FEC	See FEC	See FEC	See FEC	See FEC	See FEC	See FEC	See FEC	See FEC
feb	1,248 a	2,261,292 a	400,589 a	1,799 a	3,361,033 a	544,127 a	1,721	2,794,938	653,235
fec	6,834 a	17,646,038 a	2,300,708 a	6,933 a	22,705,650 a	1,741,233 a	7,137	22,451,650	1,871,850
fmc	67,259	134,294,405	15,560,923	66,878	127,559,752	19,316,741	67,472	131,715,210	18,427,831
fum	43,647 f	NA	NA	35,302	NA	NA	35,302	NA	NA
ggb	46,242 a	27,179,045 a	4,206,088 a	45,721 a	29,433,584 a	4,087,132 a	54,088	34,438,595	3,822,657
lca	See ELCA	See ELCA	See ELCA	See ELCA	See ELCA	See ELCA	See ELCA	See ELCA	See ELCA
lms	1,835,064	1,278,836,855	120,937,847	1,803,900	1,223,607,882	119,478,393	1,784,139	1,234,616,467	126,921,340
mch	See MUS	See MUS	See MUS	See MUS	See MUS	See MUS	See MUS	See MUS	See MUS
mgc	See MUS	See MUS	See MUS	See MUS	See MUS	See MUS	See MUS	See MUS	See MUS
mus	108,651 l	NA	NA	106,617	NA	NA	105,768	NA	NA
mca	17,554	17,869,301	1,152,271	16,733	17,264,555	1,003,550	16,352	17,198,636	1,043,314
nab	NA	NA	NA	NA	NA	NA	NA	NA	NA
opc	21,031	38,486,700	7,243,700	21,243	39,118,505	6,917,483	21,608	39,785,674	6,790,182
pch	2,209,546	2,518,402,119	398,386,295	2,140,165	2,542,921,235	378,650,258	2,077,138	2,414,721,917	358,621,774
rca	162,182	294,008,651	44,438,226	157,570	283,598,231	46,305,818	154,977	258,802,017	43,036,743
sda	1,000,472	368,356,521	890,924,215	1,021,777	321,184,421	874,235,374	1,043,606	413,465,740	862,030,314
sbc	15,858,062 g	10,815,008,893	1,292,087,965 a	15,822,728 g	10,799,510,977	1,321,709,948 a	15,763,596 g	10,612,188,360	1,299,990,953 a
ucc	1,145,281	859,744,628	77,117,434	1,111,691	869,869,656	71,683,884	1,080,199	861,387,225	67,251,700
wel	309,658 a	255,887,929 a	67,194,722 a	307,452	251,506,951	68,481,343 a	306,881	255,254,310 a	59,728,209 a
Total	28,107,432	21,120,279,588	3,493,593,506	27,749,579	20,766,213,022	3,462,815,765	27,521,086	20,454,533,573	3,370,516,969

a Data obtained from denominational source.

f Inclusive membership, obtained from the denomination and used only in Chapter 5 analysis; not included in the Total sum on this page.

g The 2007, 2008, and 2009 data for the Southern Baptist Convention used in the 1968-2011 analysis includes data only for those State Conventions that provided a breakdown of Total Contributions between Congregational Finances and Benevolences for that year. For the 11 Denominations 1921-2011 analysis, and the Membership Trends analysis, 2007, 2008, and 2009 Southern Baptist Convention Membership is 16,266,920, 16,228,438, and 16,160,088, respectively

k Data available in YACC series used only in Chapter 5 analysis; not included in Total sum on this page.

l Data obtained from denominational source and used only in Chapter 5 analysis; not included in Total sum on this page.

m 2008 membership data is calculated on the percent change from 2006 to 2007 membership data obtained from the denomination; 2009 is calculated on the 2007 and 2008 data; used only in Chapter 5 analysis; not included in Total sum on this page.

Appendix B-1: Church Member Giving, in Current Dollars, 1968-2011 (continued)

	Data Year 2010			Data Year 2011		
	Full/Confirmed Members	Congregational Finances	Benevolences	Full/Confirmed Members	Congregational Finances	Benevolences
abc	292,392 a	241,463,947	47,881,389 a	291,363 a	263,321,076 a	46,646,045 a
alc	See ELCA	See ELCA	See ELCA	See ELCA	See ELCA	See ELCA
arp	34,328 a	46,085,018 a	8,144,620 a	35,911 a	55,171,267 a	11,602,822 a
bcc	23,061 m	NA	NA	23,108 m	NA	NA
ccd	405,338 a	443,712,948	45,652,854	393,677	433,042,420	40,680,609
cga	249,521 k	NA	NA	248,722 k	NA	NA
cgg	3,121	3,692,900	465,343	3,089	3,636,000	466,502
chb	120,041	72,339,775	19,930,435	118,315	68,648,156	17,713,217
chn	640,966	648,769,174	126,057,895	641,989	628,476,287	119,449,511
cccc	33,146 a	40,777,835 a	7,294,704 a	29,462 a	45,130,561 a	6,348,168 a
cpc	71,809	43,118,256	9,412,929	67,076 a	39,636,506 a	9,599,579 a
ecc	17,557	18,183,077	2,037,928	16,779 a	16,012,255 a	2,050,297 a
ecv	133,005 m	NA	NA	NA	NA	NA
elc	3,259,371 a	2,007,197,248 a	219,215,741 a	3,107,925 a	1,954,879,486 a	212,890,820 a
els	15,301	13,842,672	1,118,086	15,041	14,200,085	1,199,216
emc	See FEC	See FEC	See FEC	See FEC	See FEC	See FEC
feb	1,720 n	NA	NA	1,718	NA	NA
fec	7,754	22,776,188	1,831,350	7,316	22,076,775	1,818,550
fmc	67,132 a	132,272,514 a	18,498,161 a	66,296 a	122,388,687 a	27,297,422 a
fum	34,472 f	NA	NA	35,500 f	NA	NA
ggb	46,367 a	31,980,744 a	3,476,780 a	52,920 a	41,051,396 a	3,267,122 a
lca	See ELCA	See ELCA	See ELCA	See ELCA	See ELCA	See ELCA
lms	1,764,024	1,254,192,118	121,592,097	1,731,522	1,255,443,938	120,711,376
mch	See MUS	See MUS	See MUS	See MUS	See MUS	See MUS
mgc	See MUS	See MUS	See MUS	See MUS	See MUS	See MUS
mus	104,687 l	NA	NA	103,529 l	NA	NA
mca	16,220	17,312,747	907,935	16,180 a	15,341,244 a	413,610 a
nab	NA	NA	NA	NA	NA	NA
opc	22,134	41,396,760	6,959,769	22,451	42,261,333	7,102,231
pch	2,016,091	2,254,593,261	359,879,672	1,952,287	2,277,643,836	343,294,225
rca	152,134	257,415,342	44,746,699	148,534	265,645,282	44,875,336
sda	1,060,386	400,622,149	867,960,056	1,074,418	401,345,082	895,724,988
sbc	14,993,567 g	10,451,810,236 a	1,269,010,084 a	15,578,291 g	10,476,354,833 g	1,328,672,872
ucc	1,058,423	867,668,652	70,331,870	1,028,324	867,082,244	67,741,866
wel	303,786 a	256,398,621	58,567,749 a	301,300 a	257,407,217 a	53,606,109 a
Total	26,401,408	19,567,622,182	3,310,974,146	26,700,466	19,576,195,966	3,363,172,493

a Data obtained from denominational source.

f Inclusive membership, obtained from the denomination and used only in Chapter 5 analysis; not included in the Total sum on this page.

g The 2010 and 2011 data for the Southern Baptist Convention used in the 1968-2011 analysis includes data only for those State Conventions that provided a breakdown of Total Contributions between Congregational Finances and Benevolences for that year. For the 11 Denominations 1921-2011 analysis, and the Membership Trends analysis, 2010, and 2011 Southern Baptist Convention Membership is 16,136,044, and 15,978,112, respectively.

k Data available in the *YACC* used only in Chapter 5 analysis; not included in Total sum on this page.

l Data obtained from denominational source and used only in Chapter 5 analysis; not included in Total sum on this page.

m 2010 membership data is calculated on the percent change from 2008 to 2009 in membership data; 2011 membership data is calculated on the percent change from 2009 to 2010; used only in Chapter 5 analysis; not included in Total sum on this page.

n 2010 membership data is calculated from the average of Data Year 2009 obtained from the denomination and Data Year 2011; used only in Chapter 5 analysis; not included in Total sum on this page.

Appendix B-2: Church Member Giving for 38 Denominations, in Current Dollars, 2010-2011

	Data Year 2010			Data Year 2011		
	Full/Confirmed Members	Congregational Finances	Benevolences	Full/Confirmed Members	Congregational Finances	Benevolences
Allegheny Wesleyan Methodist Connection (Original Allegheny Conference)	1,296	3,967,845	1,104,194	1,269	3,955,179	989,865
Baptist Missionary Association of America	137,909	43,311,114	11,226,103	110,816	34,414,814	10,251,232
Bible Fellowship Church	7,627	18,752,540	3,749,624	7,525	19,855,686	3,853,670
Christ Community Church (Evangelical-Protestant)	916 [a]	1,039,817 [a]	237,850 [a]	911 [a]	1,174,542 [a]	235,786 [a]
Christian and Missionary Alliance	198,118	399,763,262	69,963,240	202,285 [a]	415,306,459 [a]	67,167,577 [a]
Church of Christ (Holiness) U.S.A.	12,959 [a]	11,186,061 [a]	632,589 [a]	13,302 [a]	11,131,513 [a]	529,688 [a]
Church of the Lutheran Brethren of America	8,828 [a]	21,644,732 [a]	1,994,410 [a]	8,748 [a]	22,110,731 [a]	2,220,434 [a]
Church of the Lutheran Confession	6,175 [a]	5,994,978 [a]	1,087,500 [a]	5,891 [a]	5,841,800 [a]	1,024,706 [a]
Churches of God General Conference	32,560	30,369,402	6,060,476	32,647	30,953,629	6,040,626
The Episcopal Church	1,576,721 [a]	1,773,619,063 [a]	314,830,613 [a]	1,542,072 [a]	1,766,133,684 [a]	314,478,360 [a]
Missionary Church, The	37,536 [a]	74,151,397	10,085,017 [a]	37,556 [a]	73,864,998 [a]	12,814,419 [a]
Presbyterian Church in America	271,633	581,396,399	122,456,403	275,513	584,453,155	120,158,556
Primitive Methodist Church in the U.S.A.	3,294	4,503,734	503,192	3,185	4,693,340	551,554
The United Methodist Church	7,615,750 [a]	4,926,231,826 [a]	1,231,852,701 [a]	7,526,497 [a]	4,941,495,970 [a]	1,248,165,973 [a]
The Wesleyan Church	121,429	271,863,678	44,342,132	122,298	283,393,134	46,317,888 [a]

a Data obtained from denominational source.

Appendix B-3.1: Church Member Giving for 11 Denominations, in Current Dollars, 1921-1952

Year	Total Contributions	Members	Per Capita Giving
1921	$281,173,263	17,459,611	$16.10
1922	345,995,802	18,257,426	18.95
1923	415,556,876	18,866,775	22.03
1924	443,187,826	19,245,220	23.03
1925	412,658,363	19,474,863	21.19
1926	368,529,223	17,054,404	21.61
1927	459,527,624	20,266,709	22.67
1928	429,947,883	20,910,584	20.56
1929	445,327,233	20,612,910	21.60
1930	419,697,819	20,796,745	20.18
1931	367,158,877	21,508,745	17.07
1932	309,409,873	21,757,411	14.22
1933	260,366,681	21,792,663	11.95
1934	260,681,472	22,105,624	11.79
1935	267,596,925	22,204,355	12.05
1936	279,835,526	21,746,023	12.87
1937	297,134,313	21,906,456	13.56
1938	307,217,666	22,330,090	13.76
1939	302,300,476	23,084,048	13.10
1940	311,362,429	23,671,660	13.15
1941	336,732,622	23,120,929	14.56
1942	358,419,893	23,556,204	15.22
1943	400,742,492	24,679,784	16.24
1944	461,500,396	25,217,319	18.30
1945	551,404,448	25,898,642	21.29
1946	608,165,179	26,158,559	23.25
1947	684,393,895	27,082,905	25.27
1948	775,360,993	27,036,992	28.68
1949	875,069,944	27,611,824	31.69
1950	934,723,015	28,176,095	33.17
1951	1,033,391,527	28,974,314	35.67
1952	1,121,802,639	29,304,909	38.28

Appendix B-3.2: Church Member Giving for 11 Denominations, in Current Dollars, 1953-1967

	Data Year 1953		Data Year 1954		Data Year 1955	
	Total Contributions	Per Capita Total Contributions	Total Contributions	Per Capita Total Contributions	Total Contributions	Per Capita Total Contributions
American Baptist (Northern)	$66,557,447 [a]	$44.50 [b]	$65,354,184	$43.17	$67,538,753 [d]	$44.19 [d]
Christian Church (Disciples of Christ)	60,065,545 [c]	32.50 [b]	65,925,164	34.77	68,661,162 [d]	35.96 [d]
Church of the Brethren	7,458,584	43.78	7,812,806	45.88	9,130,616	53.00
The Episcopal Church	84,209,027	49.02	92,079,668	51.84	97,541,567 [d]	50.94 [b]
Evangelical Lutheran Church in America						
The American Lutheran Church						
American Lutheran Church	30,881,256	55.24	34,202,987	58.83	40,411,856	67.03
The Evangelical Lutheran Church	30,313,907	48.70	33,312,926	51.64	37,070,341	55.29
United Evangelical Lutheran Church	1,953,163	55.85	2,268,200	50.25	2,635,469	69.84
Lutheran Free Church	Not Reported: YAC 1955, p. 264		2,101,026	44.51	2,708,747	55.76
Evan. Lutheran Churches, Assn. of	Not Reported: YAC 1955, p. 264		Not Reported: YAC 1956, p. 276		Not Reported: YAC 1957, p. 284	
Lutheran Church in America						
United Lutheran Church	67,721,548	45.68	76,304,344	50.25	83,170,787	53.46
General Council Evang. Luth. Ch.						
General Synod of Evang. Luth. Ch.						
United Syn. Evang. Luth. South						
American Evangelical Luth. Ch.	Not Reported: YAC 1955, p. 264		Not Reported: YAC 1956, p. 276		Not Reported: YAC 1957, p. 284	
Augustana Lutheran Church	18,733,019	53.98	22,203,098	62.14	22,090,350	60.12
Finnish Lutheran Ch. (Suomi Synod)	744,971	32.12	674,554	29.47	1,059,682	43.75
Moravian Church in Am. No. Prov.	1,235,534	53.26	1,461,658	59.51	1,241,008	49.15
Presbyterian Church (U.S.A.)						
United Presbyterian Ch. In U.S.A.						
Presbyterian Church in the U.S.A.	141,057,179	56.49	158,110,613	61.47	180,472,698	68.09
United Presbyterian Ch. In N.A.	13,204,897	57.73	14,797,353	62.37	16,019,616	65.39
Presbyterian Church in the U.S.	56,001,996	73.99	59,222,983	75.54	66,033,260	81.43
Reformed Church in America	13,671,897	68.57	14,740,275	71.87	17,459,572	84.05
Southern Baptist Convention	278,851,129	39.84	305,573,654	42.17	334,836,283	44.54
United Church of Christ						
Congregational Christian	64,061,866	49.91	71,786,834	54.76	80,519,810	60.00
Congregational						
Evangelical and Reformed	31,025,133	41.24	36,261,267	46.83	41,363,406	52.74
Evangelical Synod of N.A./German						
Reformed Church in the U.S.						
The United Methodist Church						
The Evangelical United Brethren	36,331,994	50.21	36,609,598	50.43	41,199,631	56.01
The Methodist Church	314,521,214	34.37	345,416,448	37.53	389,490,613	41.82
Methodist Episcopal Church						
Methodist Episcopal Church South						
Methodist Protestant Church						
Total	$1,318,601,306		$1,446,219,640		$1,600,655,227	

[a] In data year 1953, $805,135 has been subtracted from the 1955 Yearbook of American Churches (YAC) (Edition for 1956) entry. See 1956 YAC (Edition for 1957), p. 276, n.1.

[b] This Per Capita Total Contributions figure was calculated by dividing (1) revised Total Contributions as listed in this Appendix, by (2) Membership that, for purposes of this report, had been calculated by dividing the revised Total Contributions by the Per Capita Total Contributions figures that were published in the YAC series.

[c] In data year 1953, $5,508,883 has been added to the 1955 YAC (Edition for 1956) entry. See 1956 YAC (Edition for 1957), p. 276, n. 4.

[d] Total Contributions and Per Capita Total Contributions, respectively, prorated based on available data as follows: American Baptist Churches, 1954 and 1957 data; Christian Church (Disciples of Christ), 1954 and 1956 data; and The Episcopal Church, 1954 and 1956 data.

Appendix B-3.2: Church Member Giving for 11 Denominations, in Current Dollars, 1953-1967 (continued)

	Data Year 1956		Data Year 1957		Data Year 1958	
	Total Contributions	Per Capita Total Contributions	Total Contributions	Per Capita Total Contributions	Total Contributions	Per Capita Total Contributions
American Baptist (Northern)	$69,723,321 e	$45.21 e	$71,907,890	$46.23 e	$70,405,404	$45.03
Christian Church (Disciples of Christ)	71,397,159	37.14	73,737,955	37.94	79,127,458	41.17
Church of the Brethren	10,936,285	63.15	11,293,388	64.43	12,288,049	70.03
The Episcopal Church	103,003,465	52.79	111,660,728	53.48	120,687,177	58.33
Evangelical Lutheran Church in America						
The American Lutheran Church						
American Lutheran Church	45,316,809	72.35	44,518,194	68.80	47,216,896	70.89
The Evangelical Lutheran Church	39,096,038	56.47	44,212,046	61.95	45,366,512	61.74
United Evangelical Lutheran Church	2,843,527	73.57	2,641,201	65.46	3,256,050	77.38
Lutheran Free Church	2,652,307	53.14	3,379,882	64.70	3,519,017	66.31
Evan. Lutheran Churches, Assn. of	Not Reported: YAC 1958, p. 292		Not Reported: YAC 1959, p. 277		Not Reported: YAC 1960, p. 276	
Lutheran Church in America						
United Lutheran Church	93,321,223	58.46	100,943,860	61.89	110,179,054	66.45
General Council Evang. Luth. Ch.						
General Synod of Evang. Luth. Ch.						
United Syn. Evang. Luth. South						
American Evangelical Luth. Ch.	Not Comparable YAC 1958, p. 292		935,319	59.45	1,167,503	72.98
Augustana Lutheran Church	24,893,792	66.15	28,180,152	72.09	29,163,771	73.17
Finnish Lutheran Ch. (Suomi Synod)	1,308,026	51.56	1,524,299	58.11	1,533,058	61.94
Moravian Church in Am. No. Prov.	1,740,961	67.53	1,776,703	67.77	1,816,281	68.14
Presbyterian Church (U.S.A.)						
United Presbyterian Ch. In U.S.A.	204,208,085	75.02	214,253,598	77.06	243,000,572	78.29
Presbyterian Church in the U.S.A.	18,424,936	73.3	19,117,837	74.24		
United Presbyterian Ch. In N.A.						
Presbyterian Church in the U.S.	73,477,555	88.56	78,426,424	92.03	82,760,291	95.18
Reformed Church in America	18,718,008	88.56	19,658,604	91.10	21,550,017	98.24
Southern Baptist Convention	372,136,675	48.17	397,540,347	49.99	419,619,438	51.04
United Church of Christ						
Congregational Christian	89,914,505	65.18	90,333,453	64.87	97,480,446	69.55
Congregational						
Evangelical and Reformed	51,519,531	64.88	55,718,141	69.56	63,419,468	78.56
Evangelical Synod of N.A./German						
Reformed Church in the U.S.						
The United Methodist Church						
The Evangelical United Brethren	44,727,060	60.57	45,738,332 e	61.75 e	46,749,605 e	62.93 e
The Methodist Church	413,893,955	43.82	462,826,269 e	48.31 e	511,758,582	52.80
Methodist Episcopal Church						
Methodist Episcopal Church South						
Methodist Protestant Church						
Total	$1,753,253,223		$1,880,324,622		$2,012,064,649	

e Total Contributions and Per Capita Total Contributions, respectively, prorated based on available data as follows: American Baptist Churches, 1954 and 1957 data; The Evangelical United Brethren, 1956 and 1960 data; and The Methodist Church, 1956 and 1958 data.

Appendix B-3.2: Church Member Giving for 11 Denominations, in Current Dollars, 1953-1967 (continued)

	Data Year 1959		Data Year 1960		Data Year 1961	
	Total Contributions	Per Capita Total Contributions	Total Contributions	Per Capita Total Contributions	Total Contributions	Per Capita Total Contributions
American Baptist (Northern)	$74,877,669	$48.52	$73,106,232	$48.06	$104,887,025	$68.96
Christian Church (Disciples of Christ)	Not Comparable YAC 1961, p. 273		86,834,944	63.26	89,730,589	65.31
Church of the Brethren	12,143,983	65.27	12,644,194	68.33	13,653,155	73.33
The Episcopal Church	130,279,752	61.36	140,625,284	64.51	154,458,809	68.30
Evangelical Lutheran Church in America						
The American Lutheran Church	50,163,078	73.52	51,898,875	74.49	113,645,260	73.28
American Lutheran Church	49,488,063	65.56	51,297,348	66.85		
The Evangelical Lutheran Church	Not Reported: YAC 1961, p. 273		Not Reported: YAC 1963, p. 273			
United Evangelical Lutheran Church	3,354,270	61.20	3,618,418	63.98	4,316,925	73.46
Lutheran Free Church	Not Reported: YAC 1961, p. 273		Not Reported: YAC 1963, p. 273			
Evan. Lutheran Churches, Assn. of						
Lutheran Church in America						
United Lutheran Church	114,458,260	68.29	119,447,895	70.86	128,850,845	76.18
General Council Evang. Luth. Ch.						
General Synod of Evang. Luth. Ch.						
United Syn. Evang. Luth. South						
American Evangelical Luth. Ch.	1,033,907	63.83	1,371,600	83.63	1,209,752	74.89
Augustana Lutheran Church	31,279,335	76.97	33,478,865	80.88	37,863,105	89.37
Finnish Lutheran Ch. (Suomi Synod)	1,685,342	68.61	1,860,481	76.32	1,744,550	70.60
Moravian Church in Am. No. Prov.	2,398,565	89.28	2,252,536	82.95	2,489,930	90.84
Presbyterian Church (U.S.A.)						
United Presbyterian Ch. In U.S.A.	259,679,057	82.30	270,233,943	84.31	285,380,476	87.90
Presbyterian Church in the U.S.A.						
United Presbyterian Ch. In N.A.						
Presbyterian Church in the U.S.	88,404,631	99.42	91,582,428	101.44	96,637,354	105.33
Reformed Church in America	22,970,935	103.23	23,615,749	104.53	25,045,773	108.80
Southern Baptist Convention	453,338,720	53.88	480,608,972	55.68	501,301,714	50.24
United Church of Christ						
Congregational Christian	100,938,267	71.12	104,862,037	73.20	105,871,158	73.72
Congregational						
Evangelical and Reformed	65,541,874	80.92	62,346,084	76.58	65,704,662	80.33
Evangelical Synod of N.A./German						
Reformed Church in the U.S.						
The United Methodist Church						
The Evangelical United Brethren	47,760,877 d	64.10	48,772,149 d	65.28	50,818,912 d	68.12
The Methodist Church	532,854,842 d	53.97	553,951,102 d	55.14	581,504,618 d	57.27
Methodist Episcopal Church						
Methodist Episcopal Church South						
Methodist Protestant Church						
Total	$2,042,651,427		$2,214,409,136		$2,365,114,612	

d Total Contributions averaged from available data as follows: The Evangelical United Brethren, 1956 and 1960 data; The United Methodist Church, 1958 and 1960 data.

Appendix B-3.2: Church Member Giving for 11 Denominations, in Current Dollars, 1953-1967* (continued)

	Data Year 1962		Data Year 1963		Data Year 1964	
	Total Contributions	Per Capita Total Contributions	Total Contributions	Per Capita Total Contributions	Total Contributions	Per Capita Total Contributions
American Baptist (Northern)	$105,667,332	$68.42	$99,001,651	$68.34	$104,699,557	$69.99
Christian Church (Disciples of Christ)	91,889,457	67.20	96,607,038	75.81	102,102,840	86.44
Church of the Brethren	14,594,572	77.88	14,574,688	72.06	15,221,162	76.08
The Episcopal Church	155,971,264	69.80	171,125,464	76.20	175,374,777	76.66
Evangelical Lutheran Church in America						
The American Lutheran Church	114,912,112	72.47	136,202,292	81.11	143,687,165	83.83
American Lutheran Church						
The Evangelical Lutheran Church						
United Evangelical Lutheran Church						
Lutheran Free Church	4,765,138	78.68				
Evan. Lutheran Churches, Assn. of						
Lutheran Church in America	185,166,857	84.98	157,423,391	71.45	170,012,096	76.35
United Lutheran Church						
General Council Evang. Luth. Ch.						
General Synod of Evang. Luth. Ch.						
United Syn. Evang. Luth. South						
American Evangelical Luth. Ch.						
Augustana Lutheran Church						
Finnish Lutheran Ch. (Suomi Synod)						
Moravian Church in Am. No. Prov.	2,512,133	91.92	2,472,273	89.29	2,868,694	103.54
Presbyterian Church (U.S.A.)						
United Presbyterian Ch. In U.S.A.	288,496,652	88.08	297,582,313	90.46	304,833,435	92.29
Presbyterian Church in the U.S.A.						
United Presbyterian Ch. In N.A.						
Presbyterian Church in the U.S.	99,262,431	106.96	102,625,764	109.46	108,269,579	114.61
Reformed Church in America	25,579,443	110.16	26,918,484	117.58	29,174,103	126.44
Southern Baptist Convention	540,811,457	53.06	556,042,694	53.49	591,587,981	55.80
United Church of Christ	164,858,968	72.83	162,379,019	73.12	169,208,042	75.94
Congregational Christian						
Congregational						
Evangelical and Reformed						
Evangelical Synod of N.A./German						
Reformed Church in the U.S.						
The United Methodist Church						
The Evangelical United Brethren	54,567,962	72.91	49,921,568	67.37	56,552,783	76.34
The Methodist Church	599,081,561	58.53	613,547,721	59.60	608,841,881	59.09
Methodist Episcopal Church						
Methodist Episcopal Church South						
Methodist Protestant Church						
Total	$2,448,137,339		$2,486,424,360		$2,582,434,095	

* Note: Data for the years 1965 through 1967 was not available in a form that could be readily analyzed for the present purposes, and therefore, data for 1965-1967 was estimated as described in the introductory comments to Appendix B. See Appendix B-1 for 1968-1991 data except for The Episcopal Church and The United Methodist Church, available data for which is presented in the continuation of Appendix B-3 in the table immediately following.

Appendix B-3.3: Church Member Giving for 11 Denominations, in Current Dollars, The Episcopal Church and The United Methodist Church, 1968-2011

The Episcopal Church			The United Methodist Church			
Data Year	Total Contributions	Full/Confirmed Membership	Data Year	Total Contributions	Full/Confirmed Membership	Connectional Clergy Support c
1968	$202,658,092 c	2,322,911 c	1968	$763,000,434 a	10,849,375 b	NA
1969	209,989,189 c	2,238,538	1969	800,425,000	10,671,774	44,416,000
1970	248,702,969	2,208,773	1970	819,945,000	10,509,198	48,847,000
1971	257,523,469	2,143,557	1971	843,103,000	10,334,521	52,731,000
1972	270,245,645	2,099,896	1972	885,708,000	10,192,265	56,968,000
1973	296,735,919 c	2,079,873 c	1973	935,723,000	10,063,046	62,498,997
1974	305,628,925	2,069,793	1974	1,009,760,804	9,957,710	67,344,298
1975	352,243,222	2,051,914 c	1975	1,081,080,372	9,861,028	75,220,496
1976	375,942,065	2,021,057	1976	1,162,828,991	9,785,534	82,681,376
1977	401,814,395	2,114,638	1977	1,264,191,548	9,731,779	94,705,448
1978	430,116,564	1,975,234	1978	1,364,460,266	9,653,711	107,508,214
1979	484,211,412	1,962,062	1979	1,483,481,986	9,584,771	116,405,701
1980	507,315,457	1,933,080 c	1980	1,632,204,336	9,519,407	126,442,425
1981	697,816,298	1,930,690	1981	1,794,706,741	9,457,012	136,991,942
1982	778,184,068	1,922,923 c	1982	1,931,796,533	9,405,164	162,884,181
1983	876,844,252	1,906,618	1983	2,049,437,917	9,291,936	172,569,488
1984	939,796,743	1,896,056	1984	2,211,306,198	9,266,853	188,372,446
1985	1,043,117,983	1,881,250	1985	2,333,928,274	9,192,172	203,047,650
1986	1,134,455,479	1,772,271 c	1986	2,460,079,431	9,124,575	211,121,271
1987	1,181,378,441	1,741,036	1987	2,573,748,234 c	9,055,145	217,708,718
1988	1,209,378,098	1,725,581	1988	2,697,918,285	8,979,139	230,013,885
1989	1,309,243,747	1,714,122	1989	2,845,998,177	8,904,824	245,281,392
1990	1,377,794,610	1,698,240	1990	2,967,535,538 c	8,853,455 c	261,434,709
1991	1,541,141,356 c	1,613,825 c	1991	3,099,522,282	8,789,101	269,248,639
1992	1,582,055,527 c	1,615,930 c	1992	3,202,700,721 c	8,726,951 c	278,990,363
1993	1,617,623,255 c	1,580,339 c	1993	3,303,255,279	8,646,595	284,654,147
1994	1,679,250,095 c	1,578,282 c	1994	3,430,351,778	8,584,125	293,637,514
1995	1,840,431,636 c	1,584,225 c	1995	3,568,359,334 c	8,538,808 c	295,102,097
1996	1,731,727,725 c	1,637,584 c	1996	3,744,692,223	8,496,047 c	296,944,022
1997	1,832,000,448 c	1,757,972 c	1997	3,990,329,491 c	8,452,042 c	310,347,506
1998	1,977,012,320 c	1,807,651 c	1998	4,219,596,499 c	8,411,503 c	319,721,285
1999	2,146,835,718 c	1,843,108 c	1999	4,523,284,851	8,377,662	328,089,751
2000	2,143,238,797 c	1,877,271 c	2000	4,761,148,280	8,341,375	338,798,893
2001	2,070,493,919 c	1,897,004 c	2001	5,043,693,838 c	8,298,460 c	359,734,860
2002	2,090,536,512 c	1,902,525 c	2002	5,242,691,229 c	8,251,042	401,465,727
2003	2,133,772,253	1,866,157	2003	5,376,057,236 c	8,186,274 c	444,210,401
2004	2,132,774,534	1,834,530	2004	5,541,540,536	8,120,186 d	462,206,590
2005	2,180,974,503 c	1,796,017 c	2005	5,861,722,397 c	8,040,577 c	466,588,268
2006	2,187,308,798 c	1,749,073 c	2006	6,012,378,898	7,976,985 c	481,453,754
2007	2,221,167,438	1,720,477	2007	6,295,942,455 c	7,899,147 c	478,982,491
2008	2,294,941,221	1,666,202	2008	6,300,722,381 c	7,819,668 c	477,863,600
2009	2,182,330,459	1,624,025	2009	6,218,009,630 c	7,724,821 c	Not Available
2010	2,088,449,676	1,576,721	2010	6,158,084,527 c	7,615,750 c	Not Available
2011	2,080,612,044 c	1,542,072 c	2011	6,189,661,943 c	7,526,497 c	Not Available

a The Evangelical United Brethren Data Not Reported: *YAC* 1970, p. 198-200. This figure is the sum of The Methodist Church in 1968, and the Evangelical United Brethren data for 1967.

b This membership figure is an average of the sum of 1967 membership for The Methodist Church and the Evangelical United Brethren and 1969 data for The United Methodist Church.

c Data obtained directly from denominational source.

d Data obtained from the denomination included this note: "Combines 2004 local church data with 2004 clergy data. In the past 2004 lay would be combined with 2005 clergy. We've been delayed in finalizing clergy figures for 2005… [Based on a check of] the past few years, that will mean a difference of less than 300 for the total number."

Appendix B-4: Membership for Seven Denominations, 1968-2011

Year	American Baptist Churches (Total Mem.)	Assemblies of God	Baptist General Conference/ Converge Worldwide	Christian and Missionary Alliance	Church of God (Cleveland, TN)	Roman Catholic Church	Salvation Army
1968	1,583,560	610,946	100,000	71,656	243,532	47,468,333	329,515
1969	1,528,019	626,660	101,226	70,573	257,995	47,872,089	331,711
1970	1,472,478	625,027	103,955	71,708	272,276	48,214,729	326,934
1971	1,562,636	645,891	108,474	73,547	287,099	48,390,990	335,684
1972	1,484,393	679,813	111,364	77,991	297,103	48,460,427	358,626
1973	1,502,759	700,071	109,033	77,606	313,332	48,465,438	361,571
1974	1,579,029	751,818	111,093	80,412	328,892	48,701,835	366,471
1975	1,603,033	785,348	115,340	83,628	343,249	48,881,872	384,817
1976	1,593,574	898,711	117,973	83,978	365,124	49,325,752	380,618
1977	1,584,517	939,312	120,222	88,763	377,765	49,836,176	396,238
1978	1,589,610	932,365	131,000	88,903	392,551	49,602,035	414,035
1979	1,600,521	958,418	126,800	96,324	441,385	49,812,178	414,659
1980	1,607,541	1,064,490	133,385	106,050	435,012	50,449,842	417,359
1981	1,621,795	1,103,134	127,662	109,558	456,797	51,207,579	414,999
1982	1,637,099	1,119,686	129,928	112,745	463,992	52,088,774 [a]	419,475
1983	1,620,153	1,153,935	131,594 [a]	117,501	493,904	52,392,934	428,046
1984	1,559,683	1,189,143	131,162 [a]	120,250	505,775	52,286,043	420,971
1985	1,576,483	1,235,403	130,193 [a]	123,602	521,061 [b]	52,654,908	427,825
1986	1,568,778 [a]	1,258,724	132,546 [a]	130,116	536,346 [b]	52,893,217	432,893
1987	1,561,656 [a]	1,275,146	136,688 [a]	131,354	551,632 [b]	53,496,862	434,002
1988	1,548,573 [a]	1,275,148	134,396 [a]	133,575	556,917 [b]	54,918,949 [a]	433,448
1989	1,535,971 [a]	1,266,982	135,125 [a]	134,336	582,203	57,019,948	445,566
1990	1,527,840 [a]	1,298,121	133,742 [a]	138,071	620,393	58,568,015	445,991
1991	1,534,078 [a]	1,324,800	134,717 [a]	141,077	646,201 [b]	58,267,424	446,403
1992	1,538,710 [a]	1,337,321	134,658 [a]	142,346	672,008	59,220,723	450,028 [a]
1993	1,516,505	1,340,400	134,814 [a]	147,367	700,517	59,858,042	450,312 [a]
1994	1,507,934 [a]	1,354,337	135,128	147,560 [a]	722,541	60,190,605	443,246
1995	1,517,400	1,377,320	135,008	147,955	753,230	60,280,454	453,150
1996	1,503,267 [a]	1,407,941	136,120	143,157	773,483 [a]	61,207,914	462,744 [a]
1997	1,478,534 [a]	1,419,717	134,795	146,153	815,042 [a]	61,563,769 [a]	468,262 [a]
1998	1,507,824 [a]	1,453,907	141,445	163,994	839,857 [a]	62,018,436	471,416
1999	1,454,388	1,492,196	142,871 [a]	164,196	870,039	62,391,484	472,871
2000	1,436,909	1,506,834	141,781 [a]	185,133	895,536	63,683,030 [a]	476,887 [a]
2001	1,442,824	1,532,876	144,365 [a]	191,318	920,664 [a]	65,270,444	454,982
2002	1,484,291	1,585,428	145,148	190,573	944,857	66,407,105	457,807 [a]
2003	1,433,075	1,584,076	145,436 [a]	194,074	961,390	67,259,768 [a]	449,634 [a]
2004	1,418,403 [a]	1,594,062	145,000 [a]	197,764	989,965	67,820,833	427,027
2005	1,396,700	1,612,336	140,494 [a]	201,009	1,013,488	69,135,254	422,543 [a]
2006	1,371,278	1,627,932	140,000 [a]	189,969	1,032,550	67,515,016	414,054 [a]
2007	1,358,351 [a]	1,641,341	147,500	195,481	1,053,642	67,117,016	413,028
2008	1,331,127	1,662,632	167,500 [a]	194,473	1,072,169	68,115,001	405,967 [a]
2009	1,310,505	1,710,560	190,100 [a]	197,653	1,076,254	68,503,456	400,055
2010	1,308,054	1,753,881	210,500 [a]	198,118	1,074,047	68,293,869 [a]	413,961
2011	1,300,744	1,755,872 [a]	217,200 [a]	202,285 [a]	1,088,756	68,229,841 [a]	416,526

[a] Data obtained from a denominational source.
[b] Extrapolated from *YACC* series.
Note regarding American Baptist Churches (ABC) in the U.S.A. Total Membership data: Total Membership is used for the ABC for analyses that consider membership as a percentage of U.S. population. The ABC denominational office is the source for this data in the years 1968 and 1970. The year 1978 Total Membership data figure is an adjustment of *YACC* data based on 1981 *YACC* information.

Appendix B-5.1: Overseas Missions Income, 34 Denominations, in Current Dollars, 2003 and 2004

Denomination	2003 Overseas Missions Income				2004 Overseas Missions Income			
	Line 1.	Line 2.	Line 3.	Line 4.	Line 1.	Line 2.	Line 3.	Line 4.
Allegheny Wesleyan Methodist Connection	$262,260	$0	$0	$262,260	$266,299	$0	$0	$266,299
American Baptist Churches in the U.S.A.	$20,562,505	$12,048,667	$0	$8,513,838	$17,250,939	$7,759,091	$0	$9,491,848
Associate Reformed Presbyterian Church (General Synod)	$3,508,682	$0	$175,690	$3,332,992	$4,453,573	$15,183	$483,815	$3,954,575
Brethren in Christ Church	$1,651,911	$45,000	$0	$1,606,911	$1,850,963	$50,000	$0	$1,800,963
Christian Church (Disciples of Christ)	$5,960,892	$1,881,873	$0	$4,079,019	$5,347,401	$1,515,309	$0	$3,832,092
Christian and Missionary Alliance [1]	$43,160,960	$0	$0	$43,160,960	$43,534,066	$0	$0	$43,534,066
Church of the Brethren [2]	$1,767,447	$203,824	$0	$1,563,623	$1,702,267	$143,947	$0	$1,558,320
Church of God General Conference (Oregon, Ill., and Morrow, Ga.)	$67,193	$0	$0	$67,193	$113,497	$0	$0	$113,497
Church of the Lutheran Confession	$182,156	$27,000	$0	$155,156	$246,896	$40,000	$0	$206,896
Church of the Nazarene	$46,334,499	$694,019	$0	$45,640,480	$49,715,273	$1,542,188	$0	$48,173,085
Churches of God General Conference [3]	$899,679	$0	$0	$899,679	$1,068,665	$21,517	$0	$1,047,148
Conservative Congregational Christian Conference [4]	$147,805	$0	$0	$147,805	$149,299	$0	$0	$149,299
Cumberland Presbyterian Church	$303,000	$12,236	$0	$290,764	$338,314	$14,974	$0	$323,340
The Episcopal Church [5]	$21,120,265	$3,507,225	$4,419,185	$13,193,855	$23,281,000	$3,000,000	$5,500,000	$14,781,000
Evangelical Congregational Church	$1,264,969	$219,732	$0	$1,045,237	$1,135,224	$193,815	$0	$941,409
Evangelical Covenant Church	$7,913,682	$0	$0	$7,913,682	$8,591,574	$0	$0	$8,591,574
Evangelical Lutheran Church in America [6]	$22,590,206	$2,952,825	$0	$19,637,381	$27,173,066	$3,741,985	$0	$23,431,081
Evangelical Lutheran Synod	$912,460	$665,873	$0	$246,587	$945,470	$679,229	$0	$266,241
Fellowship of Evangelical Churches	$912,689	$0	$0	$912,689	$847,526	$0	$0	$847,526
Free Methodist Church of North America	$9,848,924	$727,325	$0	$9,121,599	$10,817,138	$630,519	$0	$10,186,619
General Association of General Baptists	$1,893,585	$34,719	$0	$1,858,866	$1,817,715	$49,178	$0	$1,768,537
Lutheran Church-Missouri Synod [7]	$14,960,928	$1,881,887	$0	$13,079,041	$15,548,240	$2,370,861	$0	$13,177,379
Moravian Church in America, Northern Province [8]				$467,570				$528,733
The Orthodox Presbyterian Church [9]	$1,254,678	$40,229		$1,214,449	$1,417,758	$43,504	$0	$1,374,254
Presbyterian Church in America	$24,070,885	$0	$0	$24,070,885	$24,319,185	$0	$0	$24,319,185
Presbyterian Church (U.S.A.) [10]	$34,348,000	$11,046,000	$47,000	$23,255,000	$36,900,000	$12,190,000	$122,000	$24,588,000
Primitive Methodist Church in the U.S.A. [11]	$542,252	$5,349	$0	$536,903	$532,337	$5,697	$0	$526,640
Reformed Church in America	$8,159,552	$307,088	$0	$7,852,464	$7,610,120	$325,560	$0	$7,284,560
Seventh-day Adventist, North Am. Division [12]	$50,790,392	$2,565,158	$0	$48,225,234	$48,209,196	$1,456,611	$0	$46,752,585
Southern Baptist Convention	$239,663,000	$0	$0	$239,663,000	$242,140,000	$0	$0	$242,140,000
United Church of Christ	$12,990,011	$4,616,927	$0	$8,373,084	$12,125,594	$4,189,916	$0	$7,935,678
The United Methodist Church [13]	$124,800,000	$20,000,000	$22,800,000	$82,000,000	$138,700,000	$19,800,000	$27,700,000	$91,200,000
The Wesleyan Church	$8,507,914	$0	$0	$8,507,914	$8,881,386	$0	$0	$8,881,386
Wisconsin Evangelical Lutheran Synod	$11,534,079	$754,916	$0	$10,779,164	$10,707,496	$402,633	$0	$10,304,863

See Notes on page 204.

199

Appendix B-5.2: Overseas Missions Income, 34 Denominations, in Current Dollars, 2005 and 2006

Denomination	2005 Overseas Missions Income				2006 Overseas Missions Income			
	Line 1.	Line 2.	Line 3.	Line 4.	Line 1.	Line 2.	Line 3.	Line 4.
Allegheny Wesleyan Methodist Connection	$399,514	$0	$0	$399,514	$286,781	$0	$0	$286,781
American Baptist Churches in the U.S.A.	$18,837,736	$7,741,255	$0	$11,096,481	$14,701,486	$5,922,316	$0	$8,779,170
Associate Reformed Presbyterian Church (General Synod)	$4,920,208	$139,231	$264,675	$4,516,302	$4,682,925	$689,152	$172,476	$3,821,297
Brethren in Christ Church	$1,980,000	$60,000	$0	$1,920,000	$2,200,000	$82,406	$0	$2,117,594
Christian Church (Disciples of Christ)	$5,810,205	$1,587,428	$0	$4,222,777	$6,134,200	$1,712,531	$0	$4,421,669
Christian and Missionary Alliance [1]	$54,267,422	$0	$0	$54,267,422	$52,505,044	$0	$0	$52,505,044
Church of the Brethren [2]	$2,417,349	$147,215	$0	$2,270,134	$2,087,021	$199,819	$0	$1,887,202
Church of God General Conference (Oregon, Ill., and Morrow, Ga.)	$80,000	$0	$0	$80,000	$63,355	$0	$0	$63,355
Church of the Lutheran Confession	$329,823	$20,000	$0	$309,823	$314,804	$125,987	$0	$188,817
Church of the Nazarene	$54,653,601	$1,899,919	$0	$52,753,682	$52,721,095	$1,751,130	$0	$50,969,965
Churches of God General Conference [3]	$1,146,044	$15,944	$0	$1,130,100	$1,282,333	$48,490	$0	$1,233,843
Conservative Congregational Christian Conference [4]	$166,875	$0	$0	$166,875	$123,509	$0	$0	$123,509
Cumberland Presbyterian Church	$306,428	$13,082	$0	$293,346	$306,035	$15,728	$0	$290,307
The Episcopal Church [5]	$23,871,967	$3,000,000	$5,500,000	$15,371,967	$24,334,083	$3,000,000	$6,527,290	$14,806,793
Evangelical Congregational Church	$767,359	$42,270	$0	$725,089	$1,326,393	$0	$0	$1,326,393
Evangelical Covenant Church	$9,008,719	$0	$0	$9,008,719	$8,530,245	$0	$0	$8,530,245
Evangelical Lutheran Church in America [6]	$29,109,564	$3,025,562	$0	$26,084,001	$25,484,714	$3,942,905	$0	$21,541,809
Evangelical Lutheran Synod	$1,211,101	$988,897	$0	$222,204	$1,214,815	$884,164	$0	$330,651
Fellowship of Evangelical Churches	$785,676	$0	$0	$785,676	$700,159	$0	$0	$700,159
Free Methodist Church of North America	$10,831,707	$111,467	$0	$10,720,240	$12,578,589	$699,714	$0	$11,878,875
General Association of General Baptists	$1,945,215	$20,707	$0	$1,924,508	$2,082,916	$34,346	$0	$2,048,570
Lutheran Church-Missouri Synod [7]	$18,897,894	$1,722,316	$0	$17,175,578	$16,170,108	$2,737,162	$0	$13,432,946
Moravian Church in America, Northern Province [8]	$568,497	$86,340	$0	$482,157	$561,849	$49,021	$0	$512,828
The Orthodox Presbyterian Church [9]	$2,212,525	$355,996	$0	$1,856,529	$2,064,820	$358,528	$0	$1,706,292
Presbyterian Church in America	$25,890,591	$0	$0	$25,890,591	$27,627,770	$0	$0	$27,627,770
Presbyterian Church (U.S.A.) [10]	$47,223,000	$15,540,000	$65,000	$31,618,000	$35,539,000	$14,575,000	$0	$20,964,000
Primitive Methodist Church in the U.S.A. [11]	$503,286	$5,441	$0	$497,845	$568,032	$1,916	$0	$566,116
Reformed Church in America	$10,727,347	$0	$0	$10,727,347	$7,891,745	$405,218	$0	$7,486,527
Seventh-day Adventist, North Am. Division [12]	$53,745,101	$1,614,134	$0	$52,130,967	$51,459,266	$2,553,650	$0	$48,905,616
Southern Baptist Convention	$259,394,000	$0	$0	$259,394,000	$275,747,000	$0	$0	$275,747,000
United Church of Christ	$11,299,684	$3,647,313	$0	$7,652,371	$10,834,552	$3,295,428	$0	$7,539,124
The United Methodist Church [13]	$177,000,000	$23,400,000	$26,000,000	$127,600,000	$120,400,000	$21,600,000	$15,700,000	$83,100,000
The Wesleyan Church	$9,769,938	$0	$0	$9,769,938	$13,105,882	$0	$0	$13,105,882
Wisconsin Evangelical Lutheran Synod	$8,957,945	$163,652	$0	$8,794,293	$10,886,785	$418,225	$0	$10,468,560

See Notes on page 204

200

Appendix B-5.3: Overseas Missions Income, in Current Dollars, 34 Denominations, 2007, and 33 Denominations, 2008

Denomination	2007 Overseas Missions Income				2008 Overseas Missions Income			
	Line 1.	Line 2.	Line 3.	Line 4.	Line 1.	Line 2.	Line 3.	Line 4.
Allegheny Wesleyan Methodist Connection	$332,511	$0	$0	$332,511	$306,946	$0	$0	$306,946
American Baptist Churches in the U.S.A.	$15,703,238	$5,837,228	$0	$9,866,010	$16,099,000	$6,253,000	$0	$9,846,000
Associate Reformed Presbyterian Church (General Synod)	$5,088,825	$254,533	$14,670	$4,819,622	$5,838,994	$0	$0	$5,838,994
Brethren in Christ Church	$2,264,672	$92,850	$0	$2,171,822	$2,569,054	$116,556	$0	$2,452,498
Christian Church (Disciples of Christ)	$6,645,790	$1,871,786	$0	$4,774,004	$6,436,974	$1,909,503	$0	$4,527,471
Christian and Missionary Alliance [1]	$55,964,407	$0	$0	$55,964,407	$52,012,830	$0	$0	$52,012,830
Church of the Brethren [2]	$1,943,631	$206,977	$0	$1,736,654	$1,807,162	$58,642	$0	$1,748,520
Church of God General Conference (Oregon, Ill., and Morrow, Ga.)	$103,495	$0	$0	$103,495	$101,028	$0	$0	$101,028
Church of the Lutheran Confession	$313,700	$36,100	$0	$277,600	$361,641	$1,318	$0	$360,323
Church of the Nazarene	$52,195,781	$1,604,626	$0	$50,591,155	$54,573,954	$812,861	$0	$53,761,093
Churches of God General Conference [3]	$1,148,045	$29,124	$0	$1,118,921	$1,153,166	($34,087)	$0	$1,187,253
Conservative Congregational Christian Conference [4]	$169,508	$0	$0	$169,508	$84,460	$0	$0	$84,460
Cumberland Presbyterian Church	$368,334	$15,690	$0	$352,644	$322,815	$21,570	$0	$301,245
The Episcopal Church [5]	$26,940,269	$3,400,000	$8,511,710	$15,028,559	$27,589,783	$3,517,957	$9,472,472	$14,599,354
Evangelical Congregational Church	$1,464,523	$0	$0	$1,464,523	$1,583,478	$0	$0	$1,583,478
Evangelical Covenant Church	$7,954,834	$0	$0	$7,954,834	NA	NA	NA	NA
Evangelical Lutheran Church in America [6]	$26,161,433	$4,414,055	$0	$21,747,378	$27,518,419	$3,358,245	$0	$24,160,174
Evangelical Lutheran Synod	$1,389,221	$885,203	$0	$504,018	$1,070,241	$450,487	$0	$619,754
Fellowship of Evangelical Churches	$700,590	$0	$0	$700,590	$724,626	$0	$0	$724,626
Free Methodist Church of North America	$13,705,466	$1,226,998	$0	$12,478,468	$13,581,459	$336,594	$0	$13,244,864
General Association of General Baptists	$2,246,653	$67,605	$0	$2,179,048	$2,158,514	$52,673	$0	$2,105,841
Lutheran Church-Missouri Synod [7]	$16,086,361	$2,899,441	$0	$13,186,920	$17,473,964	$2,968,153	$0	$14,505,811
Moravian Church in America, Northern Province [8]	$542,968	$18,819	$0	$524,149	$504,041	$30,521	$0	$473,520
The Orthodox Presbyterian Church [9]	$1,899,674	$75,285	$0	$1,824,389	$1,820,552	$20,247	$0	$1,800,305
Presbyterian Church in America	$28,456,453	$0	$0	$28,456,453	$29,173,722	$0	$0	$29,173,722
Presbyterian Church (U.S.A.) [10]	$45,301,000	$4,935,000	$0	$40,366,000	$24,839,000	$4,920,000	$0	$19,919,000
Primitive Methodist Church in the U.S.A. [11]	$568,612	$1,802	$0	$566,810	$543,570	$1,132	$0	$542,438
Reformed Church in America	$7,931,523	$319,910	$0	$7,611,613	$8,160,053	$517,484	$0	$7,642,569
Seventh-day Adventist, North Am. Division [12]	$53,772,765	$1,734,653	$0	$52,038,112	$53,959,359	$2,457,879	$0	$51,501,480
Southern Baptist Convention	$278,313,000	$0	$0	$278,313,000	$254,860,000	$0	$0	$254,860,000
United Church of Christ	$9,800,591	$2,493,501	$0	$7,307,090	$9,943,495	$2,698,518	$0	$7,244,977
The United Methodist Church [13]	$126,600,000	$21,400,000	$25,700,000	$79,500,000	$148,300,000	$23,800,000	$10,000,000	$114,500,000
The Wesleyan Church	$13,554,996	$0	$0	$13,554,996	$13,669,461	$0	$0	$13,669,461
Wisconsin Evangelical Lutheran Synod	$11,173,147	$500,952	$0	$10,672,195	$12,107,158	$471,779	$0	$11,635,379

See Notes on page 204

Appendix B-5.4: Overseas Missions Income, in Current Dollars, 33 Denominations, 2009, and 32 Denominations, 2010

Denomination	2009 Overseas Missions Income				2010 Overseas Missions Income			
	Line 1.	Line 2.	Line 3.	Line 4.	Line 1.	Line 2.	Line 3.	Line 4.
Allegheny Wesleyan Methodist Connection	$275,139	$0	$0	$275,139	$313,920	$0	$0	$313,920
American Baptist Churches in the U.S.A.	$14,526,000	$4,941,000	$0	$9,585,000	$16,628,000	$4,507,000	$0	$12,121,000
Associate Reformed Presbyterian Church (General Synod)	$4,359,553	$124,682	$0	$4,234,871	$4,367,714	$122,084	$0	$4,245,630
Brethren in Christ Church	$2,612,767	$139,173	$0	$2,473,594	See table at the bottom of this page.			
Christian Church (Disciples of Christ)	$5,826,676	$1,848,084	$0	$3,978,592	$5,964,111	$1,668,436	$0	$4,295,675
Christian and Missionary Alliance [1]	$52,888,984	$0	$0	$52,888,984	$53,693,745	$0	$0	$53,693,745
Church of the Brethren [2]	$2,022,629	$118,492	$0	$1,904,137	$2,120,575	$98,945	$0	$2,021,630
Church of God General Conference (Oregon, Ill., and Morrow, Ga./McDonough, Ga.)	$166,433	$0	$0	$166,433	$108,017	$2,002	$0	$106,015
Church of the Lutheran Confession	$402,162	$0	$0	$402,162	$405,811	$0	$0	$405,811
Church of the Nazarene	$45,059,581	$1,688,702	$0	$43,370,879	$50,869,056	$3,600,786		$47,268,270
Churches of God General Conference [3]	$1,355,136	$19,538	$0	$1,335,598	$1,718,312	$21,024	$0	$1,697,288
Conservative Congregational Christian Conference [4]	$18,397	$0	$0	$18,397	$10,124	$0	$0	$10,124
Cumberland Presbyterian Church	$300,535	$23,123	$0	$277,412	$326,906	$17,906	$0	$309,000
The Episcopal Church [5]	$30,493,164	$4,373,291	$10,508,830	$15,611,043	$38,106,292	$4,429,106	$13,625,923	$20,051,263
Evangelical Congregational Church	$1,462,048	$0	$0	$1,462,048	$1,416,294	$0	$0	$1,416,294
Evangelical Covenant Church	NA	NA	NA	NA	NA	NA	NA	NA
Evangelical Lutheran Church in America [6]	$27,574,196	$2,908,702	$0	$24,665,494	$25,482,057	$2,573,432	$0	$22,908,625
Evangelical Lutheran Synod	$1,964,975	$820,864	$0	$1,144,111	$1,327,743	$675,405	$0	$652,338
Fellowship of Evangelical Churches	$804,057	$0	$0	$804,057	$839,881	$0	$0	$839,881
Free Methodist Church of North America/USA	$12,032,082	$311,563	$0	$11,720,519	$12,354,513	$128,003	$0	$12,226,510
General Association of General Baptists	$1,978,712	$32,563	$0	$1,946,149	$1,724,984	$27,225	$0	$1,697,759
Lutheran Church-Missouri Synod [7]	$17,687,922	$2,196,136	$0	$15,491,786	$16,992,475	$984,639	$0	$16,007,836
Moravian Church in America, Northern Province [8]	$531,872	$28,055	$0	$503,817	$516,738	$23,570	$0	$493,168
The Orthodox Presbyterian Church [9]	$2,293,701	$314,657	$0	$1,979,044	$2,329,475	$523,507	$0	$1,805,968
Presbyterian Church in America	$27,219,278	$0	$0	$27,219,278	$25,327,324	$0	$0	$25,327,324
Presbyterian Church (U.S.A.) [10]	$27,182,967	$5,196,136	$0	$21,986,831	$35,638,050	$4,175,670	$0	$31,462,380
Primitive Methodist Church in the U.S.A. [11]	$430,150	$620	$0	$429,530	$405,337	$567	$0	$404,770
Reformed Church in America	$8,367,356	$179,496	$0	$8,187,860	$9,105,639	$235,004	$0	$8,870,635
Seventh-day Adventist, North Am. Division [12]	$52,019,434	$2,480,790	$0	$49,538,644	$51,744,014	$1,351,563	$0	$50,392,451
Southern Baptist Convention	$255,427,000	$0	$0	$255,427,000	$264,924,000	$0	$0	$264,924,000
United Church of Christ	$9,531,462	$3,317,710	$0	$6,213,752	$9,380,301	$3,567,773	$0	$5,812,528
The United Methodist Church [13]	$124,120,000	$17,800,000	$9,400,000	$96,920,000	$166,640,000	$21,200,000	$10,200,000	$135,240,000
The Wesleyan Church	$14,139,092	$0	$0	$14,139,092	$14,780,950	$0	$0	$14,780,950
Wisconsin Evangelical Lutheran Synod	$10,706,565	($324,254)	$0.00	$11,030,819	$9,367,119	$99,538	$0	$9,267,581

See Notes on page 204

Overseas Missions Income Data for Three Additional Denominations, in Current Dollars, 2003-2011

Denomination	2003 Overseas Missions Income, Line 4	2004 Overseas Missions Income, Line 4	2005 Overseas Missions Income, Line 4	2006 Overseas Missions Income, Line 4	2007 Overseas Missions Income, Line 4	2008 Overseas Missions Income, Line 4	2009 Overseas Missions Income, Line 4	2010 Overseas Missions Income, Line 4	2011 Overseas Missions Income, Line 4
Brethren in Christ Church								$2,507,447	$2,357,759
Friends United Meeting	$1,314,527	$276,887 (partial year)	$863,445	$859,750	$937,142	$1,076,400	$888,142	$1,144,101	$965,104
Mennonite Church USA	$4,155,596	$3,854,139	$3,937,548	$3,876,657	$4,054,734	$4,225,771	$3,650,453	$3,303,048	$3,120,909

See Chapter 6, Note 9

Appendix B-5.5: Overseas Missions Income, in Current Dollars, 32 Denominations, 2011

Denomination	2011 Overseas Missions Income			
	Line 1.	Line 2.	Line 3.	Line 4.
Allegheny Wesleyan Methodist Connection	$244,376	$0	$0	$244,376
American Baptist Churches in the U.S.A.	$14,229,000	$4,226,000	$0	$10,003,000
Associate Reformed Presbyterian Church (General Synod)	$4,161,822	$40,172	$0	$4,121,650
Brethren in Christ Church	See table at the bottom of page 202.			
Christian Church (Disciples of Christ)	$5,384,548	$2,361,965	$0	$3,022,583
Christian and Missionary Alliance [1]	$51,740,315	$0	$0	$51,740,315
Church of the Brethren [2]	$1,855,666	$42,627	$0	$1,813,039
Church of God General Conference (Oregon, Ill., and Morrow, Ga./McDonough, Ga.)	$82,803	$1,522	$0	$81,281
Church of the Lutheran Confession	$389,457	$0	$0	$389,457
Church of the Nazarene	$46,983,907	$2,214,694	$0	$44,769,213
Churches of God General Conference [3]	$1,344,352	$14,421	$0	$1,329,931
Conservative Congregational Christian Conference [4]	$21,855	$0	$0	$21,855
Cumberland Presbyterian Church	$441,629	$12,241	$0	$429,388
The Episcopal Church [5]	$35,085,747	$3,915,786	$11,800,789	$19,369,172
Evangelical Congregational Church	$1,502,493	$0	$0	$1,502,493
Evangelical Covenant Church	NA	NA	NA	NA
Evangelical Lutheran Church in America [6]	$26,199,965	$1,812,519	$0	$24,387,446
Evangelical Lutheran Synod	$699,851	$445,562	$0	$254,289
Fellowship of Evangelical Churches	$719,573	$0	$0	$719,573
Free Methodist Church of North America/USA	$13,790,352	$156,929	$0	$13,633,423
General Association of General Baptists	$1,699,280	$28,352	$0	$1,670,928
Lutheran Church-Missouri Synod [7]	$19,170,000	$506,663	$0	$18,663,337
Moravian Church in America, Northern Province [8]	$510,848	$19,684	$0	$491,164
The Orthodox Presbyterian Church [9]	$1,870,011	$28,521	$0	$1,841,490
Presbyterian Church in America	$24,971,256	$0	$0	$24,971,256
Presbyterian Church (U.S.A.) [10]	$26,311,242	$3,359,214	$0	$22,952,028
Primitive Methodist Church in the U.S.A. [11]	$341,040	$573	$0	$340,467
Reformed Church in America	$6,858,714	$231,324	$0	$6,627,390
Seventh-day Adventist, North Am. Division [12]	$57,206,455	$1,914,301	$0	$55,292,154
Southern Baptist Convention	$256,882,000	$0	$0	$256,882,000
United Church of Christ	$9,036,727	$3,357,817	$0	$5,678,910
The United Methodist Church [13]	$132,000,000	$21,200,000	$8,200,000	$102,600,000
The Wesleyan Church	$14,788,726	$0	$0	$14,788,726
Wisconsin Evangelical Lutheran Synod	$12,012,740	$411,524	$0	$11,601,216

See Notes on page 204

Line Descriptions on empty tomb, inc. Overseas Missions Income Data Request Form:

Line 1.: What was the amount of income raised in the U.S. during the calendar or fiscal year indicated for overseas ministries?

Line 2.: How many dollars of the total amount on Line 1. came from endowment, foundation, and other investment income?

Line 3.: Of the total amount on Line1., what is the dollar value of government grants, either in dollars or in-kind goods for distribution?

Line 4.: Balance of overseas ministries income: Line 1. minus Lines 2. and 3.

Notes to Appendix B-5: Overseas Missions Income, 2003, 2004, 2005, 2006, 2007, 2008, 2009, 2010, and 2011

[1]   Christian and Missionary Alliance: "Since both domestic and overseas works are budgeted through the same source (our 'Great Commission Fund'), the amount on lines 1 and 4 are actual amounts spent on overseas missions."

[2]   Church of the Brethren: "This amount is national denominational mission and service, i.e., direct staffing and mission support, and does not include other projects funded directly by congregations or districts, or independent missionaries sponsored by congregations and individuals that would not be part of the denominational effort."

[3]   Churches of God General Conference: "[Data Year] 2008 line 2 represents a net loss in investment income included in line 1. By adding this net loss amount back, line 4 represents the amount received in contributions from donors."

[4]   Conservative Congregational Christian Conference: "The structure of this communion limits the national office coordination of overseas ministries activity. By design, congregations are to conduct missions directly, through agencies of their choice. The national office does not survey congregations about these activities. The one common emphasis of affiliated congregations is a focus on Micronesia, represented by the reported numbers." Data Year 2010: "The amount raised is down because we didn't have any missionary that we sent overseas."

[5]   The Episcopal Church: "The Episcopal Church (aka, The Domestic and Foreign Missionary Society) does not specifically raise money to support our non-domestic ministries. Many of the activities included in our budget are, however, involved, directly or indirectly, with providing worldwide mission … Many other expenditures (e.g., for ecumenical and interfaith relations; for federal chaplaincies; for management's participation in activities of the worldwide Anglican Communion) contain an overseas component; but we do not separately track or report domestic vs. overseas expenses in those categories."

[6]   Evangelical Lutheran Church in America: "Some assumptions were made in arriving with the total income, and those remain consistent from year to year."

[7]   The Lutheran Church—Missouri Synod: "The Lutheran Church—Missouri Synod (LCMS) is a confessing, orthodox Lutheran church comprising 6,000 congregations and approximately 600,000 households (2.27 million baptized individuals) across North America. LCMS witness and mercy work is carried out by two distinct offices: The Office of International Mission and the Office of National Mission. These offices encompass the work of two legacy entities: LCMS World Mission and LCMS World Relief and Human Care. The information provided in this report reflects the work of LCMS World Mission*. Annual budget income; above budget income; administrative incomes; and the special, multi-year, mission funding campaign, called *Fan into Flame*, income is included in the overseas income data. The majority of LCMS World Mission funding was supplied through direct gifts from individuals, congregations, and organizations connected to the Synod.

"(*) Note: information for LCMS World Relief and Human Care, another official LCMS entity involved in international and national ministry, is not included in the statistics provided here.

"In more recent years, the 35 districts (regional jurisdictions) of the LCMS, along with a growing number of congregations and Lutheran mission societies, began sponsoring various mission fields and projects directly. That support did not flow through LCMS World Missions. More information regarding the international work of the 35 LCMS districts can be found at www.lcmsdistricts.org and the 75-plus members of Association of Lutheran Mission Agencies at www.alma-online.org. Therefore, millions of dollars of additional support from LCMS members is raised and spent for international ministry each year which are not part of this report. Since these funds are not sent through the LCMS national office—and thus are not part of Synod's annual auditing process—the total amount cannot be verified and incorporated into this report."

[8]   Moravian Church in America, Northern Province: "Data provided by the Board of World Mission, an interprovincial agency of the North American Moravian Church. The Overseas Missions Income figure was estimated for the Northern Province by the Board of World Mission of the Moravian Church. The Northern Province is the only one of the three Moravian Provinces that reports Total Contributions to the *Yearbook of American and Canadian Churches* series."

[9]   Orthodox Presbyterian Church: "These figures, as in past years, reflect only what was given through our denominational committee on Foreign Missions. In addition, $122,166 was given through our Committee on Diaconal Ministries for diaconal and disaster relief ministries administered by our missionaries on various overseas fields. Local churches and individuals also give directly to a variety of overseas missions causes."

[10]   Presbyterian Church (U.S.A.): "Nos. 1 & 4 Year 2005: Higher for Asian Tsunami Relief."

[11]   The Primitive Methodist Church in the U.S.A.: "This only includes monies passing through our Denominational Mission Board (International). Many churches send money directly to a mission field."

[12]   Seventh-day Adventist, North American Division: "This estimate, prepared by the General Conference Treasury Department, is for the U.S. portion of the total donated by congregations in both Canada and the U.S."

[13]   The United Methodist Church: "The above represents total income received by the General Board of Global Ministries, The United Methodist Church."

Appendix B-6: Estimates of Giving

Year	A. Form 990 Direct Public Support '000s $	B. Form 990 Indirect Public Support '000s $	C. Form 990 Donor-Advised Funds '000s $	D. Form 990-EZ Contributions, Gifts and Grants '000s $	E. Giving USA Gifts to Foundations Billion $s	F. Giving USA Giving by Corporations Billion $s	G. Giving USA Giving by Foundations Billion $s	H. Giving USA Giving to Bequests Billion $s	I. Giving USA Individual Giving, Million $s	J. IRS Other than Cash Contributions '000s	K. CE Giving to "Church, Religious Organizations" '000s
1989	35,828,100	7,008,648		463,432	4.41	5.46	6.55	6.84	79,450	7,550,914	31,739,713
1990	39,395,074	8,055,551		644,613	3.83	5.46	7.23	6.79	79,000	7,494,016	30,673,887
1991	40,282,952	7,717,705		685,538	4.46	5.25	7.72	7.68	81,930	9,681,786	36,444,100
1992	43,986,785	9,110,478		813,604	5.01	5.91	8.64	9.54	87,200	9,632,779	35,159,679
1993	47,507,722	8,335,206		769,751	6.26	6.47	9.53	8.86	91,720	12,278,893	35,495,384
1994	49,238,498	8,722,141		780,896	6.33	6.98	9.66	11.13	92,280	14,739,299	37,189,109
1995	64,148,723	9,746,924		820,036	8.46	7.35	10.56	10.41	94,780	13,521,937	39,741,542
1996	69,419,764	10,230,304		988,638	12.63	7.51	12.00	12.03	107,350	21,298,819	39,053,447
1997	74,681,875	10,945,060		977,961	13.96	8.62	13.92	16.25	123,670	27,961,174	41,201,034
1998	83,359,695	12,711,938		1,053,669	19.92	8.46	17.01	13.41	137,680	29,255,985	44,831,015
1999	91,696,783	13,519,909		1,011,289	28.76	10.23	20.51	17.82	154,630	38,286,580	49,102,106
2000	103,453,445	15,176,512		1,086,099	24.71	10.74	24.58	20.25	174,090	47,256,104	48,737,216
2001	108,065,595	14,561,940		1,087,365	25.67	11.66	27.22	20.15	173,060	37,997,546	57,321,111
2002	102,802,550	15,223,713		1,095,317	19.16	10.79	26.98	21.16	173,790	34,293,125	62,476,667
2003	112,808,019	16,330,097		1,188,783	21.62	11.06	26.84	18.08	181,470	38,041,067	65,108,080
2004	124,575,951	16,947,398		1,397,630	20.32	11.36	28.41	18.53	201,960	43,373,209	65,712,121
2005	140,348,374	21,624,408		1,469,440	24.46	15.20	32.41	24.00	220,820	48,056,520	82,948,394
2006	150,214,837	26,049,161	10,368,453	1,551,098	27.10	14.52	34.91	21.90	224,760	52,631,443	89,469,764
2007	157,337,807	31,074,073	10,902,610	1,465,577	37.67	14.22	40.00	23.79	233,050	58,747,438	82,288,294
2008	145,209,711 *	26,844,533 *		13,851,212	30.14	12.40	42.21	31.24	213,760	40,421,411	89,915,680
2009	141,663,143 *	30,839,484 *		9,420,321	32.39	13.79	41.09	19.12	200,370	31,816,050	87,565,736

* Form 990 categories changed for the 2008 Form 990. For purposes of this analysis, the 2008 category, "All other contributions, gifts, etc." is regarded as "Direct Public Support." "Indirect Public Support" is the sum of 2008 data for: "Federated campaigns," $3,392,058; "Fundraising events," $5,919,225; and "Related organizations," $17,533,250. 2009 "Indirect Public Support" is the sum of 2009 data for "Federated campaigns," $3,070,589; "Fundraising events," $6,149,135; "Related organizations," $21,619,760.

Source: Columns A., B., and C.

1989	"Form 990 Returns of Nonprofit Charitable Section 501(c)(3) Organizations: Selected Income Statement and Balance Sheet Items, by Size of Total Assets, 1989"; downloaded 6/12/2007; <http://www.irs.gov/pub/irs-soi/89eo01as.xls>; p. 2 of 6/13/2007 12:26 PM printout.
1990	"Table 1.--1990, Form 990 Returns of Organizations Tax-Exempt Under Internal Revenue Code Sections 501(c)(3)-(9): Selected Income Statement and Balance Sheet Items, by Code Section"; downloaded 6/12/2007; <http://www.irs.gov/pub/irs-soi/90np01fr.xls>; p. 3 of 6/13/2007 1:48 PM printout.
1991	"Form 990 Returns of Nonprofit Charitable Internal Revenue Code Section 501(c)(3) Organizations: Selected Income Statement and Balance Sheet Items, by Asset Size, 1991"; Internal Revenue Service, *SOI Bulletin*, Pub. 1136 (Rev. 8-96); downloaded 6/12/2007; <http://www.irs.gov/pub/irs-soi/91eo01as.xls>; p. 2 of 6/13/2007 2:48 PM printout.
1992-1999	"Table 1.--[Year], Form 990 Returns of Nonprofit Charitable Internal Revenue Code Section 501(c)(3) Organizations: Selected Income Statement and Balance Sheet Items, by Asset Size"; Internal Revenue Service, *Statistics of Income Bulletin*, Pub. 1136; downloaded 6/12/2007;
1992	(Rev. 8-96); <http://www.irs.gov/pub/irs-soi/92eo01as.xls>; p. 2 of 6/13/2007 3:21 PM printout.
1993	(Rev. 4-97); <http://www.irs.gov/pub/irs-soi/93eo01as.xls>; p. 2 of 6/13/2007 3:39 PM printout.
1994	Spring 1998 (Rev. 5-98); <http://www.irs.gov/pub/irs-soi/94eo01as.xls>; p. 2 of 6/13/2007 4:12 PM printout.
1995	Winter 1998/1999 (Rev. 2/99); <http://www.irs.gov/pub/irs-soi/95eotab1.xls>; p. 2 of 6/14/2007 9:25 AM printout.
1996	Winter 1999/2000 (Rev. 2/00); <http://www.irs.gov/pub/irs-soi/96eo01c3.xls>; p. 1 of 6/14/2007 9:55 AM printout.
1997	Fall 2000 (Rev. 11-2000); <http://www.irs.gov/pub/irs-soi/97eotb1.xls>; p. 1 of 6/14/2007 10:09 AM printout.
1998	Fall 2001 (Rev. 11-01); <http://www.irs.gov/pub/irs-soi/98eo01as.xls>; p. 1 of 6/14/2007 10:17 AM printout.
1999	Fall 2002 (Rev. 12-02); <http://www.irs.gov/pub/irs-soi/99eo01as.xls>; p. 1 of 6/14/2007 10:29 AM printout.
2000	"Table 1.--2000, Form 990 Returns of Nonprofit Charitable Section 501(c)(3) Organizations: Selected Balance Sheet and Income Statement Items, by Size of Total Assets"; IRS, *Statistics of Income Bulletin*, Fall 2003, Pub. 1136, (Rev. 12-03); downloaded 6/12/2007; <http://www.irs.gov/pub/irs-soi/00eo01ta.xls>; p. 2 of 6/14/2007 10:43 AM printout.
2001	"Form 990 Returns of Nonprofit Charitable Section 501(c)(3) Organizations: Selected Balance Sheet and Income Statement Items, by Asset Size, Tax Year 2001"; downloaded 6/12/2007; <http://www.irs.gov/pub/irs-soi/01eo01as.xls>; p. 1 of 6/14/2007 10:55 AM printout.
2002	"Table 1.--Form 990 Returns of Nonprofit Charitable Section 501(c)(3) Organizations: Selected Balance Sheet and Income Statement Items, by Asset Size, Tax Year 2002"; IRS, *Statistics of Income Bulletin*, Fall 2005, Pub. 1136, (Rev.12-05); downloaded 6/12/2007; <http://www.irs.gov/pub/irs-soi/02eo01as.xls>; p. 2 of 6/14/2007 4:31 PM printout.
2003	"Table 1: Form 990 Returns of Nonprofit Charitable Section 501 (c)(3) Organizations: Selected Balance Sheet and Income Statement Items, by Asset Size, Tax Year 2003"; IRS SOI Division, August 2006; downloaded 6/12/2007; <http://www.irs.gov/pub/irs-soi/03eo01as.xls>; p. 1 of 6/14/2007 4:42 PM printout.
2004-2005	Table 1: Form 990 Returns of 501(c)(3) Organizations: Balance Sheet and Income Statement Items, By Asset Size, Tax Year [Year]; IRS, SOI Division,
2004	August 2007; downloaded 3/15/2008; <http://www.irs.gov/pub/irs-soi/04eo01as.xls>; p. 1 of 3/15/2008 9:59 AM printout.
2005	August 2008; downloaded 3/5/2009; <http://www.irs.gov/pub/irs-soi/05eo01as.xls>; p. 1 of 3/5/2009 3:59 PM printout.
2006-2008	"Table 1. Form 990 Returns of 501(c)(3) Organizations: Balance Sheet and Income Statement Items, by Asset Size, Tax Year [Year]"; IRS, SOI Division,
2006	August 2009; downloaded 4/29/2010; <http://www.irs.gov/pub/irs-soi/06eo01as.xls>; p. 1 of 4/29/2010 3:27 PM printout.
2007	July 2010; downloaded 4/28/2011; <http://www.irs.gov/pub/irs-soi/07eo01.xls>; p. 1 of 4/29/2011 9:10 AM printout.
2008	July 2011; downloaded 3/26/2012; <http://www.irs.gov/pub/irs-soi/08eo01.xls>; p. 1 of 3/26/2012 2:58 PM printout.
2009	"Table 1--Selected Form 990 Data for 501(c)(3) Organizations, 2009"; IRS; downloaded 2/12/13; <http://www.irs.gov/PUP/taxstats/charitablestats/09eo01.xls>; p. 1 of 2/12/13 10:13 AM printout.

Source: Col. D.

1989	"Form 990EZ Returns of Organizations Tax-Exempt Under Internal Revenue Code Sections 501(c)(3)-(9): Selected Income Statement and Balance Sheet Items, by Code Section, 1989"; IRS, SOI Tax Stats; downloaded 6/15/2007; <http://www.irs.gov/pub/irs-soi/89eo04cs.xls>; p. 1 of 6/16/2007 8:56 AM printout.
1990	"Table 2.--1990, Form 990EZ Returns of Organizations Tax-Exempt Under Internal Revenue Code Sections 501(c)(3)-(9): Selected Income Statement and Balance Sheet Items, by Code Section"; IRS, SOI Tax Stats; downloaded 6/15/2007; <http://www.irs.gov/pub/irs-soi/90np02ro.xls>; p.1 of 6/16/2007 9:11 AM printout.
1991	"Form 990EZ Returns of Organizations Tax-Exempt Under Internal Revenue Code Sections 501(c)(3)-(9): Selected Income Statement and Balance Sheet Items, by Code Section, 1991"; IRS, *SOI Bulletin*, Pub. 1136 (Rev. 8-96); downloaded 6/15/2007; <http://www.irs.gov/pub/irs-soi/91eo04cs.xls>; p.1 of 6/16/2007 9:22 AM printout.
1992-1993	"Table 4.--[Year], Form 990EZ Returns of Organizations Tax-Exempt Under Internal Revenue Code Sections 501(c)(3)-(9): Selected Income Statement and Balance Sheet Items, by Code Section"; IRS, *SOI Bulletin*, Pub.1136; downloaded 6/15/2007;
1992	(Rev. 8-96); <http://www.irs.gov/pub/irs-soi/92eo04cs.xls>; p.1 of 6/16/2007 9:39 AM printout.
1993	(Rev. 4-97); <http://www.irs.gov/pub/irs-soi/93eo04cs.xls>; p.1 of 6/16/2007 9:48 AM printout.
1994-1995	"Table 4.--[Year], Form 990-EZ Returns of Organizations Tax-Exempt Under Internal Revenue Code Sections 501 (c)(3)-(9): Selected Balance Sheet and Income Statement Items, by Code Section"; IRS, *SOI Bulletin*, Pub. 1136; downloaded 6/15/2007;
1994	Spring 1998, (Rev. 5-98); <http://www.irs.gov/pub/irs-soi/94eo04cs.xls>; p. 1 of 6/16/2007 9:58 AM printout.
1995	Winter 1998/99, (Rev. 2/99); <http://www.irs.gov/pub/irs-soi/95eotab4.xls>; p. 1 of 6/16/2007 10:09 AM printout.
1996	"Table 3.--1996, Form 990-EZ Returns of Nonprofit Charitable Section 501(c)(3) Organizations: Selected Balance Sheet and Income Statement Items, by Asset Size"; IRS, *SOI Bulletin*, Winter 1999/2000; Pub. 1136, (Rev. 2/00); downloaded 6/15/2007; <http://www.irs.gov/pub/irs-soi/96eo03c3.xls>; p. 1 of 6/16/2007 10:28 AM printout.
1997-2000	"Table 4.--[Year], Form 990-EZ Returns of Organizations Tax-Exempt Under Internal Revenue Code Sections 501(c)(3)-(9): Selected Balance Sheet and Income Statement Items, by Code Section"; IRS, *SOI Bulletin*, Pub. 1136; downloaded 6/15/2007;
1997	Fall 2000, (Rev. 11-2000); <http://www.irs.gov/pub/irs-soi/97eotb4.xls>; p. 1 of 6/16/2007 10:36 AM printout.
1998	Fall 2001, (Rev. 11-2001); <http://www.irs.gov/pub/irs-soi/98eo04cs.xls>; p. 1 of 6/16/2007 10:43 AM printout.
1999	Fall 2002, (Rev. 12-02); <http://www.irs.gov/pub/irs-soi/99eo04cs.xls>; p. 1 of 6/16/2007 11:22 AM printout.
2000	Fall 2003, (Rev. 12-03); <http://www.irs.gov/pub/irs-soi/00eo04cs.xls>; p. 1 of 6/16/2007 11:29 AM printout.
2001	"Form 990-EZ Returns of Organizations Tax-Exempt Under Internal Revenue Code Sections 501(c)(3)-(9): Selected Balance Sheet and Income Statement Items, by Code Section, Tax Year 2001"; IRS, SOI Tax Stats, downloaded 6/15/2007; <http://www.irs.gov/pub/irs-soi/01eo04cs.xls>; p. 1 of 6/16/2007 11:34 AM printout.
2002	"Table 4.--Form 990-EZ Returns of Organizations Tax-Exempt Under Internal Revenue Code Sections 501(c)(3)-(9): Selected Balance Sheet and Income Statement Items, by Code Section, Tax Year 2002"; IRS, SOI Bulletin, Fall 2005, Pub. 1136 (Rev. 12-05); downloaded 6/15/2007; <http://www.irs.gov/pub/irs-soi/02eo04ty.xls>; p. 1 of 6/17/2007 7:50 AM printout.
2003	"Table 4: Form 990-EZ Returns of Organizations Tax-Exempt Under Internal Revenue Code Sections 501(c)(3)-(9): Selected Balance Sheet and Income Statement Items, by Code Section, Tax Year 2003"; IRS, SOI Division, August 2006; downloaded 6/15/2007; <http://www.irs.gov/pub/irs-soi/03eo04ty.xls>; p. 1 of 6/17/2007 8:07 AM printout.
2004	"Table 4: Form 990-EZ Returns of 501(c)(3)-(9) Organizations: Balance Sheet and Income Statement Items, by Code Section, Tax Year 2004"; IRS, SOI Division, August 2007; downloaded 3/14/2008; <http://www.irs.gov/pub/irs-soi/04eo04ty.xls>; p. 1 of 3/14/2008 3:50 PM printout.
2005	"Table 4: Form 990-EZ Returns of 501(c)(3)-(9) Organizations: Selected [I]tems, by Code Section, Tax Year 2005"; IRS, SOI Division, August 2008; downloaded 3/5/2009; <http://www.irs.gov/pub/irs-soi/05eo04ty.xls>; p. 1 of 3/5/2009 4:11 PM printout.
2006-2008	"Table 4: Form 990-EZ Returns of 501(c)(3)-(9) Organizations: Selected Items, by Code Section, Tax Year [Year]"; IRS, SOI Division,
2006	August 2009; <http://www.irs.gov/pub/irs-soi/06eo04ty.xls>; p. 1 of 4/29/2010 5:34 PM printout.
2007	July 2010; <http://www.irs.gov/pub/irs-soi/07eo04.xls>; p. 1 of 4/29/2010 3:41 PM printout.
2008	July 2011; <http://www.irs.gov/pub/irs-soi/08eo04.xls>; p. 1 of 3/23/2012 9:00 PM printout.
2009	"Table 4–Selected Form 990-EZ Data 501(c)(4[sic])-Orgs, 2009"; IRS; downloaded 2/9/13; <http://www.irs.gov/PUP/taxstats/charitablestats/09eo04.xls>; p. 1 of 2/9/2013 1:47 PM printout.

Source: Col. E.

1989-2009	*Giving USA 2013*, p. 251.

Source: Columns F., G., H., and I.

1989-2009	*Giving USA 2013*, p. 248.

Source: Col. J.

1989	Internal Revenue Service, Statistics of Income—1989, Individual Income Tax Returns, "Table 2.1—Returns with Itemized Deductions: Sources of Income, Adjustments, Itemized Deductions by Type, Exemptions, and Tax Items by Size of Adjusted Gross Income" (Internal Revenue Service: Washington, DC, 1992), p. 41.
1990-2001	"Table 1.--Individual Income Tax Returns, Selected Deductions, 1990-2001"; IRS *Statistics of Income* Winter 2003-2004 Bulletin, Pub 1136; <http://www.irs.gov/pub/irs-soi/01in01sd.xls>; pp. 1-2 of 9/6/2005 8:59 AM printout.
2002	"Table 3.--2002, Individual Income Tax Returns with Itemized Deductions, by Size of Adjusted Gross Income"; IRS, Statistics of Income Bulletin, Fall 2004, Pub. 1136, (Rev. 12-04); <http://www.irs.gov/pub/irs-soi/02in03ga.xls>; p. 5 of 9/6/2005 10:58 AM printout.
2003	"Table 3.---2003, Individual Income Tax Returns with Itemized Deductions, by Size of Adjusted Gross Income"; IRS, Statistics of Income Bulletin, Fall 2005, Pub. 1136, (Rev. 12-05); <http://www.irs.gov/pub/irs-soi/03in03ag.xls>; p. 5 of 6/6/2006 3:38 PM printout.
2004	"Table 3--Returns with Itemized Deductions: Sources of Income, Adjustments, Itemized Deductions by Type, Exemptions, and Tax Items, by Size of Adjusted Gross Income, Tax year 2004"; IRS, Statistics of Income Division, July 2006; <http://www.irs.gov/pub/irs-soi/04in03id.xls>; p. 3 of 8/12/2007 1:33 PM printout.
2005-2009	"Table 3. Returns with Itemized Deductions: Itemized Deductions by Type and by Size of Adjusted Gross Income, Tax Year [Year]"; IRS;
2005	<http://www.irs.gov/pub/irs-soi/05in03id.xls>; p. 3 of 4/10/2008 7:07 PM printout.
2006	<http://www.irs.gov/pub/irs-soi/06in03id.xls>; p. 3 of 3/10/2009 11:34AM printout.
2007	<http://www.irs.gov/pub/irs-soi/07in03id.xls>; p. 3 of 4/28/2010 4:48 PM printout.
2008	<http://www.irs.gov/pub/irs-soi/08in03id.xls>; p. 3 of 4/28/2011 12:09 PM printout.
2009	<http://www.irs.gov/pub/irs-soi/09in03id.xls>; p. 3 of 4/9/2012 5:05 PM printout.

Source: Col. K.

1989-2009	U.S. Department of Labor, Bureau of Labor Statistics, "Table 1800.Region of residence: Average annual expenditures and characteristics, Consumer Expenditure Survey, [Year]"

APPENDIX C: *Income, Deflators, and U.S. Population*

Appendix C-1 presents U.S. Per Capita Disposable Personal Income for 1921 through 2012.

The Implicit Price Index for Gross National Product is provided for 1921 through 2012. The deflator series keyed to 2005 dollars provided deflators from 1929, only, through 2012. Therefore, the 1921 through 1928 data was converted to inflation-adjusted 1958 dollars using the series keyed to 1958=100, and the inflation-adjusted 1958 dollar values were then converted to inflation-adjusted 2005 dollars using the series keyed to 2005 dollars.

Appendix C-2 presents U.S. Population for 1921 through 2012.

SOURCES

Income, 1921-1928, Deflator 1921-1928, and U.S. Population, 1921-1928

Historical Statistics of the United States: Colonial Times to 1970, Bicentennial Edition, Part 1 (Washington, DC: Bureau of the Census, 1975):

    1921-28 Disposable Personal Income: Series F 9, p. 224 (F 6-9).

    1921-28 Implicit Price Index GNP (1958=100): Series F 5, p. 224 (F 1-5).

    1921-28 U.S. Population: Series A-7, p. 8 (A 6-8).

Income, 1929-2012

Per Capita Disposable Personal Income in Current Dollars: U.S. Department of Commerce, Bureau of Economic Analysis; "Table 7.1. Selected Per Capita Product and Income Series in Current and Chained Dollars"; Line 4: "Disposable personal income"; National Income and Product Accounts Tables; 1969-2012: <http://www.bea.gov//national/nipaweb/SS_Data/Section7All_xls.xls>; 1929-1968: <http://www.bea.gov//national/nipaweb/SS_Data/Section7All_Hist.xls>; 1929-1968 data published on July 27, 2012; 1969-2012 data published on March 28, 2013.

Deflator, 2005 Dollars, 1929-2012

Gross National Product: Implicit Price Deflators for Gross National Product [2005=100]: U.S. Bureau of Economic Analysis; "Table 1.1.9. Implicit Price Deflators for Gross Domestic Product"; Line 26: "Gross national product"; National Income and Product Accounts Tables; 1969-2012: <http://www.bea.gov//national/nipaweb/SS_Data/Section1All_xls.xls>; 1929-1968: <http://www.bea.gov//national/nipaweb/SS_Data/Section1All_Hist.xls>; 1929-1968 data published on July 27, 2012; 1969-2012 data published on March 28, 2013.

Population, 1929-2012

U.S. Bureau of Economic Analysis; "Table 7.1. Selected Per Capita Product and Income Series in Current and Chained Dollars"; Line 18: "Population (midperiod, thousands)"; National Income and Product Accounts Tables; 1969-2012: <http://www.bea.gov//national/nipaweb/SS_Data/Section7All_xls.xls>; 1929-1968: <http://www.bea.gov//national/nipaweb/SS_Data/Section7All_Hist.xls>; 1929-1968 data published on July 27, 2012; 1969-2012 data published on March 28, 2013.

Aggregate Income, 1929-2012

U.S. Bureau of Economic Analysis; "Table 2.1. Personal Income and Its Disposition"; Line 27: "Disposable personal income"; National Income and Product Accounts Tables; 1969-2012: <http://www.bea.gov//national/nipaweb/SS_Data/Section2All_xls.xls>; 1929-1968: <http://www.bea.gov//national/nipaweb/SS_Data/Section2All_Hist.xls>; 1929-1968 data published on July 27, 2012; 1969-2012 data published on March 28, 2013.

Appendix C-1: Per Capita Disposable Personal Income and Deflators, 1921-2012

Year	Current $ Per Capita Disposable Personal Income	Implicit Price Deflator GNP [1958=100]	Implicit Price Deflator GNP [2005=100]	Year	Current $ Per Capita Disposable Personal Income	Implicit Price Deflator GNP [2005=100]
1921	$555	54.5	18.118	1967	$2,894	21.116
1922	$548	50.1	18.118	1968	$3,112	22.015
1923	$623	51.3	18.118	1969	$3,324	23.101
1924	$626	51.2	18.118	1970	$3,586	24.320
1925	$630	51.9	18.118	1971	$3,859	25.537
1926	$659	51.1	18.118	1972	$4,140	26.639
1927	$650	50.0	18.118	1973	$4,615	28.121
1928	$643	50.8	18.118	1974	$5,010	30.669
1929	$683		10.601	1975	$5,497	33.570
1930	$605		10.213	1976	$5,972	35.502
1931	$517		9.159	1977	$6,514	37.767
1932	$393		8.088	1978	$7,220	40.419
1933	$366		7.872	1979	$7,956	43.782
1934	$417		8.306	1980	$8,794	47.769
1935	$465		8.475	1981	$9,726	52.251
1936	$525		8.565	1982	$10,390	55.438
1937	$559		8.934	1983	$11,095	57.635
1938	$512		8.673	1984	$12,232	59.800
1939	$545		8.586	1985	$12,911	61.614
1940	$581		8.687	1986	$13,540	62.973
1941	$703		9.271	1987	$14,146	64.804
1942	$879		9.998	1988	$15,206	67.031
1943	$990		10.537	1989	$16,134	69.570
1944	$1,072		10.787	1990	$17,004	72.260
1945	$1,088		11.074	1991	$17,532	74.819
1946	$1,142		12.394	1992	$18,436	76.586
1947	$1,187		13.739	1993	$18,909	78.291
1948	$1,299		14.510	1994	$19,678	79.942
1949	$1,275		14.481	1995	$20,470	81.611
1950	$1,384		14.638	1996	$21,355	83.166
1951	$1,496		15.690	1997	$22,255	84.630
1952	$1,550		15.960	1998	$23,534	85.581
1953	$1,620		16.153	1999	$24,356	86.840
1954	$1,627		16.301	2000	$25,946	88.720
1955	$1,713		16.582	2001	$26,816	90.725
1956	$1,800		17.150	2002	$27,816	92.191
1957	$1,866		17.720	2003	$28,827	94.131
1958	$1,897		18.118	2004	$30,312	96.782
1959	$1,976		18.336	2005	$31,343	100.000
1960	$2,020		18.592	2006	$33,183	103.234
1961	$2,077		18.802	2007	$34,550	106.230
1962	$2,170		19.060	2008	$36,200	108.589
1963	$2,245		19.264	2009	*$34,899*	*109.529*
1964	$2,408		19.563	2010	*$35,920*	*110.977*
1965	$2,562		19.920	2011	*$37,013*	*113.353*
1966	$2,733		20.486	2012	$37,964	115.387

Appendix C-2: U.S. Population, 1921-2012

Year	U.S. Population	Year	U.S. Population	Year	U.S. Population
1921	108,538,000	1956	168,221,000	1991	253,530,000
1922	110,049,000	1957	171,274,000	1992	256,922,000
1923	111,947,000	1958	174,141,000	1993	260,282,000
1924	114,109,000	1959	177,130,000	1994	263,455,000
1925	115,829,000	1960	180,760,000	1995	266,588,000
1926	117,397,000	1961	183,742,000	1996	269,714,000
1927	119,035,000	1962	186,590,000	1997	272,958,000
1928	120,509,000	1963	189,300,000	1998	276,154,000
1929	121,878,000	1964	191,927,000	1999	279,328,000
1930	123,188,000	1965	194,347,000	2000	282,398,000
1931	124,149,000	1966	196,599,000	2001	285,225,000
1932	124,949,000	1967	198,752,000	2002	287,955,000
1933	125,690,000	1968	200,745,000	2003	290,626,000
1934	126,485,000	1969	202,736,000	2004	293,262,000
1935	127,362,000	1970	205,089,000	2005	295,993,000
1936	128,181,000	1971	207,692,000	2006	298,818,000
1937	128,961,000	1972	209,924,000	2007	301,696,000
1938	129,969,000	1973	211,939,000	2008	304,543,000
1939	131,028,000	1974	213,898,000	2009	307,240,000
1940	132,122,000	1975	215,981,000	2010	*309,776,000*
1941	133,402,000	1976	218,086,000	2011	*312,036,000*
1942	134,860,000	1977	220,289,000	2012	314,278,000
1943	136,739,000	1978	222,629,000		
1944	138,397,000	1979	225,106,000		
1945	139,928,000	1980	227,726,000		
1946	141,389,000	1981	230,008,000		
1947	144,126,000	1982	232,218,000		
1948	146,631,000	1983	234,333,000		
1949	149,188,000	1984	236,394,000		
1950	151,684,000	1985	238,506,000		
1951	154,287,000	1986	240,683,000		
1952	156,954,000	1987	242,843,000		
1953	159,565,000	1988	245,061,000		
1954	162,391,000	1989	247,387,000		
1955	165,275,000	1990	250,181,000		

Notes